LAST RIDE

The Defeat of Lieutenant Colonel George Armstrong Custer's 7th Cavalry at the Battle of the Little Bighorn

JAMES CLINTON HUNGERFORD

PublishAmerica
Baltimore

© 2005 by James Clinton Hungerford.
All rights reserved. No part of this book may be reproduced, stored in a retrieval system or transmitted in any form or by any means without the prior written permission of the publishers, except by a reviewer who may quote brief passages in a review to be printed in a newspaper, magazine or journal.

First printing

ISBN: 1-4137-4498-2
PUBLISHED BY PUBLISHAMERICA, LLLP
www.publishamerica.com
Baltimore

Printed in the United States of America

DEDICATED

First to:

My very best friend in this life,
my wife, Brenda,

AND to:

Those men that took
that last ride, Americans all,

AND finally to:

All American men and women of all colors
And creeds who in Service to its Liberty
Have followed the Stars and Stripes
And taken that last ride....

Table of Contents

Author's Foreword	7
Introduction	26
Chapter 1: Field Commander	29
Chapter 2: When Boys Become Men	37
Chapter 3: The Boy Became a General	44
Chapter 4: Custer's Myths and Truths	47
Chapter 5: The 7th Cavalry's Headquarters & Detachment	56
Chapter 6: Manning Tables and Sourer Grapes	63
Chapter 7: Custer's Nemesis: Captain Benteen	69
Chapter 8: Everyone's Scapegoat: Maj. Marcus Maj. Reno	81
Chapter 9: Custer's Battalion Troop Commanders	89
Chapter 10: Other Members of Custer's Inner Circle	101
Chapter 11: Enlisted Men & Civilians in the Regiment	108
Chapter 12: Horses, Jackasses, and Donkeys	130
Chapter 13: Early Morning, Sunday 25 June 1876	135
Chapter 14: The 7th Deploys	143
Chapter 15: Hell Fire and Brimstone	155
Chapter 16: Major Reno Deploys	160
Chapter 17: Major Reno is Ambushed	163
Chapter 18: Major Reno's Nightmare	168
Chapter 19: The Myth	172
Chapter 20: The Valley Fight	176
Chapter 21: Speculations and Guesses	185
Chapter 22: Captain Benteen's Insight	193
Chapter 23: The Hostiles Take Control	196
Chapter 24: Custer's Battalion Goes A-hellin' Towards Destiny	204
Chapter 25: Custer's Luck Runs Out	213
Chapter 26: The Battle Plan Runs Amok	219
Chapter 27: All Hell Breaks Loose	224
Chapter 28: Keogh Takes Over	230
Chapter 29: Captains Smith and Yates Pull Out	234

Chapter 30: Breaking Out of Death's Grip	236
Chapter 31: The Deep Ravine is a Death Trap	240
Chapter 32: There is No Escape	242
Chapter 33: The Missing Men	246
Chapter 34: Retribution	247
Chapter 35: Somebody's to Blame	257
Chapter 36: After-effects	260
Chapter 37: Culpability	270
Chapter 38: Hunka Hey	275
Chapter 39: Taps	281
Chapter 40: The Congressional Medal of Honor	315
Chapter 41: Lieutenant Bradley's Gruesome Find	322
Chapter 42: Official Battle Reports	351
Chapter 43: *The New York Times* Newspaper Report	370
Chapter 44: Court Martial of Major Marcus Reno	377
Chapter 45: The Custer Legacy	388
Chapter 46: Epilogue	397
References	405

AUTHOR'S FOREWORD

Author's Note: The swallow-tailed flag above is Custer's personal Battle flag. The top half of the flag is scarlet red, the bottom half is Navy Blue. Centered between the two fields are two crossed white sabers. After Custer was promoted to brigadier general, this flag was flown whenever his command went into battle through the rest of the Civil War and during the time he spent on the froniter. To the Confederates it was a sure sign that they should take caution for their personal well being. The flag remained a permanent fixture all the years he was stationed in the West on the frontier. He and his wife Libby designed it and she hand-sewed it for him. When Custer ordered that his flag be unfurled and displayed, a sergeant was appointed to carry it. The flag bearer always rode close to the commander at the head of the column, always close to the right side of the commander. This flag was lost on the battlefield that last day and never recovered.

The flag above is a Troop Guideon; it too is swallow-tailed and closely resembles the American "Stars and Stripes". In the blue field are 34 five-point gold stars, one for each state of the Union. Each troop of Cavalry carried their own guideon. This guideon was used from the late 1860s through the 1880s by all cavalry units.

These two flags were the only ones that Custer and the 7th Cavalry took to the Little Bighorn.

The Last Ride will try to dispel many of the legends, half truths, and falsehoods that surround the man, Lieutenant Colonel George Armstrong Custer. At the time of his death, Custer held the rank of lieutenant colonel; however, during the Civil War he held the rank of a brevetted major general (two stars).

In this book the term "brevet" will be used from time to time. It is as interesting a term as it was practical and almost impossible to manage in the Union Army during the Civil War. There were more than 1,400 brevet promotions from the rank of major to lieutenant colonel and from lieutenant colonel to colonel and from colonel to brigadier general were made. That is somewhat of an interesting fact even if it is not well known. That being said, there was only one case where a lowly first lieutenant was promoted to brigadier general in all of those brevet promotions. That one man, of course, was George Armstrong Custer.

In reality, the Civil War is blamed for destroying the idea of allowing the brevet promotions. The practice was used prior to (the Mexican War) and during the Civil War and for a short time thereafter. The brevet rank was usually an honorary promotion given to an officer or occasionally, but very rarely to an enlisted man in recognition of gallant conduct or other meritorious service. They served much the same purpose that medals play today. The military did not have a system of medals at the time of the Civil War per say.

In a preponderance of cases being brevetted to a higher rank was almost meaningless in terms of real authority.

For example, a major who was promoted to a brevet lieutenant colonel collected the pay as a major and not of a lieutenant colonel. His shoulder boards showed him to be a major; he could not give orders to lieutenant colonels and was authorized only commands that would fall to other majors. About the only difference was that in written correspondence he was allowed to use his brevet rank title.

However, there were some unusual circumstances where the brevet rank did carry authority. One such case concerned, again, Lieutenant George Armstrong Custer. In 1861, he went from being a courier during the first battle of the war and later served on the staffs of Generals McClellan and Pleasonton from then until at Aldie, Virginia, June 1863, when the company commander was killed and he took it upon himself to lead the Michigan 3rd and 5th Cavalry in numerous attacks against a strongly entrenched Confederate force. He was successful in breaking through and routing them while having a couple horses shot out from underneath him in the process.

For this action he was promoted to Brigadier General of Volunteers in command of the 2nd Brigade, 3rd Division, Cavalry Corps, on October 19, 1864. His cavalry met and defeated General JEB Stewart twice on the battlefield, once at Gettysburg, July 3, 1863; and again at Yellow Tavern where General Stewart was killed. Ultimately, it was Custer's cavalry that cut off the General Robert E. Lee and his Army of Northern Virginia's last escape route from Appomattox Court House. For that action he was promoted twice; once to the rank of Brevet Major General of Volunteers, and on the same date, March 13, 1865, to Brevet Major General, U.S. Army. Both ranks are identical but in two separate Army structures, one the regular Army and the other in the huge volunteer Army. His rise to his highest attained rank was obviously something more than honorary.

Sometimes, and it was more customary than not in those days, an officer was retired at what would be his next higher rank if he had been promoted before retiring. It was a sort of thank-you for your service gesture of the country he had served. For example, that was the case of one Colonel Fredrick Benteen. When he retired from the service he was retired as a brigadier general rather than "just a full colonel." He was never paid a retirement that a brigadier general would be authorized; but he would be forever known as General Benteen nonetheless in private life, even though he had never served a day as a general. Somehow, that irony is fitting for the man.

During the Civil War, attrition was the main reason for officers being promoted rapidly to higher ranks than would have possible otherwise. The Union Army as well as the Confederates often had difficulty backfilling leadership positions because replacements with the proper rank just were not available. The brevetting of younger, more capable officers was one way to fill the hole in a command's officer corps and was a common practice in the North and almost never used in the South.

Custer's entire class resigned en mass from West Point Military Academy on the eve of having to sign an affirmation and sworn statement of allegiance to the United States of America. Custer would spend the next nearly two straight days and nights to make sure he did not miss the first battle riding from West Point, New York to Manassas Junction (Bull Run), May 23, 1861.

A little more than two years later we see him as one of the most popular, as well as youngest brigadier (one star) general in command of an entire brigade of cavalry in the Army of the Potomac. Within fifteen months of that he was this nation's youngest major general ever, at the age of twenty-four, leading the 3rd Cavalry Division. He was an example of what the Army needed then. He was a fighter and he was a survivor and he was rewarded with the rank that far exceeded his age.

To see what the officers and men under his command said of "Old Curly," the "Boy General," as he was sometimes referred to, would inspire the biggest doubter that George Armstrong Custer was anything but unworthy of his rank, prestige, and fame. He earned his rank; it was not given to him as a "thank-you for your years of service."

Soon after the war, the Army began to downsize. Nearly all the officers given brevet commissions, earned or otherwise, were either forced to leave the Army altogether or retired on the spot. Many of these officers did not have what it took to stay in the army or friends in high places or had not distinguished themselves enough to be saved from being kicked out.

Those who were allowed to stay were allowed to but most would be reverted back to their former official entitled ranks they held prior to the Civil War. In Custer's case he had not held any rank prior to the Civil War. Had he been anyone else and all things being equal, the Army would have allowed him to count his years of service as time held in grade. He would have been a reduced back to Captain, that being a rank he held only briefly as a staff member for General McClellen when he served on his staff shortly after his first battle.

His case was as unique as he was; he went from being a shave-tail second lieutenant to brigadier general, skipping the four ranks in between at the convenience of the Army. It was certainly a SNAFU that the Army would have to clean up someday; they knew that. But at that particular time, what the Army of the Potomac needed were officers who were willing to fight, and George Armstrong Custer could certainly do that.

When the Army finally got around to acting upon his case, two years after the war, he was reduced in rank to a lieutenant colonel. It was a rank, oddly enough, that he had never held during the war. He was only one of a very small handful of officers who was not busted all the way down to their last former officially held rank.

After being reduced to the rank of "light colonel" (the Army's euphemism for lieutenant colonel) he was placed as second in command of the newly formed 7th Cavalry, in July of 1868. The commander of the

7th Cavalry was Colonel Samuel Sturgis (more about him later).

Post-Civil War officers who had held higher ranks were often addressed by their former brevetted rank by their brotherhood officers in the field. That is why it is sometimes confusing when you hear or read accounts concerning this era and the Army's officer corps. In the movies or even in many of the books that flood the bookstore shelves you read about General Custer this or that. When that happens, the writers are either confused or do not know what he was to begin with.

If ever a man was born to be a general, George Armstrong Custer was the man, and he earned it the old fashion way—displaying the characteristics of an outstanding field commander at the highest standard. His greatest moment in his life occurred when he was given command of his own division of cavalry. Everything from then on was down hill from the moment he pinned on his second star and the war ended. At age twenty-four he had been to the loftiest peak of his life.

The man and the story of his life appear now, as much of a paradox as it was then, more than 125 years ago. Except for the American fascination with the events of that bloody Sunday afternoon, June 25, 1876, this man may well have been long forgotten.

No one in his battalion survived the short but savage fight that day. That fact alone adds just enough spice and mystery to the drama to keep his name and that of the 7th Cavalry legendary and a focal point of American folklore. The part each played that day has stayed alive in America's minds after all this time.

Many of the other past heroes in American history, some who had accomplished more with their lives than Custer ever did, are sadly all but forgotten. Perhaps, it is the kaleidoscope that future generations of Americans view their pasts with that gives each succeeding generations differing views of our American past. However, of this one fact I am sure: Let no one talk you out of the idea that Custer was not a real American hero, then or now. He was one while he lived, he was one when he was killed, and he is still one today. There are not many who can be counted that way.

As to the Little Bighorn fight, those who live through something like that will tell you that a thick, smog-like, strangling, blinding fog hangs over every battle man has ever fought. That same blurring fog—so thick one would have to slash through it with a saber—sticks to many of the details surrounding the Custer fight like badlands gumbo to a man's boots on a soggy rain-soaked day. The confusion that hangs on nearly all attempts at sorting fact from fiction is exhausting, imperfect work.

The years following the battle are some of the most sorrowful times in American history: the dismantling of a race of people occurs across the fruited plain in the land called America. Since then, time has fought against some of the very important facts concerning this particular saga, the Custer fight at the Little Bighorn River. The facts concerning this fight are as hard to catch as the wind-driven clouds that blow across the great Montana sky before a thundering storm in the summer time.

Some of the important information surrounding this near free for all fight simply evaporates. History has shown that some of the information was withheld by design–men like Major Reno and Benteen, battalion commanders in the 7th Cavalry that day, were inveterate liars. Others later, like Captain Wallace, fabricated facts and "truths" during the court of inquiry in 1879. Some knowingly withheld the truth, though perhaps to a lesser extent, men who knew better but did it anyway and should have been far above such things–Generals Terry, Crook, Sheridan, and Colonel Gibbon. Some of the truths were never heard because of bad timing like in the example of D Troop's commander, Captain Weir's untimely death. Some simply remained silent for protection of their commander's wife, Libby. Some withheld information for fear of destroying their own careers. Lieutenant Godfrey was one. To each they were disappointments all, they knew more than they ever admitted.

As for the hostiles, the Teton Lakota Sioux and the Shahiyala–the Tse-tsehese-staeste or Southern Cheyenne, (their name translated into, "Those who are hearted alike"; their Northern Shahiyala or Northern Cheyenne–Ohmeseheso, when you evaluate that point in time, in an effort to be fair, they had a legal right to the land they called home. They had a signed in a treaty by these same *wasichu* ([waz I chû]—the Indian's word for white man) who were coming to steal it from them.

You might say, "What the hell is fair with that?" Good Question. The answer is more complex and cannot be answered within the next few pages, perhaps another time I will address that issue.

But for now, we find that in less than a year after the Custer fight, the Lakota and Shahiyala people were in total disarray. The people are starving to death because the buffalo are all but gone; or, their old people and children are dying of disease and exposure; what few warriors are left among the tribes have nothing to hunt. No one is safe from the horrors brought on them.

After only a handful of years beyond the fight, these Native American people had assassinated many of their once-powerful Indian leaders. Even Sitting Bull would fall from an assassin. Sitting Bull, perhaps the most respected of all of the Lakota, was not immune to the destruction of the people that seemed to implode in on them all. The once-mighty spirit and pride of this battle's victors is broken and remains so to this day.

Only a few years after that historic fight, an entire race of people is trampled like plowed up prairie grass behind a massive buffalo stampede. Like a punch-drunk fighter staggering around from corner to corner in a boxing ring, being hit from every angle, the American Plains Indians still have not recovered—by the looks of it today, they never will.

To this day, the United States government has not honored even one treaty it has signed with the Lakota or Shahiyala. Instead, the government has created a class of people who have for the most part have lost their dignity and honor by systematically building a welfare state on the reservations across this land that was once theirs. Today, in this politically-correct environment, we, the citizens of the United States of America, would demand the government declare war against any nation that did what we did by our own accord to the Native Americans.

We would clamor and demand justice for no other reason than human rights and common decency of any government other than our own for doing what we did then more than a century ago. It continues on to this day with no end in sight.

When looked upon in that vein, what happened to the Native American is far worse than the defeat of Custer. The loss of five troops of essentially immigrant, green-horn, largely untrained, and ill-equipped cavalry is not much in comparison to what happened to this vanquished victor.

What happened to Lieutenant Colonel Custer and the 7th Cavalry was nothing more than a sign of the times in which these men lived. For Lieutenant Colonel Custer's part, he was not unlike all men we have ever known. He certainly had many outstanding qualities. Along with those attributes was a darker, ominous, and threatening side. He was in the end what all men are, the sum total of all the pluses and minuses.

His commander ordered him to the field with half as many men—and most of these mostly young experience-wise and not fully trained—as he should have commanded. Most of his officers were without any Indian-fighting experience; his troops were armed with outdated weapons.

As one might expect, the Army finally blamed him for the fiasco that occurred in the middle of that hot Sunday afternoon. By doing so the U.S. Army tried to place this man along side the likes of William Crawford or William Fetterman who had blundered their way into something they could not get out of and whose commands were wiped out to the last man. Poor leadership, they would call it. What is worse, most believe it to this day. That was a sad commentary and poor reflection of the Army then, and is, in some instances, now.

At first glance, it is human nature to blame someone for failing that last day during critical times during the fight. The truth is more elusive, and less obvious as to who should shoulder the blame. The burden of the disaster should be borne by more than just those on that field under his command that day. For the most part, historians tend to whitewash certain events by saying the other battalion commanders did not have a choice.

My perspective is different, though if given the choice, these men may have wanted to fail Custer the commander, rather than Custer the man. For most men they could not make the distinction or separate the two from one another. Most often, those main officers, Major Marcus, Major Reno, and Captain Frederick Benteen, are framed as trying to do what they could. They had their day in a military court of inquiry and were found innocent of all charges for dereliction of duty. That same court found that at critical times these two so overcome with near death struggles of their own that they could not have come to their commander's aid.

You have been led to believe they were simply overcome by events—light years beyond their control. In the end, that was the simple truth, but far from being the whole truth and nothing but the truth.

In the end the defeat of Lieutenant Colonel Custer was simple—the river was too wide and the hill too tall, the prairie too wide, and there were just too damn many hostiles to have any hope of winning. The question was, "How in the world could they have ever seriously contemplated trying to get to him and his command to help?"

At the same time, a great many other young and inexperienced officers and their own green, under-equipped troopers, were for the first time facing the vaunted Plains Indians—Shahiyala, the world's finest horse cavalry, and the fierce Lakota, or what they became known as by the white man, the Sioux Nation, the Lakota nation—Brulés, Oglalas, Unkpapa (Hunkpapas), Minnecoujous (Minniconjoux), Sans Arcs, Blackfeet, Two Kettles; plus the Arapaho, Gros Venture, and other sub-tribes.

Further, many of the officers and troopers had no experience at fighting Indians, any Indians. For these men and even many of the old, grizzled veterans, they would only get this one chance–and that one would not be a pleasant experience for them. As for their commander, he had paid his dues to be allowed to go the way he would have wanted to go, leading his last charge on his last ride.

While no one who really knows about what he or his men faced, they can not seriously say he was the oaf he is often portrayed as being today. Many who have claimed expert status on the subject have simply failed to look past the seemingly obvious shortcomings of the commander, and have judged him unfairly and thus, wrongly.

What they have based their reasons on has nothing to do with facts or truth; one does not automatically beget the other. The story most often told of the Custer fight builds its foundation, as you will see, on falsehoods and misrepresentations of facts.

Lieutenant Colonel Custer's greatest failing, perhaps, was that to the end of his life he dared to dare. It made him seem impulsive and at times almost adolescent in his actions. His personal history only reflect that he was willing to stand on the thinnest branch of the tallest oak tree around and wave in the wind when no one else would have even considered it.

However, he was a natural leader who learned how to command during nearly one hundred battles and engagements he was a part of during the Civil War. His deeds between his youth while in the Academy and his command of a cavalry division at the end of the Civil War show growth of gigantic proportions. Even his tactics at the fight of the Little Bighorn River command begrudging respect and admiration of many notable peers.

Folks have gone to great lengths to point out his shortcomings to illustrate how incompetent he was. He was a man who did always what he thought was right for him at the time. He would be officially hooked for such thinking several times during his career. His first such offense occurred while he was a cadet at West Point. That one almost caused his missing being engaged during the first battle of the Civil War because he was ordered to stand a court martial (one of three in his career). That was a convoluted truth after a fashion. He was charged for failing to stop a fight at West Point when he was officer of the guard for no better reason than he wanted to watch the fight himself as the charges read.

Soon-to-be officers and gentlemen, as ordained by the United States Congress, did not take part in such things–but Custer did. The incident was more than just a fight between brother cadets, he and a few of the guards (his friends) had decided to go to an off-limits bar for a quick drink of warm rum while on guard duty and sneak back before anyone found out (it was in the dead of winter, and these cadets had drag duty). They were shanghaied as they came back by the officer of the day. A spirited discussion (fight) broke out between the catchers, and the caught.

Custer took the blame for it if the others were spared. Before his actions could be tried by a Courts Martial he and the entire senior class resigned and went their separate ways. Over half, forty-three cadets went south to Dixie, while only thirty four went to Washington or Manassas Junction to volunteer in the Army of the Potomac.

His actions were always subject to closer scrutiny by those jealous of his many successes. At the same time his loyalties to his men can never be questioned.

Concerning the plight of the Plains Indian, he wrote in an often-quoted passage in his unfinished biography, *My Life on the Plains*, "If I were an Indian, I would greatly prefer to cast my lot among those of my people who adhered to the free open plains rather than submit to the confined limits of a reservation."

In the end, on that blood-soaked hill, he would get his wish. Custer and nearly a third of his regiment lay dead and mutilated at the feet of these same Stone Age people he was talking about.

You see—something that perhaps he had not counted on was that the Indians loved their freedom and their way of life every bit as much as the *wasichu* who were trying to take it from them did. In a sense, it was fitting that his military life should end the way it began—on a Sunday. The first battle of Bull Run was on a Sunday also.

Lieutenant Colonel Custer had his orders, as outlandish and ambiguous as they seem now, after more than 125 years of reflection and study by hundreds of "experts," he would try to follow those orders, even if it killed him.

Regardless of what one thinks of George Armstrong Custer, the man, or the cavalry officer, he was pure unadulterated hell on the back of a horse. He died pitching into his country's enemy as the point of the spear against impossible odds that the vaunted American Plains Indian held that day.

He would not have chosen any other way. Those who did not personally like him could be nothing but impressed with his tactics, tenacity, and courage when facing an enemy of his country in battle. What happened that day, June 25, 1876, and many others like it on the frontier must never be forgotten, or counted as insignificant.

Often, with the passage of time, that is what historians do. They portray older historical events as less important than other more current events. That is wrong. Shame on the history book writers, and shame on the history teacher who thinks he cannot teach relevancy to his students by teaching his students about our American past. Though the picture of our past may not be pure of heart and as clean as storm-driven snow on a cold winter morn, it is still ours, from whence we came, and how we got to where we are today.

A long time ago I read, "Those who forget their past have no future."

LAST RIDE

I was twelve years old and visiting one of my first Civil War battle sites. Those few words have stayed with me ever since that time. My older sister had taken me to Vicksburg, Mississippi. The epitaph was over the doorway leading into a courthouse in that once-embattled city. It was fitting then, and it is more fitting today.

Past events should always be important to us as Americans. All of us, as one people, regardless of our skin color, for the good, as well the bad of that past. Whatever the situation, what it was then, and what it is now is why we (as Americans) are what we are today.

The injustices of that time, against not just the Plains Indians, but also all Native Americans, cannot be denied. Denial will never change a situation any more than the injustices of an earlier time concerning the slavery of African Americans will go away or change if we do not talk about it. It is too easy of an answer to say that in those days, everybody could be a slave. It did not then, and does not today, make a difference what one's skin color was or is. Slavery was wrong. The point being, Americans decided to make this country different, and were willing to fight and suffer nearly a million casualties to change the idea of enslaving a race of people. It was white Americans fighting white Americans, brothers fighting brothers to solve that issue between Americans. Slavery was wrong-headed. There have not been white men standing up to fight for the American Indians. That is wrong-headed also.

The danger comes from rewriting the past so the truth is hidden, or misconstrued, or deemed unimportant and in time, with apathy being an added ingredient into the mixture, the wrong is, and has been, forgotten. That is one of the reasons why the Custer story and others like it are so important. We should never forget our past, whether it is our personal past or our nation's past. We will become stronger as individual people and as a nation if we remember from whence we came.

Most times, the writers themselves lose track of what is important, and what is not. History counts; it is why we are what we are. The Battle of the Little Bighorn River is just one of literally hundreds of events that could have just as well have been forgotten. But it was not, and it should never be forgotten.

The Battle of the Little Bighorn will always leave just too many unknowns to suite us *wasichu*. There are just too damn many missing pieces to the puzzle to know for sure what really happened at the end of Battle Ridge, or down some gully on the edge of Custer Hill. To me it really does not matter where the last soldier may have fallen, or even who it was that fell last. Dead is dead.

On the surface of the incident, the fact the superior forces of a nearly Stone Age people overwhelmed the then-modern civilized man's 7th Cavalry is almost unfathomable. How could this have happened? This was, after all, the "modern age" white man fighting the "Stone Age" prairie- dweller. We have been led to believe by historians and movie-makers the 7th Cavalry was a veteran Indian-fighting force.

Lieutenant Colonel Custer led his regiment down the divide of the Wolf Mountains, and into the valley of the Greasy Grass. The Greasy Grass was the Indian's name for the valley of the Little Sheep River–the Indian name for the white man's Little Bighorn River. What happened next would make the British charge of the Light Brigade against Russian canon at Balaclava in 1854 seem like a well thought-out, and perfectly executed military operation.

In their myopic view of the situation, the United States Army saw an enemy. The 7th Cavalry was sent to fight a rag-tag bunch of beggars who would not and could not fight such an organized force, much less stand up to Lieutenant Colonel George Armstrong Custer's mighty horse soldiers. The Army, after all, was this mighty military force that had brought the Confederates to their knees as they begged for mercy. These beggars would not know that and what is more they did not care. The Army's kind of thinking is what started things going into the crapper. Somebody was mixing apples and bananas and calling them the oranges.

The U.S. Army was during the Civil War a tried and true military force. That was during another time, eleven years earlier. What that day in June of 1876, had to do with the years of Civil War that this same U.S. Army had waged, was exactly nothing. It was not the same Army.

What most do not often understand is the rag-tag bunch of beggars was better equipped, fighting on their own lands, and had a ten to twelve times larger fighting force than the 7th Cavalry Regiment. Not only that, if it was not enough; these Indians were going to protect what was theirs by reason of ancestry and personal possession—possession being nine-tenths of the law—to the death if necessary.

If the Indians had not fought the blue coats, what would have happened to them? Where were they going to go? What would they when they got there? Many had tried doing what the *wasichu* had wanted and many had died either by starvation or white man's diseases and sickness.

These people did not have trades that they could go out and earn a living. They had no concept of the white man's term. They earned their living for themselves and their families and other needy folks in their tribes by hunting and fishing on lands that had always been open to them. They took care of their own. Everybody ate; if one went hungry, they all went hungry.

Many, many of these Indian people had tried the white man's way already, and had either been attacked at night while they slept, or nearly starved to death believing the Great White Father in Washington DC would provide their food and take care of them. Throw in two or three, or thirty treaties (the Fort Laramie Treaty of 1868 being the main one) signed by the white man establishing the Indians rights to the land they were on as a people casts a different light on the subject.

The government had not kept even one treaty signed by their well-meaning agents or Army officers. Nor did the government really have any intent in keeping its promises. It is not hard to believe under the leadership of Red Cloud, Crazy Horse, Gall, Lame White Man, and Buffalo Bull Who Sits (Sitting Bull) the Indians were a little more than tired of listening to the white man's promises.

As for the fight on the Little Bighorn River, we should accept the idea for what it was; a defeat for the U.S. Army and the government of the then United States and its white people. Unfortunately, it was little more than a whisper in the wind. About all the battle accomplished for the Indians was to stave off the inevitable for a few months; the end would come fast. Like the buffalo, the Plains Indians would nearly become extinct very quickly.

What happened on the hillsides just east of that gently-running stream one Sunday, just after noon, June 25, 1876, is an American saga. Even after a century and a quarter plus years. That is good. We should never forget our American history and how we, as Americans, got to where we are today as a people and a nation.

Men like Custer, and later our parents, and later still, you and I, got us where we are now, like it or not. What we are today, for better or worse, is the America we now claim as our home. Each of us, no matter how great or small, has had a hand in shaping the story our children and their children take into their lives as Americans. What we have learned from our mistakes and successes, we will pass on to future generations of Americans.

Let us hope the story they tell about us will be the way it really was, and as we knew it to be and that it was above all, the best we could do.

This rendition of that last ride of Lieutenant Colonel George Armstrong Custer and his battalion of the 7TH Cavalry Regiment will hopefully not place too much blame on anyone who does not deserve it. Not because it is not politically the correct thing to do—kicking the dead, but because it is not necessary—the facts speak for themselves. Custer's superior commanders, acting upon circumstances beyond their own control, doomed the 7th Cavalry to its own fate. Custer did what everybody knew he would. He fought.

If they did not want a fight, they should have left him at home with Libby, his pack of hounds, and his band, and let Major Reno take the U.S. 7th Cavalry to the field. What happened should not have surprised anyone, then, or even now.

Last Ride hopefully puts to rest some of the misnomers and innuendoes concerning this battle in particular, and the man specifically. In the end, you will have to draw your own conclusion as to whether George Armstrong Custer was a real American hero, or nothing more than a glory-hound and fool.

Author's Note: Before I even get started, I need to clarify something. It is of absolutely no import as far as the story you are about to read, but while I was researching the material for what you are about to read, I came across numerous references to Custer's horse (of all things). It is and was a complete bafflement to me, why would anyone even stop to think about such a thing as the gender of the horse he was riding that last time.

Perhaps, if you were like me, I had never once ever thought about his horse, in nearly fifty years; that is a long time not to have ever wondered about something, but I never did.

However, you may have wondered about the lieutenant colonel's horse that he was riding that day. And if you have, here is what I found:

As a very minor point of interest here, it seems these types of things come up over and over again as an attempt to distract researchers, rather than to add substance to the event we are trying to uncover.

People have wondered, "Was 'Vic', the lieutenant colonel's horse, a boy or a girl?" For those who do not want to sound totally unaware, a boy horse is either a stallion (meaning the male horse still has them "hanging"), or gelding, meaning that they do not "hang;" they are missing, snipped off as it were); all "girl horses" are called mares.

A little dull-witted perhaps, but maybe even a fair question for those who get easily distracted. Why folks would even wonder that is beyond me? I do not know.

However, in such cases, it depends on who you want to believe! I do not know why anyone would even ask! Perhaps, people have too much idle time on their hands or in these times of women's lib and NAGS we want to always be politically correct, who knows? It certainly did not make any difference at all, but here goes...

The lieutenant colonel had two horses he rode during this campaign; both would survive the battle. One would never be seen again. Libby was told that, "he lay dead beside his master," presumably as a way to comfort the poor distraught woman when told of her husband's demise. In researching this particular point, I found about as many folks who thought the same thing as Libby was told as there were people who thought it was the he should be a she and not the other way around, "she lay beside her dead master." It was nearly a draw.

First of all, "she" or "he" did not lie beside "her" or "his" master—even though someone a year later cut the hooves off a skeleton of an animal lying close to where Custer (they said) and his brother were buried, calling the new trophies "Vic's' hooves." The man turned them into bookends and inkwell holders (in memory of the event I suppose).

In comparing the pictures of the two horses together and assuming the captions beneath the pictures are correct (the sources don't even agree most times with which horse was called by which name) I would have to say, that one of the animals is definitely a male and the other definitely a female. Now, which is which?

'Vic,' the animal's name, is irritatingly interesting because it was the horse's name that the lieutenant colonel was riding that last day. The question now is, "Was the name short for Victor or Victoria?"

If we can trust pictures, I would have to say as someone of fair authority on male and female physiology of livestock, that 'Dandy' was a 'he'. In other words a gelding or a stallion—meaning he may have been castrated; or no, he may not have been. Perhaps you have heard the expression, "He's a Dandy!" Meaning of course, that it was a very fine "whatever," in this case, "horse" is credited with getting the lieutenant colonel to the battlefield.

'Dandy' was a smallish dark sorrel with a small blaze on his forehead and three white stockings. He was a beautiful animal. He had the look of a thoroughbred and substantiates Libby's claim that one of the animals was a Kentucky thoroughbred, though she could not remember which one. She thought it was Vic who was the Kentucky thoroughbred (more about that later) and was, (at least in my mind in looking at the pictures) beautifully structured piece of horse flesh—gallant, well rounded, strong of spirit, tough, and well-bred, would be the phrase that would describe him. In other words, the horse was fitting for this lieutenant colonel to ride to, or in, battle, and one that you would expect to see prancing between the legs of this lieutenant colonel.

Vic, on the other hand, has the look of a plow horse, perhaps one step away from a Clydesdale. Vic was a much larger, bigger-boned, and heavier duty animal than little Dandy. Vic looked to be about 300 pounds or so heavier than Dandy. In other words, Vic was what the Army bought for use as a "warhorse," three white stockings, blaze-faced, the animal just looked strong and powerful. The horse was strong, well muscled-shoulders, broad-beamed, strong-neck, large-head; two, or two and a half hands taller than Dandy. If you wanted to ride over the top of someone in your way, Vic would do that without any problem for the lieutenant colonel.

In conclusion, I would have to say, Dandy brung the lieutenant colonel to dance. Vic was to tote him home; it just didn't work out that way. 'Vic' was short for 'Victor', and not 'Victoria'.

For those who might have wondered even further…it was rumored that a Shahiyela warrior by the name of 'Walks Under the Ground' rode her off the field after the fight. The tale goes the Indians had not messed with Vic until after the fight because his reins were still tied around the lieutenant colonel's wrist (standard procedure for cavalry soldiers when mounted for charges or combat—they tied the reins around one wrist, not their shooting hand, rather than risk dropping the reins in battle.

The Indians, being sort of a spooky lot about dead folks, were just a little jumpy about taking a horse when the dead owner, after a fashion, still had a hold of it. Apparently though, while the hostiles were stripping the lieutenant colonel's body after the fight, the reins became "untied" or at any rate the reins "gave way" and it was then safe to take the beast then.

As for little Dandy—later, after the survivors of the 7th Cavalry got back to Fort Lincoln, the gutsy little stallion was sent back to the lieutenant colonel's father in Monroe, Michigan. What ever became of Vic was never determined.

Supposedly when Libby was asked what gender Vic was, she said, "She was a Kentucky thoroughbred stallion…." That clears it up for me, she was a stallion!

For now, I will flip a coin; John Burkman, Lieutenant Colonel Custer's striker, said when asked this question, "Vic? Why hell, man, she was a mare, because I had washed and curried her coat a thousand times, I ought to know, bud." Normally, that would have sewed it up for me…an actual live, first hand opinion from a source who would have known. But, alas, everything is not as it seems. John, when asked that question, was a pretty old man, and had fought many a bout with the bottle for a number of years prior to that. He had some trouble from time to time even knowing what day it was, or for that matter, who he was for sure. In a passage concerning the horse Victoria or Victor, Custer refers to the animal as a "him." So who do you believe? I guess I would go with George and not Libby or John.

INTRODUCTION

Through the course of time, from the early settlements of the eastern coastlines of the present day United States, many thousands of pioneers had pushed for the settlement of the western lands. They lay claim to all that was before them as their own.

The Indians who lived on these lands could never understand how men could own the land. How could some white man (*wasichu* to the American Indian) claim it as theirs? The red man had lived on all of the lands for as long as the sun had risen in the east and set in the west. In a more perfect world, these people, though "Stone Age," when the wasichu invaded their ancestral lands had more of a right to call the land theirs. These white-eyes had no rights to it, and yet they were taking it from them in giant gulps. The American Indian continually gave way, fighting the best fight they could, but always backing away from their lands, piece by piece.

How things have changed. The mere mention of the terms "imminent domain" or "manifest destiny" were then, just as repugnant of terms as they are now. In today's world we do not talk in these terms. We sugarcoat them, and call them something else that means the same thing; "liberating." Everything goes down better when we swallow if we do not call it by what it was.

It was then, and is now, a natural law. The law is Only the Strongest Survive. This natural law is most unpopular, and not now politically correct. We do not like to think in those terms. It disturbs our sensitivities if we happen to think on it too long.

This natural law, "manifest destiny" applies to all forms of life, and is as old as life itself. Roughly translated, it proclaims, "What is yours is yours; as long as you can maintain physical control of it. Once you lose that ability, or physical strength and/or power to possess it—it (whatever "it" is) belongs to someone else."

It matters not one bit at all if the rightful owner takes a hundred, or two hundred, or even a thousand years to lay claim to what is rightfully theirs. It is the law of the jungle—only the strong survive; it has nothing to do with individual human rights, or national honor, or being fair, or anything like that. It is the way it is.

This unwritten law was in effect by those same Indians who were found in the Americas long before the *wasichu* found the lands. They may not have thought about it in the terms expressed above, but they practiced its tenets among themselves for thousands of years.

The first time a Viking ship landed on some barren ice-covered northeastern shore, or a Spanish Conquistador landed on the beaches of the Yucatan in Mexico, or even much later when the first Englishman stepped out on to the forested lands of New England, the ownership of these vast lands, from "sea to shining sea," changed hands. Not a shot had to be fired or an arrow shot into anyone, ownership changed hands.

Of course, it did not play out that way; folks do not take kindly to other folks taking what they think is theirs to begin with. Nobody likes to be kicked around, and the American red man, "Stone Age" and uncivilized or not, was no different.

The many tribes of the North American Indians, as they became known, no longer controlled the land from sea to shining sea. They had lost the right to roam as they had for thousands of years. The realization that they had also lost any right to that land's bounty was slow in coming and they would not accept it without a fight. No red-blooded white men would accept such a thing any better than they did. It would be a fight to the bitter end and at the end there would be no glory in the outcome.

The natural law does not make exceptions. It never has and never will, and it would not change for the American Indian in the 15th and 16th centuries. To this day the law is still in place. The white settlers did not make up this law so they could become the masters of North America. They were perpetuators of it. It is the law of pack. At that point there were too many to fight and defeat.

In time, that could change; men of a different skin color may wrestle control away from the white man just as the white man wrestled it away from the red man. Things change, and as evolution goes, perhaps a change has already occurred, and we just do not know it—yet.

These kinds of things do not just happen like lightning striking from the sky. They have to percolate for a spell before fact becomes reality.

As for the often-cried Indian savagery, how soon we forget. It was not very long ago when my own ancestors were doing worse to their fellow man, or had the same thing done to them in the towers of London. They were white-skinned folks doing the same kinds of things to each other. It only is mutilation, when one mutilates someone of another race or nationality. Then it becomes savagery, and then really offensive to the defrocked individuals.

So much of what we think about what is right or wrong comes from our perceptions of justice. A very old and wise man whom I respected greatly once said to me, "...the veneer of civilization is very thin; you only have to scratch the surface of it off before you find out that not long ago we used to eat each other and think nothing of it."

—1—

FIELD COMMANDER

LIEUTENANT COLONEL GEORGE ARMSTRONG CUSTER
Seventh Cavalry Regiment, Field Commander, Montana Expedition

It was May 5, 1876. The re-united 7th Cavalry (formed July 8, 1868) was finally together at Fort Abraham Lincoln, North Dakota Territories at long last. It had been many years since the whole regiment had been in one location. Its field commander, when held to the same candling-light as his fellow brethren, is more renowned than any in the Army at the time. Oh, there are a few— the Grants, Shermans, the Sheridans and even JEB Stewart and Mosley, that history has not all but forgotten. But for the most part, none will achieve the long-lasting fame his name etches in American history books, and the minds of America's youth from his time on.

Those others remain now unnamed, and most times forgotten, while General George Armstrong Custer's legend lives on and on. On the surface of it, it hardy seems fair his name and deeds surrounding the Little Bighorn Battle should be so stained and misunderstood. For whatever reason, many of his critics have chosen to believe the worst concerning this officer's actions that last time out. It is more understandable today than at the time he and his regiment made that last ride.

Historians and military experts have labeled the man, George Armstrong Custer, as a "glory hunter." He was, but, also, more than just that. They have called him "an insufferable ass," and he could certainly have been that. No one had to tell him how great he was; he had already convinced himself, and his wife Libby for that matter. Others have likened him to the "Napoleon of the West." During the Civil War he was called the "Boy General," and later, "Murat of the American Army." He had lots of names: Curly, Fanny, Iron Ass, Son of Morning Star, and many others as well.

Sometimes, folks would get overzealous about the superfluous titles they heaped upon him. He would let them do it; he had an ego as large as a hungry ape in the wilds of Africa who needed something to eat. It mattered little to him if the facts were a little overstated sometimes; he rather enjoyed folks thinking he was great.

His troops sometimes referred to him as "Old Iron Ass" because he could stay in a saddle so long. Everyone else in his command would be nearly delirious from fatigue, saddle sore, and bone-weary, but not George; he was just getting started.

The word "ass" is often used when his several critics attempt to describe him. In truth he was one, sometimes. But, who among us are not, at times, asses? Sometimes, he was much worse; sometimes, we all are.

Some who served with him saw him as their knight in shinning armor. They would follow his battle flag through the gates of hell itself if he was their leader. Others saw him as some sort of beast in sheep's clothing. Or worse, they would think him the devil incarnate. In the final analysis, he was undoubtedly a glory-hunter. Most times he was an "insufferable ass" or a much worse modifier.

He also fell far short of being close to resembling anything like a "Napoleon of anything"…and certainly not of the West. He would not live long enough to become that. George Armstrong Custer was something else—he was most of those things mentioned above, and then a great deal more; sometimes even a great deal less. He was then, and is now, an enigma.

Nonetheless, George Custer is a true American hero. More often than not, Custer is misunderstood, misquoted, or worse, out-and-out lied about. The truth of the matter is that dead men do not talk—and they certainly cannot defend themselves. Their actions are often misunderstood, and always left personally undefended from the grave.

You can say what you want about them, and they will do nothing about it. They are, hopefully, above responding. History leaves the final analysis for the future generations to work out. In this particular case, the last word has not been written about the man, or the part he played in the events of that day he and his command fell.

More will surely come who will try to explain, justify, or damn him in the part he played as a soldier during that last Indian campaign. He served his country for a good part of fifteen years, faithfully. In every year of service he did so with valor, and breathtaking bravery. I certainly would withhold the temptation of adding honor to everything he did.

George Armstrong Custer was a good soldier. He was an excellent field commander. He was an iron-assed, tough-fisted taskmaster as a combat field commander. His experience as such taught him to be that way. His methods were technically sound. His combat experience made him a very skilled, tactical officer during four long years and nearly a hundred military operations against the Confederates during the Civil War.

He then turned his ire against a half dozen or so separate Indian tribes from Texas: Comanche, Kiowa, Apache, Pawnee, Arapaho, Cheyenne, and Sioux, to name a few. When he could catch them and make them fight the way he wanted them to, he defeated them, except for that last time. You can argue about his tactics and methods, but not the results.

Most of his career in the military, or the many facets of his personal life, are not discussed at length in many books or articles concerning him. Most of the time one would believe he was born, raised, and then somehow managed to find himself on that battlefield all in one quick breath.

What one perceives of the man from these snippets of his life seem to somehow be unrelated–or even colored to prejudices the audience being catered to or the writer as he writes. To believe he had no life before going to the Little Bighorn is obviously short-sighted.

One usually never gets a feel for George Armstrong Custer, the man. What was it that made this man the firebrand he was? What did he think about? What did he care about? Most of what you hear or read about this man's life as a soldier and his life as just a man is one dimensional. Often, that side of him is discarded as non important. His story was built with his own sweat, tears, and ultimately his own blood.

Just as there are for all of us, there was more to him than just a shadow of the man the public knew about. Though, for most of us, we ourselves would be happy with a mere shadow to be remembered by.

His military career may have gone better had his political affiliation been different. He was somewhat stymied by the fact he was not personally wealthy and happened to be politically affiliated with the Democrat Party.

In those times, he needed to be a Republican if he wanted to succeed in the Army. He was never very astute that way. Wrongly, he guessed, and was just stubborn enough to believe his deeds on the battlefield would cover his debt politically. He was wrong about that, and he found the going hard, especially after the war.

When Custer was given command of a brigade during the Civil War, and along with it his first star, he took with him the childhood friend to whom he had always been closest. Custer was like that; he depended on friends to be unshakably loyal. Lieutenant George Yates, his adjutant, was that. Over the fifteen years they served together, George Yates was always at the General's side.

George Yates and a little brother, Thomas Ward Custer, never left his side when in the field–especially once he moved to Fort Abraham Lincoln (near present day Bismarck, North Dakota), in the Dakota Territories. It also establishes a president that would follow Custer all through his life as a soldier. He surrounded himself with family or close military friends when in command of a force in the field.

Only the closest handpicked officers and men would serve with him directly. These few men were trusted by him to do their jobs, and fight as he fought. For commanders, making hard decisions concerning life and death issues he wanted men who would make those decisions as he would if he were in their place. Sometimes, it put tremendous pressure on those men, their friendship, and loyalty to the general. Most of the time, it kept men alive when under fire.

Those who served with him that last time out and lived to talk about it later remembered one thing distinctly about their last night before the fight. They said the only time they ever heard him justify himself to his officers was that last night. He never did that before, and of course, never would again.

He had his methods, and as harsh and unrelenting as they seemed at the time, they worked for him. They may not have for someone else who was not as inwardly driven as he was.

As for his treatment of troops, he gave no mercy to deserters. After the Civil War, the Army was experiencing terrible desertion ratios—as high as seventy percent in some outfits. Custer's rates approached that temporarily while in Kansas and Colorado. He put a stop to the problem in the 7th Cavalry by promptly having three deserters shot dead, hanging three others, and putting seven in the hospital from wounds sustained from trying to out run the men who were sent to bring them back to face charges of desertion.

The word was out in the 7th: do not desert— if you do, you take your life in your own hands at Custer's leisure. His rates fell in the 7th Cavalry to a more acceptable twenty five percent.

As for the soldierly skills, he had mastered as many as his peers had; the rifle (he was an expert marksman), the saber, and horsemanship (he was a superb rider). He could line up an artillery piece or design and build a bridge to move his cavalry across most any stream in his way. At the same time, he would have preferred to blow up that same bridge with his self-aimed artillery piece once his troops had crossed than ever retreat back across it. He hated to back up.

That made him a little different than most men in the Army at the time. Usually they went out of the way to avoid a fight. Not Custer; he never thought about the retreat, only the charge. His fervent desire was to trample his enemies, whoever they were, beneath his cavalrymen's horse's steel-clad hooves.

Simply, he was a fighter, and he was born for it. In those days after the Civil War not many men like him were left alive. For that reason probably, to most men, he was a little scary, he did not plan on losing, and never thought about a way out of a fix if he got into one.

He was a superb shot with a rifle, though probably two others in the 7th Cavalry Regiment were better, his adjutant, Canadian-born, Lieutenant Colonel William Winner Cooke (Custer always misspelled the man's name, choosing to write it "Cook"). Apparently, it did not matter to Cooke; he knew who the general was talking about; and the regiment's lead scout, Lonesome Charlie Reynolds. Both died at the Little Bighorn the day Custer fell.

His side-arms would appear more for show than shooting something to death—matching, self-cocking pearl-handled .38-caliber nickel plated, British Parrot Bulldogs. As weapons they might scare the hell out of you when they went off, but would lose accuracy past thirty to forty yards. They would have been good for close-in work, to which he was not averse. Sword-fighting did not bother him either; he was excellent at either the sword or pistol.

It was said that he had small hands. The Parrot handle-grips (horned) fit his hand better than the larger block-handled Army standard issue .45-caliber Colt pistol's blocky grip.

Picture him with his custom-made, shortened-octagonal barrel, repeating .44-caliber rifle, and his two nickel-plated .38 caliber pistols. Neatly tucked down the inside of his floppy-eared knee-high Wellington ridding boots was a nine-inch-long scalping knife he had taken from an unfortunate Indian enemy.

Add to that (though he did not take it with him that last time out) a longer-than-regulation cutlass. It too was taken from the first man he killed during the Civil War. He had chased the man (an officer) down and finally shot him in the back as he was making his retreat across a stream when Custer rode him down and shot him in first engagement.

Nobody ever would accuse George Custer of not getting his "blood up" during a fight. Throughout his career, he gave no quarter, and in the end, he never asked for any.

Mounted on either of his horses (Dandy or Vic), a pack of hunting hounds barking at his horse's heels, he would have been an impressive sight. Dressed in his bleached buckskin pants and jacket over a dark blue navy shirt and red flowing neck tie, George Armstrong Custer would have been outstanding to look upon.

Standing flat-footed, he stood nearly six feet in height in his stocking feet, and was a little on the thin side of 165 pounds. His Wellington knee-high boots helped create a near comical image of a cavalier, or perhaps one of the missing French Musketeers. His broad-brimmed hat covering sometimes long reddish blond hair; a bushy, long, droopy mustache that covered his almost invisible lips; below a straight and pointed nose and bright, piercing, steel blue-gray eyes, and your mind's eye has captured what Custer must have imagined a consummate savior of the West would look like.

When unleashed onto his enemies he was like an aroused cobra that would strike you in a New York second. He would not back up; his enemies would have to beat him back. It was not over for him until he had his hot little hands around his enemy's neck, strangling the very life out of him. He liked to fight!

He said once that, "his voice was for war," so too then was his total being.

He had a warrior's heart; he could love you, or kill you. He was passionate either way. He always gave his best shot, held no grudges, and made no excuses if things went the other way, which sometimes, not often, happened.

To his many military critics he was just about everything good officers were not, in their opinion. They would say he lacked the gentleman qualities of his brother officers. They would say he had a spotty education at best in his youth, scarcely passing most of his subjects, and then only by the skin of his teeth. They would say that he was precocious, reckless, a bothersome troublemaker, and a constant tease to everyone close to him. In truth, he was, particularly to little brother Tom and any other family member within his grasp. He had a hard time "growing up."

Others have said his parents could not handle him as a youth and shipped him off to other members of the family just to get him out of their hair. It was passed around that even those members of his family had pawned him off to one another while he was growing up in Ohio. Then later in Michigan he had many of the same problems his own mother and father had with him. He was a handful for sure. One would think, rather than a future soldier, they were raising the first cousin of Dutch Shultz instead.

To say he was a precocious child would have been making light of the fact young George Custer was a handful and then some. As many rural folks did in those days, as soon as the boys could work, they were put behind a plow and mule to help put food on the table. Schooling would have to come second.

His father, a blacksmith and farmer from Ohio before moving to Michigan, would have been poor by most standards in those days; modest would have been too kind.

When his father's fields were squared away, and that work was caught up, he was also sent to help his two older sisters' men with their field chores. Sometimes, that interfered with schoolwork, and young George Custer was not opposed to missing out on a few days of school if he could work it out.

Daddy Custer was a dirt-poor German immigrant farmer with a large two-marriage family to feed, and in those days, men did what men had to do: Providing a roof over everyone's head, and making sure the children got fed were the basic priorities, followed by cleanliness and godliness.

—2—

WHEN BOYS BECOME MEN

Boys became men at a very early age in the 1800s. Life did not allow them to look back on a childhood lost. Instead, there were crops to harvest, homes to be built, a frontier to tame and a life to carve out of whatever was before them. The girls fared no better for that matter. This country was a baby nation filling up with immigrants from Europe who were looking for a better life, and a way to make a break with their past. The new start often meant getting out onto the frontier and pushing across it to a better place than the tenements in the industrialized East. The western frontier was usually just beyond the back doorstep.

For not having very much of the finer things in life during their children's growing years, the Custer family had an uncommon closeness and love within the family. His relationship with his stepmother was also uncommon—she would become his dearest friend, even after his marriage to Libby.

Often times, if not every time, he would break down in tears when at home on leave from the service and he had return to the military. He was unabashed about it, even after he and Libby were married. Libby would have to help him pull himself together so they could leave. Once on the road to where they were going, he was fine and would never discuss why it was so hard for him to leave his dad, his mother (step-mother), sisters, and brothers.

His getting into the Army's Academy at West Point may have been his only true accomplishment as a youth, and he nearly wrecked that. Once there, he set the Academy's record for demerits (he and George Pickett, who would later lead a Confederate Division against the Union center at Gettysburg—still hold that dubious record, though both were there at different times).

Both men seemed to be on a different page than their brotherhood while at the Academy—the record still stands to this day. Both the Georges (Picket and Custer) were pretty much free spirits—rules were for their lessers to abide by, they would say. Perhaps, these two were right.

If you wanted to make a case of George Custer having a spotty education, one could. It was not because he was stupid or dull-witted. He was not. Poor families operated differently than families with money and titles. At West Point, money was prestigiously important.

Perhaps, George Custer's biggest problem during his young life, after he got into the Academy, and then forever afterward, was his seemingly stark insubordination to his superiors. It could be argued that this was because in Custer's mind, he had no superiors. In different times, the future general would never have been allowed to finish at West Point, much less be given a diploma of graduation from that storied institution.

While at the Academy all of his faults could be recited at great length. One could go on and on about what a nincompoop a goodly number of people thought he was. That being said, it must also be stated he enjoyed a strong following amongst a good number of his classmates, an almost cult following of several even while at the Point.

He seems to have kept most of his virtues a secret from his superiors while at the point, and to those who attended to the cadets. Robert E. Lee, Superintendent of the Academy at the time Mr. Custer entered, would probably someday regret having not kicked him out long before he became a senior. He was by all accounts a natural-born leader if there is, or was ever, such a thing.

His friends and associates seemed to be cut from the same grade of cloth that he was. He seems to almost be their mascot, or champion—he became their leader because he would stand up and be defiant when the other cadets saw retreat a better part of valor. He was loyal to them, and they were devoted to him because of it. Because his ego (probably) would not allow him to show fear, he displayed only bravery, and had no fear of man or beast.

Retreat was not a popular remedy as a youth growing up in Ohio or Michigan. Standing up to threats by those senior to him as a young man at West Point only made him more determined. Later on the fields of more than sixty-five Civil War engagements, and countless run-ins with the hostiles on the plains of America, those traits would come in handy. They could not teach those things in the classroom.

Personalities aside, he was a superb horseman and cavalry commander at the end of the Civil War. At the end of the war, only one Union cavalry officer would have come close to his finely honed skilled at cavalry tactics. That officer, though older, was General Wesley Merritt, commander of the 3rd U.S. Cavalry. Ironically, Merritt would become the new commander of the 7th Cavalry Regiment upon Custer's death.

Lieutenant Colonel Custer's biggest problem, his whole career, was that he just never respected, even modestly, the enemies he faced in all those previous engagements over all of those years of military service. That fault of seemingly being reckless and careless is evident time and again during the Civil War. It carried over in nearly all of the actions against the Indians from 1866-1876.

He was purely audacious. He once led his 500-man Michigan 3rd Cavalry against Thomas Rossier, a former classmate, roommate and close personal friend, at the Academy. That day, Rossier's cavalry had 2,000-men in it, and after learning Rossier was the Confederate's Division Commander he faced; he rode out in front of his own cavalry by himself.

Lieutenant Colonel Custer proceeded forward to about halfway between the two opposing lines of cavalry. Upon identifying Rossier, Custer doffed his large-brimmed hat to his former roommate, and bowed in the saddle. Slowly, he turned his warhorse back to his own units, formed them, and charged headlong into Rossier's 2,000-man division— leading the way into the thickest fighting. The result was Custer's regiment sent Rossier's men pell-mell in retreat back to whence they came.

Numbers had no impact on Custer, or the men who rode behind him. This kind of action made him seem irresponsible to many of his peers. At the same time, he worried his enemies greatly. Time and time again, up and until that last day, he had been lucky— only very, very lucky! He had been able to snatch victory out of the jaws of defeat many times because of his tenacity and bravery. His bulldog-like instincts and bravery saved him time and time again during the Civil War; and with his brushes afterward with the Indians. That and boundless personal energy and fortitude saved his bacon.

The fact he had a nearly inexhaustible supply line and manpower not one of his enemies ever had until that last day, probably never crossed his mind as being one of the reasons he was so good or lucky. Strangely, it seems, he never considered those as the reasons his luck held for as long as it did.

You would not accuse George Custer of being a deep thinker, because most times he was not. That is not to say the man could not think. He could—and did—spend long periods of time thinking about battle strategy, and the role he and his cavalry would play in an upcoming fight. As was said earlier, he was a tactical officer, not a strategic planner. On the battlefield he could move his commands where he wanted them, and would expect his sub-commanders to get their jobs done in support of his objective.

He had learned from experience just how important his logistical trains were during an incident earlier on the plains of Kansas that had nearly cost him his command. That last time out he took great pains to ensure they were protected against the loss. He instinctively believed it was his skill at soldiering and his "Custer luck" brought his enemies to their knees.

He was mistaken, of course; luck would have nothing whatsoever to do with it. Lady Luck, he would find, was a lying, cheating bitch. If he ever learned this lesson, it was too late to do him any good.

The Army would learn a valuable lesson at the hands of Crazy Horse, Gull, Dull Knife, White Bull, and many others in the battle's aftermath. The Indians taught him his final lesson on the Little Sheep (as they called it) River.

He had become famous during the Civil War by attacking whoever was in front of him. He had been sent in retreat only a few times because he picked on the wrong boar for eating his cabbage during that war. It never stopped him from getting seemingly in over his head. His spar with friend Rossier and his boys showed that. It seemingly did not make much of an impression.

Perhaps it made an impression when he bit off more than he could handle that Sunday afternoon in 1876. But that was a different matter; he did what did because in that situation, soldiers do what they have to do sometimes. They do not have to like it—but they do it.

Some have tried to make something out of the fact he graduated last in his class at West Point in 1861. That is not the truth. There was no official graduating class at West Point Military Academy in 1861, so let that be the end of the lie.

However, how you look at that set of facts tells what truth you want to believe. Truth is usually a perception in one's mind; it is not necessarily reality. The truth is there would have been seventy-seven graduates in his senior class had the Civil War not come along the same year he would have graduated. Fully forty-three of the other graduates went south to accept commissions in the Confederate Army rather than having to take the oath of allegiance to the United States. The next day the remaining members of the class of 1861 resigned to a man, weeks before commencement, and enlisted into the Army of the Potomac.

The truth is, with the fall of Fort Sumter, the entire class resigned in time for the first land battle of the war—Bull Run/Manassas. The Southern boys, out of a high sense honor, resigned so they would not have to take a required Oath of Allegiance and the Northern boys resigned so they could get into the fight that was coming on the side of the Union.

All of this negative talk about being last in his class, as if it made some big difference why he was defeated at the Little Bighorn, makes no sense. Using that sort of logic one could also say Abraham Lincoln should not have been President of the United States because he did not have a high school diploma—much less a license to practice law—but he did both.

Years later, Lieutenant Colonel Custer's wife, Libby, would show him his diploma from West Point that had been sent to his home of record. He would look at it, and in typical Custer fashion, just smirk. The Academy would present honorary degrees to the thirty-four members of the 1861 class who had enlisted into the service of the United States.

Having said all of that, by nearly all accounts, he was a not even an average student academically. His mind was always on something more important (to him at least) than his studies to pay much attention to what an instructor had to say. It had been that way even when he was a little boy going to elementary school.

Being saved by grace alone, he was on the verge of being kicked out of West Point on poor grades. Added to his poor academic record, the perceived slothful way he conducted himself in nearly all other activities would have been enough for him to get the boot, under normal circumstances. And if that was not enough, he had about one hundred more demerits than were authorized for a senior cadet to have. There were a host of reasons he should have been kicked out the front gate. But, those were far from normal times, even the Commandant of the Academy, Colonel Robert E. Lee, could see that.

By war's end, everyone who had graduated with a higher grade point average in his class from the Point were either dead, crippled, or still field grade and below officers, or out of the service altogether.

It is ironic is it not that at the end of the Civil War, the man who Robert E. Lee should have kicked out of the Academy long before his senior year, would be the officer who literally ran Lee's Army of Northern Virginia down with his cavalry?

Finally, at the end of the war, he was selected as the officer most deserving of accepting the great Southern general's battle flag at Appomattox Court House to end the War Between the States. The troops he commanded during the Civil War captured more regimental battle flags than any command in American history. He was also the youngest of the Union generals.

There were three things that separated and distinguished George Armstrong Custer from his peers after leaving West Point—brilliance under fire, courage, and valor. Those qualities, in that combination, are uncommon in most any man. It was not math, science, the study of classic literature, bridge-building, nor other scholarly things that won on the battlefield. Those three qualities overshadowed everything else about Custer.

He may not have been willing to learn or quote long passages of Shakespeare or Chaucer; or to clutter his mind with such rubbish, though he could have. He was simply a soldier; those things of academia would not help in his future trade—war. He was an engineer officer by trade; he could build a pretty good bridge by himself—at least one good enough to get his cavalry across a stream. But, given a horse, a saber, men to lead, and an enemy to his front, he was magic. He was a fighter of the first magnitude.

It was his cavalry that met and defeated the South's great cavalry leader, James Ewell Brown (JEB) Stuart, twice—the first time on the East Cavalry field at Gettysburg, in 1864. The second time he met JEB Stewart was at Yellow Tavern. That was the last time JEB fought, he was killed by one of Custer's men. There were not many better cavalry officers than Custer still alive at war's end, north or south.

Of the South's survivors, Nathan Bedford Forrest, an illiterate, could come close to his abilities as a combat commander. General Forrest was but nineteen years of age at war's end. His most remembered accomplishment in life was that he was the founder of the Klu Klux Klan after the war and would become that infamous organization's first Grand Dumas.

—3—

THE BOY BECOMES A GENERAL

Lieutenant Colonel Custer had a well-earned reputation as a glory-hound. Few could have argued with that appraisal, and lesser men would have been glad to jump on that bandwagon to believe the bad about the "Boy General." To him, it was all a game, and at the same time, he was deadly serious about it. There are not many men who, as a twenty-three-year-old kid, could get men much older into battle risking life and limb.

He dressed the way he did and acted with great bravado in order to get men to follow him in life's deadliest game, the cavalry charge. This "Boy General" led men into battle the way they should be led—from in front; always from the front.

In some respects, his critics were right in their judgment of him: He was overconfident, arrogant, and the exalted grand master of the prima donna society of the world. He was a glory-hound, but he had the intestinal fortitude to push his men and himself beyond the breaking point and then almost as if by magic, not allow his command or himself to break. Most of his contemporaries never developed the taste for war he had acquired.

Men whose careers were mired in quicksand would find a way to blame their failure on the success of someone else. Many tried to pin the rose, for their shortcomings, on him, and others like him. Even General Crook had taken a spin at Lieutenant Colonel Custer after Custer and his Wolverines saved General Crook and his cavalry at Sailor's Creek during the Civil War. As it worked out, it was a problem for the red-bearded general the rest of his life. As it turned out, many have suspected that it may have been why Crook was so slow in coming down the Rosebud to join up with the other forces converging on the Little Bighorn and have to face the kid who had bailed him out in an entirely different war.

The qualities that counted most, as far as his superior officers were concerned during the Civil War, was the passion for the rudiments of war—the killing, fighting, hard living, loneliness, and deprivations. He was willing to take on all of these to be their personal warrior, and he was very, very good at it.

Both General Sheridan and Sherman admired him greatly during the war. During those last days of that terrible war in the spring of 1865, it was Custer's cavalry under the orders of General Sheridan which struck day and night at the Rebels' heels. Time and again, unrelentingly and unmercifully Lieutenant Colonel Custer struck at the General Lee's retreating rag-tag Confederates. His cavalry drove the Rebs back time and time again, never giving them a chance to catch their breath, or to even tend to their dead and wounded.

He continued attacking even at the Appomattox Court House. It was his cavalry striking nearly-defenseless men one last time that brought General Lee to the bargaining table. Lee had only one choice: surrender what was left of his shattered remains of his army. That relentless pursuit of his nation's enemies, real or imagined, became Custer's way. It became his most-used operational tactic—to drive and attack the enemy until there was no more fight in them. And then to keep on kicking them until there was no more resistance from them before he would stop.

As for his superior officers, both Sherman and Sheridan were cut from the same cloth. Once the first shot was fired, and there was fire and brimstone in the air, blood on the ground, they were ready to strike. They had given the boy general command early on because he had earned their respect as a fighter and battlefield commander.

The real question concerning him after the Civil War was, "What do you do with men like Custer created by the gods of war? When there is peace, and the war is over, and one has no more enemies to his front—what happens to these brave men who live only for its sanctity?

You cannot put them in a box, and put it in the attic until the next time you need their particular angel of death skills. Men like him, the General

Pattons of the world, are the misfits of society when there isn't a battle to be fought or a war to be won. Our country needs men like them—even if we don't need them most of the time.

Thankfully, for both him and the nation, there was the American frontier that needed taming. Out West there were Indians to be fought. Lieutenant Colonel Custer never split hairs about what was right or wrong about a situation. Given the order to attack, he attacked whoever was to his front. He lusted for the fight, and he was an aroused cobra ready to strike whenever he could.

As for the Indian problem, he was just the man for the job. The Indians loved to fight, and a fight they would have from this *wasichu*. He would show them fight. Like him or not—he could, and would sink his teeth in an enemy.

Almost without taking a breath for himself and Libby, he answered his country's need again. Custer went after the American Plains Indians like he had the Confederates, first in Texas; and then in Oklahoma and Kansas. He chased them, and they frustrated him with their methods, but he never stopped; he just kept coming.

—4—

CUSTER'S MYTHS AND TRUTHS

Custer loved to gamble in nearly every facet of his life as a soldier and as a man, yet he was a terrible card player, and did only slightly better when betting on the ponies. He just did not allow himself to fold or quit when he was ahead. This trait slopped over into his professional life and when carried to the extreme usually caused big problems for him and his superiors.

He hardly ever drank after he met and married Libby. He had promised Libby he would stop, and by most accounts, he did. Libby probably save him from himself; most men in his profession were closet drunks by the time their careers in the military was over. He was on the same path and was a wild man before he met and married Libby Bacon. Before that time, he had a reputation as a rounder–he liked the ladies and they were wild about him. What woman wouldn't be crazy about a wild-eyed, long-haired, cavalier cavalry officer, riding a horse as high-strung as its rider?

If we are to believe some of the stories about this man concerning this subject, he had dallied around from time to time with a few ladies of questionable reputations while a cadet. He had gotten syphilis while on leave in Washington. In those days when a man took the cure for the disease, the medicine cured lots of things besides, but the most notable of these was making babies—the man who underwent the treatment was usually left sterile. Not long after that treatment, he met and married Miss Bacon, and from all accounts that really counted, that was the end of his being a "rounder."

Rumors would pop up from time to time, mostly just cheap talk among the soldiers themselves, usually traceable back to his most noted hater, Captain Benteen.

At least once, he is supposed to have had a passionate affair with a fair little Indian maiden, a southern Cheyenne named Me-o-tzi. He met and employed her as a translator for his command while on duty in Kansas in 1868-69. After the battle at the Little Bighorn the rumor at the time was she saved his body from mutilation. As we shall see later, you decide if that is a fact.

As for Me-o-tzi and her babies (there were rumors that she had two), there was a story about her leaving the United States with Sitting Bull and going to Canada for a year or so after the battle, finally returning and settling in Wounded Knee, South Dakota just before the 9th Cavalry burned the place to the ground. They killed all the men, women and children they could get their hands on.

He was (at least by his wife Libby's account) a fantastic husband. It is hard to argue with her; she lived another 57 years after his death. He had endangered his wife many times by allowing her to be a regular camp follower across the plains of Texas, Oklahoma, Kansas, Nebraska, and the Dakotas.

She obviously did not see it that way—she wanted to be at his side whenever it was possible, even during the Civil War. Her wish was always his command, and he would move heaven and hell to make sure she got what she wanted!

The two of them spent as much time with each other as they could. She went to his station in Kentucky during the reconstruction days immediately after the War Between the States, which was far from safe for pretty young damsels from the North. He once even stood before a court martial for leaving his duty station without authorization to ride 300 miles across Indian-infested lands just to see her. There was, of course more to it than just a horny soldier wanting to see his wife. The fact was he had not heard from her for sometime, and there was a rumor cholera had struck Fort Leavenworth after she had gotten to the post while he was chasing Indians in eastern Kansas and Colorado. With no way to substantiate the story, and the health conditions of the love of his life perhaps hanging in the balance, George Custer followed his heart. That was also the time Captain Weir apologized for overstepping his bounds with the general's lady.

Coupled with a situation where he had six of thirteen deserters shot or hung without a trial during the trip back to Leavenworth got him kicked out of the Army for a year without pay. There is more to the story, but the point is, George was a good and faithful husband from the day he married Elizabeth Bacon in 1863 until the day he died in 1876. And for Libby's part, she was loyal to him and his memory until her death in 1933—for about seventy years.

George Custer, the famous "Injun Fighter," was created in the mind of a woman. General George Armstrong Custer was a lot of things. Perhaps, even in his own mind, he was a "Famous Injun Fighter." Two out of three might not be all that bad, if the issues of life and death are not at stake. He was famous and he was a fighter. His Civil War record and his ten years of warring with the Indians on the Great Plains proved that. But he obviously had a ways to go to be called a Famous "Injun" Fighter. He would not live long enough to be called that.

Before that last time out his record against the hostiles had not been that impressive. In most instances he had beaten them because of superior numbers, and attacking Indians who had been nearly run into the ground first. That would come to a halt at the Little Bighorn.

The last incident of note on a rather long list (and as it turned out was indeed his last) was he was ordered by Congress to testify against Orville Grant who happened to be President U.S. Grant's brother for stealing and embezzling funds from the U.S. commissaries at the Army post he commanded, Fort Abraham Lincoln.

What was he supposed to do, not go? It was because of his throwing the President's brother off his post, and then making such a stink about the fact the commissary was ripping off his soldiers he was obligated to tell what he thought was going on. After he got back to Washington, and in front of Congress, did he do what was he supposed to do—lie to protect the president's honor, and his crooked brother? Not Custer; he always stepped up!

He went, and he testified—telling the committee what he thought had gone on with the commissary and soldiers not getting the provisions they were supposed to. Finally, when they did get the goods, his men were being overcharged for them. All of the charges were very incriminating for the president's brother. Lieutenant Colonel Custer would have been better served had he just kept his mouth shut and gone about it politically through the back door.

The damage he had done to his former commander, and now the commander and chief, President Grant, had him in a terrible position. President Grant was so angry with the General he kept him waiting for three weeks in Washington cooling his heels. When Lieutenant Colonel Custer decided to return to his post, the president had him arrested on his way back in Chicago while changing trains. He was put under house arrest, cooling his heels again, for nearly six weeks. Major Marcus Reno was temporarily put in command of the 7th Cavalry, and was given the task of making ready to lead it against the vaunted Sioux and Cheyenne. President Grant was so furious with him; he forbids Custer any contact at all with his command. He ultimately took his command away from him.

It was only upon pleas from General Sheridan and General Terry that he was allowed back to his command. Being stripped of command of the expedition, he was allowed to only command the 7TH Cavalry Regiment. The biggest problem was that, in true Custer form, he said what he thought. That was so un-political of him, but then, he was an unpolitical man.

Unfortunately for him, he said those things to the wrong people, Congressmen, and they were very political, for President Grant's part, while never popular in either the north or the south. But, he was still the president, and presidents sometimes have short memories about favors owed to former associates who had a hand in making them great.

Besides, U.S. Grant was cut from the same cloth as Custer, and when barked at, Grant would snarl and show his teeth, and then take a big bite out of someone's backside. Since he was the biggest dog in the junkyard, his bite was the worst. Perhaps that is the best way to describe their lack of cohesion. When the two warriors looked at each other, it was like looking into a mirror at themselves; often as not, what they saw, they did not like.

Grant, of course, being the president, would have the last word, and wanted Custer's backside to barbecue over a slow white-hot fire. (Grant was a member of the warrior brotherhood, also.) Only General Sheridan, and finally General Sherman saved George if you could call it that, that last time.

George Custer may not have been the best politician of all the cadets to sashay under the archway of the North Gate at West Point, or the smartest. However he clearly understood the situation he had created and he knew he had stepped on it big time. He did not have the patience for politics, and above all things, he was just too honest to himself. He had a desire to be president, and in those days, he very well may have been one if he had been successful on the last campaign.

At the same time, let no one say he was not a great leader of men; or, he was not brilliant with military tactics of his day on a battlefield. His men would ride into hell with him, and in the end, many of them did. If Custer was intolerant of lesser, fainter-hearted men, then so be it. He was not some country bumpkin fresh off the farm. He was not a fool or foolhardy when it came to fighting, and getting his command ready to fight. Custer would always fight, and so would those he led.

His superiors knew that about him, and that was one of the reasons why he was sent to the West—to fight the Indians. To push, pull, kick, or kill the red bastards, and make them go to the agencies and reservations and keep them there, or kill them, whichever came first.

For his part, Custer's solution to nearly everything was to sound the bugles and charge. If pressed, "To hell with the bugles, charge!" he said once. "My voice is for war." Tamer-hearted men just do not think that way. With Custer, that attitude permeated throughout his entire being, just as sure as ice ran through his veins when tamer men retreated. Lieutenant Colonel Custer charged, again, and again, and again.

As long as he had men to lead, horses to ride, bullets and cold steel to fling at the enemy, he would fight. That philosophy had worked his entire military career. He had no reason to believe it would not work there and then, against this rag-tag hoard of beggars (Indians) he had been ordered to catch, as he prepared for what would be his final battle.

Truly, Lieutenant Colonel Custer was not a complicated man. Dynamic would almost be too complimentary of him. He had base instincts he trusted and followed. Those instincts in his mind had kept him alive for thirty-six years. Everybody else, well, they could be damned, for all he cared. He simply did not care what everybody else thought.

The loss of five half-strength troops of the 7th Cavalry, plus his headquarters staff, was a small price for relative peace within a year of that battle. What this defeat actually accomplished shortly after the fight was the claiming of the entire Great Plains from Canada to the Gulf of Mexico; from the Missouri River to the mountains in Utah. In his death, he brought about the beginnings in the taming of the great American West.

His record as the division commander, at the tender age of 23, of Michigan Cavalry at the conclusion of the Civil War, justifies much more notoriety than his accomplishments as a "great Indian Fighter." The highest rank he attained was during the closing months of that terrible Civil War, and when literally within days of the armistice being signed, he was promoted to Major General (two stars). Even that was not unusual for the crisis that this country was facing from 1861-1865.

There were several "Boy Generals" during the Civil War, so he really was not an anomaly even for that time. Going back nearly a hundred years before Jean Lafayette was George Washington's right hand man, and was also a "Boy General" even more so—he was just nineteen.

At least two Confederate "Boy Generals"—young Fightin' Joe Wheeler (he promoted himself to Major General at the end of the war) and Nathan Bedford Forrest whom I have mentioned earlier was a superior cavalryman commander, and was even younger than Custer. All three earned the rank and the responsibility of leading men into battle.

"Old' Fightin' Joe," as Wheeler was known in his later years, would later be known (or forgotten) as the commanding general of U.S. Forces in Cuba during the Spanish-American War. Unfortunately, George Armstrong Custer will always be remembered for being massacred at the Little Bighorn, and his glittering Civil War record, all but forgotten.

We Americans will always walk away with the idea that only reason George Armstrong Custer was a hero was because he got himself and half of his command massacred. On the surface that sounds silly, but when one thinks about it unless he has done some research on the subject he will not know that this man did more than get killed at the Little Bighorn.

Unfortunately, many of us will not remember or even know, or, worse, really care about the whole truth of the matter.

Usually, our heroes have only good things said about them. They are created to have lived model lives that instill in our youth the promise of, "Good things happen to good people, just look at...." For an example, when our children are told of a favorite hero and how they should act more like the hero if they want good things to happen to them. Perhaps someday, by chance they can become heroes also. Real heroes are common everyday people who happen to do uncommon things, at uncommon times, when no one else will. Todd Beamer, of the September 11, 2001 Pennsylvania plane crash, is just one example.

While people died following him, George Armstrong Custer could and would do the things no one else could on a battlefield that might keep them alive. Of course, keeping men alive was really very, very important. That thrown in the mix with fear made men do a lot of stupid things which under normal circumstances they would not dream of doing.

You can be assured on that day, June 25, 1876, there were heroes who died aiding their fellow soldiers. Those soldiers that rode with Custer whose acts of bravery and valor died on an uncaring wind unnoticed, lost for all time. Acts of kindness, and true heroics fell with the men on the northern edge of Battle Ridge. Just so, there were acts of cowardice and cover up of the true facts of the battle, and the events of the fight from one end of the battle line to the other. Untold truths run untold by those who knew better but lacked the same courage and intestinal fortitude as the man they slandered. Rather than stand up and be heard the ghosts in valley of the Little Bighorn wonder forever across the wide Montana skies.

On the 25th of June the whole battle probably lasted three or four hours from the start at the south end of the Indian encampment when Major Reno attempted his feeble attack, to when the last man fell somewhere four miles northwest of Major Reno's hill.

The soldiers on Major Reno Hill would continue to battle the Cheyenne and Hunkpapas, latter to be joined by Crazy Horses' Oglalas and the rest of the tribes down in the valley through afternoon. Major

Reno and Benteen's boys would get plenty of action from about five in the afternoon 'til around dark on the high plains (about nine that evening). For the most part though, the fight was over; for some hangers on the Red Man's side, some really hot-bloods, the outcome—a foregone conclusion.

The Indians could have taken out Majors Reno and Benteen any time they were ready, or wanted to. The issue was not when, but how much would it cost in terms of lives—Indian lives, not *wasichu* lives. Some of the Indians who took part in the battle gave an accounting of the events of that day, and their testimonies of the day's events were lost for all time. After all, there were some 2,500 to maybe as many as 5,000 hostile warriors (probably closer to 4,000 to 4,500) on that battlefield that day. It has only been rather recently that historians have started to believe what those who were there and lived had to say about that day. Many of them told the white man of their part in the fighting as they faced the soldiers that day. Unfortunately, many of those testimonies were shunned as unimportant or "a damned lie" when it didn't fit the official government take on the situation.

The Indian testimonies given shortly after the battle were usually given out of fear of reprisal or threat of death if the white man didn't hear what he wanted to hear. Sitting Bull and Red Cloud's statements pertaining to the fighting of that day are examples of that type of patronization.

Sitting Bull, while in no attempt to cheapen his memory or to defile his prestige among the Sioux, never got to the battlefield that day; he didn't leave his tent, nor did Red Cloud. He was at his agency in Nebraska. For everything that the old chiefs were–one, once a famous warrior in his younger years and then a medicine man, and the other one an old man, too old to be a war chief, they were also smarter than the average white man gave them credit for being. They both knew it was infinitely better to put the soldiers on the field that day in a perhaps brighter light than they deserved—or it might threaten their livelihood. Part of the confusion is that *wasichu* and Indians do not now—and surely did not then—think in the same terms. The idea to the Indians was to protect the women and children in the encampment. It did not matter who deployed where, and with whom. The Red Man fought largely independent of each other or in small groups.

—5—

THE 7TH CAVALRY HEADQUARTERS AND DETACHMENTS

From a tactical standpoint, there were three tactical battalions, or "Wings," as they have sometimes been referred. The center wing, commanded by Major Marcus Reno, included 112 troopers from Companies A, G, and M.

Attached from the 7th's headquarters to this Center Wing was the lead scout for the regiment, "Lonesome" Charlie Reynolds, who was Custer's favorite scout and a personal friend of the Lieutenant Colonel and his lady. Charlie was perhaps the bravest man of all the men in the regiment. He was the second best shot. No one knew much about Charlie then—as to where he had come from, or anything much about his past. Charlie never said and it was not polite to ask in those days.

We have learned more about the man after he died than the folks he worked with, fought with, and finally died with did while he was alive. Since his death, it has been learned that he was born and raised in Kentucky, Illinois, and finally Kansas. His father was a doctor and his mother died when he was but a very small boy. Before coming west he completed three years college in Abingdon, Illinois and later enlisted in the 10th Kansas Infantry from 1861 to 1864.

Following his enlistment, he served as a scout and guide for the Army, hunted buffalo, and served as a dispatch courier between Fort Laramie and Fort Abraham Lincoln at a time when no one else would have dared to even attempt to travel the route without a battalion of cavalry as escort. Lonesome Charlie did it alone, all 844 miles one way and then back again. Not only did he do it all alone but he did it in the dead of winter, through blizzards and hailstorms. Not only did he do it once, he made several trips during the time he was contracted as courier.

The 7th Cavalry quartermaster, at Lieutenant Colonel Custer's request, hired him on for a $100.00 per month for this expedition to the Little Bighorn. He was the second-best rifle shot in the regiment, next to Winner Cooke, Custer's adjutant. He had been Custer's main guide on three earlier expeditions: The two Yellowstone Expeditions, 1873 and 1875; and the Black Hills Expedition in 1874. He was never married.

During the fight in the valley, he was shot through the heart and killed instantly. Very close by was Doctor Porter who was attending a wounded man when Charlie went down. Doctor Porter said that Charlie was dead before he touched the ground.

Also attached to this Right Wing was the regiment's translator, Isaiah Dorman—the only black man in the regiment. Just that morning he had been assigned to Major Reno's command. Isaiah, like most of the men in the regiment, had lived through some pretty hard times before he got to the 7th Cavalry. It was thought that he was a runaway slave who had ended up on the frontier. He had knocked around for a number of years, sometimes working for the Army as a guide or scout or as a common laborer for the quartermaster. Another story had him being taken in by the Sioux as a child (how that happened is not clearly explained) and in time he had married a Santee Sioux woman. One of his Sioux names was Black Hawk. It was rumored that they also called him "Teat" because when they said his name "Isaiah" it came out like their word for a buffalo cow's smooth black teat, "Aizini."

During the valley fight, Isaiah's horse was shot out from under him; he barely cleared the horse before it fell and caught his leg while still in the stirrup. If the horse had fallen with him still in the saddle, his leg could have possibly been pinned him beneath the animal, making any attempt to escape impossible. Perhaps it would have been kinder to the big black man to have broken his neck in the fall.

As it turned out he was quick to his feet, scrambling; a short distance he kneeled and began carefully aiming at the closing hostiles. Only getting off a couple shots, Black Hawk was promptly shot in the chest. Somehow, he managed to crawl through the bushes and tall grass until he could pull himself upright and lean against a tree next to the river bank. There he stayed slowly bleeding to death. The rest of the men in the battalion fled past him; he waved his good-byes to them and them to him.

When squaws saw the man leaning against the tree mortally wounded, a couple of the women recognized him and he them. In the end his fate would be the same as that of Charlie Reynolds. The two men went down about the same time and Isaiah was found within 30 feet of the scout. When found Dorman had been shot-gunned in the legs; it could not be determined if he was still alive when these wounds were sustained.

Even before Major Reno and the survivors of his battalion got out of the valley, the Sioux and Cheyenne women started going among those wounded *wasichu* to finish them off. They found "Teat." They asked him why he had gone against his people and was coming against them with the *wasichu*. He told them that he needed work and that he did not do the scouting or the guiding of these soldiers. In fact, the Army was paying him $100.00 a month for his services as a translator. He was their "Sioux talker." He asked the women if they could spare a drink of water and mercy.

That, of course, made the women giggle to each other. As one could guess, that did not go over too well with the gals at hand. They were bent on killing any of the wounded *wasichu* as pay-back for everything the *wasichu* had done to them up to that point in time. In the end they cut his throat and slashed and mutilated his body. When Isaiah's body was identified, it had been mutilated before and after he was killed. He had numerous wounds to his lower legs, probably with something like double-ought pellets to his legs. He had a horse's picket spike driven through his testicles, and a bouquet of a dozen arrows splayed across his chest along with a couple rifle slugs also lodged in his chest. The man had suffered greatly before having his throat cut by the squaws from the encampment. That was the end of poor Isaiah but not the end for the brutality visited upon his person.

A young Cheyenne warrior named Wooden Leg was riding past the women as they were doing their handy work and watched them rid the world of this black-white, *wasicun-sapa*, as the Indians called the black-skinned men. Wooden Leg was totally absorbed in the color of the man's skin. Isaiah was a very black-skinned man and Wooden Leg had never seen a black man before. He asked the women how it was they knew him and how he could speak their tongue. They told him he had been in their tribe for many years before going on to help the *wasichu*.

Wooden Leg, rather than scalp the hair on Black Hawk's head, scalped Black Hawk's beard on his face and took the gory mess back to his mother as a trophy. At the time, Wooden Leg was but fourteen summers old.

A large contingent of Indian scouts and guides, thirty-nine, was lead by 2nd Lieutenant Charles A. Varnum, also went into the valley with Major Reno. Varnum would live to retire as a full colonel after having had a tremendously exciting career. At the time of the battle he was twenty-seven years of age. He would later be awarded the Congressional Medial of Honor in the 7th's fight with some of these same Sioux in a little remembered battle known as White Clay Creek, 1890. At the Little Bighorn fight he would be wounded during the withdrawal from the valley in this fight. He would live another sixty years. When he died, February 26, 1930, he was the last surviving officer in Custer's command.

Under Varnum's command was Custer's favorite Indian scout, Bloody Knife. Bloody Knife had ridden with the lieutenant colonel for a number of years. On this day, Custer ordered him to lead Major Reno's Wing to the hostiles. He had gone on several scouts for the major in the past and it must have seemed to Bloody Knife like some kind of punishment. Before he left the Lieutenant Colonel's side, however, he told his friend, Custer, "Today, you and me together will leave this earth."

Bloody Knife would also fall in the valley fight near where Charlie Reynolds fell. A hostile's bullet entered the Arikara's head between his eyes and splattered his brains all over Major Reno who was standing near the man talking to him when the bullet smashed through his guide's head.

Major Reno's command also had two of the three Regiment's doctors, two assistant surgeons, Henry R. Porter and James M. DeWolf. DeWolf was killed trying to escape during the valley fight. All totaled, no more than 130 men, not counting the Indians, rode with Major Reno as they forded the Little Bighorn River late that morning, the day of the battle. The Indians guides and scouts were told they could keep the ponies they caught from the Lakota and Cheyenne herds.

The second of the three battalions is identified here as the Left Wing, comprised of Troops D, H, and K, under the command of Captain Benteen. This commander was also assigned the operational control of Troop B. Within the three troops of cavalry, excluding B Troop, the wing were about 120 troopers, plus the 146 men and six officers (plus Lieutenant Hodgson and Captain McDougall) from Troop B, though they would operate largely independent of each other for most of the first day of the fight. Second Lieutenant Hodgson was assigned as Major Reno's adjutant and was killed in the valley fight during the escape to what is now known as Major Reno's Hill.

The third and final battalion was the Right Wing of the command and included the remaining five troops of the 7th Cavalry, E, F, L and I.

I Troop was known as the "Wild-Eye" because many of the troopers in the other troops thought their commander, Captain Myles Keogh had a crazy streak in him and a mean, glaring eye when he was drinking, which was frequently. These five troops comprised Custer's Wing that additionally included a small contingent of his headquarters and headquarters' company (HHC). Within this wing, he named Captain George Yates, F Troop commander, as a battalion commander comprising his own troop and Captain Fresh Smith's E Troop. The Lieutenant Colonel attaching the HHC to Troop C, assigned Captain Tom Custer, his brother, commander of Troop C, as his adjutant. He moved First Lieutenant Winer Cooke, who usually was the lieutenant colonel's adjutant, to act as his executive officer.

Troop B was the special detachment company. Its commander was charged with all of the logistical "trains" for the regiment in the combat zone of operations. Captain James McDougall commanded Troop B. Captain McDougall had in his troop 69-men, plus an additional seventy-seven men (six enlisted and one sergeant from each of the remaining eleven troops) augmentation drawn from within the regiment to enhance this troop's strength. These "extra men" were detailed daily per

Lieutenant Colonel Custer's orders to bolster the command strength in support of the substantial supply trains.

Captain McDougall operated throughout the day of the battle largely out of contact from the three wing commanders. In other words he had to sit on his thumbs while the rest of the regiment deployed against the hostilities. They had arrived at the regiment's last stop early the morning of the 25th around 2:30. His command had been in the saddle for over thirty-hours trying to catch up to the command. The captain, one of Lieutenant Colonel Custer's trusted few outside of his own battalion command, had no direct contact with Custer after Major Reno's split from the main column later that morning, between 11:00 and 11:30 AM.

In retrospect, some of the chair-warmers have argued that Custer left too many men in B Troop to protect the trains. It is an argument that lacks much substance, however. Hindsight is always twenty-twenty. As things turned out, most anyone could say that and not be far from being right upon first blush. At the time, under the conditions the 7th Cavalry faced, Lieutenant Colonel Custer was utilizing his troops prudently. The loss of the trains would have and could have spelled doom to the entire regiment. In the trains was the food and forage for the men and horses, mules and jackasses, ammunition, extra equipment, replacement horses for the regiment and the necessities of life that kept the regiment in the field. That number of troopers in the "trains" was a necessary evil in the colonel's mind; he could ill afford to lose his supply lines especially the ammunition packs that the 1,000 plus mules and donkeys carried.

Past experience had taught him his supplies were the lifelines for the regiment and they must be protected at all costs. Following standard military practice of the day and from his experience, Custer ensured he had the firepower this time out to protect his 200-wagon supply-trains.

CUSTER'S THREE COMMAND WINGS AND TROOP STRENGTH UPON DEPLOYMENT FOR THE BATTLE

```
┌─────────────────────┐   ┌─────────────────────┐   ┌─────────────────────┐
│ Lieutenant Colonel  │   │       Major         │   │      Captain        │
│  George A. Custer   │   │ Marcus Major Reno   │   │  Fredrick Benteen   │
│   Troops C, L and I │   │  Troops A, G, and M │   │  Troops D, H, and K │
│   (138 men, scouts, │   │   (112 men, plus    │   │     (120 men)       │
│ Guides and Civilians)│  │  scouts, civilians  │   │                     │
│                     │   │     and guides)     │   │                     │
└─────────────────────┘   └─────────────────────┘   └─────────────────────┘
```

```
┌·····························┐                     ┌·····························┐
: Captain George Yates        :                     :  Captain T M. McDougall     :
: Troops E and F (76 men)     :                     :    Troop B (146 men)        :
└·····························┘                     └·····························┘
```

TOTAL MANPOWER STRENGTH OF EACH WING

Lieutenant Colonel George A. Custer: 214
Major Marcus Reno: 112
Captain Frederick Benteen: 266
Total Combat Strength of 7th Cavalry on the Morning of June 25 1876: 592

—6—

MANNING TABLES AND SOUR GRAPES

One of the Lieutenant Colonel's critics was General "Red Beard" Crook. When it was all over, General Crook said Custer overprotected his trains. He would discover later that summer and fall that Custer was not necessarily wrong in doing so. When General Crook took up the chase of the Sioux later in the fall of 1876, he managed to lose his logistical trains to the Indians. Crook's men were down to literally eating their last jackass when the cavalry arrived and saved what was left of him and his men.

General Crook, you will remember, had been highly critical of Lieutenant Colonel Custer all along anyway. The reason seems to stem back to the Civil War days when a brash young major saved General Crook during another fight. That brash young major then, was now Lieutenant Colonel George Armstrong Custer. General Crook never quite lived down the embarrassment and ribbing he received afterwards from his brother commanders for having to be "saved by such a youngster."

It was General Crook's way of paying back the jaunty major from all those years before. Crook was sure he could have gotten out of the mess he had created when Major Custer came busting through a passel of Confederates and saved Crook and his command just as Crook was trying to save himself. General Sheridan gave the then Major Custer the credit for saving Crook's command. Crook had egg in his red beard and did not like it one bit, he would never forget the slight of the brash young major.

Before starting out on the campaign from Fort Abraham Lincoln, the regiment would be short thirteen assigned officers: two ranking field grade (majors) officers (Joseph Tilford and Lewis Merrill), three captains (Ilsley, Tourtellotte, and Hale) and seven lieutenants (Braden, Eckerson, Nave, Garlington, Jackson, Learned, and Bell). These officers were on detached duty or on leave in other parts of the country during the time of this expedition. The commander tried to get these officers back to the 7th Cavalry before deploying to the field. He was told that the officers in question could not be spared from their temporary duties nor could they be replaced with equivalent ranking officers in time before the 7th Cavalry deployed to Montana.

It was the way it was. This was a post-war Army that had been stripped of its officer corps at a time when every man was needed on the frontier, more times than not, temporary duty had them someplace else when they were needed. These men could not be moved back to the 7th Cavalry in time for the regiment to move out.

When the regiment left Fort Abraham Lincoln on May 17, 1876, Lieutenant Colonel Custer had in his command a complement of twenty-nine officers out of the forty-two authorized from the tables of manpower for the regiment.

Custer was faced with the daunting job of trying to fill the vacant officer slots the best he could with what he had from within the regiment and any volunteers within Fort Abraham Lincoln. With over thirty percent of the regiment's regular officer corps missing, he moved younger, untested and inexperienced officers into those positions that the missing officers had occupied. He would know at the outset that leadership in the field would be spotty at best. If he could hedge his bet by placing younger men he trusted in those command positions, why not? He would be chastised for it later, but he simply had no choice other than to do what he did.

The lack of an adequate officer corps was not the reason the 7th Cavalry failed that day, the point is he just did not have a fully experienced officer corps in the regiment when the 7th deployed to the field. Men fight best with officers who they know and trust and who have been with them for a time; men who have shared the good and bad times together and officers that the enlisted men would trust and follow through hell's doorway.

On the day of the battle he was forced to have newly appointed and promoted first lieutenants and captains from outside of the command leading troops who also lacked combat experience against overpowering, numerically superior Indian hostiles. Experienced captains and majors should have held those leadership positions. The other point is that the 7th Cavalry was under strength by nearly a full third of its manning table's total strength. When the regiment should have had about 900 enlisted it had just fewer than 570 men when the 7th Cavalry faced its toughest assignment since its formation in 1868.

One of the only a few bright spots as far as combat command was Captain Benteen. He had been in through the rigors of combat many times before. His record as a combat commander was very impressive. He had faced the hardships of long expeditions, the terror of combat not only on the plains but during the Civil War as well.

The fact he was a true leader of men cannot be disputed. That was the good side of Captain Benteen, but every coin has two sides. For his part, Benteen was much relieved when the two majors could not be returned. His good spirits were brought on because the two majors' in question dates of service preceded his own, and both were West Pointer's and would have out ranked him not only within the regiment but also in the field. Theoretically, all he had to contend with was Major Reno for second in command and he had been a full brevet colonel during the Civil War and in his shadowy mind that might account for something if a second in command was needed.

Lieutenant Colonel Custer promoted a few first lieutenants to captains McDougall, Myles Moylan, and Fresh Smith, to fill in for three of the four missing captain troop commanders. He also recruited a infantry type who had volunteered for service in the 7th Cavalry rather than spend another summer training green infantry: Second Lieutenant J. J. Crittenden, whose father had served as a major general during the War of the Rebellion would be one of the newest members to Custer's officer cadre.

Both Crittenden and Moylan had served as infantry officers earlier in their military careers during the Civil War and for a short time afterward. They had since come to their senses and had joined the cavalry, Moylan long before Crittenden. The then Lieutenant Moylan had been with the Custer's 7th Cavalry since before the Washita assault on Black Kettle's

Southern Cheyenne back in the winter of 1868. In the time between then and now, the Montana Expedition, Moylan had been brought into the Inner Circle. He had been found totally reliable and trustworthy by the Custer Clan. This would be Crittenden's his first action against Indians.

Captain Thomas Mower McDougall and First Lieutenant Edward Settle Godfrey (later to become General of the Army) were also promoted to troop commander status.

Both of these young officers thought a tour with the active 7th Cavalry would break up the monotony of pushing walk-a-heaps, the Indians' name for infantry ground troops, during training in the hot summer sun.

Probably against Custer's better judgment, he also took a couple shave-tails (fresh new lieutenants) who had just graduated from the West Point just the month before: Second Lieutenant James C. Sturgis, second in command of E Troop on the battle rooster, but who had been assigned to M Troop, under Captain Thomas H. French; and Second Lieutenant Henry M. Harrington, second in command, C Troop). As it turned out on the day of the battle these two young officers would get no more experience than the charge down Medicine Tail Coulee.

In short, Custer made do with what he had, and did not worry about the rest of it. Most of the troop commanders, aside from Major Reno and Benteen, were loyal to Custer to a fault, or at least, neutral. Many had not been around long enough to hear Captain Benteen's ranting and raving enough to be influenced against the Lieutenant Colonel. Few of them would have paid attention to Benteen if he were not in their food chain (he did not rate them on their yearly Officer Efficiency Reports).

There were exceptions. One would be First Lieutenant DeRudio; even Captain Benteen did not like this man, saying once that he was, "no gentleman." His only redeeming quality as far as Captain Benteen was concerned was he did not like the Lieutenant Colonel, so he could not be all bad even in Benteen's mind.

DeRudio used the name John De Sylva from time to time. He was born Carlo Camilio di Rudio, and was known as a consummate liar and near-scoundrel. As sometimes happens with men like that, he also lived through enough of the bad times to be thought to have a charmed life. At the time of the Custer fight, he was forty-four years of age.

By the time he got to the 7th Cavalry, however, he had fought against Napoleon III at twenty-six years of age, served time in prison and sentenced to death on the guillotine in Paris. He had worked as a dock worker and immigrated to the United States in time to fight in the Civil War as a private. Late in the war he was appointed as a second lieutenant in Company A, 2nd U.S. Colored Infantry in 1865. He had been with the 7th since 1869. He retired as a captain and advanced to a major upon retirement.

Captain Thomas McDougall newly-promoted and new commander of B Troop was assigned shotgun for the logistics company that guarded the supplies and ammunition trains plus the horse and mule teams. All four of Custer's sub-commanders were experienced Civil War officers. It was the only thing they had in common.

Captain McDougall was an interesting bird. He commanded a unit of the 10th Louisiana Infantry Volunteers of African Decent during the rebellion. From 1863 to 1869 he served as an infantry officer. After the war, he had grown weary of foot-slogging with the infantry and transferred to the 7th Cavalry when the call for officers came. He earned extensive experience fighting Indians prior to joining the 7th Cavalry as an infantry officer. He won an appointment as captain in the 7th only six months before the battle on the Little Bighorn.

Captain McDougall became a fast friend of the Lieutenant Colonel. One can only surmise that it was McDougall's past history of having no aversion to a fight that brought him to the colonel's attention in the first place. Captain McDougall enjoyed fighting above most anything the Army had him do. He retired as a major from the military in 1890. His father had also served during the Civil War as a Brevet Brigadier General, the same as Custer, though the two generals never met.

At the time of the deployment of the 7th Cavalry, he was junior in rank and was one of the newest members of the Lieutenant Colonel's inner circle. Captain McDougall and Custer's brother-in-law Lieutenant James Calhoun were very close friends and in 1874 he married Calhoun's little sister.

Only those members of the Lieutenant Colonel Custer's inner-circle were commanders and sub-commanders (lieutenants or captains) within

Custer's third wing battalion. These men would follow their leader that last day. That is all, except Captain McDougall. The Lieutenant Colonel told McDougall that he would be his command's lifeline in the event he needed one so to be ready to ride through the gates of hell to get to him when and if he was called.

At the end of the day, he could not get to his friends or his commander; but it was not because he did not try. After the battle, nine men from McDougall's B Troop would be recommended for, and awarded, the Congressional Medal of Honor for their part in the battle.

—7—

CUSTER'S NEMESIS: CAPTAIN BENTEEN

Captain Frederick Benteen was a thorn in the side of Custer from 1868 to the last day that Custer lived. After the battle, Benteen was accused of doodling, and not following his direct orders from the Lieutenant Colonel concerning his part in the battle. Other charges were that he let his personal relationship with his superior officer stand in the way of performing his direct orders, and for starting malicious gossip concerning the Lieutenant Colonel and his lady. Apparently, all the charges were true, yet no punishment or loss of privileges was ever recorded for those offenses.

This officer, more than any other in the 7th Cavalry, was one of its best and ablest leaders. It cannot be denied that Captain Frederick Benteen had a truly unabated hatred of his commander. This man could hate, and he really hated Lieutenant Colonel Custer. If telling a little fib now and again along the way helped tarnish his commander's memory, Captain Benteen could live with it.

In Benteen's past, before riding with Lieutenant Colonel Custer that last time, he had emerged from a rather difficult past and managed to land in the Army at nineteen years of age. In his first battle during the Civil War, he had turned and run in mad flight with his unit as the Confederates were overrunning them. It was the first and last time Fredrick Benteen ever ran from anything, man or beast, for the rest of his life.

He was raised in an ultraconservative family that had eventually settled in the south. When the Civil War broke out, only Fredrick Benteen would answer the call as a Unionist, both his father and brother would go the way of their adopted state. As a result his father banished him forever from ever returning to the family because young Frederick turned against his family to fight against them and states rights, and the Confederacy.

Later in the war, 1863, as luck would have it, his father was captured in the same battle that son Frederick, (now Lieutenant Benteen, U.S. Army) was fighting in. The Yankees won the battle, and as the prisoners were being rounded up and sorted out, son Frederick saw his father being marched along as a prisoner.

Lieutenant Benteen went to his commander and told him that his father was a prisoner of war and he knew if his old man was granted amnesty the old fellow would be right back at the nearest recruiting station the next morning. He asked that his commander deny amnesty to his father. The commander accepted Benteen's argument and had Papa Benteen moved to a Union prison for the rest of the war for his own protection.

On the surface it would seem a mean-spirited thing to do to his father. It was not that way at all. In Frederick the Younger's mind, it was the surest way to ensure Frederick the Older would survive the war. Ensuring Frederick the Younger's mama would get her husband back in mostly one piece. Son Frederick knew his old man, and knew the old fool would reenlist the minute he was out of sight of them "damned Yankees." The next time his father might be shot out of hand, or blown to smithereens and Frederick the Younger's mama would be a widow. Rather than risk that, son Benteen did the next best thing under the circumstances. He arranged for his father a nice long rest for the remainder of the war.

It did not endear Frederick the Younger with Frederick the Older, and until the day Frederick the Older died, he never forgave his son for fighting for the other side, or making him a prisoner all those years. Through the years, daddy Benteen's son took financial care of him and the rest of the family—even after the war. Thus, young Benteen was set adrift of his family early in life. Captain Benteen was not the perfect man most history books or accountings say he was. He had his faults.

In all the years after his first battle, no one ever saw Frederick Benteen even duck when shots were fired his way. It was as if he defied someone to shoot him. Perhaps, he never went to "cover" when shots were fired his way because he was so upset with himself for running that very first time he came under fire. Men like him never seem to last very long in those situations, but Benteen did time and time again. To prove he was no coward to himself, it was his way to cover up the fact that once he had shown the sign of the "white feather" when just a boy of nineteen.

Who knows what makes men tick? Frederick Benteen was certainly a different kind of clock. He was a soldier's soldier, who always took his men into account first. The men who served with him, or were under his command, thought he was the bravest of any man on a battlefield.

Later in his life he had a drinking problem, which was not uncommon for frontier soldiers in those days—most of them were hard drinkers. Captain Benteen could usually control his hard drinking for appropriate times. He then would go on binges that would last for several days. His men would usually take care of their commander until he had drunk his demons under the table, or after he had chased the last of them far enough away so they would not bother him for a time. When his blood got up, or he felt a mean drunk was necessary, no one could control him. While it did not happen often, once was enough for most of those who were around when it happened.

He was an able leader and undeniably the stronger, steadier, and more reliable then Major Reno. He had attained the brevet rank of Colonel during the Civil War and was brevetted to general just as the war ended as recognition for his contributions to the Union effort.

He, like everyone else in the officer corps, lost his brevet grade after the war. He was reduced back to his highest earned rank, the rank of captain. He often served in the capacities above his rank, as did most of the officers in the post-war era. Fate had kept him from ever attending West Point. For that reason, on the day of the battle, he probably missed being Custer's second in command or even being in command of the regiment himself.

Captain Benteen was a vain man, and most always had a dislike for those who he thought were beneath him in abilities — which seemed to be just about everyone he ever met. Lieutenant Colonel Custer was number one of those whom Captain Benteen hated with an unbridled, never-ending, bile rising, purple passion. During the Civil War, Frederick Benteen had been a regimental commander in the western theater, and a member of the 7th Cavalry in its early days after the Civil War in Kansas-Oklahoma territories in 1868-69.

It was here; in those early frontier days he had his first personal dealings with Lieutenant Colonel Custer. Ultimately, his feelings of hate worked against him as Lieutenant Colonel Custer sent him to isolated postings for his remarks concerning his handling of the Washita affair, and leaving Major Elliott hanging on a very tenuous branch all by himself and nineteen men. That incident, probably more than anything else Custer did, put him on Captain Benteen's outhouse wall.

The icing on the cake, however, happened about the same time. Captain Benteen's wife had taken seriously ill while he was on one of Custer's "I'll get you list" remote postings in western Kansas. When Captain Benteen applied for emergency leave, LTC Custer, his commander and rater in the Army's food chain disapproved his request. Benteen swore to get even for this slighting but Custer was only pointing out to the Captain that there were prices to be paid for talking behind his commander's back.

Benteen was the same age as Major Marcus Reno, forty-two, though he looked much older because of prematurely stone-white hair. He cared deeply for his men and their welfare; and was an outstanding commander and leader both in the field and in garrison.

He made a point to never raise his voice louder than a normal tone when speaking. To hear what he said one had to be listening very carefully because he had uncommonly quiet voice under normal circumstance and he only said it once—even under fire. If he should need to talk louder than that to make his point to a soldier or a junior officer, or to a commanding officer for that matter, Captain Benteen could, and would, rip the heart out of the offender and feed it back to him piece by piece to make his point. He very seldom had to do that more than once.

The offender who had committed the cardinal sin of disappointing this man never forgot it. His men would never cross him, and he would guide them splendidly with intelligence, courage, and valor.

After the Civil War he was assigned as a troop commander in the 7th

Cavalry under the command of the Lieutenant Colonel George Armstrong Custer. Custer was reduced in rank shortly after taking command of the 7th Cavalry from Major General to Lieutenant Colonel. For Benteen to be reduced from Brigadier General to Captain was a slight he never got over. What was worse, in his opinion, at least, was a prima donna, six years his junior, was in command of his regiment, and worse — was his new commander.

In Benteen's mind, Custer had command only because he had skated through West Point. That was wrong-headed, of course; Custer was every bit as much a leader of men that Benteen fancied himself to be, plus a bit more. His being a "ring knocker," of course, did not hurt either.

Fredrick Benteen's choice was either put up with the way things had gone or get out of the Army. Rather than do anything else, he took command of a company in the newly formed 7th. He had heard all the stories of his new commander's lightening quick rise to Major General and of all the exploits of the "Boy General." He had heard that Custer's uniforms were self-designed and hand-sewn by his wife. To Captain Benteen's keen sense of priority, he saw his commander as a self-edifying, sanctimonious, half-educated creation, not worthy of leadership. More to the point and especially in Benteen's mind, he was not worthy as his commander, even though they had never met and Benteen had not had the opportunity to appraise him in person while in a commander's role.

His experiences with his new regimental commander, George Armstrong Custer, were not good from the very first evening they met in Oklahoma. It seems Captain Benteen was a card player of some merit. Since no one personally knew him, or his reputation, when he got to his new posting, as far as his brother officers were concerned, he was just fresh meat for the weekly card game. Usually, someone knew tidbits of information about men. But in Benteen's case, no one had a clue that Captain Benteen was a poker player from hell; that little fact was not out for public consumption.

Out on the frontier in 1868, playing cards was the favorite past time amongst officers and enlisted men alike, though they never played together that would have been against the military code. To Custer's inner circle Captain Benteen was the fresh lamb to be lead to slaughter. Not knowing that Benteen was the next thing closest to a card shark before the big game caused some surprises for the unsuspecting pack of waiting want-to-be-wolves. Custer's weekly card game just so happened to be "one-hand" short the night Benteen reported in.

Captain Benteen's new commander thoughtfully asked him the new captain to sit in on a little friendly game. Of course, the officers who invited him considered themselves as the best the Army had to offer with cards. It did not take long before the friendly game of poker turned serious. As the evening wore on the old-timers started dropping one by one.

Captain Benteen won pot after pot. First, Custer went broke (he was a terrible gambler, always had been, always would be). The commander then wrote a chit for $200, and promptly lost that. He retired to his own home to face Libby's wrath.

Next, card-shark Benteen summarily broke each and every one of his new acquaintances and brother officers at the table that evening. To the newly arrived captain, it was quite amusing; however, he did not necessarily win any friends that evening. The last man to fall was Captain Thomas Weir; who took it particularly hard. Captain Weir told Captain Benteen it was not a gentlemanly thing to do. That being new on post and then taking advantage of everyone he would serve with, especially to brother serving officers who were just trying to make him feel at home.

Benteen just smiled, and kept counting his winnings. The new captain told his peer if he didn't like the heat, to stay the hell out of the kitchen. Captain Weir never had much use for the guy afterwards.

Captain Benteen came to the command with some pretty damning conclusions concerning Lieutenant Colonel Custer. First, Benteen had heard the stories of how Custer drove his men in the field and in garrison. Benteen's personal opinion was that Lieutenant Colonel Custer was overly harsh and demeaning to the men in his command in both places. He thought Custer expected too much of them, and was willing to sacrifice any or all of them to satisfy his near bloodlust for glory and victory.

The trouble was Captain Benteen had a point. All of that was true, or at least seemed true the way he looked at it. The other side of the coin was that Custer had been successful when other officers had failed because he took no pity. Not on the enemy, and not on his troops. If others thought he was tough on his troops, his enemies knew him and his men would be tougher on them.

The most damning of all of the events occurred in the Oklahoma Indian Territories at the Battle of the Washita in the winter of 1868. The ordeal along the Washita River was to become Custer's lasting shame. The Lieutenant Colonel always saw it, as he said in his own autobiography, as one of his most shining moments. To many who witnessed it, it was something far, far short of that.

During the shameful affair, Lieutenant Colonel Custer lost track of one of his favorite troop commanders, Major Elliot. Major Elliot had led a company of men during the early morning attack on Black Kettle's peaceful Southern Cheyenne.

The 7th Cavalry's Osage Indian scouts had tracked these "unknown hostiles" for days before finally just barely catching a whiff of them on the late afternoon wind in the Valley of the Washita during a snow storm. Without following them to their camp to be sure to whom they belonged the scouts reported back to Custer. While the three white scouts with the Osage were not sure they belonged to old Black Kettle's Southern Cheyenne it did not really matter that much to Lieutenant Colonel Custer. Indian's were pretty much just Indians and their pedigree did not really matter that much. His scouts thought it was the same bunch they had been tracking that led to Black Kettle's camp. It would have been damn hard to prove they had found the same bunch they had been tracking at the time without going in and asking before they attacked. As for this band of Southern Cheyenne, they had suffered once before at the hands of other white men who had attacked them on Sand Creek and nearly whipped them out four years earlier. These folks had been then, and were now, on the lands the Great White Father had promised that they would be safe.

Custer sprung a surprise attack on the encampment before sunup on the freezing cold morning of November 27, 1868. Not knowing for sure who he was attacking seemed to be less important an issue than being right in which band he attacked. His command put to the sword and cannon shot the entire almost defenseless village. Unfortunately, it just so happened that most of those that were killed more were women, children, and old unarmed men. It was not an issue, at least not to Custer, or later, to Sheridan, who had said in the past that the only good Indian was a dead Indian.

The 875 to 900 horses that Custer had ordered to be shot afterwards and the few hostile warriors that were killed in defense of their village was just part of the dirty business called war against the hostiles. It did not matter to the Lieutenant Colonel if the folks he killed were armed or not. He knew, as few others did, that honor has no place on a battlefield; shameful things did occur; and in the end, if enough of them took place against the Indian then ultimately the wars would end and the immigrants could pass through the Great Plains without "Injins liftin' their hair, raping their women folk and stealin' their kids."

The slaughtering of all the camp's horses should have been enough one would have thought. But then Custer ordered all the hundreds of buffalo robes and many tons of dried buffalo meat the Cheyenne had stored up for the winter to be put to the torch. If there was glory to be found in the fighting of the Indians, glory was not found there in the valley of the Washita River that Christmas morning, 1868.

Custer was not hunting glory or honor that day; he was hunting Indians, any would do. Most important, he following orders and fighting a war that he understood even if his men and the other officers did not.

It was this tactic Custer would use over and over, time and again when attacking hostiles—divide his force and hit from two sides at once, leaving a strong reserve to come to the rescue either of the attacking forces on an as-needed basis. Today, military strategists call this technique the hammer and anvil. It worked then and it still works to this day.

The point of the attack was to kill Indians and destroy the encampment. To Lieutenant Colonel Custer, the mission was accomplished—he had killed Indians, lots of them. It did not necessarily matter to him if they were good, bad, or ugly, young or old, women or children, and nearly defenseless or full-blooded, honest-to-goodness warriors. He believed in total war and always said as much.

After torching the encampment, Lieutenant Colonel Custer rounded up the few survivors and marched them off in the freezing temperatures with what they had on their backs, leaving old Chief Black Kettle, his wife and nearly two hundred more lying dead and frozen stiff in the snow next to the Washita River.

While the issue of killing all the Indians before they could escape was still up in the air, Major Elliott had taken a squadron (eighteen troopers) off on his own to round up several "hostiles" who had been seen fleeing up a dry creek bed that led off from the river. A couple hours, maybe, as many as three, would pass after the attack as Custer order the slaughtering of the horse herd and burning and sacking of the village. As the command began to reassemble Captain Benteen discovered his friend Major Elliott was missing. A few of the men had said that they Major Elliott and a squadron take off after some of the escaping hostiles.

Because the defeat of old Black Kettle's harmless band of Southern Cheyenne had been so easy—only two soldiers killed—during the attack, it was barely noticed Elliott was missing to begin with. Because Major Elliot had been so popular in the regiment with the other officers as well as many of the enlisted men, the officers of the command, especially Benteen, pleaded with Custer to go out and scout the area filled with gullies to find the major and the missing men.

At the same time, Custer's Indian scouts were telling him there were hostiles coming toward them in force from up and down the Washita and that if the cavalry wanted to save its hair they had better be for getting out of that valley very quickly.

Looking along the ridges above the encampment, they could see that angry hostiles were gathering in significant force along the rim of the valley. Upon seeing the forces gathering along the ridge lines Custer realized he might have led his command into a trap. In his military mind, if they did not get out immediately they may never get out of at all. He ordered a quick march out of the valley, deciding Major Elliot had probably seen the same thing, and would have skeedaddled out ahead of them—and they would probably meet somewhere on the trip back to their own camp, of course, that never happened.

Custer refused to let anyone go reconnoiter the area to find out if they could find the missing members of the regiment. In fact, no search whatsoever was ordered during the operation for the missing command. To the men, it would be Custer's lasting blemish, and would always be remembered, even after his death. It may have been Custer's only time in his life that bravery, courage, and dedication to duty failed him. He tucked tail and ran as fast as he could to get out of the valley. This valley had death written in its snow and Custer even if no one else could see it, he could see.

In Custer's defense, there were military considerations for his refusal to go find Major Elliott and his squadron. His command was about to be attacked by several of the other tribes camping along the same river as Black Kettle's band of Southern Cheyenne. While Custer did not know he was hitting Black Kettle's camp specifically, he also did not know that nearly a half dozen other Indian encampments were also camping along the Washita during that same winter. Black Kettle's band just happened to be the one that the 7th Cavalry had stumbled upon, and being so, it was attacked with the full force that Custer had at his disposal (six troops, about 250 men). While he had not considered the size of the camp before he attacked; he did in fact attack. He had surprise and cannon balls as advantages.

He also knew he could not withstand a drawn-out fight if he did not hit hard and fast. Not knowing there were several other tribes close gave him a false sense of security. He thought he could take his time afterwards and destroy the total encampment at his leisure. After his scouts had told him what was going on around the valley, his best move, in his military mind, was to get away from the river as fast as he could. He wanted to keep his hair after he had taken care of the grisly business of killing nearly 900 of Black Kettle's horse herd. Each one was shot, wasting what would have been sorely needed ammunition had he had to fight the other bands in the valley in order to get away.

Two months later, while on a routine patrol going back over the battleground around Black Kettle's old encampment Captain Benteen' patrol found the remains of Major Elliott and his squadron of men. They had been ambushed and wiped out to the man. The ambush site had shown the squadron had formed itself into a wheel with spoke like pattern, each man positioning himself a few degrees off the next man's right arm, feet pointed to the center and their weapons pointed out. The evidence was clear; these men had died like soldiers should—fighting to the end. From the positioning of the remains when found each man had died defending his fighting position.

Each of their bodies had been mutilated, as was customary with the red man. It was not a personal thing that the Indians did; it was as much spiritual as it was ceremonial. Each man had been scalped and hacked, their bodies pelted with arrows.

From that day on, Lieutenant Colonel Custer had a real enemy at his back wherever the command went—Captain Benteen.

Captain Benteen's real problem with the "Custer boys" was that in his mind, they were in it for the glory they could heap upon themselves. If a few men got killed along the way, well, it was unfortunate, but killing and dying happen in wars—do they not?

As for Frederick Benteen, he remained a soldier until very near the end of his life. He died at sixty-three of cancer. Upon retiring he was promoted to the rank of brigadier general. He finally got the rank he felt he had so long deserved, even if it was after he had been turned out to pasture. In his mind he deserved it, and Custer did not.

Captain Benteen's dislike of Custer would fester as time went on from the middle-1860s, and he carried that grudge with him the rest of his life. To him, Custer was not fit to push cattle—much less troops.

On a rather long list of things and people that Benteen hated were Mormons. Later in his career he would face a court marital for slandering and fighting with them. It would cost him a half-year severance from the service, and half a year's pay. Needless to say, Mormons tried their damnedest to stay the hell away from the then-Colonel Benteen.

If Fredrick caught someone on the wrong side of the way he saw things, he could make their life seem like a living hell. It did not matter who it was, or what the situation he did not like was, he came smashing and blasting. Mormons or anyone he did not like, or that he saw no utility in, learned the same thing.

The Battle of the Little Bighorn would bring some of those shortcomings out. That would not be so unusual–combat brings out the best and the worst in most men. For Benteen the fight would also bring out his qualities as a field commander in a hostile environment. When all facets of this complex man were considered, one would look a long way before finding one to measure up to Captain Benteen in a matter of life and death.

The downside to Captain Benteen was that if someone tweaked his pride or threatened his self-admiration he could be as mean-spirited as a two-headed rattlesnake and as dangerous as a gut-shot bull buffalo. Being moved to a secondary role during the deployment of the regiment did not set well with the captain. He would not forget what he perceived a slight, though not intentional, by the Lieutenant Colonel during the deployment for battle.

In Lieutenant Colonel Custer's mind it was a matter of military protocol; Major Reno outranked Captain Benteen. It was easy—at least for Custer—to justify the way he divvied out the operation's missions. Besides, had Benteen looked at the way Custer probably did, he would be in relief of either or both battalion's before the sun set that day. But, as usual with Captain Benteen in matters between him and Custer, he had a skewed way at looking at things. The man could think and act at the same time on his feet. His attitude towards the Lieutenant Colonel would influence his otherwise clear thinking capability.

For Lieutenant Colonel Custer's part, he did not have time to play games; he was all business when it came to getting men ready to face the enemy. Thus, Major Reno was put in second command to Lieutenant Colonel Custer. Captain Benteen would avenge his slight in the fight at the Little Bighorn, and again during the Court of Inquiry, later, and then, to the end of his mostly unhappy life.

Cut to the spring of 1876, Fort Abraham Lincoln: Captain Benteen was forty-two years of age, still with the 7th Cavalry, and still a troop commander—the oldest one. Major Marcus Reno was the acting regimental commander during Custer's absence. The Lieutenant Colonel, you will remember, had been called back to Washington to testify about the much discussed swindling by the post's commissary mercantile owner's personnel. In his absence, Major Reno became the acting commander.

—8—

EVERYONE'S SCAPEGOAT: MAJOR MARCUS RENO

Major Marcus Reno had an almost colorless personality. Seldom, if ever, did anyone remember of hearing him laugh or tell a joke. To say Major Marcus Reno was boring would be to add new definition to the word itself. He had his own ghosts in his private closet, and he kept those buried in his soul. He fought those demons constantly, losing usually at the wrong end of a whiskey bottle.

He too, like his commander, had attended but had not distinguished himself at the Army's academy. He established his own notoriety for demerits and general misconduct much the same as Custer would a few years later. Much to his embarrassment, he had to attend the institution an additional year in order to complete the curriculum requirements to graduate. Some sources say that it was more like two additional years, but it was really just one, to receive his commission as a Second Lieutenant. While he had attended the Academy he had established a record in his own right of having received more demerits than anyone in his class.

During the Civil War he had served mostly undistinguished but somehow had survived. That was an accomplishment in and of itself. Just to live through the Civil War as an officer was no easy task. For doing his duty and in the process not getting killed he was eventually brevetted as a brigadier general during the war. Afterwards his rank was reverted back to Captain. For the next ten years he then was posted to several lonely (non-accompanied) outposts before. Finally, he put in for and received a station at Fort Abraham Lincoln and the 7th Cavalry Regiment in the fall of 1875. He had no combat experience against the Sioux or any other Indians before his assignment to the 7th Cavalry. Unfortunately for everyone in the 7th Cavalry, he had not gained any before the 7th deployed to the Little Bighorn.

Major Reno's wife died in 1874 leaving a young son for the major to try to raise or find someone to leave him with to take care of while he was stationed in outposts far from civilization. His wife's sister in Illinois was raising the Major's son at the time of the expedition to the Little Bighorn.

A notorious drunk much of the time, when he was not, he was simply a capable officer—nothing more, or less. Seemingly brave enough, from past efficiency reports, he was just pasted along. No one in the past had seen him operate under stress of combat or whether he could act on his feet when the enemy was upon him.

In other assignments such as scouting in front of the expedition he did only what he was asked and not one thing more. He was not noted for doing anything above and beyond what his orders required him to do. Major Reno had gradually been moved up the ranks because of his tie back to the Military Academy at West Point. In other words, he followed his orders to the letter, no more, no less—and that my friends can drive a commander nuts sometimes, especially when the fortunes of war are hanging in the balance, as they oft times are as forces move toward combat.

He too, like Captain Benteen, did not like Custer or his methods and was never a part of the Lieutenant Colonel's inner circle. What is more, he had no desire to ever be considered for such an asinine thing as being a part of someone's "good ol' boys club."

When asked about Lieutenant Colonel Custer's ability to lead, he said something to the effect of, "I had no confidence in the General's ability to soldier or as a leader."

As for the two battalion commanders, Lieutenant Colonel Custer had to leave Fort Abraham Lincoln with, about the only thing that Major Reno and Captain Benteen could agree upon between themselves was that neither man had any use for "Old Iron Ass." The ironic part of these two's relationship was they did not even like each other.

Their liking or disliking each other should not have mattered once in the field where military men did their jobs, and to hell with everything else. Back at the post, the point remains that neither socialized with the Lieutenant Colonel and his lady, or with one another. Libby was somewhat intimidated with these two men who did not think her Lieutenant Colonel walked on the water and as a result did not like either of the officers as men, or officers. Their attitude toward her was politely, "So what?"

    This expedition and fight on the Bighorn was to be Major Reno's first real "live" action against Indians. That being the truth, he fit in with about forty percent of the regiment, they had exactly as much as he did, and that was not a comforting thought going into battle for the enlisted men under his command. Major Reno's feeling was that he and the men he led would get the job he was tasked with done if it could be done. He would do what was asked of him, no more, no less, and don't expect any heroics along the way. Major Reno was not a hero; he made no pretenses of being one, he was able, and that was enough in his mind.

    On the day when a little bit of heroics would have been nice, both he and his men would find the job could not be done, and the few of them who were left at the end of the day were only the really very lucky. Major Reno would relate later, when help finally did come on the afternoon of the 28th, both he and Captain Benteen thought it was Custer coming with reinforcements from the north. Who is to say, not he or even Benteen would have thought that they hostiles would kill him—not Custer! They even believed in the Custer magic.

    Major Reno very well may have thought just that.

    On the one hand, the good major was not anywhere near the caliber of leader that Captain Benteen was. Major Reno more than once was accused of dropping the white feather, though that could have been due to more circumstance than fact.

    Major Reno was a "ring-knocker" (a West Point graduate) and was given the privilege of attacking the village. He had always been an able commander up to that date in time. He had served as a staff officer during the Civil War and had managed to survive any combat he may have been a part of. Afterwards, out on the plains when serving with the 7th Cavalry, and even before on outposts on the Pacific coast his raters and said he "seemed" brave enough but that you could not prove it by them. In all that time though he had never had to fire a shot in anger himself or had he had to fire one in his self-protection.

In nearly every capacity when evaluating the two officers, Major Reno fell far short of Captain Benteen's ability, even counting Benteen's self-serving ways. The only difference in maintaining a rank higher than Benteen seems to be that Major Reno was a West Point graduate, and Benteen was not, and the Army took care of its own, deserved or not.

There is only one time that Captain Benteen mentioned that Major Reno had lost his courage during the fighting. The Captain would say something like, "He (Major Reno) seemed to have waved the white feather, by the time me and my boys got to him and his command." It suggested to the board Major Reno was not on top of his A-game. Suggesting such a thing means, of course, that Major Reno had lost his courage during the valley fight and was thus unfit to lead the defense of the hills above the valley.

It also says loads about Captain Benteen; he was always willing to drop the dime on those who failed to meet the expectations of a situation, no matter what the reason. It was not necessarily a character flaw in Captain Benteen. He just would not tolerate excuses from anyone, especially his supposed superiors; or anyone, for that matter who out ranked him. Benteen expected better of not only his commanders but also of the men who served under him.

In that respect he was not much different than a very strict coach of some athletic team during training. He pushed everybody to their limit and he expected them to perform at that high level regardless of what the circumstances were. To his way of thinking, demanding high performance is what kept people alive when things got dicey. Battle situations have a tendency to do that in any battle. On that hill above the Little Bighorn River with thousands of hostiles ready cut the throat of every living one of the men in the 7th Cavalry at any moment, it got a little dicey.

When things got rough, like they did that first day a long the Little Bighorn River, and later on Major Reno's hill; Major Reno gave way to Captain Benteen's presence. Benteen's presence brought order to the defense of the hill. Whether the enlisted men saw it that way or the other officers present saw it that way, and just did not say anything, does not change the way it was. The fact is Major Reno had been stretched beyond his capacities at that time he led the charge down the valley toward the southern end of the encampment and then for the next two and a half days.

Usually, the major was a quiet man who kept alone. He drank by himself and would get sloppy drunk when he did. He was not close to anyone in particular, as far as that goes he was the new man on the block. He needed orders to follow, and when he did not have orders seemed to toddle along or wait very still until he got some. That is not necessarily a bad thing under most instances. But during the valley fight, and later, in the defense on the hill when it really mattered, it was not a good thing.

What happened in the valley had shaken him to the very inner part of the man's soul. Perhaps, he just snapped mentally for a time, and was not really in command of himself, much less his troops. That is bad timing, and fortunately for his men, Captain Benteen was there, and could take up the slack for the idle major.

Major Reno, like Benteen, had been a part of the 7th Cavalry since 1868. After that tragic War Between the States, before the 7th Cavalry was even born, units were sent to serve throughout the South to aid in maintaining order during reconstruction. After the Battle on the Little Bighorn, the very capable General Wesley Merritt was placed in command of the 7th Cavalry over the recommendation of the surviving enlisted men and officers. Major Reno was placed in field command of the 7th until the new general could assume command.

Perhaps, in Custer's mind, Major Reno was expendable. Going into harm's way, as every man in the 7th Cavalry knew they were, it was imperative men trust each other, and especially important it was imperative that commanders are trusted by their subordinate leaders and vise-versa.

Many have thought Major Reno did not fight hard enough to maintain contact with the southern end of the camp. His failure to maintain pressure on the hostiles was the main failing to the final act in the Custer story.

In Major Reno's defense, it would be damned hard to prove. All that Major Reno would have accomplished was his command's total destruction had he tried any harder. Waiting even five minutes longer at the front of the beehive, so-to-speak, would have been too long.

It may have kept the hostiles busy killing and butchering all of Major Reno's men while Custer attacked where he did. If how the battle ended, with only Lieutenant Colonel Custer's command being wiped out, his attempt at striking harder would have only made a bad ending worse. The whole of the 7th Cavalry would have been buried on the side of those hills and in the valley next to a sleepy little river the Indians called the Little Horned Sheep.

Instead of five troops of cavalry being destroyed running up the sides of those hills, there would have been quite possibly eight; or as many as all twelve troops left soaking up the hot summer sun. No, had Major Reno or Benteen tried any harder to get to their commander once they got into their earthen dugout dish, they would have been totally wiped out.

On that day, if these hostiles got close to a *wasichu*, they were going to rip his hair off as they killed them. As time went on that afternoon, those men holed up on Major Reno Hill simply could not move, even if they had wanted to. The worst part was that the hostiles knew it. The two commands (Major Reno's and Benteen's) had fallen into a giant spider web and the harder they tried to move, the more they got tangled and snared. The Indians kept them there mired in the web to suck their life juices from them at their leisure.

The Army was looking for a scapegoat after the mess-up on the Little Bighorn. They needed someone to take the hit for Custer's possible bad decisions, someone to cast the evil eye away from any shortcomings the Army may have a hand in. The excuse of a numerically superior force simply overmatched this legendary Lieutenant Colonel was not a good enough reason even for the Army nor would it be for the public. However, if they could pin the calamity on someone living for not coming to the aid of his commander, the guilty might be branded a coward the rest of whatever life he had left. At the same time it took the heat away from the armchair generals back in Washington and Chicago.

Add to that, if a brother commander stated, after it was all over, that he, Major Reno was a little over-wrought by the events leading up to the events of that terrible day, the die would have been cast. It would not be unreasonable to have felt betrayed by the brotherhood. Major Reno stood before the Courts of Inquiry in mid January 1879 and listened to Captain Benteen explain his personal impressions and observations to the court concerning his commander. Much to his credit, the major said nothing in his defense of Captain Benteen's assessment of him to the court. Perhaps, understanding more than Captain Benteen, the best way to show innocence (if that is what it was) is to say nothing at all. Retreat and holding the best ground on the field was the only responsible thing he could see to do. He simply did not have any options if he wanted to live, and he did.

For Major Reno's part, he was simply lucky his command was not annihilated during his attack on the southern end of the encampment. Surprisingly, it would be only one of the few times in life that he was lucky.

Major Reno never stood up for himself; maybe, in part, because deep down in his soul he felt he really was a coward and felt personally responsible for Custer's fall. He probably felt a little betrayed also by the situation at the same time. We will never know, Major Marcus Reno never said one way or the other. He is, however, the only officer of all of the officers that were on the field that day, and lived through the trauma of the battle that requested to be buried with his men when he died. Perhaps, there was more to Major Reno than we will ever know.

In the end, it would matter not one iota. Lieutenant Colonel Custer was the field commander and field commanders have great flexibility once in the field. Very seldom are the decisions of a commander questioned by anyone when they move against the enemy. Commanders move to a different drummer once in the field against an enemy. They could shoot their underlings for not following their orders. Custer would not have been above shooting his own brother had he thought it necessary to complete his mission.

Men of war do not mess around, and combat commanders are the next things to a living god as man will ever get. If the combatant commanders are not gods, then they sit on the right hand side of the Great War God when they move their commands into harm's way. As the events of that day unfolded, there were only two things that would have saved Custer that Sunday afternoon upon the hillsides of the Greasy Grass:

(1) If he had not been there in the first place (and well he should not have been).

(2) A biblical rapture had occurred, removing him and his twelve troops of cavalry by the Almighty to heavenly places.

—9—

CUSTER'S BATTALION TROOP COMMANDERS

Within Lieutenant Colonel Custer's Wing (battalion) there were five troop commanders. Within his battalion, he had split it into two parts. Captain George Yates, commander of F Troop, led one small battalion comprised of two troops of cavalry, E and F. Newly promoted First Lieutenant Algernon (Fresh) Smith would command E Troop (Captain McDougall's old Troop).

Lieutenant Colonel Custer would command the other three troops, C, L, and I. His brother, Thomas Ward Custer, who would double as the Regiment's Executive officer that day as well, commanded C Troop.

Lieutenant Colonel Custer once said that his brother, Thomas Ward Custer, should have been the general, and he should have been the captain. That may have been an overstatement on the Lieutenant Colonel's part, but it can be understood. George Custer admired his little brother almost as much as his little brother admired him.

Thomas entered the U.S. Army as a buck private infantryman, with the Michigan Volunteers as soon as he was old enough to do so. At seventeen years of age he enlisted to get into the Civil War where his big brother was. As luck would have it, their cousins, the Johnny Rebs, were waxing the Michigan boys along with the rest of the Yankees fairly regularly.

Brother George, out of his own fear for his brother's early death, and upon the plea from his scared-to-death mother, got young Thomas moved from the infantry over to the 7th Michigan Cavalry, his own regiment. George told his momma he would keep an eye out for his baby brother. After all, he wanted to save his momma's heart from breaking with the loss of her youngest baby boy. It must have been an unbelievable headache for George, because Thomas was every bit as "wild and crazy" as George ever had been, more so, if all the stories are true.

Thomas, or "TW" to his friends, was just seventeen years of age when he came into his older brother's command as a sergeant. He was without the benefit of a college education that his big brother had received. That had left Thomas a little rough around the edges as far as anything intellectual, but like his brother he was a natural born leader of men and also like his brother he knew no fear. The boys shared a remarkable relationship. As the boys grew into men they were selfishly loyal to one another.

"TW" had an uproarious and often outrageous sense of humor. George did too, but had learned to control it most of the time, at least in public. "TW" never quite mastered the art of when and where to pull his often-times mischievous pranks. His personality allowed for a lot of daredevil and orneriness mixed in for good measure and made it nearly impossible for big brother to control very much of anything he did.

Hell, he was just a kid. "TW" drank hard, chased anything with a skirt, fought anybody (officer or enlisted when he was either), and was full of piss and vinegar from the beginning of his military career to its end beside his brother.

For his part, Thomas quickly rose from private to sergeant within weeks of joining up with his brother in the cavalry. Not only was Thomas an excellent horseman, he was a natural leader like his brother. Plus, the fact that officers, especially cavalry officers, had a nasty habit of getting killed. So did sergeants. Thomas was in an outfit that needed sergeants, and ultimately, officers with Thomas' daring.

He was awarded his first Congressional Medal of Honor (CMH) a year after he got into the cavalry. The second presentation came late in the war while he was still an enlisted man, after being shot in the face.

During the action leading to his second award, Thomas had tried to take a battle flag from a Rebel. The rebel took exception to this young stud trying to steal his flag, drew his revolver, and shot Thomas full in the face at point blank range. It was a good thing he was not a great shot, or that Thomas tried to dodge the round, because the bullet struck him in the jaw, breaking it before exiting just below the right ear.

While the wound was indeed serious, it looked a lot worse than it really was. It was very bloody and messy. The round, fired at such close range to his face, had left powder burns covering much of his face and embedded spent gun powder beneath the skin surface. The physical effect was that it made TW's face seem as if it had been partially blown off and terribly disfigured, like some ghastly modern-day Halloween creature.

In addition to really getting TW's ire up and in defense of his own life, the assaulted youth drew his revolver and shot the man dead; grabbing up the flag he galloped off to where George was to show him his new prize. In a fight, any fight, TW was a very serious and a deadly dangerous contender. His personality would not allow him to back up, not from his enemies or even his brother. TW remained the wild, untamed mustang all the days of his life. If anyone could control him, it was only his older brother, George. TW idolized George. Interestingly, the opposite was also true.

Since the injury occurred during an attack, brother George was leading. Upon seeing the action and then seeing his little brother look as if he might bleed to death, George ordered him from the field. TW, of course, apparently having too much fun, had hardly noticed that he had been shot in the face and refused to leave. Upon refusing to leave, his older brother ordered him arrested by the provost guard. He was to be bodily taken from the field by force, under an armed escort to the first surgeon's tent the guard encountered, or he might have continued to fight.

When the armed escort corralled the officer, one of the guards asked the Lieutenant Colonel what they should do if he would not stay put once they got him to the doctor's tent. George looked at the poor bleeding soul that was his brother, and coolly said, "Shoot him."

George looked long into TW's eyes, nodding his head that his order would be carried out he tipped his hat to his brother, and rode back to the fight without looking back. Whether or not he was serious was beside the point. Both the guards and little brother Custer thought he was, and that was enough to keep TW under the doctor's care.

Anything that big brother did, Thomas was going to die if need be, to outdo him. He would show his big brother he was every bit as brave, or just plan better. Whether it was riding, shooting, or charging into the very teeth of hell, it simply did not matter to Thomas. Whatever George could do, little brother Tom could do it better, and if not better, then faster.

Well, that was fine—but George would never let his little brother be better at anything than he was. The net result was they pushed each other everyday they rode together during the war of the rebellion, and then for nearly eleven years afterward.

First one, then the other would do some eye-popping, astonishing thing that would naturally challenge the other to do something grander. The only reason George didn't have three Congressional Medals of Honor when the war ended was that officers were not authorized medals or badges until 1878.

With all of the competition between the two men…brothers, they were first and foremost friends and were very, very close. "Libby" Custer thought of Tom as her only baby brother, and often referred to Thomas as her brother. Thomas' promise to Libby was that he would keep an eye on her "Autie" for her, and not let him do anything that was apt to get him injured in anyway.

With the end in sight on the side of what is now known as Custer's Hill, it was Thomas who put the .38 caliber bulldog parrot (his brother's own gun) up to Autie's left temple rather than let some "Injin" do him. Thomas would have faced the Indians by himself if need be, "Hell, the red buggers don't scare me!" he might have said and thought. He would never have let hostiles have his big brother alive. He had promised Libby he would take care of Autie, and he would. It was probably one of the last things he ever did.

Captain Keogh, like his boss, Lieutenant Colonel Custer, was thirty-six years old. At the end of the Civil War he held the brevet rank of a one-star brigadier general. He was a good looking, well-built, cocky, unmarried, rough-talking, hard-drinking, women-chasing man, in other words, a model of a then, and as well as now, cavalryman. Captain Keogh, like the two Custers, was brave to a fault; he knew no fear. He was tough, smart, dashing, and as natural born a leader as there was in the 7th Cavalry.

If you were lucky enough to have him as a friend (and there were not many who could be counted as his friend) he would be your huckleberry in any bar room brawl, your closest ally in any fight. The fact that he had the morals of an alley tomcat when it came to women was softened somewhat by the fact that he was a soldier first and foremost. If you were his friend, he cut you no slack; a friend had to toe the line with Keogh the same as someone he did not know. In other words, right was right, wrong was wrong, and a man stood up for himself and his honor at all costs to himself personally. Captain Myles Emory Keogh epitomized the consummate idea of a modern day cavalry commander; he had been with the 7th since 1868 when it had been newly formed. He trained his men in the "Wild Eye" to be some of the best troopers in 7th.

In many respects, his tactics with his men mirrored those of his boss. He was relentless with their training. In those days, it was the captain's job to ensure that the men in the troop were trained. As a consequence he was especially hard on his sergeants and his new replacements. Heaven help the men in either group who did not measure up to Keogh's lofty standards. He could be brutal to the transgressors who missed the point of his directions and often was. Drunk or sober, he could get a man's attention, if, in his mind, he needed to be reminded of the finer points of obeying his instructions.

Unpopular in the regiment by most accounts by the enlisted men, and some of the officers because of his drunkenness, and pure mean streak. He was nonetheless a leader of men in tight situations. He could size up a situation immediately, and assume command as naturally as he could cuss the rising of the sun, or the way the moon was hung. Captain Keogh was a fighter, and had proven himself time and again during the Civil War rising. His ability to command was his strongest suite, that and chasing good-looking women, married or otherwise.

Even his brother officer, Captain Benteen, who Captain Keogh only slightly acknowledged, was even alive, admitted to his wife that he had dreams about Captain Keogh. He told her after the 7th returned from the field that while he was on the expedition he had a nightmare of "that damned Keogh" whisking her off her feet and ravaging her in place, had he lived. Benteen admitted upon seeing Keogh's dead body not far from that of Custer's; he had a feeling of relief because he had been killed. His Mary would be safe at home when he got back.

Captain Benteen was really a very insecure man. He was probably a realist at the same time. He knew Captain Keogh in the true cavalry tradition, there were no limits and Keogh was not picky. He was good looking with the devil-may-care look in his eyes.

When it came to women, with most any of them, he never had to chase very hard.

For whatever his private life may have been, Captain Keogh was a cool head in tight situations. When the men needed leadership at the ford or at the end of the ridge, they had to look no farther than to the commander of the Wild Eye Troop.

Unlike most of the other officers in this battalion, Captain Keogh was his own man. If he thought the "Old Man" (Custer) was off base, he, in his inevitable way would say so without mincing words. He was straightforward, and a man of few words when it came time to 'fessing up and holding men and himself accountable for their actions.

He was born in Ireland, as had a good share of the enlisted men in the regiment had, having left home at fifteen. He was a devout Catholic, and decided that the best way to serve his faith was at the foot of the throne of the Pope in Rome. While still very young, seventeen, he became a member of the Papal Guard in Rome. Before leaving three years later, he would be awarded the Medal of St. George by the Pope himself for his service and bravery in carrying out his duties as a personal body guard. It was a medal Keogh prized above everything else he owned his whole life, and would afterward carry all the days of his life. He never wore the medal because it was too big to wear around one's neck, so he carried it around in his pocket in a leather pouch.

About the time the Civil War started, Keogh decided he needed to be apart of the fight against the rebels, and he became an Irish immigrant to the United States. Once in America, he joined the Union Army and shortly afterward accepted a commission as a cavalry officer. One thing you could count on concerning Keogh was if there was a fight to be had–and Keogh was close to it, he was going to be in it. That reputation followed him and won for him promotion after promotion until he became a brevetted brigadier general leading a division of cavalry.

In retrospect, he was purely a mercenary soldier of fortune, and once the Civil War ended he was looking for work and adventure again. He would look no further than the newly formed 7th Cavalry and its new field boss, Lieutenant Colonel George Armstrong Custer.

It was not long afterward that he became a fast friend of Custer. The two of them, the Lieutenant Colonel and the captain, were a perfect match for one another—like the twin British bulldogs patriots that Custer carried on his hips, they were a matched pair.

He once testified against Lieutenant Colonel Custer in 1868, when the Lieutenant Colonel had been on trial during the Court Martial for abandoning his command in Kansas. The courts martial found the lieutenant colonel guilty mostly on Captain Keogh's testimony. It cost Custer a year's wages and one-year suspension from the Army.

Even so, the Lieutenant Colonel and the captain remained close friends. In Custer's mind, at the time, abandoning his post was wrong, while going AWOL was justifiable to ensure the safety of his wife for his own mind's satisfaction. He never quibbled about being disciplined for his misdeeds, nor did he hold it against the venerable Captain Keogh.

If Custer did wrong, folks had to do what they had to do. It was the way it was, and the way it should be. He would not hold it against men who he considered his equal and Keogh had won the right to be his commander's equal.

Tough-talking, rabble-rousing, Captain Myles Emory Keogh, commanded what had become known as the "Wild Eye" Troop, or I Troop. Some of the officers in the regiment would say that everybody better get out of Captain Keogh's way when he was drinking because when got that "wild eye" of his going, there was bound to be trouble and on more than one occasion he had fought with anyone with in his range, officer or enlisted. He was a mean drunk.

He was purely mean most of the time when he was enhanced with the evil spirits, and was a stickler for perfection within his own command. He was as demanding of his men as he was himself and perhaps that was his saving grace.

His men under his command took on the same characteristics as their leader, they were just as hard-living, hard-drinking and had an attitude that said, "to hell with everybody else" as was Captain Keogh. The name stuck and the troopers of the I Troop adopted the moniker, "The Wild Eye" as their own. The old timers in this troop had been together for several years and the troop was one of the toughest, best disciplined units in the regiment.

At the time of his death he was thirty-one years old. James Calhoun missed most of the Civil War traveling in Europe after graduating from Mt. Pleasant Academy, Ossining, New York, from 1860 to 1864. Upon returning from touring Europe he enlisted as a private in the 23rd Infantry. At the age of nineteen he applied for entry into the Naval Academy at Annapolis Maryland. He was denied entry by the board, and was appointed first sergeant in February 1865. He served in that capacity until October 1867. He was appointed as a second lieutenant in new regiment, the 32nd Infantry. He was assigned to the 7th Cavalry, where he married George and Thomas Custer's little sister, Margaret Emma Custer, in 1872.

His friendship with the Custers and their taking him into the family began immediately. They became his brothers, and he theirs. It was the Custer way. Prior to leaving on what would be his last expedition, he had been on two expeditions with the Lieutenant Colonel. The first one was the Yellowstone expedition in 1873; and after that, the next year, the Black Hills expedition in 1874.

His experience at Indian fighting was very limited, even though he had been with the 7th Cavalry for nearly four years before the Montana expedition. Until being assigned to Fort Abraham Lincoln in 1873, he probably had not seen too many Indians that were angry enough with him to want to take his hair. He, like many of the officers mentioned thus far, was loyal only to Custer. For Calhoun's part he idolized his brother-in-law. He told the Lieutenant Colonel if ever he was needed, or that his life was needed to protect his, the Lieutenant Colonel would not find a better man. That Sunday afternoon, James Calhoun's and his troop fell fighting to the last man trying to protect the regiment's rear at the top of Battle Ridge.

When General Terry and Colonel Gibbon's troops arrived on the battlefield and the bodies of Custer's men where being identified and readied for burial in their shallow graves, all of these named men were found clustered within a few feet of their commander. Only one, First Lieutenant Calhoun, would be found where he and his Troop fell trying to protect the command's rear, along the ridge spine, a quarter mile from where the others fell.

From where he and L Troop formed their final skirmish line and made their final stand along the ridge line before being overwhelmed on all sides, it is a little more than a quarter of a mile from where the others would end their day. The young lieutenant would only nod at the men who were like his brothers as they rode by. He, like them, knew the score. The men who were left in I and C Troops hurried unknowingly toward glory on Custer's Hill at the end of what would become known for all time as Battle Ridge.

Captain George Yates and Lieutenant Colonel George Custer grew up together in Monroe Michigan and over the years had developed a strong friendship that would endure all of their lives. In many ways the two men were closer than brothers.

During the Civil War, the then Captain Custer asked his commander, General Pleasonton, if he would appoint Lieutenant Yates to his command. His whole life, George Custer, wanted close friends and relatives to serve beside him. George Yates and Lonesome Charlie

Reynolds (he would ride with Major Reno that last day) were the closest of the non-family and relatives who rode with him into the valley. The two Georges had ridden together in the Army for fifteen years, fought many fights against a common enemy, and had always been at one another's side through the good times and bad.

Not much is known about the depth of the relationship between First Lieutenant (Fresh) Smith and the commander of the 7th Cavalry. However, Lieutenant Colonel Custer attracted certain types of personalities. Actually, he recruited certain types of men to his command's leadership. Given time he would have handpicked each of his regiment's troop commanders, and their seconds as well as all of the men on his headquarters' staff. He made a good start of it. Most of the men in key positions were handpicked. Not all of them were, mind you, but a good share of them were the type of men he could count on when he needed them. Leading up to the last fight he had managed to place seven or eight officers in command of his troops, and was working on finding more.

These five commanders were Custer's most trusted officers. All had proven themselves worthy of the Lieutenant Colonel's trust and had never failed him in battle. They had been with the Lieutenant Colonel a long time, some since the regiment had been formed, a couple even longer than that. All held brevetted ranks much higher than lieutenant and captains they wore that last day. One had been a brevetted brigadier general; two had been full colonels, and one, a lieutenant colonel.

Within the battalion, only James Calhoun had not seen action as an officer during the Civil War. He had served in the last year of the war as a non commissioned officer in an infantry unit.

Of those who held brevetted ranks, each was cited for gallantry while in command of a combat force in the presence of their nation's enemy. As soldiers, they were outstanding, as leaders they were imminently qualified. These men, in short, were the core of the officers in the 7th Cavalry, and all were members of Custer's inner circle. They were totally committed, and loyal to him. On that last day they would not fail their commander's expectations of them.

The officers who served these commanders as seconds in command were youngsters in terms of years in the service and had seen very little or no action against anyone much less the vaunted Sioux or Cheyenne. It was hoped and felt that these youngsters would be molded into the type of officers their commanders were. In the end it would matter little what the expectations were; every man would be overcome by events far beyond their wildest imaginations just past noon on Sunday, June 25, 1876.

Whatever would happen, each of these senior commanders would be near the point of spear, George Armstrong Custer. The boss could always count on that from this group that he had assembled around him that last time.

Some said Custer played favorites. On the surface that intended slur and criticism sounds bad, but analyze the statement. While it is intended to slander, the individual making the statement has probably never heard a shot fired in anger that was aimed in his direction, and then had to react to it. Playing favorites in those situations makes a lot of sense.

It could be argued playing favorites in that situation was prudent. Custer played favorites? No, Custer went to war with people under his command who would fight; it kept him alive a long time when he lived in dangerous places. This business of war was then–and is now–about life and death and destruction. In many cases, it is not some sort of children's game like "Red rover, red rover, may I send my man over?" The Army, then and now, is a place where people are trained to break and kill things.

Sometimes, even the breakers get broken and destroyed. It, the Army's business is a serious life and death game. If one was really serious about wanting to live, they stacked the deck when they could. As a commander, it makes sense. Why is that a bad thing?

The boss played favorites all right. These five commanders were in his deck. He never had to worry about his six (his back) when he led these men. If he got hit from behind, it was because they were all dead.

The type of men Lieutenant Colonel George Armstrong Custer wanted in his command were pretty much mirror images of himself. Algernon Smith, as were all of those who rode with him that day, cut from the same clothe. The man would fight, and did not like backing away from any man or situation. He had served as an infantry officer during the Civil War and had been through the meat grinders at Cold Harbor, Fort Wagner, Petersburg, Darbytown Road, and Fort Fisher. At Fort Fisher he was severely injured, and nearly died. When fully recovered, he had lost most of the use of his right arm. By war's end he held the rank of brevet major, U.S. Volunteers.

He came to the 7th Cavalry in 1868 as a second lieutenant quartermaster. That he was a quartermaster had more to do with his crippled arm than it did his fighting spirit. Lieutenant Colonel Custer could see that, and put the man back where belonged, at the head of a troop of fighting men, the box band troop of the 7th Cavalry, the Gray Horse Troop, idealistically, the best of the best. It was also Custer's favorite Troop, thus, all the horses in the troop were grays. Matching the color of the mounts within the regiment was a Custer innovation. He felt that matching colored mounts added *esprit de corps* to the 7th and that the Gray Horse Troop should be commanded by one of his best officers. The fact that Smith commanded the Gray Horse Troop is an indication of what Custer thought of the Lieutenant.

—10—

OTHER MEMBERS OF LIEUTENANT COLONEL CUSTER'S INNER CIRCLE

Captain Thomas Benton Weir is often not discussed by many who are students of the battle, or when they reference the 7th Cavalry. He was not one of Lieutenant Colonel Custer's battalion commanders, but he had a history with the Lieutenant Colonel that went back nearly twelve years. He had first served with the major general in 1865, as acting assistant inspector general. He had earned the brevet rank of major early in 1865, shortly after lieutenant colonel had picked up his brevet rank of major general. Weir was mustered out of the service in 1866 and then recalled by the Army, and assigned to the 7th Cavalry the day the regiment was formed, July 28, 1866 as a first lieutenant.

Prior to that, during the Civil War, Captain Weir was subsequently brevetted to major and then lieutenant colonel for action against Nathan Bedford Forest during the Civil War (1863—news traveled slowly in those days). He was promoted to the rank of captain in July of 1973, the rank he held until the day he died only six months after the battle on the Little Bighorn from exposure and exhaustion. He died in New York City while convalescing from a mental collapse. No one in those days wanted to talk about such things as mental collapse. It was not a manly thing to have happen. None the less that is what happened along with a severe bout with a bottle of whiskey or two everyday for six months since the battle had been the real reason he was put on temporary duty recruiting in his home town.

Captain Weir was as loyal to the Lieutenant Colonel as any of the Lieutenant Colonel's closest associates and family members. Perhaps, because of a very close relationship with Libby while the Lieutenant Colonel was out chasing Indians in Kansas had kept him from being brought into the full brotherhood of Custer's Inner Circle.

During the time (1867-1868) when gossip was being passed around Fort Leavenworth their friendship had gone farther than just visiting, and Weir was taking advantage of the boss being out chasing hostiles became the only strain on their relationship.

Of course, Custer was maddened by the very idea that Libby would do such a thing, and his vision about her sashaying about with a "friend and brother officer" would make him nearly crazy by the time he ridden clear across Kansas to find out about it. The whole affair had been blown completely out of proportion by the time the lieutenant colonel had heard about it and without permission other than that granted to himself he took off for Fort Leavenworth.

The escapade earned the Lieutenant Colonel a Courts Martial, and he was suspended for a year without pay, cooling his heels in Monroe, Michigan and New York City).

When confronted about the situation by Custer, Captain Weir admitted perhaps he was being inappropriate with his boss' lady by spending so much time with her while he was gone. While not admitting he had been inappropriate in any way, Weir begged the Lieutenant Colonel to forgive him from even letting someone start the gossip. On his knees before his commander he assured him that in no way would he take advantage of the colonel's absence or his lady. This he swore to as an officer and a gentleman.

As far as it is known, or ever written about, that was the end of it. There may have been more to it than that, but who knows? Custer accepted the man's apology. It was never brought up between the two men again. Custer was like that. A man's word was his bond.

Lieutenant Colonel Custer never approached his wife on the subject. He accepted the man's word as a statement of honor. As for the two officers and gentlemen, Weir and Custer—remember, Custer, never held grudges; men did what they had to do. Weir was a good officer and a staunch apostle of Custer's during his entire service with him.

Captain Weir, and Lieutenants Edgerly of D Troop, and Godfrey K Troop commander (were with Captain Benteen's battalion) but were considered junior members of the Custer Inner Circle. The inner circle disbanded after the fight, and the men had to fend for themselves.

When the battle was over, Captain Weir wrote a short note to Libby telling her he had much to tell her. "The whole story about the battle and the Lieutenant Colonel is not what you have heard, and I will tell it to you, when the time is right." He made it sound as if what the others were saying, Major Reno and Benteen was not the whole truth, and nothing but the truth.

It had been up to that time and forever afterwards, the only time Captain Weir contacted Libby since the day he told his commander he would stop talking to her eight years before. Unfortunately, Captain Weir never fully recovered from his own battlefield combat stress and the trauma of having to bury the commander and his men.

Upon returning to Fort Lincoln he had taken sick leave and returned to New York. From that point on, to end of his life (only six months later) he seems to have been emotionally crippled. The loss of the commander, coupled with the nightmares of the mutilations of the men in the field, and even his own perceived failure to get to Custer was too much for the man to handle.

In the end, he never got around to telling Libby what he wanted to. He died a tormented and sick-minded man. He was only thirty-eight years old at the time of his death. The one woman, whom he may have loved as much as he loved his commander he had served, never heard his side of the story. Perhaps, if he had told her what he knew; or even written it down, what really happened on that ridge would have been known. The drama that has played out all these years afterward may have ended had Captain Weir ever told his side of the battle as he knew it to be.

Captain Weir would play a part in the final act of the battle late in the afternoon of the 25th when he and his D Troop tried to break through the hostiles who had gathered around Major Reno's hill and on Sharpshooter's Ridge. Major Reno would say that he tried to send a troop of cavalry in Custer's direction in his after action report, but he had not.

Captain Weir had requested that his commander, Major Reno, allow him to go find Lieutenant Colonel Custer; Reno neither gave verbal permission for him to go or even a nod of the head. He just looked blankly into Weir's face and said nothing. Captain Weir took the no answer as an affirmative and issued orders to the men of his troop who still had horses to mount and follow him. Formally, Captain Weir took the response as to mean go ahead and try. In fact, no permission was granted and Weir tried to go anyway.

Captain Weir and his D Troop would not get 500 yards before they were on the verge of being surrounded by hostiles who had in the mean time reorganized themselves along what is now called Sharpshooters Ridge. By doing so, they had only to close the door behind Captain Weir and his D troop who had nearly gone to a point of no return and making it impossible to withdraw once they were out in the open. Though Captain Weir's heart and loyalty were in the right place, it was far too late. Unknown to him or any one else in the command, Lieutenant Colonel Custer and his command had already fallen to the last man. Had it not been for the ever-alert Captain Benteen seeing what was about to happen, D Troop would have suffered the same fate as Custer's command. Captain Benteen ordered his other two companies of men to charge, on foot, to break Weir's D Troop out of the encirclement.

Benteen's men had already shot their horses and were using them as breastworks to keep the hostiles away from them when they attacked on foot to break D Troop out of its trap. The only options were to let Captain Weir and his troop being wiped out, or attack and try to get them back if he could. Captain Benteen took care of his men.

On the day of the battle, only those closest to Custer, the most loyal to him within the command, the ones he trusted the most, were with him and not with other troop commanders.

There were two exceptions. Second Lieutenants James Sturgis and Harrington rode with the Custer's battalion so he could take care of them as best he could. That, of course, included Second Lieutenant Sturgis; Custer did not trust anyone but his brother and himself to ensure young Sturgis survivability.

Sturgis was the son of the 7th Cavalry's official commanding officer.

Colonel Sturgis personally asked Lieutenant Colonel Custer if he would take the young man under his wing and teach him the ropes of command. Colonel Sturgis was the assigned commander of the 7th Cavalry.

He commanded it in St. Louis, Missouri in abstention; Custer commanded the regiment from the field. The good Colonel apparently had some rather shallow understanding about going into harm's way. That the colonel was a quartermaster during the Civil War, and had, through political connection managed to stay in the Army at his same rank after the war, says something about his ability to survive politically. He obviously did not have a full grasp of what could happen to men venturing into harm's way. His son must have seen this foray into Indian territory as an opportunity to make it on his own rather than follow in his father's footsteps.

That says something profound about young Sturgis, perhaps Custer saw this and decided the world needed fewer daddy Sturgis' and more son Sturgis. If the boy, just fresh out of the Academy, wanted to be a real soldier, Custer could and would help him become that, if he could.

Colonel Sturgis, of course, thought that was a grand idea at first, in fact, had even went to Custer on his son's behalf, requesting the lieutenant colonel take his own son under his wing and teach him to become a leader and officer. Though privately (being a former logicistician) Colonel Sturgis thought that Custer took too many chance and went through men and horses too fast, he thought the tutelage under a man such as Custer would only benefit his young son's career. On the surface of it, he could not argue with his success during the Civil War and the lore that followed the lieutenant colonel during the string of expeditions staged from 1872 until this last movement. He did, at least acknowledge the fact that Custer was a fighter (and he, Colonel Sturgis was not). If his son were to have half a chance on the frontier, it would be better putting him with a man who had fought a lot and lived.

He thought Custer could teach his son a few things and get him back in one piece. As it turned out of course, young Jack (James) got himself killed in C Troop's escape from the River.

For Custer's part, at least in the way it turned out, it was not necessarily a bright thing to do, to go out and get the commander's kid killed the first time he is in a fight, but that is what happened. It earned Custer and his brother Tom a permanent spot on Colonel Sturgis's hate list.

On the day of the fight, the commander ordered Sturgis to ride with Tom Custer's C Troop. Though originally assigned to M Troop, young Sturgis was raring to go. The idea, apparently, was so both of the Custers could try and avoid the situation that did ultimately occur. At least, the lieutenant colonel did not have to explain to Colonel Sturgis, his boss, why he let "Little Jackie" get killed. All of it was only the tip of the ice burg when measured to what Young Lieutenant Sturgis' ma would think. She never forgive either the dead lieutenant colonel or the live colonel.

There were other officers in the Regiment that, though newer members of Custer's inner circle were loyal to a near fault to the Lieutenant Colonel. Captain James Moylan, Troop commander of A Troop was one.

Benteen picked on Moylan after the fight on Major Reno Hill. Captain Benteen had intimated that perhaps this fellow officer was not as brave as he should have been during that situation. However, the other side of the story is, Moylan was a friend of Custer's—and that would have never set well with Captain Benteen.

Moylan had served in the Civil War, coming in as a nineteen-year-old private, working his way up to a sergeant with the Second Dragoons. In 1863, he was offered a commission as second lieutenant in the fifth Cavalry, but was dismissed from the service for going AWOL. Why he was not shot is not clear.

Soon afterwards he came back into the Army. This time, enlisting as a private under an assumed name he again started working his way up to sergeant major, and then later he was commissioned again as a second lieutenant. He became a captain before the war ended. It was a rank he kept until being mustered out after the war.

Again, he re-entered the Army; again as a private, in the regular Army this time and was assigned to the 7th Cavalry 1868. Upon hearing his story, Lieutenant Colonel Custer promptly promoted him to sergeant major, and within a very short time endorsed him for a commission. Within six years of that commission, he was promoted to captain, and later during the Nez Perce Wars he would be awarded one of the first Congressional Medals of Honor awarded to officers. He was married to Lieutenant Calhoun's sister.

His war record and his actions against the hostiles never showed him to be afraid of a fight, rather, quite the opposite, he liked a good fight. Perhaps, his only sin was that he liked George Custer, and that was an unpardonable sin in Captain Benteen's eyes as the unofficial master of all things good and bad.

—11—

THE ENLISTED MEN AND CIVILIANS IN THE REGIMENT

The 7TH Cavalry Regiment left Fort Abraham Lincoln on the morning of 17 May 1876, for their action against the Indians in southeastern Montana. The regiment was comprised of twelve companies (troops): A, B, C, D, E, F, G, H, I, K, L, and M.

The bright observer will notice the letter J is missing in the alignment of the alphabet letters that were assigned for each of the troops. The military, in their finite wisdom, made it was standard military practice not to so assign the letter JAY (J) to any troop or company in the U.S. Military Service. It was felt that the letter could be miss-identified on a troop guidon as an EYE (I), or possibly an "EL" (L), in the fog of battle. Rather than risk misidentifying a troop, or perhaps, confusing one with troop another troop which had a similar look to it, the letter J was never used. According to Regimental Adjutant Lieutenant Edward Godfrey, on the morning report of May 17, 1876, the assigned strength from the roster for the 7th Cavalry Regiment had the following troop strengths:

LAST RIDE

Troop Strength on:	May 17, 1876	June 25, 1876
A-	55	47
B-	71	129*
C-	66	60
D-	64	49
E-	61	53
F-	68	61
G-	69	44
H-	55	46
I-	65	49
K-	69	41
L-	69	57
—	63	55
Total	775	661 Authorized

Troop Strength: 840 plus scouts, guides, teamsters, doctors, and civilians.

*Troop strength bolstered by the addition of 6 enlisted men and 1 sergeant from each of the other 11 Troops additionally the pack train escort had 6 civilian packers assigned to B Troop.

In addition to those numbers, the Regiment had an authorized officer cadre of forty-four officers on the same day, May 17, 1876. The total number of assigned enlisted and officers brought the total troop strength of the regiment to 820 uniformed solders. To that total would be added fifty-one Indian scouts, twenty-one packers, guides, interpreters, band members, civilian contract doctors, and just plain civilians for a total number of all human beings under the command of Lieutenant Colonel Custer the day the regiment left Fort Abraham Lincoln at 913.

In passing, it should be mentioned that there were more horses, donkeys, and jackasses on this trip to southern Montana than there were soldiers.

Technically all of these extra non-military men on the expedition were expected to be Indian fighters should the need arise and there was not going be any question about "if" the need arose, they all knew it would. The real question was only, "when?" They all had weapons and they all knew which end went where when it was necessary to get down to business. Part of their job on this expedition was to protect not only themselves; but also, as in the case of the packers, they and their weapons had been hired to protect the pack wagons in the trains and extra animals that they had to bring with them.

Horses' hooves wore out just like tires on a truck would, usually at inopportune times. When a horse lost a wheel, so to speak, or went down out of just being worn out, or went lame, if you were a cavalryman you either had to have a spare horse or you walked. For this bunch it would not work well at all to walk.

Not every trooper had a spare horse, of course, but enough extra mounts were taken to get by on if things went right. Even if that number would have been one horse for every five troopers, it would have been close to 200-head. Then when you got to counting jackasses to pull the wagons and donkeys to tote the ammunition you had the numbers that got seriously almost overwhelming. Custer had with him over 200 wagons that needed to be pulled from point A to point B.

As for the guides and scouts it went without saying, these men knew how to take care of themselves and had many times. Lonesome Charlie Reynolds was a master at taking care of himself against the elements as well as hostiles.

The most questionable element would have been the other civilians, the contract doctors, and those who just went along for the ride, Arthur Reed and Boston Custer, for example.

Doctors were not combat trained even though they had been out many times with the troops of the 7th Regiment. These men had patched the men up when they were injured and mended their broken bones. That would have been about the extent of their combat experience. Up and until that last day they had not needed more.

When they did need more, it would not have mattered if they had one day or ten years. They would have fought and fired a weapon, they were not above that, but how effective they would have been is anyone's guess. When it was all over, it mattered little at all, except for Mrs. Dr. Lord and Mrs. De Wolf, their widows.

Boston Custer and Autie Reed were very young. Only Boston would have had any experience at all on the frontier and that would have been beside with his two bigger brothers. His brothers would not have allowed him off by himself or even out of their' sight for very long. What little true wild-west experience he had would have gained would not have helped in the fight at the side of Last Stand Hill where he and his cousin were found....

"Little Autie" as young Mr. Reed was known by the family was only just eighteen years old and severely asthmatic. Because he was the youngest member of the Custer clan on this expedition, he was to stay close by and well within contact with either of his uncles or the "more experienced" cousin. This adventure would be his first and last.

As for the newspaper man, Mr. Kellogg, the jury was still out on him, and is even today; perhaps, even for all time. Somehow though, he was with the last bunch as they made their stand not many yards from either Boston or "Little Autie."

Custer had made a deal with the Ree and Sparrow Hawk (Crow) scouts, before they would agree to go along on this expedition. He told them they would be allowed to leave once they had located the enemy, the Lakota, Shahiyela and Ohmeseheso. They would not be expected to fight them. The Lakota and Shahiyela scared the wits right out them. In the end, a handful of these Rees and Sparrow Hawks would go war against their ancestral enemies and lose again.

The Ree and Crow scout's home tribes had been traditional enemies of the Lakota and while they hated them enough to lead the *wasichu* to them, they were mostly afraid of having to fighting them. Their were exceptions to that because on the battlefield that day Bob Tail Bull, Little Brave (also called Stab or Little Soldier) Ree scouts; and Bloody Knife (a Crow) would fall with the men of the 7th in the valley fight while with Major Reno, while Goose and Strikes Enemy, who were Sparrow Hawks, would be wounded also in the valley fight.

The doctors, of course, would not be put in line to fight but if it came to shooting and staying alive they would have and probably did. The civilians were not treated any differently than anyone else by the hostiles. The law was, if you had to fight and kill someone to stay alive it would probably in you best interest to do so. In other words, this was a "war party" not some backyard social and everyone was expected to hold up their end of the deal if they wanted to keep their hair. That included everyone but the band.

The Regimental Band added another twenty-one men assigned. Only five members were officially authorized on the 7th's Organizational Chart for the band. But, "Ol' Curly", the Lieutenant Colonel's nickname, liked his music, and he would have his band, so they went along with him and the regiment to entertain the men after a hard day in the saddle.

These men were musicians. Though they were part of the regiment, if they had to perform the duties of a regular trooper, most of them would have been as useful as teats on a boar hog. With the exception of two, or maybe three, the band members may not have known which end of the carbine to aim at the enemy. By and large, they were non-combatants and they liked it that way. They would march with the regiment for three days and then would go by the wayside when he got to the remount station three days out of Fort Abraham Lincoln.

Even the lieutenant colonel believed band members were not really soldiers in the accepted definition of the term. In most soldiers' minds, the band made music, not war. Troop and Regimental buglers were not considered part of the band. They were soldiers first.

Charlie Reynolds and Mitch Bouyer, the teamsters, and the other five civilians the total number would be close to 725 to 730 bodies, give or take a few here or there. No one knows for sure.

The recruits didn't have time to become acquainted with their horses, much less train them how to not jump when they shot their carbines from their backs, or how not trample the soldier when he shot across his horse's back while standing at the animal's side. Now jump ahead twenty-seven days, probably fewer than 350 of the men have been in armed conflict against Indian hostiles.

Nearly all of the officers present and accounted for have at least been in contact with the enemy, but not all had actually been in combat against them. Major Reno, second in command, Lieutenants Sturgis, Harrington, McIntosh, Reily and Porter are some of the "green" officers. For nearly half of the twenty-nine available on the day of the battle, they will only get one chance to do it right and still live to talk about it afterward.

For the trooper's part, these same nearly-new recruits who are going into combat for the very first time have never seen that many Indians in one place at one time as they will on the 25th of June 1876. They probably didn't know there were that many Indians in the whole world. And suddenly, all of these hostiles were all bent on killing each and every one them and everyone dressed like them on that Sunday afternoon.

Even if they did know, they would not have been all that afraid. After all, this was the famed 7th Cavalry. The Indians would flee for their lives once they saw whom they were up against—or so the green and inexperienced troopers may have thought.

The total number of men in the Regiment the morning of 17 May 1876 was 899 men before they left the fort. That is not saying they all left the fort together all in one grand parade under the portals of the post. They did not. It would have been a very impressive sight, indeed, but alas, everything that sparkles is not gold.

Custer's eyes must have glazed over at the site that unfolded before him that morning as he sat beside his wife watching the spectacle unfold before them. She would go with him as far as he could get that first day out of the post. The next morning she would return to the post. He had led large expeditions before, but nothing like this. His Black Hills expedition in 1874 had been nearly this big. Nothing would compare, not even the Yellowstone Expedition in 1872.

The question that must have popped into his head was, "How in the hell am I ever going to sneak upon Indians with this gaggle with me?"

Before Lieutenant Colonel Custer left the fort, General Terry asked him if he wanted to take a couple extra troops of 5th Cavalry (another 120 men or so), and a squadron of Gatling guns (three more wagons, ten more horses and thirty-four men) — just in case he might run into trouble. The troops might have come in handy, but they were not 7th Cavalrymen, and the feeling prevailing within the 7th (rightly or wrongly) was there were not that many Indians in the whole west they would need any extra help whipping. That assessment, of course, was a wrong answer. An entire corps of cavalry would not have been enough for what they were going to ride in to.

The short haired, blue-eyed general just thanked his boss and said, "We can handle it, sir."

As for the Gatling guns, now, they would be a real pain in the butt. As far as being an offensive weapon, they were not. Besides they were resource intensive. Meaning of course, the extra wagons and mules to haul the three weapons and extra ammunition would be a real drain on his manpower and the most crucial element—time. They would have only slowed him down, perhaps as much as three days riding time could be lost if he took those damn guns with him because he would have to go slow to protect the weapons and personnel assigned to the detail.

Destiny was calling and he could not take a chance of them breaking down and delaying him even more. Besides, Gatling guns were defensive weapons in those days. It took about ten men just to serve each one of them—much the same way artillery was resource intensive. Often, the Gatling guns were mechanically unsound in those days; they were not the mechanical wonders they are today. Sometimes they worked and sometimes they just did not. The wagons that hauled them were often over weighted and by their very nature, slow. He did not want to be always waiting on them. He did not feel that he was up to having to worry about them, all the way out and back again. Trying to provide protection for them during the 700-mile trip would have not only stripped his command of manpower more than it already was, but the biggest reason for the "no" was they would have slowed him down. Custer, once out the gate of Fort Abraham Lincoln, was not about to be slowed down by anyone, or thing. To the offer from his commander Lieutenant Colonel Custer said simply,

"No," again.

The lieutenant colonel would lighten-up the 7th to get it down to the fighting strength he had five weeks later. Of the twenty-one-member band, one of members volunteered to ride on with the 7th after the band was sent packing upon reaching the horse depot. He considered himself a soldier first, and told the commander that. The commander got a kick out of this feisty little Italian telling him, he wanted to fight if the he could find a place for him.

True to form, Custer allowed the man to stay on with the regiment. His new duty was that of a courier for the regimental headquarters, and he was put on the manning list officially assigned to Captain Benteen's battalion in Troop H. The man spoke very broken English, and had nearly non-existent conversation skills. But he was dependable, and could play a bugle better than most of the troops' buglers.

His Americanized name was John Martin, alias, Giovanni Martini. He had only recently emigrated from Italy. Being unable to speak English, and with meaningful work to support his young family was hard to come by in New York. He arrived in the United States less than two years before, married, with a wife and a baby daughter in tow. As a youngster growing up in Sola Consalina, Italy, he had enlisted into the Italian army at the age of fourteen, and fought against the Austrians in 1866.

Upon coming to America there were two things he could do to earn money to support his wife and daughter. He could try and join the American Army and fight who ever they were fighting, and he could blow his horn. He enlisted into the U.S. Army, and was assigned to the 7th Cavalry in June of 1874.

Not during this upcoming fight against the Sioux and Cheyenne, but later, the stuttering Giovanni Martini would be awarded the Congressional Medal of Honor (all five-foot-six of him). In another fight in a dry, dusty canyon the 7th would face the Nez Perce in 1879, at Canyon Creek, Utah, and he would prove his mettle. He ultimately would survive all of his battles, and his twenty years in the Army and would retire from the regiment as a sergeant in the band. In his post-cavalry years he would work as a subway ticket agent in New York City.

One cannot assume a man being assigned to the regiment means the individual was on duty at the battle site the day of the battle. One can only know on a given day the soldier was assigned to the regiment. His duties and situation (sickness, detached duties, etc.) may have had him elsewhere.

We have already established that Custer's 7th Cavalry was very short of having the manpower the commander would need to do the job against 4,000 to 5,000 warriors. In this case about one-third of the regimental strength was assigned on detached service, sick call, special duty, or detailed away from the regiment. The number included thirteen of the assigned officers who were on detail duty elsewhere and 289 enlisted men otherwise occupied somewhere other than the Little Bighorn.

Some of those missing men, nearly, if not more than 200, would be walking back to Fort Abraham Lincoln behind the tunes of the twenty-piece band. Those band members who had gone as far as the last depot on the Powder River would act as hospital stewards for the wounded men on the "Far West" river boat as she made her way back to the post.

In those days, an Army regiment was lucky to have an Army surgeon, most would have to settle for contract docs who may or may not have been bona fide and certified doctors. When it was all said and done it was a hell of a way to run a railroad, but what was a commander to do?

Concerning the enlisted man, his average height was about five-feet-seven-inches tall. That would be considered short by today's standards. The average trooper was about, twenty-five years of age, and mostly uneducated beyond elementary school. There were exceptions of course. The average trooper weighed about 135-145 pounds.

By contrast, these men were shorter and lighter than the enemy they were fighting; these men were not big, burly lumber jack kind of guys. These men were on the small side. The men in the cavalry tended to be a little on the light side. They were recruited that way to save the horses their lives would depend on.

Other characteristics that seem striking are how many men came from foreign countries, and ended up in the U.S. Army. Just remember, this was not the same America we know today. During that period of time in our nation's history, most folks were immigrants, or just second-generation descendants of immigrants.

On the marble monument that stands on Custer Hill there are the names of men from fourteen different nations who died that day. Ireland being the most prominent, Germany second, followed by: England, Canada, Switzerland, Russia, Wales, Greece, Denmark, Prussia, Bavaria, Scotland, and Italy.

The states that the other men were native of represent: Pennsylvania, New York, Ohio, Massachusetts, New Jersey, New Hampshire, Rhode Island, Connecticut, Kansas, Wisconsin, Kentucky, Georgia, Iowa, North Carolina Missouri, New Mexico Territories, Virginia, Indiana, Maryland, District of Columbia, and Dakota Territories.

Nearly one hundred years later a range fire burned over the battlefield giving the National Geographic an opportunity to do an archaeological survey of the surface area surrounding the site where the battle was fought. One of the most interesting facts was that bullets fired during the battle came from as many as forty-seven different weapons. We know what the soldiers had. We were never sure what the Indians had until the fired bared the earth enough to do a real search of the area.

The soldiers had essentially two basic types of weapons: the .45-caliber pistol, and the .45-.70 Springfield carbine. The officers would have by and large used the same weapons. A few would have their own favorite rifle, or as in the case of the general, non-standard pistols and rifle. That means of course, everything from muskets to buffalo guns, from single shot ball and cap to Winchester repeaters were used by the hostiles on the field that day.

Granted, there were some were old musket balls, but a lot of the shell casings and spent bullets were from different, modern (then) repeating weapons the soldiers did not have access to. The hostiles did though—and in many cases the Indian Agencies where they came from supplied them. In addition to those, they also had thousands of steel-tipped arrows, lances, hatchets, axes, and stone-headed clubs, all of which were effectively used that day.

The last point is a slug from a .50-caliber musket ball would kill a man as sure as a .45-caliber bullet fired from a Winchester repeater would. The hostiles were not short-handed that day. The weapon of choice that day was the "Stone Age" bow and arrow, though they had plenty of other things to do the job.

The 7th Cavalry left Fort Abraham Lincoln undermanned and outgunned to begin. The manner in which it was outfitted, manned and trained should indicate several things about the seriousness of the government it served. Going out, rather being sent out half dressed was not the way to catching and putting an end to the hostile problems on the high plain prairies.

Neither the U.S. Army, nor the U.S. government had quite caught on to the seriousness of the task that lay before them. By the end of that summer's campaign they would understand their shortsightedness. They would not make the same mistake twice. They would take the steps necessary to put an end to the matter once and for all.

It is on this occasion a delicate and somewhat sensitive topic needs to be discussed before continuing on. The idea of men committing mass suicide would have not fit the politically correct idea of the 7th Cavalry Regiment fighting heroically to the last man we have ingrained into our minds. That idea would not have flown any better in 1876 than the picture that the American public has even today.

It would be bloody hard to prove they did not if we believe everything our history books and the movies about this affair tell us. Most of those stories about the gallant 7th battling it out, and sending as many of the heathens to hell as the hostiles killed of them just is not so. If we just listen to the *wasichu* tell the story, or watch the television stories, or the movies it was an even fight until all of the pony soldiers were killed. We can believe that, but reality illustrates a different set of facts.

The Indians had a different version the *wasichus* did not like to hear. According to many of the hostiles on the battlefield that day, many of the soldiers did try to fight but were simply just overwhelmed before they could turn and counter strike the hostiles—some of these men died facing their enemies. Just so, a goodly number of men did not try to defend themselves or even attempt to fight—these men died at the hand of and without remorse from their killers. These were not fit to be on the same field with the other brave ones. These men, the non-fighters instead they relied on the frontier axiom—"Save the last shot for yourself," except for several it was not the last one but the first one that was used.

To the Red Man, this was a very strange occurrence to witness and tended to only anger them more. There are just too many Indian accounts backing up the idea of *wasichu* shooting themselves, or seemingly worse one another before the hostiles could get close enough to kill them with their own hands. To the Indians, suicide was almost an alien subject–they did not have a word for the act in their language. To their way of thinking, sane humans did not do that. To them, the blue coats went crazy, and that is why many of them killed themselves. Afterwards, the Indians went to great lengths trying to understand why they would do that.

After the fight and the warriors were going through the effects of the dead they decided it must have been the water that the *wasichu* was drinking, because it had the same effect on them. It made them crazy! It seems that the sutler at the Powder River Depot had sold some of the soldier's alcohol and some of the soldiers had filled their canteens with booze rather than the brackish water that they had been drinking.

The last of the men, those fifty-four souls who were found at the north end of Battle Ridge where Lieutenant Colonel Custer's body was found were like tethered goats. They had come to the end of their rope. They had no place to go and no way to get there. They could go no farther. These, the last of the Custer's battalion of the 7th Cavalry, were surrounded on all sides on the side of that hill. They could see hell–it was only 400 yards away.

It would have been better to put an end to it yourself than to have a half-naked snarling beast gut you alive, and then maybe kill you when he got around to ripping your hair off by the roots.

Put yourself in their place as you see what they saw…

"…Holy mother of Jesus, the bastards are on us before we even get off our sorry horses…"

"Hurry, boys!"

"Shoot! Come on boys, hurry, here they come!"

You hear the heathen bloodcurdling war cries screaming in your ears. In fact, you cannot hear anything except a giant blood-curdling roar amidst the sound of gunfire that seems muffled by comparison. The dust raised by the horses' hooves on dry prairie is burning your eyes and choking you at the same time. Everything seems to be in dusty fog and you are only firing unaimed shots into the air. Of course, you do not know it; many times you have just pulled the trigger thinking you are shooting your weapon, not realizing it is not shooting any more. It is empty and you have forgotten you have to load it. The smoke and dust-induced fog has reduced visibility to just a few feet in front of you. Past that, everything seems a mirage, or somehow out of focus. Whatever you are doing is automatic now. You are not thinking. Your brain has just clicked off.

Fear has overtaken you, and you know somehow you have transcended into the very bowels of a living, burning hell. The Indians have blackened the sky with hundreds and hundreds of arrows and are firing bullets point-blank at you and your bunkies. You wonder why you are still alive in this man-made hell.

The heathens you were sent to destroy are in fact scalping the less fortunate *wasichus* closest to them, some even before they are dead. Vaguely, you notice some of the men are being butchered are alive. You see the horror in the soldiers' eyes, and see the blood spurting from their bodies—that's how you know they are not dead. Blood is running down their faces and hideously inflected wounds. You see the men's mouths open to scream but you cannot hear them. You know they are screaming because if it were you, you would be screaming. All around you there is no sound, just a jumbled up mass of noise.

Off handedly you cannot quite make out the sounds you are hearing. Other sounds are going into your ears but they are not registering in your fear-ravaged brain.

The Indians to your front are naked or nearly so, only wearing a breechclout to cover their manhood, some not even that. Few are painted, you notice, but the ones who are put the fear of an angry Jesus in your heart. They remind you of nightmare creatures you used to dream about when just a little boy or maybe just last night.

You hear strange sounds coming from your own throat, and you notice the sounds coming from your throat are almost animal-like. The sound is just as savage and ferocious as anything you have ever heard. You do not recognize the sounds; they are inhuman...you have never made or even heard those sounds before...can they be coming from you, you ask yourself.

Those heathen bastards not running your friends down on their ponies and trampling them to death, are beating their brains out with a rock-headed clubs or gutting them while still standing. Others are just shooting arrow after arrow into already-dead bunkies.

You see your friends one by one being hacked down, and some nearly butchered like a side of beef in the process. Nothing is making any sense to your mind.

Almost casually, you see others around you either point their pistols to their hearts or brains. You see the smoke from the weapon as its bullet rips into your bunky's chest and then exits out the back in a bloody, fog-like, red-clouded burst or see the blood, brains, bits of bone, and tufts of hair blow away from what is left of another's head and you say, "Why not?"

In that mere moment, you regain your senses just long enough, maybe for just long enough to ask that same question again and in that one moment you....

What would you do? Why expect those men to do something damn few of us would not do?

A dead hero is still no less dead than a dead coward, if that is what those men who killed themselves were. One would not want to be almost dead in that situation–that would be worse than being really dead, cowardly or not. A bullet to the heart or brain settled the matter.

On that hillside that afternoon under the glaring hot sun, many men asked the same question. If you think about what you would have done in their situation, it is not much of a stretch to imagine putting a bullet in your own head when you are nearly insane with fear.

Try putting yourself in the average trooper's place that day. You are a nearly new recruit—more than a third were. Chances are probably pretty good that you are foreign-born—at least forty percent were, and if you are real lucky you can understand English, at least well enough to know that when someone wants you to do something, you can figure out what it is.

Nearly twenty percent of the regiment cannot clearly understand English. Some of these new guys have been in the Army less than ninety days, but compared to the 122 who came in less than two weeks before leaving for the Little Bighorn to round out the regiment, these men are old timers.

On top of everything else going on around you at that instant, you are exhausted, hungry, and dying of thirst; you would almost sell your shirt for a drink of water.

The average recruit has not had what is called basic training in today's Army. His basic training was anywhere from two weeks to two months of drilling with his company's first sergeant and officers screaming in his ears as they are learning how to ride a green-broke (partially broke) horse. These "old-timer recruits" have barely learned how to wear their uniform properly, how to salute an officer, how to clean and take care of their mount, and how to make a bunk.

If the recruit was really lucky, he got to fire a carbine a few times, and his pistol a few more times—but he still could not hit anything with either one consistently. One truly critical error in the recruits training was that they never were taught how important it was to keep their weapons clean and their ammunition, bright and shiny for if they had, they may have got a few-well aimed shots in before their weapons jammed when they needed them the most.

Custer failed that day but it was not because his men's weapons jammed when dirty. The truth hurts here though. The cavalry carbine did jam from time to time. If the ammunition was not kept shiny clean. Usually the Springfield trapdoor single shot carbine was as reliable as any weapon the army had ever issued up to that time.

The weapon had an assortment of short comings but given them these short comings could be worked around. All-in-all it was a good short-range weapon that could be fired from the back of a horse, provided that the horse and rider were so trained to do such a thing. The key was training, both the man and the second part of the equation, the horse.

A great deal is made about the lack of training many of these men had acquired thus far in the short time they had been in the cavalry. The old axiom, "If you want to make real mayonnaise, you got to break some eggs." Meaning of course, the more training these men got, the better their chances of survival on the plains fighting hostile Indians and nature were going to be.

It had more to do with time in the saddle and on the rifle range and the recruit being taught the ways required to make him into a bona fide horse soldier while in garrison or on the drill fields outside the post gates. No easy thing to teach under the best of conditions to English speaking recruits; for the immigrant recruit with a language problem to begin with, it was a hundred times harder to learn because of the language barrier for starters, army customs for another, the adapting to a new culture, and getting used to the life on the frontier. None of that would be the fault of the frontier army or the new recruit. None the less, it all took time and time was a commodity these men did not have.

One would be remiss if they did not discuss what it took to train the horse to the ways of what was expected of a cavalryman's horse. A great deal was expected of the horse, in some ways the horse's training was more taxing than that of the recruit's. To train a horse under normal circumstances is no simple manner and it was not as easy as it sounds.

Because so much was expected from the animal it took a great deal of time and patience of the trooper to teach the animal all that it had to learn. Shooting off the back of the horse had a tendency to spook the animal, as did shooting across its back or along side its neck and head. Horses are not dumb animals; just the same, they ain't the barnyard's brightest star, either.

Most of the horses the Army bought for the Cavalry were "green broke" or at least they were sold to the Army as "green broke." "Green broke"—now, if there was ever a term that needed a definition it is "green broke." It meant different things to different folks, obviously.

One would only have to be around horse traders for a short while before they discover that those folks come from the far reaches of civilization and usually are a little short of scruples and ethics when it comes to judging and selling horse flesh. Green broke usually meant that the animal could be haltered and led around a corral and that a saddle could be placed on its back, cinched up, and the rider could climb aboard and not expect to land on the moon or be thrown into a fence headfirst. Nobody ever said that the animal could be ridden anywhere. It normally could not be ridden anywhere without throwing the rider in to a horse tank or fence along the way first. That was fine with the Army and its remount stations; they liked the horses raw. The idea being that the Army wanted its horses just like it wanted its new recruits, dumb to the ways of the Army.

The Army would teach its horses everything they needed to know from that point on. But it took time and they, the horses, and the Army did not have time this time around. The regiment's new stock would not learn to respond to the bugle calls the way most well-trained cavalry horses would have. That in itself is a marvelous sight. Just watching a troop of cavalry on horses that only respond to a bugler's calls is something to behold. Without a word being uttered, well-trained cavalry horses go from just standing kind of disinterested to a formed up troop going through its drills just on the bugler's tunes that he plays. If you love horses, it would be enough to make you proud. It was an art unto itself, and one that every horse worth its salt mastered.

That would only be the beginning of the cavalry horse's training. They would have learned how to behave with someone shooting from their back or along their necks. Normally, any horse gets a little spooky with sudden movements. They damn sure would get spooky when hostile Indian ponies were running beside them and trying to bite them as they did so. They would not take to seeing half-dressed or naked monsters rising up out of the ground yelling at them no matter how well they were trained; even a horse had its limits.

There was a lot to learn if a horse was going to be a useful mate to its master. Mastery of horsemanship would take longer than most of the newbies had, unfortunately. There were other problems just as big as trying to get along with a green-broke horse. Another issue would take on new meaning during the fight on the Little Bighorn that the rookie horse soldier would struggle with. Those who survived would only have to experience this problem once and the lesson would become a lifelong one that he would never forget.

It was the use and care of the Army's cavalry sliding-trap door, .45 caliber carbine rifle. This weapon fired the same 45-caliber round as the standard Army issued single action revolver. The rifle was very accurate up to 50 yards, beyond that then the trooper would be lucky if he could hit anything he was aiming at. It was best for "short- in" work off the back of a horse or for short range fighting. It was reliable if taken care of and relatively light. Its one critical problem was its ammunition.

The bullet casing was copper, not brass; it was the Achilles Heel of the weapon. Copper corroded easily and would turn green if not looked after and wiped off on a regular basis. For those young soldiers who did not pay attention to such details, it was a terrible fix to find oneself. For those men, they only had to forget it once. They got no second chances.

During sustained firing of the carbine, the corroded particles that were on the shell casing would stick to the insides of the firing chamber. When the breech was flipped open, the spent cartridge was supposed to be ejected. Over a surprising short mount of time, this build-up of melted sludge would turn into rock-hard greenish-blue resin in the chamber. A few more shots and the spent casing would become part of the breech itself. The sludge caused by the corroded rounds being fired through the weapon and the breech becoming very hot was a bad combination. It might only take ten, maybe twenty rounds fired rapidly before the young soldier would experience his worst nightmare. The weapon's sliding trap door that was supposed to clear the breech of the spent round would open half-way and lock up. The mechanism would only halfway extract the shell casing. That would cause the round to become stuck in the chamber rather than be ejected when the trap door was opened.

The young inexperienced soldiers were told about this problem and why it was important to clean their ammunition. They were expected to ensure it did not happen. For many of the men it was apparent that they may not have taken the lesson to heart until it was too late. In the middle of a fight the situation would cause them untold grief.

After being in the saddle for over thirty days of forced marches, looking after one's ammunition would have probably one of the last things a soldier did when he had a few minutes to rest. It all would make sense later that day. The sergeants' braying at them like one of

McDougall's damn jackasses about making sure their weapons were clean and that the ammunition in their pouches was in good order was like water off a duck's back. At the last minute all of that would take on new meaning.

When hundreds of hostiles were running straight at them with murder in their eyes, for instance, it was not a time for a problem of this nature to raise its ugly head. For the trooper's part, they hadn't had a chance to fire their weapons for over a month. These troops were for the most part "green." "Green" had nothing to do with the age of a man; it referred to life and death experiences, military discipline, tactics, techniques and procedures that all cavalrymen were supposed to know. Most of the men in the regiment had never been close to an Indian, much less try to kill one. When they got their chance, on this day, the "green" part became instantly apparent and a good many of them would remain that way.

Good veteran troopers who had lived long enough on the frontier to have the "green" ware off would find time to feed and take care of their horse first before they would let themselves even think about eating or sleeping. Sleeping was something a man in the cavalry would do after everything else was taken care of.

One of the reasons they could be called veterans was they knew their lives depended on the "other more important things" and they did what they had to ensure they could keep the moniker. After ensuring their mount was taken care of, they would make sure their weapons were in shape and their ammunition was ready when they needed it. Then the veteran would worry about eating even if that meant slurping some terrible tasting stuff someone euphemistically called coffee and busting their chops on hardtack. If time allowed they could do some sleeping or just ball up and catch some winks later when they had time.

In the end it would not have mattered had they been a regiment out of the old 3rd Cavalry Division that Custer had chased down Bobby Lee with at the end of the Civil War. These men were worn to a frazzle and their horses were put up wet lots of times. If the truth of the matter be told, the horses were probably in worse shape than the men or the Army would admit later.

If that was not bad enough, time-borne experience had shown that the carbine would jam if care with the ammunition was not a priority. In those days, copper shell casings were the least expensive casing for the round. The Army has always been in the mode to go cheap, at least as cheap as it could on ammunition.

During the battle this idea would cause a serious problem, especially if the soldier had to try to pry the spent copper shell casing out of the breech with a knife or spoon or whatever was handy at the time—his teeth—while trying to keep a hostile away long enough to reload. It says something about time-management at moments of high stress.

After the fight, the only carbines left on the battlefield were those whose breeches were stuck open with a round casing tightly jammed in the mechanism. There were too many to miss.

This same problem happened many times to Major Reno's and Captain Benteen's commands when they were pinned down on the river and then again on Major Reno's Hill. After the battle on Battle Ridge several weapons were found on the battlefield in Lieutenant Colonel Custer's battalion, which were jammed open with the spent casings showing signs of trying to being pried out and trooper obviously failing to dislodge the jam. The hostiles, seeing the problem, left the weapons on the field—they were useless.

The 7th U.S. Cavalry up to this time had not been tried and tested. True, a certain few companies of the 7th had been on the frontier for nearly eight years but only five or six had any real sustaining battle experience against the red man. Men's enlistments would end and sometimes a large portion of a troop would have to be retrained by the old-timers so that some day they could repay the favor.

And true, parts of the 7th had chased Indians from Texas to present day North Dakota. However, that being the case, this regiment on that day, on that expedition, was essentially an untrained and untried gob of men, led by largely inexperienced officers. By the time they left Fort Abraham Lincoln, Dakota Territory, they had barely learned how to ride a horse in a military manner when on a march.

It would only be afterwards that the regiment would truly learn its lessons of that day. Many of enlisted men that lived through this day would be promoted to become two strippers and first shirt sergeants to replace those who had fallen with Custer. In time, these now "experienced" non-commissioned officers would teach the replacements what their former sergeants had tried to teach them. The difference being they had the time.

The 7th Cavalry would ride again and it would win the next fight, and the next, and the next. Ultimately they would run down the Lakota and the Cheyenne and fight them until there was no one left to fight. Crook's 5th Cavalry would learn in time as the 7th Cavalry had. Each had hard lessons to learn.

For the 7th, they were lucky they would learn under the direction of its new recently promoted commander Colonel Wesley Merritt, Lieutenant Colonel Custer's friendly rival in the Army of the Potomac during the Civil War days. Both had been young lions during the Civil War, both had been division commanders, though Merritt was short of accomplishing all that Custer had. Often, the two men had been favorably compared by other general officers and enlisted men alike. Colonel Merritt was outstanding as a tactical commander, but when compared to Custer, there were no comparisons to his equal.

When rebuilt, the 7th Cavalry would rise out of the ashes of the Little Bighorn valley and hillsides that led down to the Little Sheep River to become soldiers again. This time they would know how to fight and have a reason and a new battle cry, "Remember Custer," "Remember the 7th." George Armstrong Custer's memory would be all they would need to do the work that was a head of them and dirty and hard work it was going to be.

Basically, the recruits learned, somehow, to stay in that damnedable McClellan saddle, and put their pants on—and that was about it. More than eighty men in the regiment knew less than some of these older new recruits. They had been in the Army fewer than sixty days. What is more, they didn't even have horses for all of them at Fort Abraham Lincoln and a thirty-day march to the Little Bighorn. The command left Fort Abraham Lincoln with a small herd of replacement horse stock, but certainly not enough for the new recruits to ride on the expedition without shorting the rest of the regiment.)

These men will have to march out of Fort Lincoln on foot behind more than 625 mounted cavalry (including the regimental band of twenty men) two squadrons of Gatling guns; a company of mounted artillery—fifteen men); a 200-wagon pack-train; a 200-mule pack-train. Throw in two companies of regular foot infantry of 172 men and these 122 green untrained foot cavalry—Custer must have been fit to be tied. It is hard to imagine what these men might have been thinking as the walked under the fort's portals, leaving for parts unknown believing when they reached the depot six days later, they would get horses.

When they reached the depot, of course, the horses they were supposed get after walking a hundred miles were not there. Several other members of the regiment's men would become ill, injured, suddenly overcome with some phantom disease along the way, or have been ordered to details while the rest of the regiment went off to fight the Indians. Some of these duties would be tending the officer's gardens to detail duty for the post. As for those men who left with Custer on foot, they were about as useful to him as teats on a boar hog, and could not continue with them for the obvious reasons.

This infamous "foot cavalry" were marched back to Fort Lincoln. They would get their chance at chasing the Indians Custer was going after without them at another time. Slim Buttes, South Dakota, was not that far away. Unknown to them at the time, it probably saved most of their lives. By the time they ended their careers in the U.S. 7th Cavalry they would make up part of the replenishment troops to replace those men killed on the Little Bighorn.

—12—

ABOUT HORSES, JACKASSES, AND DONKEYS

When the 7th Cavalry took to the field on 17 May 1876, Custer's command had about 700 horses. What boggles the mind about that figure is not the number of horse flesh but the amount of grain that it would take to sustain just the herd for the march to the Powder River Depot. The regulations stated that each horse would be fed either 14 pounds of hay or 12 pounds of oats for each day of the deployment. That comes to very nearly five tons of hay or 8,400 pounds of oats per day just to feed the regiment's horses, not to mention the jackasses and donkeys that went along to pull the wagons and haul the ammunition. It would take the command nearly a month to get to the depot. All totaled, it amounted to 252,000 pounds (126 tons) of grain if the force's horse flesh was to be fed according to regulations. Of course, it would have been impossible to haul that much feed for the command's need of rations for its horses.

The command's horses were fed one-third of its authorized limit of grain, or only 42 tons of grain, and expected its horses to be get the rest of its needs by eating grass along the way. You see, horses were by and large expendable in the eyes of the U.S. Cavalry. In the early days of the Civil War, for example, when the Army had just six regiments of cavalry, they had used up and destroyed 284,000 horses by 1863. Custer's command upon leaving Fort Abraham Lincoln did not bring very many extra horses for those who would be lost along the way. If a man lost a horse, he was to become a member of Custer's ever growing "foot cavalry" that brought up the rear of the long, long column until they could reach the remount depot 318 miles away. In the end, 77 troopers would belong to that growing troop.

On a good day, with the sun shining, no clouds in the sky, when no one was shooting at anyone, and no red-skinned savage was trying to lift a soldier's hair, one plain ordinary mule could be a real pain in any man's butt. This sterile, single-minded, long-eared, cross-eyed beastly beast of burden, could give new meaning to the word stubborn. This cantankerous curse did not have to even try to be stubborn. It was born for obduracy. For no good reason, just out of the blue, this four-legged, bay-nosed, hee-hawing scourge could bring tears to a grown man's eyes for the utter refractoriness it could cause. Putting 200 of these grain-consuming, contrary, tetchy, and unreasonable critters together for a month, carrying heavy ammunition packs, and trying to get them to go anyplace in a hurry, would have taken a saint with the patience of Sister Teresa. How Captain McDougall, with his Irish ancestry, renowned temper tantrums at the drop of a hat controlled them is still a mystery. His short-fused anger at even the slightest provocation was somehow diverted when dealing with these beasts of burden. Somehow, they must have reached a part of the captain that gave him a special touch with these animals.

When something went astray while his soldier drovers and packers and mule-skinners lead and herded them and jackasses, he would just shrug and shake his head. His deportment while he managed the task is a testament to the man's un-before-mentioned, but obvious, sainthood. The long eared, moon-eyed cuss has what we could call an independent mind and its own way of doing things. The beast was chosen by the Army for its toughness and perseverance under the most austere of environments, and last but not least as a food source as the Army managed its operations. From the deserts of the southwestern United States, to the upper reaches of the Great Plains and all points between there, to the Pacific Ocean these brave and tough little critters served with distinction.

Donkeys were a different story. There was not enough meat on those little stiff-legged turds to be worth the bother of trying to eat fresh meat. They were game, tough little animals, though. Donkeys, though they shared a single-mindedness of their distant cousins, were gusty little critters and hard workers. At the same time they can make a man wish to hell he had never been born. Along with all of the good qualities these two breeds of animals the Army owned did things, usually on their own terms. They did not care what mere humans thought or demanded and certainly not those of some irate trooper who had not the temperament, patience, or required understanding to handle their particulars. The naked truth of the matter is the 700 miles that the expedition traveled to the Little Big Horn would not have happened without either the mules or donkeys in the command.

The biggest problem with these two beasts, you see, is that neither has a sense of immediacy. Being fast at anything, except the pace they set in their own mind, is what they gage what their speed should be to do anything. Everyone should have the experience. Simple things like scaling Mt. Everest for example, without the aid of climbing boots, or ropes, or oxygen masks, or, perhaps, taking a stroll across the Mojave Desert barefoot, without water on a nice late summer day when the desert floor reaches 130 degrees in the shade. Either of those tasks would be easier than to try to get a gaggle of jackasses all headed in the same direction at the same time and at anything that approached the same speed.

Trying to get them to hurry just because some poor trooper might need the ammunition they were toting was a waste of everyone's time, theirs included. To a jackass, time was irrelevant. Fact is, you could whack it at either end (the tail end or the head), and get the same result—nothing. Laying the wood betwixt their ears, or whompin' 'um with a switch would give the critters not one more ounce of "hurry-up—quick." In fact, most times it has just the opposite effect on their mind set; the downside to all of the fuss would be that a body could get kicked in the gut or bitten on the buns when they weren't looking as a payback. In doing anything adverse to what a jackass had already committed its mind to do usually just made them just want to get even with the perpetrator. It took time for the jackasses to teach McDougall and his men who was boss in the outfit known as Company B. In time, the men learned, and it all would work out in the end. It could be said, the jackasses ran B Troop. Captain McDougall and his men just went along for the experience, and did they best they could to keep things packed on the critters.

On the night before the battle, one of the packs broke loose, unbeknownst to the soldiers, and probably much to the relief of the jackass. This pack carried in part, foodstuffs (a couple cases of crackers or hardtack) among the packing.

Early the morning of the battle—actually it was during the short stop the command made at about 2:30 AM—one of McDougall's men reported the missing pack had somehow become lose. Apparently, the pack had fallen off the donkey during the movement in the dark. Captain McDougall immediately sent men to find and retrieve it in the event that the hostiles found it and at the same time sent a rider ahead to inform the lieutenant colonel of the potential disaster. It was well beyond first light before the troopers could find and locate the lost pack containing the hardtack crackers.

The problem was that a new band of Indians had moved across the Cavalry trail made during the forced march the night before to the Valley of the Little Bighorn. As luck would have it, this unrelated band of Indians had happened upon these packs just before the soldiers could get to them. To the Indians, it was like manna from heaven.

They had no idea where they had come from or how they had been so fortunate to happen across the packs. From here on it things started to go down hill for the 7th Cavalry. This band of Indians were not part of the village following the gathering of Sioux and Cheyenne, this band had come from distant Fort Laramie and had no inkling that Custer was about to attack their cousins in the Valley of the Greasy Grass. Somehow, Custer's command was still under the impression the hostiles in the valley had no idea the 7th Cavalry were hot on their trail.

The troopers who found the cases, along with several hostiles who were snacking on the crackers, chased them off. The Indians, feeling lucky not to have been killed, did not know who the soldiers were or where they had come from. The soldiers were happy to have recovered the missing supplies but very concerned that they had been seen by Indians, who in their minds were part of those they were fixing to attack in the valley. The newly arrived hostiles made their getaway without a shot being fired.

Hearing of the broken packs and that Indians were already into the packs, Lieutenant Colonel Custer was fit to be tied. When the "train" men reported what had happened, Lieutenant Colonel Custer assumed the hostiles in the camp that he had not yet located would know that the Army was close by and spoil the colonel's surprise attack. The 7th Cavalry was sliding down a slippery slope; they had past the point of no return from then on. As for this small Indian band, they were just on its way to the great encampment and had no idea that there were *wasichu* within a hundred miles of them or the valley just ahead.

These people would not reach the encampment until late the afternoon of the 25th of June, after the battle. When they arrived in the encampment they were almost killed by their own people. Those who had fought thought they were spies or traitors that had escaped the same fate as others who had betrayed them. It was for that reason—the loss of the packs— that Lieutenant Colonel Custer decided to attack the hostile camp at noon rather than wait for an early morning attack on the 26th. He was sure he and his regiment had been discovered, and surprise was a moot point. The matter at hand was how he would deploy his regiment to affect a surprise and still have a chance for victory.

The lieutenant colonel need not have worried. The hostiles in the valley were setting up their ambushes long before he got there. They may not have known whom it was Custer and his 7th Cavalry; if they had it simply would not have mattered. The hostiles knew the *wasichu* were going to come knocking. They were ready for them when they tried.

In the end, you could not say it was only a broken chinch strap on a Jackass's pack harness that gave the 7th away. Murphy's Law was in full bloom from this point on, "Anything that can go wrong; will go wrong." As little and insignificant as it was or should have seemed at the time, it caused the wheels to start to come off of the 7th Cavalry's wagon. In this particular instance, the 7th Cavalry had only begun to feel its sting.

—13—

EARLY MORNING— SUNDAY, 25 JUNE 1876 DAY OF THE BATTLE

The 7th Cavalry had been roused up at 0330 the morning of June 25, 1876. The day before, they had tracked the hostiles for eighteen hours. They stopped only because the scouts could no further in the dark.

An hour after the sun had gone down, several of the men had actually fallen off their horses asleep. Once it was pitch dark, more and more men embarrassed themselves in front of the other members of their troop. On the 24th the regiment had ridden fifty-five miles before stopping at 2300 that night. Only Lieutenant Colonel Custer seemed undaunted by the long ride. The man had an iron ass. His impatience with lesser souls had to be tempered by his brother, and his lead scout. Finally, he relented, and ordered a short breather for the horses and men.

For that break, a few of the beleaguered souls attempted to eat a few bites of hardtack and drink a few gulps of foul-tasting alkaline coffee. They all wanted sleep for whatever time "Old Iron Ass" would give them. Most of the men did not unsaddle. They just loosened the chinch a little and fell down beside their tired horses and tried to catch a few winks.

Eating anything was wasted effort. Those who tried the hardtack biscuits were rewarded with nothing more than mouthfuls of crumbled chunks of stuff stuck to the roofs of their mouths. The hardtack only dried them out even further; the alkaline-tasting coffee only made them sick to their stomachs. The coffee chaser did nothing to relive the flour taste, and turned the crumbs to near glue in their mouths. In good American soldier tradition, grumbling could be heard from one end of the regiment to the other. The pack trains showed up just in time to move out again with the rest of the regiment when it went to boots and saddles (moved out) four hours later. It was not a happy time for the men of the 7th Cavalry on the early morning hours of the 25th.

The regiment's horses had not had a good long drink of alkaline-free water for more than two days. They sorely needed one. As tough as it had been on the men, it had been tougher on the horses. They had carried their riders a long way, and that was a lot of hard work. They were starting to show signs of fatigue, and a few more were breaking down every mile they went. They had carried the regiment since the 17th of May more than 350 miles from Fort Abraham Lincoln, in the Dakota Territories to this spot in southeastern Montana at the foot of the divide. Now they would carry the men into the valley of the Little Bighorn.

This last meal, as it was for so many that night, was a sorry plight for the men who would be expected to fight on the next day. A few of the men may have taken time to feed, water, and curry their mounts before eating or finding sleep for themselves. These were the men who knew their lives depended on their horses.

Perhaps, a few others would remember to ensure their weapons were in shape for the following day's work that was sure to come. But those men would have been the exceptional ones, men with experience on the frontier—there were not many of them in this lot. This regiment was nearly half-full of new recruits; men who barely knew where they were, much less know how to fight Indians. Unfortunately, most of the good ones and many of these other new men, obviously unknowing what a new day would bring, need not to have bothered. Nearly half of them would be dead by sundown that day.

As the camp settled for a rest, some of the old timers went through their valuables, and started to give away what few things they had. A few of the men had an uneasy feeling about what the next day would bring. Somehow, they kind of knew the crap would hit the proverbial fan sometime after the sun came up. Some men just know when their number is coming up; it spooked the others around them. Their friends would react differently to such goings-on. Some would try to talk their bunkies out of it. Some would get angry. Some thought hanging around the guy would bring them bad luck.

Lonesome Charlie Reynolds, the lead scout and one of the lieutenant colonel's closest, and most trusted friend, was one who gave away whatever he had to anyone who wanted it. Charlie was the best shot in the Regiment and one of the bravest men that the lieutenant colonel knew. It was not like Charlie to act so. But Charlie knew. He would ride with Major Reno's battalion on the morning, and die at almost high noon in the valley fight.

There were not many takers; the very thought the "giver of gifts" would be dead gave a body kind of a spooky feeling, and many thought it was bad luck to take a man's valuables while he was still alive. They would wait to see if the "giver" was right or not before they divided up the man's possibles.

George Custer, on the other hand, was like a blue tick bloodhound hot on the trail of a coon he wanted either to catch or to tree. Many of the men had just simply fallen asleep where they stopped, some not bothering even getting off their horses first, but just falling off and sleeping where they fell.

When the regiment went into that short camp, there was a quick officer's call. As the officers gathered around the lieutenant colonel's tent, the wind picked up, and the lieutenant colonel's battle flag was blown from its stand, landing crumpled on the ground.

John Burkman, his striker, had almost gotten to it before it hit the ground, but he did not quite make it. He immediately picked it up, and jammed it angrily back into the ground. Almost before he straightened up, the wind kicked up again and promptly blew the flag over again. After the flag had fallen a third time, Burkman fixed it by piling rocks around the standard to keep it in place. Some of the officers would notice what had occurred. At the time they would just look at each other and shrug. None would comment on it until after the meeting and they were walking away from the meeting.

Once the officers had gathered, Lieutenant Colonel Custer discussed his general plans for attacking the hostiles when they found them. He told the officers the next morning they would find what they had been hunting for the past five weeks. To more of them than would admit it, the lieutenant colonel's voice and actions seemed uncommonly subdued about the impending fight that was going to occur.

The men could not decide what would have that sort of effect on usually upbeat driving personality of their commander. Maybe, he was not made of iron after all. Maybe he was just tired. Maybe, like his friend Charlie Reynolds, he felt something his ego would not allow him to admit to himself, or anyone else.

Lieutenant Colonel Custer could be no more than speculative about what they would find. From the trails they had seen and crossed all day long, the hostiles were just up ahead. Some time tomorrow, the lieutenant colonel did not know when, but soon they would have them where he could fight them. He did not know how many warriors they would be facing—but obviously he said, "…more than the 800" they had originally thought they would encounter.

During the brief meeting, they were astonished by Captain Benteen and the lieutenant colonel bantering back and forth for a few minutes. Under normal conditions they said the lieutenant colonel would have locked Captain Benteen's heels, and read him the riot act. The other officers withdrew after being dismissed in small groups of twos or threes. A few would comment on the lieutenant colonel's tone, and how almost depressed he seemed to them.

Others were taken aback by his unusually mild-manner in which he had handled the outspoken often foul-mouthed and cantankerous Captain. The superstitious ones like the guides, scouts, and even a few of the officers who had seen the lieutenant colonel's flag fall thought it was a bad sign, and would tell their friends about it.

To the Indian scouts who were with Lieutenant Varnum's detachment, the fallen flag was a really bad sign, they would tell their boss. The great soldier chief would fall on the morrow, or whenever the battle was.

When his officers were dismissed, the lieutenant colonel seated himself near a small fire. He would get a few lines written to Libby before falling to sleep. They would be the last words he would write to his Libby.

Using his knee as a desk—he would fall asleep this last night sitting upright, writing his, "My Dearest Libby" letter....

Three hours later at 0330, his striker, John Burkman, awakened him. Then Burkman sent runners off to the officers with orders to get their men up and ready to get back into the saddle. The false sunrise on the morning of the 25th betrayed the earliness of the hour. It was about 0430 when the long blue column started to snake its way down the divide onto destiny.

The days had melted together for Lieutenant Varnum, Chief of the Indians scouts. He had not been to sleep for a couple days now. His scouts had found the encampment by 0330 the morning of the 25th, and had summoned Lieutenant Colonel Custer to a lookout point known as the Crows Nest that overlooked nearly the entire Little Bighorn valley at 0430.

It would have been a grand view, even at that time of day. The Ree and Crow Indian scouts pointed out the massive pony herds far in the distance—about twenty or more miles distant—and told the lieutenant colonel there were more Sioux in the Valley than Custer would be able to defeat in many days of fighting.

When the lieutenant colonel got to the lookout, he could not see a blamed thing, and accused the scouts to losing their courage. Custer, wittingly or not, teased Varnum's scouts of being afraid of the Sioux they were supposed to be tracking. His scouts did not think it funny; they did fear the Throat Cutters and among themselves decided he should also.

They only thought the blue-eye lieutenant colonel was blind, or he simply did not want to see what they said, "a blind man could see."

Whatever the problem was, it was a bad sign for Varnum's Indian scouts. Many of the scouts started talking excitedly to themselves. Some even began to sing death songs among there own kind. The white eyes never understood when an Indian sang his death song what it meant exactly.

The Native Americans were, and are to a great extent today, spiritual people. If they had an opportunity to sing to their spiritual father about a possible ending of their lives, they sang songs to the Great Spirit asking to be admitted into the next life. They probably wondered why the soldiers did not do the same thing, since it was obvious to them at least a great many riding with Custer would not see the sun set. They were unabashed about it. To them it was as natural as drinking water or breathing. What seemed strange to the Red Men ridding with Custer's 7th was that the *wasichu* did not feel the same need and do as they were doing.

The Indians could see it just confused the soldiers or frightened them, or both. It was at times like this they did not care what the *wasichu* thought. They wanted the spirits on their side when they went into battle.

Custer told his officers to get the men moving again and the regiment was again on the move by 0500. It would not be long now, and they would move to the attack.

By 0800 that morning the regiment had moved to the bench lands out of the Wolf Mountains some thirteen miles from where they had stopped the night before. Lieutenant Colonel Custer summoned Captain Benteen to him.

It was already too damn hot for being so early in the morning. The column of men, horses, and equipment were creating a dust cloud high over column as they stopped and waited for whatever was going to happen next. Most of the troopers in the ranks were thinking their brains would be boiling by noon. Those men with the new straw hats that were sold to them at the Powder River Depot were glad that they had made the purchase. Maybe $1.25 was a lot of money for an old hand-made straw hat but it was a darn sight cooler than the felt hats that had been issued back at Fort Abraham Lincoln, even some of the officers had bought them and had discarded the felts along with the overcoats and other unusable equipment. That gear would be stored away and they could collect it on their return from the dance. A soldier did not have a lot of money; $14.00 a month was all they got, plus their beans, bullets, horse, and bunk when in garrison. Spending that kind of money for an old straw hat was still a good deal to them. Besides, what good was money out in the middle of where they were, which was nearly at the end of the world for all they could tell?

A goodly share of these troopers would not be around to be picking their gear up in a few weeks or ever. Others those who would severely wound would wish they had not.

Captain McDougall and the reinforced B Troop (146 men) was left with the wagon trains, mules and horse herd, and ordered to stay close—but not too close by the commander. McDougall was a good friend of the lieutenant colonel's, and teased his commander about making him stay back and missing all the fun.

McDougall had commanded E Troop before he had been promoted to Captain. As was protocol, once promoted, an officer would be moved to another command even if it was in the same regiment or unit. The reason for it was so as to give the newly promoted officer fresh faces and a fresh start. First Lieutenant Algernon "Fresh" Smith, another close friend of the lieutenant colonel's was commanding E Troop. The tall, rangy, good humored captain with the droopy mustache, sort of tickled the commander. Besides, Smith had paid his dues. He was capable of leading troops anywhere, anytime. He and his bum arm had shown up at the 7th's Quartermaster depot as its new chief, but it was not long before the word was out about "Fresh" Smith. It was obvious that Smith had been retained in the Army because of his prior service in the War Between the States. He was a fighter and there were not many like him around.

He was a veteran Civil War Infantry commander that like many of the other Custer Inner-Circle knew his way around the battlefield. Always good for a laugh or two, you did not want to anger the man. He was like a bull in China closet when angered or sensed danger. He was also a natural born leader who men would just naturally follow. He feared no one or thing, good humor or not, kindly, warm eyes and all; he was a dangerous man when his blood was up. As far as the lieutenant colonel was concerned, E Troop was in good hands. Smith would cover his back if the need came.

The lieutenant colonel told his friend, "You have done a masterful job, Mac, getting the wagons and those blasted mules to this point. You have had the toughest job in the regiment, but your work is not done."

It was rare for the lieutenant colonel to hand out complements. McDougall looked at the lieutenant colonel to see if he was really serious.

Going on, the commander said, "Captain, your Troop is under the operational control of Captain Benteen, should the need arise. You are the 7th's lifeline, and you must be ready at a moment's notice when called, so stay ready." The call would come, but McDougall would never hear the call until it was far too late.

At this point the lieutenant colonel made his first split of the command. He ordered Captain Benteen to take his battalion (Troops D, H, and K—175 men) and scout the area to the south, at least ten to fifteen miles south of where they were then. He was to ensure the hostiles were not escaping to the badlands southwest; or back to the southeast and the mountains they had just left. The lieutenant colonel wanted to be sure that he followed his orders to constantly scout to the south of his advance and also to be sure that none of the hostiles in the encampment had tried to run.

He had deviated from his orders a wee bit; General Terry told him to continue on down the Tongue River, and then onto the Little Bighorn to be sure the hostiles were not getting in front of him, and away to the south.

The lieutenant colonel and his scouts knew where the hostiles were headed, or had already gotten to, so he changed those orders—it was his right of command to do so. Though he had not scouted the area to the south himself, Major Reno had only a week earlier and he had said it looked like to him the hostiles were headed to the Little Bighorn River valley. General Terry's orders suggested he should scout the entire Tongue River drainage before turning up into the Little Bighorn. Not that he had to.

When it became obvious to him the Indians had turned into the Little Bighorn basin, he chose to move toward the hostiles rather than risk their making a break away from his cavalry. He covered his bet, so-to-speak, by sending Captain Benteen to the south to see if anyone had tried to get away from the encampment.

This order angered Captain Benteen. It seemed to him it was a waste of time and horseflesh to go wandering willy-nilly up and down hillsides looking for Indians who were running away from them when it was obvious where the hostiles were.

—14—

THE SEVENTH DEPLOYS

Shortly after 0800, Lieutenant colonel Custer ordered Sergeant Major Sharrow to send riders back to the battalion commanders, present his compliments, and have the three battalion commanders join him at the front of the column. When they presented themselves, he issued his final orders for deployment.

The operations plan had been issued the night before. Each of the battalion commanders and their troop commanders were aware of what was going to happen when they found the village. They were going to attack the hostiles were they stood, bringing hell with them when they did.

This last hurried meeting between the war chiefs would ultimately be a bone of contention after the fight. For as long as people talked about the mistakes that were made causing the 7th's defeat, people would doubt what transpired. Both Major Reno and Captain Benteen would swear to a court of inquiry no such meeting took place. Who was left alive to argue with what was the truth? Captains George Yates, Myles Keogh, and Tom Custer, along with Lieutenant William Cooke, and the lieutenant colonel had been killed during the ensuing battle. Of course, none of those men could testify otherwise.

However, it cannot be disputed the meeting took place. Some have argued that it did not. The comments by the other officers about the flag falling over are the cinchers. The substance of this last meeting between the seven officers who were present—Custer's own commanders and Captain Benteen and Major Reno—is not known.

It must be assumed the lieutenant colonel gave all of his commanders their final orders and the roles they were to play in the upcoming fight. The lieutenant colonel was all business when it got down to pulling up the shirt-sleeves and getting ready for a fight.

As for the lieutenant colonel, his part in the operation, would, of course, lead the main attack into hostile encampment; that was what he had always done. Captain Yates and his battalion (Troops E and F) would serve in the lieutenant colonel's support. He would lead Troops C, I, and L.

To think otherwise is asinine. Commanders do not go into combat, with sub commanders not knowing exactly what their part is in the upcoming fight. They insure the support commanders know full well in advance what was expected of them, and their role in the battle. No one in that situation has a death wish.

When the three commanders came forward, Lieutenant colonel Custer along with Brevet Lieutenant Colonel (now lieutenant) Cooke, Major Reno, and Captains Benteen, Keogh, and Yates and the lieutenant colonel's brother Thomas, rode off a short distance ahead of the halted regiment.

The men gathered noticed the lieutenant colonel seemed a bit agitated—the lieutenant colonel's voice a bit higher-pitched, and maybe a little shakier than usual. Perhaps, it was from lack of sleep. After all the man was human, even if he and most of those who rode with him did not think so. On this day, all of the officers were feeling the effects of the last few days' long march, and lack of sleep.

He told his commanders they would strike the Indians along the Little Bighorn River by noon. At the news, both Major Reno and Captain Benteen face's registered noticeable surprise, Captains Yates, Keogh, Thomas Custer, and Lieutenant Cooke just nodded. They would follow the boss to hell if he told them that is what he wanted to do. The other two kept the eyes riveted on their commander, before finally nodding they understood.

Here again, as was becoming a rather bad habit with Captain Benteen, he questioned the lieutenant colonel's motives. Benteen said like, "Hadn't we oughter wait for the other columns that will be coming up the river tomorrow, Colonel?"

The lieutenant colonel eyed his captain for but a brief moment, and went on with his orders for the deployment of the regiment without comment to the question Captain Benteen had asked.

Not to be put off, and not caring if the lieutenant colonel liked it or not, Captain Benteen felt the bile rising in his throat. He interrupted the lieutenant colonel again, "Sir, begging your pardon."

The lieutenant colonel was stopped in mid-sentence by the abruptness and tones in the questioner's voice, the lieutenant colonel caste a scornful glance at the persistent captain. The captain asked why they were going to attack now.

The lieutenant colonel must have blinked; Captain Benteen had a point.

Catching it the captain continued his diatribe. He was just getting warmed up, "Lieutenant colonel… sir, the tracks we came across yesterday and then again this morning; plus, what we saw from the crows nest clearly show that the intelligence given only four days earlier was all wrong. The tracks indicate that rather than a few hundred Indians being in that valley down there ahead, there are going to be thousands of them."

The lieutenant colonel waved him off with an irritated frown and a flick of his hand as if he was a swatting a fly buzzing around his head.

Not to be denied, and the man's warrior blood starting to bubble, Captain Benteen interrupted the lieutenant colonel for a third time, this time to recite General Terry's orders to his boss. That last part about "his orders" got the lieutenant colonel's attention. His jaw was set, and his eyes narrowed as he formed his answer.

In a steadied voice, gained by the years of making perfectly clear what he wanted his battalion commanders to accomplish in an attack, he said, "Captain Benteen, You are NOT granted permission to question those orders or my judgment ever again while we are on this campaign. As for what my orders tell me to do, that is none of your concern."

"You and these other six officers have read them the same as I have, and what my orders tell me is I am to pitch into these hostiles whenever and where ever I can. I am to prevent them from escaping back into the mountains we have just come down or to the south and the open plans and badlands."

"That, Captain, is exactly what I plan to do. I do not have to wait for anybody."

"We are to strike them when we find them, and by gory that is what this regiment is going to do!"

The captain's face was starting to take on a light pink color, as he was not used to being verbally reprimanded in front of his peers. Angered by the lieutenant colonel's rebuke, he started to move his mouth before any words could be formed to ask a question concerning the deployments. At the last second thought better of it and remained quiet.

The lieutenant colonel, not accustomed to being interrupted even once, much less being disagreed with, shot an angry eye at the captain. The captain blinked. The discussion was over.

From that point on, the lieutenant colonel completely ignored any action of the captain. The lieutenant colonel continued without interruption giving his orders for the battalion commanders to follow. He had both Major Reno's and Benteen's full attention. For their part they were looking at each other out of the corners of their eyes trying to read the other man's mind. The two men just sat on their mounts, saying nothing, their eyes riveted to the lieutenant colonel's face.

As for Captain Yates, the lifelong and stubbornly loyal friend, a member of the esteemed inner-circle of loyalists to the lieutenant colonel, eyed both of the men with contempt. He did not trust either of them any further than he could throw them and their horses.

Suddenly, it came to Yates as he sat astride his little gilding watching their reactions to what they were ordered to do, he realized why. First, Major Reno was a garrison rat; he did just fine if you could keep him sober long enough to get the job done. To Yates, the man was no fighter. He did not even look the part of grizzled frontier horse soldier. Clean-shaven, and sort of chubby, he looked as if he belonged in a store, stocking shelves. Captain Yates had heard through the grape vine from some of his own men that he seemed almost sissified somehow.

As for Benteen, Captain Yates had no use for him because of his avowed hatred for his best friend, George Custer. That made Benteen a natural enemy of Yates as a man, if not as a soldier. He feared slightly that Benteen would try to find a way to get back at the lieutenant colonel for the verbal lashing he had just received. Captain Yates stuck that thought in the back of his mind.

Captain Yates' gaze next landed on Major Reno. Yates understood what Major Reno was being ordered to do would be a monumental task, perhaps, even impossible. He was not sure he could do what was being asked of the major…but he damned sure would try, or die, if need be to get it done for the lieutenant colonel.

That was the difference, Yates would lay his life down for the lieutenant colonel–and he knew Major Reno would not. That was the difference, in combat there is no room for "trying"—you "did it"…or died trying to get it done; other men's lives depended on it.

With the outsiders—Captain Benteen and Major Reno—their eyes communicated what their minds were thinking. Both knew what their commander would never totally know, or if he thought it, he would never admit what they were up against was a slippery slope they could not climb. This operation was going to be as tough a fight as any of them had ever been in. Once they struck the hostiles waiting in the valley below, for all they knew, might be waiting down there for them right now.

If either Major Reno or Captain Benteen, had dared to think about what lie ahead, they could almost guess the Indians were laying up a perfect ambush to swallow them all up like a giant dragon waiting for its prey.

These two men, Captain Yates, and Lieutenant colonel Custer knew the element of surprise had long since evaporated like dew off buffalo poop on the prairie days before. They had heard the Ree and Crow scouts tell Second Lieutenant Varnum about the thousands of horses, and the gigantic vastness of the camp they were planning on attacking. They had seen, just as all of the men had, the enormous trail cut deeply into the ground by the Indians ahead of them the day before.

They also knew these signs had no effect at all on the lieutenant colonel. It was as if he never noticed them past the part that they were hot on the hostile's trail. If he had, he gave no credence to the deep and wide cut in the trail they had crossed not twenty-four-hours before as if they were not worthy of even his contempt.

"Captain Benteen, you and your battalion plus B Troop will be our reserve. However, McDougall is to hang back and support us all or whoever needs him and his supplies first. You will take D, H, and K and scout the watersheds to the south, southwest. Part of my orders is to ensure that none of the Indians escape to the southwest out of the valley, and into the badlands, or back into the mountains.

"You, Mister, will ensure that does not happen. If you run into any of them that have gotten away, you have the men to pitch into them and herd them back this way. Stay in visual contact with Captain McDougall as long as you can. Order him to stay in your line of march, but well behind your battalion.

"Do not get too far ahead of him. We must protect our trains and supplies at all costs.

"You will have to break contact with the major here, but do not get so far away as he can not support you; or you, him, if there is a need; or me, in the event I need support.

"You are ordered to scout at least the first two drainages, and perhaps more to the south of our current line of march; use your best judgment. You must not let them escape to the southeast to the mountains."

Turning in his saddle, the lieutenant colonel looked over his shoulder and continued, "Do not let any of them get to the southwest and the badlands…we'll never catch the buggers then. If you see them, pitch into them and push them back toward us in the encampment."

Captain Benteen, never one to be shy about asking questions of anyone—especially to this man who made his skin crawl at the mere thought of him, piped up a last time. "Lieutenant colonel, I should be allowed to lead my boys into this upcoming fight you got dreamed up. I have the largest battalion between the two of us, and it is my military right because of my former rank."

The lieutenant colonel looked at Benteen, and a small smile crossed his mustachioed lip., "Captain Benteen, I may have underestimated you. I appreciate your wanting to be in on this fight at the start, but in this fight you are a captain and Major Reno outranks you; we will follow military protocol on this subject. The major simply out ranks you. You are ultimately our reserve; we'll need your troops when the time comes."

Completely misreading the captain, the lieutenant colonel continued, "You'll get your chance at these hostiles, there will be plenty of fighting for us all."

"What you were way back when is not important to me right now. The major will lead his battalion against the head of the encampment."

That settled the issue. Major Reno sat stone-faced on his horse, watching, but barely listening to the two men haggle about whose military right it was to do what, to whom, and when. He was not offended by the captain's request or complaints; he could even understand it, almost. Privately, in fact, if anyone had asked him, he would have preferred Captain Benteen's mission to his own. Hell's fire, if anyone had asked him, he would have told them both straight up. He was not too proud of a man to admit what he had to do scared him so bad he was almost ready to pee down his leg.

He had just gotten a fresh supply of rum while at the Powder River Depot from his friend, the quartermaster, who always had a fresh stash for him when he was anywhere near. He had been into his new supply a time or two since then, but now all he could do was wait until his first opportunity. He patted his saddlebag to make sure the pint-sized flask was still there. As soon as he got back to his battalion and when he had a minute's peace from these two idiots, he was going to take a big swig of it.

What Benteen was really saying was, "If this thing—this ridiculous attack—was going to have any chance at all of working, his command might be able to pull it off". He had almost a hundred more men in it than Major Reno's did. It was times like this when numbers mattered.

As the commander, the regiment would have a better chance of success than Major Reno and his command would. Having failed to make his point, or to change a damned thing in the lieutenant colonel's donkey-headed mind, the captain saluted.

Nodding to Captains Yates and Keogh, and the lieutenant colonel's brother Tom, he said as he passed them by, "Keep your heads down, boys," and rode off.

Captain Yates was ordered to bring his battalion of two troops (E and F), along in support of the lieutenant colonel's three troops C, I, and L). Captain Yates saluted, wheeled about face, and left the meeting to go back to his battalion.

Captain Benteen turned his mount and as he past the last of the battalion commanders, Major Reno he nodded and said, "Do the best you can, Marcus." Spurring the mare he headed back to his battalion. The two officers barely nodded as Benteen passed.

The battalion commander rode back to his companies. Some of the men saw him coming, and there was a stirring in the columns of Captain Benteen's battalion.

A short distance away Captain Benteen got their attention, "Captain Weir, Gibson, and Godfrey we are to take the battalion, and scout the area south and west of this line of march."

Barely noticing their commander's return, the three troop commanders were jerked out of a near sun-struck daze when they heard his voice. Gibson had just about fallen asleep, hunched over his saddle like a hulking raptor settling over his dead meal. Captain Weir and Lieutenant Godfrey were absorbed in some inconsequential discussion about some play they both had seen on Broadway in New York the last time they were there. It was idol chatter, just to help them stay awake.

As soon as they heard the battalion commander's gravelly voice, their attention was diverted to him. The cadre of officers had gathered ahead of the Benteen's battalion column waiting for their commander. When they heard their orders they continued to just sit there looking at one another.

Two of the battalion's company commanders, Lieutenant Godfrey and Captain Weir looked like deer caught in the head light of an oncoming freight train, both thinking the same thing. Captain Weir gathered his senses enough to say the first thing that came to his mind.

"What in the hell are we going to do that for Captain?" Pointing with goat-skinned gloved hand to his straight front, "The bleepin' Injins are over there, not running up river from the encampment!"

Captain Benteen commanded H Troop; Weir, D Troop; and Godfrey, K Troop.

Nodding his head in agreement was enough of an answer, Captain Benteen said, "My thoughts exactly, sirs. Gentlemen, you have your orders, prepare your troops to move."

The young officers saluted their commander, and turned back toward the troops to make ready for the deployment.

Major Reno watched the white haired warrior Captain Benteen as he galloped the short distance back to his command.

Lieutenant colonel Custer turned his steel blue eyes and full attention to the pudgy Major. The major immediately came to attention in the saddle.

"Major, you've got a big job…" Major Reno's attention was now full on the colonel.

"Marcus," the commander started, "I know this is your first real action against hostiles, but you have good officers, and some of this regiment's best men. I am sending Charlie Reynolds with you as the lead guide. He'll take good care of you. Don't worry where to cross the river; Charlie will know. He has been in this country before, and can get you to where you are supposed to be as painlessly as possible, listen to him."

The lieutenant colonel began giving his orders for the attack to the ranking battalion commander. Major Reno eyes wandered past the lieutenant colonel, and watched Captain Benteen as he reached his battalion. He could not hear what Benteen was saying, but he saw the troop commanders' salute, and ride back to their separate commands. Immediately their orders to mount up and to go to boots and saddles were issued using the cavalryman's hand signals. Whirling an arm overhead, and then pumping the arm up and down from the elbow, translated into, "Off your ass and into the saddle; form on me."

Without a bugle to blow the men into formation, they knew what their captains wanted, and they complied.

Custer was giving the major his orders for deployment for action, "Your battalion of cavalry are to cross the river at the nearest ford and attack the encampment. Keep your noise down as long as you can, Major. Get as close as you can, and then you have to go all out."

"You buy us the time here; me and my boys will take care of the rest. But you must attack hard; you must make it stick. Make them think your attack is the main assault."

It can be substantiated by witnesses who observed Major Reno during this time just before he led his battalion down into the valley. The Major was nearly beside himself, almost overcome with fear, and at the same time knowing he had never led an attack, he had no idea what to expect.

Finally he admitted to the lieutenant colonel he just could not do the job. Ignoring the major, he said, "I will send Captain Keogh with you for a ways to make sure you are on track. Remember to listen to Charlie; do everything he says, and you'll be fine."

Accepting his orders with a nod, and without uttering another word, the major saluted, turning his bay he galloped the short distance back to his battalion's column. Major Reno would do what he could to get the job done, and trust providence for everything thereafter.

The major wanted to protest his orders, not because he was afraid of dying, hell he had died when he lost his wife in 1874, and then again, when he had to leave his young son that last time with the boy's aunt, his wife's sister, who lived back East.

Maybe now, someone would finally kick a little dirt in his face and make it official. He was ready... or so he thought. He would save his words for the right time. As far as he could see, his dying was a real possibility in this operation.

Though the major was no genus, he did not need to be, today. He would have to be a fighter though—and he was no Attila the Hun, either. Simply put, he just could not see any way for his attack having any success in his attempt at following his orders.

Major Reno was a lot of things. He was also not known to be a fighter who lusted for a fight the way his commander did. He could fight and would, but he did not relish the battle the way combatant commanders should. He was never a stupid man, and he could see his chances for success were going to be worse than a snowball's chance in hell.

All he knew about fighting Indians he could stick on the tip of a pinhead. Captain Benteen would have been his choice of leading in the initial charge into the encampment. But hell, what did he know; he was just a field grade major trying to get by the best he could. With a shrug he thought, "Perhaps everything would work out for the best." He would worry about that later.

After Captain Benteen's column broke to the southwest, the remaining columns moved on down the bench lands until about 11:00 that morning when the remaining nine troops of cavalry reached the bench that broke to the Little Bighorn River below. A ridge line followed the river, making it impossible to see the river. From that location, neither the commander, nor the troops could see the village, and what lay before them.

The column had been moving on the bottom of a wide saddle and could not yet see the hostile encampment either. The regiment's Indian scouts had, and came scurrying back to tell the Chief of Scouts, Second Lieutenant Varnum. In sign they told him that they were near. Lieutenant Varnum relayed the news to the lieutenant colonel. Immediately the lieutenant colonel summoned Major Reno one last time.

"Major you may take your command from here, and attack as soon as you are ready," the lieutenant colonel said.

This was the time to speak his mind to his boss, before returning to the battalion, the major stopped his horse, and turned back to face the lieutenant colonel, his staff and Lieutenant Varnum, "Colonel, I want your word as an officer you will be in my immediate support."

It was obvious what he meant: The lieutenant colonel would be in support directly behind his line of attack. This request, made within earshot of the men and other officers, must have totally infuriated Lieutenant colonel Custer inside, but he made no notice that it did so.

Caught up short by the demand, Lieutenant colonel Custer reined in Vic. He was not used to having his integrity put on the spot by his lessors, and looking directly at the officer who had questioned it he relented and said, "Major Reno, we will be in your immediate support."

Of course, help and support would never come. At least, help would not be coming directly from behind Major Reno's charge as he thought it would. That was how Major Reno would have supported the lieutenant colonel, from directly behind. Lieutenant Colonel Custer's command would support the major. Though in a different way than the major would have thought if he was running the attack. Indirectly, the support, or the drawing-off the hostiles trying to get after Major Reno's battalion did occur.

Only the survivors would ever know it afterward, and then only comment about it among themselves. It was a curious affair; a sub-commander requiring a near written guarantee a senior officer supports his attack. It was very un-Custer-like for the lieutenant colonel to relent in the first place—and even answer such a question. Secondly, it was surprising that Major Reno got away with the affront without being relieved of command on the spot, or worse, shot by this commander.

Major Marcus Reno was not a Lieutenant Colonel Custer-type of a leader, who under better times than these had never really distinguished himself very much the eyes of his enemies, or in the minds of his commanders before coming to the 7th Cavalry. To many of the men in the 7th Cavalry however, the fact he may have impressed others did not impress them. "…but what have you done lately?" was the question they wanted answered. They knew Major Reno had absolutely no hostile (Indian) battle experience, and that bothered old and new soldiers the same.

This was to be his first action against Indians. That being the truth, he fit in with about forty percent of the regiment, they had exactly as much as he did. At the same time it put the enlisted men as well as the officers ill at ease because of his lack of experience…and that was bad.

—15—

HELL FIRE AND BRIMSTONE

Lieutenant Colonel Custer's command consisted of five troops—C, E, F, L, and I. No one knows for sure just how many men were in that ill-fated battalion at the time it struck the encampment. On the surface of that statement, it may seem strange.

However, since no one who went down Medicine Tail Coulee with the lieutenant colonel survived, it is acceptable. What we do know is who was present and accounted for after the fight was over in the other troops of the 7th Cavalry and who those men were who were assigned to other units that had previously been members of those ill-fated troops.

All troop accountability documents went with the individual troop sergeants. They knew who was in the individual troops. Since nearly all men in Lieutenant Colonel Custer's battalion were nude when found, the paperwork the sergeants carried on their persons was lost.

Battlefields are messy places. Today, we know who is going into battle, and what their names are before they go. Forensics can give us an exact accounting of each fatality even many years after a soldier's death. In those days, it was a moot point. They did not know anything about forensics. The best thing that could be done was field-expedient burial. Get the dead soldiers covered as best as the survivors could, and the survivors of the 7th Cavalry back to Fort Abraham Lincoln as soon as possible.

The plan was to send Major Reno's battalion into the lion's own den to kick the sleeping simba. That would get things going. However, the lieutenant colonel made what was to become one of several miscalculations at critical times.

What happened was, of course, a real-life double nightmare for Major Reno's command unfolding before their very eyes. The outcome would not have been any different had it been Captain Benteen's battalion striking the encampment. Had Lieutenant Colonel Custer's battalion been in support behind Major Reno's attack the way Major Reno said he thought they would, it could have been worse for the 7th Cavalry.

At this point, Major Reno and Captain Benteen's accounting of the battle in their after-action reports differ from what the facts show now.

They said they did not know what the lieutenant colonel's plan was. The plain and simple truth of the matter is, they did.

Lieutenant Colonel Custer all but spoon-fed the Major all the way up to the time for his attack. He and his command headquarters staff waited just long enough to watch the major deploying his battalion for the attack before resuming their own line of march to Medicine Tail Coulee. It was that wait which caused a great loss of time for Custer's battalion. In the end they would pay for it in blood.

Major Reno stated he saw Lieutenant Colonel Custer wave his hat overhead to him for the last time just as he ordered the charge. Custer's headquarters staff gave a great hurrah, turned their horses north behind the cover of a ridge, and galloped away. That would be the last time Major Reno would see Custer's men alive.

Not one of the men galloping away would ever see the immense size of the camp until it was right in front of them. One would have thought someone would have gone just a little further around the hill to look at what Major Reno had been ordered to attack; but no one did. There was a ridge line blocking their view from the obvious. For that matter, Major Reno would not see how large the camp was until after he had charged to the bluffs to get away from the hostiles.

The encampment was still two and a half miles north of where Custer's battalion was then!

As for Lieutenant Colonel Custer, as far as he knew, Major Reno's attack was going to be totally successful. He planned on the feint to the front of the camp buying him some time. It would be time he needed to get around to the back of the camp, and hit the enemy where they least expected it.

If he hurried, at the gallop—he was using up what strength his command's horses had left—he could get to the north end of the camp and initiate his own attack. The plan, had it worked, would have pinned the hostiles against the river. Held there by two cavalry forces, Custer's and Major Reno's, at their flanks; with a third force (Benteen's) blocking any escape out onto the plains to the west. Had there only been 800 warriors instead of 4,000 to 5,000 of them, and 12,000 to 15,000 total people in the encampment, the plan may have worked. Reality has such a nasty way of showing up just at the wrong time.

The wheels started coming off the lieutenant colonel's wagon almost before Major Reno got started. First, the lieutenant colonel misjudged how long it would take to get down to the river. Custer thought he could spring a compound attack against the camp in concert with Major Reno's attack.

His hope was to catch the hostiles in between Major Reno's and his own force. Next, he misjudged the lay of the land. In doing so, he made, perhaps, his most fatal of mistakes. He thought he could initiate his own attack sooner than he did.

He never dreamed it would take him so long, nearly thirty minutes of hard riding—to get to the break in the ridge they were behind, and then swing around and start down Medicine Tail Coulee to cross the river.

"So far, so good," the lieutenant colonel must have thought. He would attack them from behind, and finish them before they finished off Major Reno. He would hit them where they were not looking. Racing down Medicine Tail Coulee his command went.

With a shout, "We got 'em now, boys, follow me," the lieutenant colonel would yell. The men followed with a great hurrah.

His command's horses' hooves were throwing dirt clods, and raising a huge cloud of dust as they raced down the dry ravine. He would have barely made out the sounds of gunfire coming from his left. It would be the sounds of Major Reno's attack.

The sounds of rifles rattling could not be distinguished from the men who were fighting for their very lives over the sounds of the enemy slaying Major Reno's men almost where they stood. He may have even seen the hostiles further to his left on their way to the Major Reno fight as his cavalry hurried on.

He would know Major Reno's command was having a whale of hard time of it. It would not be long now, and he would be in support of Major Reno, and his command.

In so doing, perhaps, he would once again catch the evasive glory he so desperately craved. It was right at his fingertips. It was his for the taking. He could taste the sweetness of victory from a hard-fought victory. Almost! But between there and the victory was hard work to be done first.

It would make victory all the more sweet. It was that lust for victory that drove men like Custer to charge headlong into the unknown. A wild-eyed, gut-wrenching, slobbering creature was now riding the great warhorse named Vic. Danger be damned; he was someone's worse nightmare. Worse, he had come as death itself to his enemies.

It may have seemed a strange way to support your subordinate commander—moving away from the sounds of the battle just on the other side of the ridge—but that was the Lieutenant colonel plan. At the bottom of the coulee, the giant warhorse Vic leaped into the Little Bighorn River; Lieutenant colonel Custer could see the part of the village rising up right in front of him on the other side.

"Hell," he must have thought, "this village is huge, there must thousands of the red buggers here...not just hundreds."

He was now totally committed, he could not go back, so he did what he always did in situations like that. He had his bugler sound the charge.

It was then he would start to realize the encampment was bigger than he would have ever believed possible. Still, there were only a hundred or so Indians in plain sight, though many more were running as fast as they could toward the river crossing, shooting as they ran with more and more on the way.

He did not see all of them. Some of the chiefs had considered the natural river forge created by the confluence of the coulee and the river would be an avenue of attack when the *wasichu* came. The hostiles had gone there, and hidden men with rifles at the river's edge in the underbrush along the slow-moving current. The hostiles were used to being patient. They waited just out of sight in case what was happening happened.

It would not have mattered at this stage of the battle if the lieutenant colonel had seen those hiding long the other side. In his mind, he was like a ghost in battle. No one had yet made a bullet that would drop him.

"By glory—we got the buggers!" he might have said to himself, he very seldom ever swore aloud. "Right where I want them...sleeping in the noonday sun."

Almost grinning, he was mid-river, his face set in grim determination. He felt the bottoms of his boots being splashed wet as he and the big warhorse waded through the deepest part of the ford. He yelled to encourage his horse, "Come on, Vic, harder, and give me all you got! A little further and we'll be on dry ground!"

He did by most accounts surprise the Indians, but only because of the speed his troops got to the coulee, and started down it. In the end it would not matter; they were waiting in ambush for him.

But, alas, the biggest surprise may have been what happened next. It is obvious he thought he could divert some of the pressure from Major Reno by attacking where and when he did. In the end, one could say his attack was the only thing that saved Major Reno's battalion.

The lieutenant colonel saw at once as he came down the coulee how the camp spread far to the north, and he was going headlong into the center of the encampment.

"...Damn...too late to change the attack. We'll have to make the best of this, and get through them and out onto the flats of the valley. We'll scatter the horse herds. Then we can tear into them as fast as we can," he might have said to himself.

Turning in his saddle, he waved those behind him to follow his lead. He would not know the dye had been caste. He was about to be one of the first casualties in his battalion.

Lieutenant Colonel Custer initiating his attack when and where he did, in a roundabout way, gave Major Reno's command a little breather. In fact, it probably saved Major Reno's command from being wiped out. Custer's attack provided enough of a respite for Major Reno to get back to the other side of the river. Major Reno leadership—or lack thereof accomplished all the wild-assed retreat to the bluffs overlooking the river.

—16—

MAJOR RENO ENGAGES

The casualty statistics from Major Reno's two separate engagements were staggering. His disastrous assault and almost immediate withdrawal from the river had taken no more than twenty to twenty-five minutes. His command's attack and subsequent day and a half holdout in a barehanded scooped-out earthen dish on the bluffs overlooking the river had cost his battalion of the 7th Cavalry a total of sixty-two men killed and wounded.

That total could have been much worse. In reality, when the final numbers were tallied up for that first day, thirty-six had been killed in action (29 percent), another twenty-six were wounded (21 percent). Twenty-two men (nearly 18 percent) had been left in the valley and were missing and assumed to have been killed in the valley fight and the subsequent "charge" to the bluffs.

Frankly, no one knew how many men had been left alive and horseless in the valley to face the hostiles when the command left. Only one officer (Lieutenant Charles De Rudio) was in that group. He had been assigned to E troop but on that day he was second in command of A troop under the command of Captain James Moylan who had also been reassigned (to B troop) to that troop as its commander.

The twenty-two missing and presumed killed would somehow turn up the next morning at the crest of the bluff where the rest of the battalion was dug in. They had miraculously survived the rest of the afternoon and all the night of the 25th. By hiding in the thick brush or downfall timber next to the river from the hostiles they had somehow escaped detection of the hostiles who combed the area for survivors. Some of the men had even been in the river hiding under the banks until it was safe for them to move up to the bluffs in small groups of three or four at a time. These men's horses had either bolted while they were dismounted, or had been killed while being held by the troop holders. When the order came to "Charge" these men did not have a horse to charge with and were left to their own devises as to surviving until they could get to the battalion's fortifications on the bluff.

Major Reno's "withdrawal"—he would call it a "charge"—was in truth, a retreat. The "charge" as he called it, turned into a wild-assed, screaming "run for your lives men" scramble. Whatever it would be officially called in the reports afterwards, it was not an orderly military movement away from the enemy. From start to finish, his assault and retreat to the bluffs had spanned no more than forty-five minutes to an hour.

Somehow, to all the soldiers who had participated in it, the attack and the withdrawal had seemed at least several hours in length if not the whole day. One of the oddities of the adventure was that no two men could when asked could say how long the battle in the valley had lasted. Nearly all of the men did not even know what time of day it was or for that matter say how long they were in the valley. For others, those that did not make it out of the valley alive it was a lifetime.

Strangely, the time it took for Major Reno and his command to move the two miles down the river to the forge and then the three miles back up the other side of the river had taken almost enough time for Lieutenant Colonel Custer's five troops to skirt around the ridge line that had hidden the village from the soldiers earlier.

Custer had to delay his movement to ensure that Major Reno and his command got to where they were supposed to be. Had he not have done that, it may have worked out about right for Custer and his men to get to the Medicine Tail Coulee. If he had not spent the time he did ensuring Major Reno got to the designated spot for his attack, he may have been able to mount his attack at the same time as Major Reno launched his ill-fatted assault. The end result may have been a little bit different.

There was another problem that Lieutenant Colonel Custer had. He had miscalculated the time it would take to reach a point where he could attack the village from what he perceived would be the encampment's most vulnerable spot, the rear.

Instead of being less than a mile, it was a mile and a half beyond where he thought he could go down toward the river. Even then, he still believed he would be hitting the village from behind with his rabbit punch attack. At the trot, the five troops of cavalry could have covered the first mile in about fifteen minutes. The next mile and a half would take nearly twenty-five more minutes. Then to form the battalion for the attack and then to attack the village, another half hour more was taken. The point is: If Major Reno's commands' attack was to draw the hostile warriors to the southern end of the camp; it almost worked—except for a couple small points.

First, the camp was bigger than anyone could have imagined. The fact only 1,500 warriors struck and overwhelmed the major's out-manned command just as it started its own attack destroyed the lieutenant colonel's tactical strategy before it ever got on track. Custer, of course, would never know that. Instead of drawing the enemy away from the heart of the camp by using Major Reno's command as the diversion it only fragmented his force once again.

—17—

MAJOR RENO IS AMBUSHED

The hostiles were waiting in ambush as Major Reno approached the southern end of the encampment. So much for the surprise attack! Custer would never know that either. This collapse of this strategy would also help seal his own fate as those warriors on the way to the Major Reno fight would be able to reverse their movement toward Major Reno's men and double back on the unguarded left flank of Custer's command.

From the start of Major Reno's attack at the southern end of the encampment until Custer's last man fell nearly four miles away, the 7th Cavalry was out-run, out-gunned and out-manned and finally out-generaled. Miscalculation can be cruel at times; in combat, it is often fatal.

Is it any wonder Major Reno was so overwhelmed so quickly? Not only was the element of surprise gone, the hostiles know he was coming. They were waiting in ambush when his command charged.

The hostiles had over a twelve-to-one advantage in manpower against Major Reno's command. In terms of firepower, it wasn't even close. The 7th Cavalry were firing single action .44-caliber six-shooter Colts, and single-shot carbines.

On the other hand the hostile's arsenal consisted of steel tipped arrows, short and long war lances, stone headed war clubs and steel cast trader store tomahawks for close in work. In addition to those, many had Winchester sixteen-shot repeaters and a host of other weapons at their disposal that the Army did not have.

For a long time after the fight many experts argued that point of superior fire power. However, for the past nearly forty-years since the archeology survey of the area after a fire in the mid-sixties conducted by National Geographic Society the truth of that fact can not be denied. The Society identified at least forty-seven different powder-charged weapons were used by the combats on the battlefield. We know what the Army used that day; they fired just two of the forty-seven different weapons. What was not known at the time of the battle, or until the study was conducted by National Geographic, was how much more firepower the hostiles had than the Army. There may not have been the quality of weapons throughout the hostiles force on the field that day, but a great many would have been armed with fire sticks that far exceeded the number held in the hands of the U.S. Army's 7th Cavalry.

In summation, those two points (numbers and firepower) sometimes get overlooked when one tries to figure out why Major Reno did not attack harder. Custer would have had no knowledge of the number of hostiles Major Reno would meet, and no idea Major Reno could not hold the hostiles attention for more than a nanosecond. He would have had no idea the hostiles were waiting in ambush of Major Reno.

Had Major Reno been just a little braver, or had he stayed in the valley just five minutes longer, the hostiles would have handled the issue the same way as it they would handle Lieutenant Colonel Custer's battalion. Had Major Reno been a braver man, his command would not have lived to complain about him not being brave enough to lead them; they would have all been dead. Does that make Major Marcus Reno a coward, or simply a prudent commander looking after the welfare of his command?

Major Reno would have envisioned when Custer had told him before splitting the regiment the final time he would be in the major's direct support. Direct support in Major Reno's mind meant something other than what it apparently meant to Custer.

Direct support in Major Reno's mind meant to follow on right behind his attack. That meant to Major Reno that Custer should have been directly behind him not ridding to God only knew where to back up his charge into the encampment. He said as much during the Court of Inquiry that was convened nearly two years later concerning this matter, Major Reno said that he thought Custer would come behind him with a second charge—following behind the Major's battalion assault on the southern end of the encampment. That was not the truth, the whole truth, and nothing but the truth; but, the court let it slide, though they had to have known better.

Major Reno's idea concerning direct support never occurred to his lieutenant colonel, or…if it had, it was only a momentary flash through his mind. Custer's whole motive for attacking the southern end with Major Reno's three troops was to draw the hostiles away from what Lieutenant Colonel Custer thought would be the northern end of the encampment.

Custer's thinking must have been that though Major Reno's force was small, if he pitched into the encampment hard enough perhaps the Indians would think the entire column of the 7th Cavalry attacking. Major Reno or anyone in his command would not see the real size of the village they were attacking until they were actually attacking. The survivors of the Major Reno fight would not see the immense size of the village until they had scaled the buttes and dug their rifle pits. They would then know how really lucky those who had lived through the affair really were.

The hostiles in the upper part of the camp—the south end—were not surprised by the attack. The hostiles had planned on and had been warned ahead of time by the young boys who had been guarding the horse herds. The boys had watched the *wasichu* as the battalion splashed across the river to get onto the west side of the river. Perhaps, the hostiles would not have reacted quite as fast as they did had if it had not been for the boys racing ahead of the troops to warn the village that the soldiers were coming.

The command had covered the three of the three and half miles to the village after crossing the river at the ford. As Major Reno ordered his battalion in battle formation for the charge an overwhelming force of hostiles smashed into them. Totally unsuspecting such an action from the hostiles, the battalion began to deploy, two attacking companies abreast of one another and one, G Troop, directly behind as a reserve, in line to attack. Just as they began their charge, they, themselves were attacked by an attacking force.

More than 1,500 hostile and very unhappy Indians would join in the brief, overwhelming, fight. One hundred and twelve mostly green troops against arguably "the best light cavalry in the world" who, besides that, were really very angry, hostile, and highly motivated Cheyenne warriors. Fifteen hundred armed hostiles bent on killing them all must have seemed to the men advancing to the attack as if they were riding into the bowels of hell. No one had to tell the *wasichu* the odds for success were not good.

The British famous "Charge of the Light Brigade" had better odds against the Russian cannon than these troops against better rifles than their own. Not only better firearms, the close in weapons like the short bows and arrows and handmade stone, brain-splattering clubs and lances, and tomahawks were also available to the cavalry's enemy. The biggest difference, though, was the experience from the top down on both sides.

The Indians were born to this kind of fighting; their leaders were leaders because they had proven themselves as warriors first. They had trained many years as a warrior learning the trade, developing fighting skills, distinguishing themselves as warriors first, and then possibly as leaders who lead others into battle against the enemies of the Indians. The warriors themselves fought to save their homes, and loved ones.

On the other side, many of these men in blue had never been in any kind of attack, ever. Most had not heard a shot fired at them in anger, much less from someone seriously wanting to kill them. They were worn out physically, hungry, tired, and confused and above all scared out of their wits.

That was not the worst of it. The officer leading them had never led an attack against anyone in his entire twenty-year military career. He had no idea what to expect, or how to fight Indians.

It was too late to learn now, he was doing it, and his men would pay the price for it.

Of course, the lieutenant colonel was not counting on the fact the Indians knew what was up, and were just waiting for them to come in. To the lieutenant colonel, the fake in the south was to get the Indians going one way. His action would strike in their rear while they were fighting Major Reno. Though no one knows for sure, Custer probably assumed that Benteen would be in support of Major Reno's battalion by then. That way the entire 7th Cavalry's manpower and military bearing could be brought to bear against the encampment effectively locking them in place. The river and hills above the encampment would seal the hostiles escape to the east. His command would block any escape to the north. Benteen's force would be able to hold the southern end of the encampment. It was all nice and neat.

That had to be what he would think, it was a classic cavalry tactic. Nothing fancy, but it did not need to be fancy. After all, Custer was fighting ignorant savages unskilled at fighting modern day military tactics. They had not been to a military academy, or fought hundreds of fights against others who fought as the *wasichu* fought. That he held the upper hand on that account was another miscalculation.

Who would think the hostiles would have anticipated the move, and been waiting for them to try to spring it on them? Obviously, Lieutenant Colonel Custer believed he had out-thought them.

—18—

MAJOR RENO'S NIGHTMARE

Try to imagine being in Major Reno's boots for a moment as he mounted his attack. He would see his lieutenant colonel on the hill watching his force deploy for the attack. He would see his peers from Custer's battalion wave a hearty salute to him and his boys. He would carry out his duties as a cavalry officer— smartly, after all, his commander was watching. God Himself, in the form of a man dressed in buckskin. You would think to yourself, " …Well, Major Marcus Reno of the 7th Cavalry do this smartly, the old man is watching you …" Thinking while doing what by now has become almost second nature to you, your mind starts to wander, "I could do what he is doing right gawd-damned now and do it just as good.…"

If you were him you almost see yourself order the battalion bugler, to sound the charge. Rather than do it, somehow, now, you are almost transcending the ground above your horse. You are watching your men tie the reins of their mounts to their gun free wrists, so as not to drop them during the charge. The troopers form, and spread in line for the charge when they hear the first note. You really do not hear the bugle yourself, but you know the bugler is blowing it, he is right beside you. You watched him put the horn to his lips and his cheeks puff out. You see your boys dig their spurred heels into the sides of their mounts. You see them reaching forward, hunkering down in their saddles, so as to make less a target. You hear that near rebel yell as their horses dig in. Your mind hears it all. Your eyes see it all, magically.

You and those men around you are on another level now. You and your horse are tearing across the prairie. It is as if you are somehow floating above what you see happening around you.

You are unconsciously bracing yourself for the possible impact should a bullet, or worse, an arrow, find its mark on you. Privately, you have seen men hit with an arrow, and it scares you to think of one of them slamming into your body. You scream through clenched teeth at the top of your lungs, "CHARGE."

Then, at a dead run, on horseback, with pistol drawn and cocked you are doing what you knew you would truly love to do. You feel the wind blow past your face; you hear the horses grunt and fart as they strain tired muscles to get the last drop of speed.

With your boys yelling at the top of their lungs, the dirt flying beneath their gallant war-horses hooves, you are thinking to yourself, "…this is why I stayed in the Army …no…screw the friggin' Army, the gawd-darned cavalry…."

The next nano-second, in the time it takes to blink, a mere 400 yards from your objective, you see twelve of your men being flung from their horses, obviously dead. "No man just falls off his horse that way," you think. In the next moment you see three or four more of them slide off the backs of their mounts, obviously wounded but your mind thinks almost nonchalantly, "Those men, MY MEN are being killed." In a flash, because you have never seen anything like it before, your mind wonders if somehow the hostiles could have stretched a rope across their path.

Everything is a whirl now; a few of your men over in M Troop horses start to bolt. You see the horses taking the riders too far out in front of the rest of the charge. At full speed, they are the first to smack into the attacking devils you thought you were supposed to surprise. Only now, you realize they are attacking you. And you wonder how it could happen. It was supposed to be a surprise attack.

Your brain has not caught up to what your eyes are seeing. "Why are my men falling off their horses, what the hell is going on?" you ask yourself.

"I don't even see …or hear gun fire."

Your ears have a feeling like you are deaf. Everything you hear seems to be coming from down in some old well back on the farm when you were growing up. Everything you hear sounds like it is a long, long way off.

With your ears, you hear nothing, but your brain hears everything, the sound of the guns as they are discharged, the screams of your men being dragged from their horses, the horrible sounds of your enemy as he rips the hair off a man who is not yet dead. Your brain goes completely blank. You should be doing something, but you are at a loss as to what it should be. Animal instincts start to take over; after all you are a survivor and the leader of men. Some where in your brain you try to use logic to straighten up the picture before you, "Well, maybe I am not a great leader of men, but I can get us through this," you argue with yourself.

You hear nothing, but somehow your brain clicks into gear as your men continue to fall. You hear the screams of the ones whose horses bolted. They are being ripped from their horses. Literally, these three or four men are hacked to death by naked painted-up monsters you don't recognize as even being human.

"Freakin' creatures, that's what these bastards are, the dirty sons-of-bitches are killing my boys," your brain screams you back to reality.

Through all of that, somehow you become what the Army is paying you for, a commander, and you have to save who you can. Instincts take over, and you must try to get those still alive back out of danger. You order the command to "dismount"and immediately your brain tells you that is the wrong thing to do. So you immediately change the order, "mount!" Your conscious mind is arguing with your unconscious mind and you stand there arguing with yourself, aloud.

The back of a man's head just ahead of you, before your very eyes, explodes into a bloody mass, but somehow the dead man manages somehow to stay in his saddle for a few seconds before he falls over the back of his mount with blood, bone, and brain spraying over the back of his horse.

Somehow, someway, you realize you have charged into hell, and the gates have slammed shut with you caught on the wrong side. You start to realize you are going to die. The idea scares you worse than being blown to bits by cannon shot, or shot with a Minnie ball. Worse though, is to be hit with one of those heathen devil's arrows; that would really hurt. Reality is not real anymore and you just want to run away, for some reason though you know you can not.

That idea makes Major Reno lean a little closer to his mount's neck and to slow down just a little.

"Oh God, I don't want to die," your mind says. You finally admit it; you do not want to die.

Now you are screaming, "Stop this. Please, dear God! Stop this!" Your mind hears what the screams of dying men and their killers have now drowned out. Gunfire is filling the air around you.

Major Reno tried to carry out his attack, only to have it literally blow up in his face in less than five minutes. It must have been the equivalent of being caught in a rowboat in the middle of the ocean when you see a tsunami wave perhaps 200 feet tall, and you are sucked into it within seconds. Or perhaps, sitting on Mount St. Helen's enjoying a nice peaceful, sunny day the instant it blows up.

No matter how hard you try to avoid what is coming next, it doesn't matter: You died. You knew it before it happened, you watched it happen—it may take another twenty years for someone to kick the dirt in on your face, but you died right there and then; and so did Major Marcus Reno. Whatever happened afterwards in your life would not matter, your life simply ended that hour and day.

—19—

THE MYTH

Overall, Custer's tactics may have worked except for one thing, the Indians had been tracking General Terry's column including the 7th's movements since they had left Fort Abraham Lincoln. They were fully apprised of the soldiers dividing their force earlier in the morning. To put a point on it, they were waiting for him. They may not have known who exactly was attacking it did not matter. Custer, Crook, Terry, Gibbons, or someone else, it did not matter—whoever it was, was going to pay.

As a point of explanation here; the Indians had a system of communication unequaled by anything the U.S. Army had or would have for years to come. Agency Indians from northwest Nebraska and southeastern Wyoming, many miles to the south of the fight on the Little Bighorn, claimed to have known about it only hours after it happened. On the other hand, it would be days before the Army would learn what had occurred at either Fort Laramie or Fort Robertson in those same locations. The Army never did figure out how they could do that, and the Indians never told them. Anything the soldiers did, including moving against them from even as far away as Fort Abraham Lincoln in the Dakota Territories, they knew about it long before it happened.

In the first place, most of the Indians could not believe the *wasichus* would be goofy enough to attack a village their size. Only a crazy man would do that. What the Indians did not know was that this army of *wasichus* did not know how big their encampment was.

For the cavalry's part, they did not know this encampment of warriors had nearly wiped out Red Beard Crook's command a week before. Their surprise attack on General Crook and command had been an utter surprise. While the death toll from the attack had not been anywhere near what this battle would claim, this command was so shocked by its furiousness Crook decided the better part of valor was to withdraw from the valley of the Rosebud back to safety at Fort Fetterman.

These same Indians had struck and defeated Red Beard's force only a week before. The hostiles could not conceive the same wasichus would attack them out in the open in mid-day.

The Indians did not know "X" part of the equation. It would not have mattered who it was coming to visit, though, and it would not have mattered to them if they had. For all they knew, it was Red Beard Crook trying to hit them again. So there was surprise on both sides, but it was not the type of surprise Lieutenant Colonel Custer had hoped or what the Indians themselves had thought it was. They would only learn about who it was sometime long after the fight. The significance of who they had defeated would be lost on them. Supposedly the 7th U.S. Army Cavalry was the best there was on the frontier at the time. That was, of course, a myth that to this day is believed. Up and until this time the 7th Cavalry had done nothing to distinguish itself in the eyes of enemy or even the U.S. Army. It did not that day on the Little Bighorn River. It would however, become a force worth its stars later in its long and historic history.

If Crook was the *wasichu's* best officer, the hostiles were beginning to wonder what they were afraid of. Often, General Crook has been accused of not telling anyone how he and his force were withdrawing from the campaign. That is not true. He had sent word to the Powder River Depot that a huge force of hostiles had attacked him, and he had to withdraw from the area in order to reorganize.

Since he was not under the command of either General Terry or Colonel Gibbon, he could come and go as he saw fit. Another misnomer was he had been routed by the Cheyenne. It was not Cheyenne warriors that Red Beard's troops fought on the Rosebud. It was Sioux, led by the Ogalalas' war chief, Crazy Horse. In the Rosebud fight, Red Beard Crook had only lost eight troopers, while the Indians lost about twenty-five men.

The surprise attack on Lieutenant colonel Crook's encampment so shook up Crook and many of his officers he really had only one option:

Withdraw and get out of the region as fast as he could to regroup. Before leaving, however, General Crook advised General Terry by way of sending a trio of couriers. Each one left at a different time and on a different trail to ensure that at least one would get through. His message to Terry was that the hostiles were in far greater strength than any previous reports had indicated. Going on Crook said that Terry's command should be aware of the potential of underestimating the enemy strength. It would reach the Power River Depot on the evening of the 25th of June 1876.

The near-enough defeat Crook imagined was really a mental one. It was nowhere near a defeat. It was a fight, one, the Army was not prepared to fight then and there. The hostiles hit Crook's command in camp, and it was a totally confused, mixed-up affair the officers could not unravel. They had lost some of their supplies and some of the command's horses. It was enough of a fright, and near enough to a real defeat Crook's force retired from the field, and lived to fight another day. It was about twelve hours too late for Lieutenant Colonel Custer's 7th Cavalry.

The lack of communications and current military intelligence when added together spelled a deadly elixir for Custer's command. His problems were to be the same as Major Reno's faced. As for who should have known, no blame can be dealt out to any man in the 7th Cavalry. As to who would be given the blame, Custer would always be looked at as the man who should have known what was going on. Major Reno would become the scapegoat.

Custer's problems were compounded by the fact that his command faced a far greater disparity in numbers. His command faced the full blunt of the Sioux and Cheyenne force as well as all of those of the lesser tribes in the encampment. His men would be out numbered nearly twenty-three to one for starters at the river's edge and at the end, on the side of Battle Ridge, nearly 100 to 1.

The Army's single-shot carbines that had a habit of jamming when fouled munitions were used and single-action pistols are not much to counter those kinds of odds.

He would have no inkling that they too were waiting for him at the bottom of Medicine Tail, the same as they had for Major Reno at the outer fringes of the encampment. He would have heard all hell break out off to his left front as he started down the coulee. Even at that distance, the sounds of rifle and pistol fire would have been largely muffled, but he would have heard a lot of small arms fire nonetheless.

He would have assumed it was the major attacking. He would have been right, but not totally right. He would not have known only a very small contingent of what was available from the hostile camp was overwhelming Major Reno and soon would be part of the force that would be led against his own command.

In the meantime, Lieutenant Colonel Custer still had not seen the entire camp. His scouts and guides had seen its immensity, several times before the column had moved on behind the ridge that led them to Medicine Tail Coulee. The scouts having seen what they had a few of the scouts got off their ponies and started singing their death chants. They knew that their leader was taking them down to where there would be no escape, even if the boss did not. Custer and a few of the officers had made fun of the Crow and Ree scouts for being afraid.

Finally, after moving his command at the trot for a half an hour he saw what he thought would be a pathway to the northern end of the encampment. For that much time to pass when he knew Major Reno was knee-deep in hostiles must have tormented the lieutenant colonel. There was nothing he could do about it. He would hurry his troops as fast as he could.

He would attack the camp as soon as he found a passageway to it. The coulee led to a natural ford on the river below. It could not have come fast enough. In his mind, he would begin an attack on the north end of the hostiles' camp. Lieutenant Colonel Custer's force would support Major Reno's attack—albeit different than what Major Reno had in mind.

—20—

THE VALLEY FIGHT: CUSTER DETAILS WHAT IS EXPECTED OF MAJOR RENO IN THE VALLEY

Earlier, before Major Reno deployed, the lieutenant colonel had sent both Captain Myles Keogh, commander of I Troop and Lt. Win Cooke, his adjutant, from the headquarters detachment, to encourage and to assist the major in setting up for the attack. These two officers had taken quite a bit of time answering all of his questions and showing him exactly what he was to do once he got to the other side of the river and then began his attack.

Those who criticize Custer often overlook that one point. The lieutenant colonel verbally explained his orders as they pertained to the major. With near hands-on instruction, the lieutenant colonel discussed the issues of how Major Reno should conduct his part of the operation. In Major Reno's after-action report, and later during the court of inquiry, he denied either of those situations as having occurred. For Major Reno to say later that he had no idea of what the battle plan was is malarkey; there were other officers who did live through the fight in the valley and hilltop to contradict the major's testimony.

On the day of the battle Major Reno's battalion strength originally consisted of 125 men in the three companies under his command, Troop

M numbered forty-one troopers; In Troop A forty-three all totaled; and Troop G had the same number as Troop M, forty-one.

After giving up his ten percent to the operation of the regiment and three of Major Reno's battalion's sergeants consisted of 112 armed combatants. Major Reno moved in columns of four after crossing the river for about a mile and a half. Then he formed his battalion for the attack when he was a little less than a mile from the outskirts of the encampment.

He placed two troops of cavalry, Troop A nearest the trees and the river, and M stretching out onto the prairie to the west away from the river. He then positioned himself beside Troop G directly behind the first two to serve as the reserve troop for the other two.

According to his own account of the battle plan he developed, he had to move some two and one-half miles before coming within a mile and a half of the edge of the hostile encampment. As the battalion moved up the river after crossing it to the west side, the battalion moved at the trot.

Unknown to the battalion, three Indian lads observed Major Reno's movement as the battalion came across the river. They had been sent to stand guard, and watch over the encampments horse herds. For the youngsters, this was a great honor. It showed them their parents saw them old enough to be out all night and responsible enough to do this very important task among their people.

The boys were seen and apparently largely ignored by anyone in the battalion (even the scouts or guides did not give them much of a second thought). The boys, upon seeing the *wasichu*, took off as fast as they could run to warn the village. They reached the encampment perhaps twenty minutes before Major Reno's battalion were forming to attack what they thought was going to be a walk in the park.

The hostiles were expecting them, and had been getting ready by the time the youngsters got to the camp. Rather than attack blindly, Major Reno kept the men at the trot as the battalion closed on the encampment. They covered the first mile in less than fifteen minutes, cautiously.

Twenty minutes would pass, and the battalion was within a mile of the village. Lieutenant Colonel Custer was at least two miles away from reaching the Medicine Tail Coulee. The general had hoped to get there just as Major Reno was beginning his attack.

A large band of warriors, perhaps seventy-five or so, rode out of the village and pretended to threatened to attack the battle-positioning battalion. The unit braced for an attack, while continuing its movement forward.

There was a brief, but hot, exchange of fire. The hostiles only feinted they were coming out in strength—and it had been convincing to the inexperienced major. Slowly, the hostiles began backing off, withdrawing slowly to the village drawing Major Reno's force in to the trap.

The major, encouraged by the seemingly light resistance, ordered the men in the two ranks forward at the canter.

The trap was set.

The cantering cavalryman plunged head long into the hostile set trap. As the force moved forward, the major must have felt his confidence go up about a hundred points when he saw only three of his men; two sergeants and a private, killed from this brief but hot exchange. He had not noticed that none of the warriors were shot dead by his men. At least, for the time being, the hostiles' withdrawal was a positive sign to the inexperienced Major Reno.

"Hell's fire," he might have thought, "maybe Captain Keogh and Lieutenant Cooke were right after all." The hostiles were backing away from his battalion's show of strength, "…you show these red-skinned devils who is boss and they back off of a guy," he would remembering somebody telling him.

As if almost drugged by such success during the first show of force, Major Reno must have thought from all appearances the hostiles were afraid of him and his troopers. Caught witlessly in a trap, like so many of the others before him, Major Reno allowed himself and the battalion to be snookered in just far enough that the trap door almost closed behind them. Only by the barest of margins were the survivors of this ill-fated tactic able to get out.

Suddenly, at the outer edge of the hostile's encampment, these retreating Cheyenne warriors stopped and turned and attacked the major with great vigor. When they begin their attack, it was not the seventy-five warriors Major Reno had seen originally, it was more than a thousand of half-naked demons that rose up out of nowhere. They charged straight at Major Reno and his pitifully thin line of troopers.

The hostiles were almost upon *wasichu* before many of them could react. That is when the wheels started coming off of Major Reno's wagon. Several of the half broke Army horses bolted taking some of the green trooper's straight into the attacking force. Some of the horses would go to bucking and snorting in wild confusion when the soldiers tried raining them in. Others would just put their heads down and race headlong into the avenger's path, their riders would be delivered straight into hell.

These men were never seen again, except in pieces and parts. Heads were severed. Bodies of the slain men were torn and ripped open. Throats were slit. Right arms up to the elbow were hacked off. The men's private parts were hacked off, their torsos and thighs gashed and laid open, their scalps ripped off their skulls. No fallen *wasichu* in this charge was spared once the hostiles got their hands on them. Those who fell under the onslaught of the hostiles attack and not killed outright would only pray later they had been killed rather than just wounded.

That little juke by the hostiles was enough to put Major Reno, all by himself, in full retreat back to the relative imagined safety of the trees that ran along the west bank of the river. It was only within minutes afterwards, when his absence was noticed, that he was joined by what remained of his command.

For their part the men in this unannounced retreat started by their commander were justified in what they did—they ran too. What was the point of staying? If it was too hot for the boss what were they doing staying in the middle of hell, they turned tail and headed back to join him in his newly found safe haven and its relative safety.

It would not stay safe for long, for once they got back to the trees along the river the hostiles were amongst them, they followed the retreating *wasichu* right up to and into the trees. These *wasichu* had drawn an unwanted crowd of folks all bent on killing every last one of them. For the soldiers' part it was obvious that they would have to fight or die where they were. If they were to live they would have to retreat further. The Little Bighorn River became almost an impassable object to the soldiers in getting back across the river. Once getting across the river would not stop the hostiles from killing them; they would then have to try to get on top of the bluffs perhaps a mile beyond. The mere thought of that alone must have been nearly overwhelming to many of the men, veterans and new men alike. There would have been not one man alive to see that they were in a live or die situation. Staying would mean a terrifying death.

It could have been almost funny watching the drama unfold, had it not been so deadly serious. Many of the fallen men had died horrifying and terrible deaths at the hands of these red-skinned savages. Many more would fall under the hostiles' arrows and rifle shot into the tree defense because of the ineptitude of not only the inexperienced battalion commander but many of the other officers as well.

When the hostiles had suddenly stopped retreating, and turned on the dime, and then struck back at Major Reno's advancing force the jig was up. They hit the blue coats with such ferociousness the lead troops had the blazes scared out of them. Things went from pretty good to near panic in a heartbeat.

The hostiles began to rapidly encircle the shattered force, working themselves in behind the near panic-stricken, often as not, leaderless, men. Once in the trees and thickets that ran along the river, the men tried to deploy in squads. The hostiles were starting to lay down a murderous fire into the remaining soldiers as they attempted to gather themselves and regain some sense of military bearing.

It took a few horrifying heartbeats and a couple gulps of air for the major to realize he was the victim of a rather rude trick. He was like a walleyed fish out of water gulping for oxygen. His eyes were bugged out, he was sweating profusely, and when he tried to talk or give a command, his throat was so dry that the only sounds from his mouth were chirps and squeaks.

Somewhere along the way, from the beginning of the attack to the short distance to the trees retreat, he had lost his dammed straw hat. The sun was boiling his brain and he could barely stand on his own two feet. The man had lost all composure and was nearly ready to pass-out from heat exhaustion and fear.

He had walked straight into an ambush rather than the obvious rout of the heathen red men his commander had proposed to him not forty-five minutes to an hour earlier. If Major Reno could have remembered that far back is not known. It must have seemed to the rookie Indian fighter that Lieutenant Colonel Custer had spoken several days before and not less than an hour before. From that point on Major Reno, though in command of the battalion was not in command of even himself much less the survivors under his command.

Command fell to the lower-ranking officers in his command, even though it was never suggested in an after action reporting. If it had not, Major Reno would have been the only one to escape to the bluffs that must have seemed a life time away. The mentally stronger and more experienced troop commanders (Civil War veterans started getting the troops together in squads and ordering them into the perimeter of their shrinking by the second battle space. The command's horses were turned over to the holders. Every fourth man was detailed this dangerous and unrewarding duty taking twenty-five percent of what was left of the command's fire power off the battle line. The other soldiers turned to deploy skirmish lines as best as they could by themselves or as directed by their sergeants, young lieutenants, and captains, Major Reno was stumbling about making no sense in his orders that he was barking to the wind.

The Indians now moved on a more aggressive attack. They would prefer it here in hand-to-hand, war ax to empty rifle. They had this foe where they wanted him, scared out of his wits, and running out of ammunition. First, they went after the holders and the horses in order to keep the *wasichus* locked in place. They wanted to take their way of escape away from the *wasichu*. They nearly succeeded.

The trees allowed the *wasichus* within their confines relative safety for only a very short time, just bare minutes. The hostiles never let up the pressure on those still left alive. Gradually, they began flanking the individual squads of Major Reno's command. By doing so they were making the noose around Major Reno's command tighter and tighter. The troopers holding the horses were placed behind the squads. These men and the horses they held were like pigs in a poke with no place to go.

Once totally surrounded, the men in blue would have no way to get out of the predicament they had put themselves. In the end, most of these holders would fall quickly, and over half of the horses would be taken by the hostiles or run off.

For Major Reno's part, in the few minutes he had been engaged, he had been stopped cold, stampeded in retreat and had lost all sense to what he was supposed to do next—he could have used a drink here to steady things out a little. He just did not have the time to think of his old friend in his saddle bags or wits enough to remember he was most times a drunk. Things for Major Reno would not improve, as time nearly stood still. The hostiles crept closer and closer to the main body of his men.

A curious issue, brought out later in his after-action report, is that Major Reno did not mention he was a little rattled by the sudden turn of events on that otherwise bright and cheery day. He never mentions the fact he went from being the commander leading the charge of more than a hundred men to running for his life—and to hell with everyone else.

He never mentions that he led a retreat on his own behalf to relative safety in the face of the enemy. Nor does he mention that once, in the trees and talking with Bloody Knife, that the scout had his head literally blown apart while discussing what he, as commander, should do next.

Right in mid-sentence, the scout's head exploded from a round meant for Major Reno. Unfortunately, Bloody Knife happened to step into the speeding bullet's path at the perfect time. The scout's brains, blood, bone, tissue, and hair were splattered all over Major Reno's face and chest in mid-sentence. The two men were using hand signs and pidgin English discussing Bloody Knife's assessment of the situation.

The effect this incident had on Major Reno must have been the proverbial last straw that broke the camel's back. One of the enlisted men would later say, "…that had they been led by anyone other than a coward, we would have all died then and there," at the Court of Inquiry two years later. It was by following him back into the trees along the Little Bighorn River, then across the river, and to the bluffs that any of them got out alive.

Bloody Knife's death occurred only moments before the major, so shaken by what was going on around him, ordered his troops to mount and then dismount three different times in rapid succession. Finally, getting horsed, he mounted another "attack" (as he called it) in his after-action report.

This time, the major "attacked" through the hostiles nearest the river. He and his horse successfully leaped into the river and he continued his "attack" to the bluffs east of the river nearly a mile away from his point of attack. The men nearby the major wore themselves out mounting and dismounting while at the same time trying to keep the hostiles at bay, and away from them.

By that time however, many of the men's horses had been stolen or run off by hostiles, leaving many soldiers afoot. Those who did not have a mount had to fend for themselves, and escape as best as they could, if they could. Many did not make it out of the valley. That situation is not discussed in Major Reno's after action report.

One could come down hard on Major Reno, he clearly deserves it for his actions during the initial attack and then for his actions once he gets into the threes. Civilians, folks like you and I, might think that way. "After all," we might say, "this was Major Reno's first contact with hostiles."

That is not how the Army views matters of this nature. It was not that he was some rookie trooper, or some young inexperienced shave-tail officer. He had been a field-grade officer for nearly twenty years; what is more, all officers are held to a higher standard than what we civilians would consider as acceptable behavior in front of an enemy. To the U.S. Army, then and now, an officer grabbing his ass and running like a scalded dog is not an option. An officer is expected to be the first one to lead by example at all times. An officer considers the safety of his command first and his own safety after he has assured his first responsibility is met.

For his first combat action to be against the vaunted Cheyenne and Sioux was just bad luck doled out to another wise very, very unlucky man. That did not excuse him from his first priority and that was to follow his orders of his commander and second to his men. The very idea he was spearheading the attack into an enemy encampment that he had never really seen, or that he had no idea of how large a force he would be likely to encounter, made him nearly insane with fear and self-doubt when reality grabbed him literally by the ass and throat at the same time.

Lieutenant Colonel Custer informed him of this fact at eight o'clock that morning. He was to lead the assault against the southern edge of the village. To most it would be a major honor to be the point of the spear. To Major Reno, it was a thought wrought with horror.

For Custer's part, it had nothing to do with his liking Major Reno better than Captain Benteen or visa-versa. He did not trust this almost nondescript officer any more than he trusted Captain Benteen but for different reasons. It was military protocol.

In the end, it was a mistake made by Lieutenant Colonel Custer to put Major Reno in that position. And it certainly was not fair to him or to the command that he was expected to lead. There was no way this man, Major Marcus Reno, could have been even remotely successful in that situation. Of course, hind sight being what it is, twenty-twenty, we can say that now. At the time, it was a simple matter of protocol.

As commander, Custer should never put a junior officer in a position where he could not expect to succeed. Major Reno did not have the ability to lead or protect his command even if there had only been 800 hostiles as they had originally thought. Custer should have known it and placed the officer who would have had the best chance of making the attack successful. The officer he placed in that position knew that, Major Reno and so did Captain Benteen. Officers at war were in the business of making war, killing and breaking things, not committing suicide. Major Reno could at least tell the difference even if Lieutenant Colonel Custer chose not to pay any attention to the fact.

—21—

SPECULATIONS AND GUESSES

To speculate as to what would have happened had Captain Benteen been ordered to assault the village instead of Major Reno we should expect the same result. Captain Benteen was a far superior commander than Major Reno; that should not be questioned by anyone. The man had been battle tested and tried many times not only in the Civil War but out on the plains against hostiles for years and years. Benteen's combat experience was virtually the same as his boss'. He would have met the same number of hostiles and would have faced the same difficulties as Major Reno. However, he would have handled each differently; but, in the end he would have had to do what Major Reno had done, "charge to the bluffs"; he would have done so in a more acceptable military manner. He would have "withdrawn," as opposed to "attack" with all of his men wounded and otherwise. Words and their meanings are important at such times.

The only difference would have been that rather than Captain Benteen coming to Major Reno's rescue, the rolls would have been reversed. That is an unsettling thought. He could have better dealt with the firestorm the hostiles were directing at Major Reno's command, and he would have directed orderly fire in response to their assault and he would have ensured that all his men that were alive would have at least had a chance to get to the other side of the river. His retreat would have been orderly and militarily correct.

In the end he would have had to still abandon the position he held along the river, but he would have moved his whole force at once. It would not have been the "helter skelter, grab your ass and run, boys" dash as it was for Major Reno.

Captain Benteen was a lot of things, not all of them good. One of the things he was however, was a seasoned pro that had faced withering firestorms from enemy lead. In doing so, he was always the coolest head in his command. He had faced nerve shattering situations many times before and knew what to expect of himself. For him, he was like his boss, daring someone to shoot him. They, the enemy, would not have even considered it, least wise they really make him angry.

Major Reno had zero experience with being shot at. Captain Benteen would have made a better stand at the river causing a longer delay for the hostiles to get back to Custer's attack down Medicine Tail Coulee. What would have happened had Benteen made the charge instead of Major Reno is purely speculation.

Within only minutes of his initial contact, Major Reno decided in his military mind that to stay in the trees amongst so many hostiles trying to kill him personally and all who looked like him was a sure way of getting his mama's son and his command destroyed. He simply got on his horse and ordered G Troop to follow him; most of those men tried to do just that, at least those with horses tried to comply. That left Moylan's A Troop and McIntosh's M behind to catch up when they figured it out, that those of G Troop had bugged out.

The line of "attack" through the hostiles meant the men and horses had to navigate the jump from the banks of the river into the water below. They did not have the luxury of a ford to assist the horses or men to cross.

Several things were wrong with this path Major Reno decided to "charge" on. The first was he left two-thirds of his command behind him in the trees with the hostiles. Second, the charge to the river was about thirty yards long before the horses had to literally jump and fall six to ten feet to the river below. Next, they had to navigate the river. At the point where they jumped into the river, it is just deep enough to make them swim for a ways because they could not find bottom.

The men had to plot a course up the steep banks on the east side of the river once across. Not one of those tasks is impossible to accomplish in and of themselves. However, while the men "charging" are struggling to stay saddled on their horses after leaping and falling into the river, the fighting did not stop so they could successfully escape. The fighting and the firing intensified all along the perimeter as the hostiles saw what was happening.

The men had to fight off the hostiles trying to pull them off their horses as they mounted them and made for their escape. Once horsed, those soldiers who could find horses were being shot at from both sides of the river at the same time. It had to be one of the most harrowing and frightening experiences seared into the memory of each man who had lived to tell about it.

Just as some of the soldiers reached the other side of the river young First Lieutenant Donald McIntosh, commander of G Troop, has his horse shot out from underneath him. He had just about reached the relative safety of the other side of the river and began climbing up the steep bank to get to flatter ground so he could continue his "attack."

Unhorsed now but otherwise unhurt, he crouched down attempting to avoid detection in the higher grass and thickets waiting for the next horseman to come by. Soon, another rider came up the slot that McIntosh had used and the young officer grabbed on to the rider's boot and stirrup nearly pulling both the horse and rider on top of him.

Both the rider, a man from his own company and horse managed to regain their balance with McIntosh still clutching the man's leg. Together, the three of them tried to get away from the bank and thicket.

At that point McIntosh lets out a scream as a bullet rips into his back, almost instantly he loosens his grip and tumbles head over heels to the ground. The rider never looked back to see if he was dead, the trooper just knew. He heard the scream and saw the blood spout from the man's back. To stop and see if he was would be near instant death for the rider.

Back home at Fort Abraham␣␣Lincoln poor little Molly, the lieutenant's wife, now his widow, would be one of the many who would get the news that their man had been killed. She, like many that day, would receive a pension of $30.00 a month until the end of their life. In Molly's case it would be thirty-four years later that her days would end, however, her life really ended that day when her Donald was killed, she never remarried.

It is not difficult to see how one would tend to get a little distracted. Picture yourself trying to load a weapon while trying to stay horsed. At the same time you are kicking at and swatting at naked, or half dressed screaming, demons out of the way as you try to attack in another direction. All the while, the soldiers were trying to follow their leader—who was running full speed away from the fight. It would have made for a perfect nightmare. It does not take many distractions like that to make a lot of good brave men turn tail and high tail it to somewhere safe.

Once on the west side of the river, the "charge" was resumed to the bluffs, nearly a mile away. The troopers were fighting hostiles all the way…many were losing both the fight and their lives. Upon seeing G Troop charging to the river, the remaining men left in the trees on the west side of the river instinctively searched out something to "charge" on with the rest of the command to wherever the troops were "charging."

To the troopers, these now, newly-tested Indian fighters, taking any available horse whether the owner needed him or not, had now become mission number one. The fire wall began to slacken as the men retreated freeing the hostiles on those still left without horses in the woods almost before they could blink. The ones they caught had their heads whacked and nearly flattened with solid stone headed war clubs, or their torsos filled with arrows or bullets.

Major Reno screamed for his bugler to sound the "charge" (retreat). Before the man could get a full note out the end of his horn, his face exploded into a red mush. Major Reno again ordered "charge" verbally, at a very high shrill voice. The command (only those few soldiers closest to the major) responded to the "charge" order. Those men who heard the order and still left alive and were able to respond, grabbed the first horse they could get to. They knew that life would be short if they remained in the valley another minute.

Still others did not have the where withal to do any thing but try to defend the ground they stood on. Many of the men, trying to maintain troop integrity in the trees and brush along the stream did not hear the order. Those who heard, or saw the other men leaving the skirmish lines did the best they could to get out of the instant hell they had escaped into.

Those men who still had horses made a beeline to the river to face the same dilemma as the men in G Troop had faced only moments before. The rest of the men ran on foot trying to cover themselves as best as they could as they too "charged" to the east away from the hostiles to their front. The tree line that ran along the river was filling with hostiles.

All of the hostiles at that point were bent on killing *wasichu*, and all those with them, the scouts and guides and anyone else that traveled with this unlucky lot.

Within minutes of Major Reno's second attack, and the hostiles counterattack, twenty-nine enlisted men would be killed, mere moments, literally. Seven more were severely wounded either during the attack or once in the woods, but somehow these seven had managed to still stay horsed. Somehow, they would manage to get away when the command "charged" toward the river bank and finally up to the bluffs above the river.

By the time Troops A and M caught up to Troop G now on top of the bluff, at least twenty-two more men would be missing, and presumed dead. These men, one of whom was Lieutenant DeRudio, his real name was John de Sylva.

It is not clear even at this point whether someone "borrowed" the lieutenant's horse to charge with Major Reno or whether his horse was killed or stolen by the hostiles trying to kill those still on the wrong side of the river.

It did not matter at this point in time, the lieutenant was horseless and that was decidedly a bad position for him, an officer and gentleman, as proclaimed by an act of Congress, to be in. Lieutenant DeRudio was not a popular man in the regiment by either the officer corps or the enlisted men.

Taking his horse, if that is what happened, would have been payback and good riddance as far as either of these two groups would have looked at it in this situation.

It just so happened that he was one of the group of men, the twenty-two troopers and scouts that were listed as missing and presumed dead. All of these men were on more or less equal grounds; rank meant nothing in this situation. If they were going to continue to breathe they would have to do it on their own.

As a group, they had a lot in common, though they would not know it during the entire time, they were trapped in the valley; they were all without horses; they were all without food; they did not have ammunition and could not have fired anyway even if they would have a boxes of ammunition, or had lost their weapons all together; and they all were totally defenseless in an area teaming with hostiles.

These twenty-two men would have to fend for themselves either individually, or as groups of two or three hiding together. They would not know even if they, in the groups of two or three, or even as individuals how many men where in the same position as they were. All they knew was that they were trapped in like fish in a barrel in a valley full of red-skins and cut-off from what was left of Major Reno's command.

What was left of the command had abandoned them and its location was only a guess at best. Somehow, these men would survive the rest of the afternoon and into the night. Amidst hundreds of hostiles and their women and children swatting the brush looking for survivors to finish off or slay and then mutilate any that they found. These men would sweat out the time, they had no choice. Some of these orphans would see their fellow bunkies killed and often as not, literally butchered in the process. They would hear their cries for help, their begging for mercy, and hear and see the aftermath of a world gone mad before their very eyes.

By grace only, these twenty-two men would scale the bluff over looking the Little Bighorn River, one by one. Miraculously, these men would show up on the bluff just out of view of the hostiles guarding the river. In groups of twos or threes, or even individually, they would slip into Major Reno and Benteen's earthen and carcass-rimmed perimeter early the next morning.

They had spent the night hiding between fallen dead trees and thick brush next to the river, or lay hidden in the rotted and hollowed-out trees along the river. A few had only escaped by lying in the brambles of wild blueberries and choke cherry bushes, or dog hair of young seedling box elder and cottonwoods. A couple had even had to get into the river itself and slide under the concave banks of the slow-moving stream to avoid detection.

In this valley fight of Major Reno's, the hostiles literally just sprung up out of the ground. They were not just in front of the troops, they were among them before they could get turned around, or do anything but what they did—run.

The Army does not like the term "run." The more militarily correct term, "retreat" is an orderly process by which the retreating force does so, while facing its enemy, and returning fire as it withdraws from the line in an orderly and military fashion. Grabbing your ass and running away from the fight has a bad connotation to it. Running means you are a coward— you turned tail and skedaddled as fast as your legs or horse could carry you.

Let me tell you, these boys ran as though their very lives depended on it—and that was exactly what those left alive tried to do.

A few of the trooper's horses went mad. It was never determined how many men died when their horses bolted toward the enemy. Eyewitness accounts indicate that there were a few who were that unlucky. Who would have had time to count how many?

Horses that are not used to seeing naked, fearsomely painted creatures screaming at the top of their lungs and rising up out of the ground, waving blankets, and shooting at them at point-blank range, have a tendency to spook anyway. Some of the survivors mentioned seeing poor ol' what's-his-name get run into the Indian camp on a crazed runaway animal. Of course, that was the end of ol' what's-his-name; nobody ever saw him again. If that was not bad enough, these demons attacking the troopers scared the bejesus out of all the *wasichu*.

It was one thing to attack an enemy not unlike yourself, that is fighting the same way you fought; it was something altogether different fighting naked and half-naked, painted-faced demons jumping up and yelling in their faces. All of the sounds associated with the fight in the valley would have made any man perhaps doubt his manhood. The blood curdling screeches aimed at giving the red-skinned attackers strength while sending fear and trembling into the hearts of those being the victims of the surprise must have sent some of the horses over the edge also.

Some of the horses went to bucking, and throwing their riders into the midst of this horrific scene. Some of the inexperienced riders simply fell off their horses, or where clubbed off their mounts by hostiles riding right beside them as they tried to break away.

Others, less worldly, would try to just surrender. That was dumb—

what was an Indian going to do with a prisoner? One quick whack with a stone mallet or a U.S. government-provided ax between the eyes took care of the stupid ones quick. The Indians took to beating the frightened troopers with their bows or buffalo-hide whips that knocked several *wasichus* out of their saddles. Once on the ground, those not killed before they got there were brutally killed as they begged for mercy.

The Indians did not give mercy this day. As a matter of fact, it was not a notion ever very popular with the red race; they did not take many prisoners. If they ever bothered, it was usually children, or every now and then, maybe a woman, but not men prisoners—for what could, or would, a white-man prisoner serve?

Perhaps, in Major Reno's military mind then, this was an "attack." Whatever it was that he did, he would call it forever after and refer to it as an attack. It worked at least well enough for him to escape death at the hands of the hostiles sneaking up on his men along the west side of the river. To put a better face on the "wild-assed retreat" it really was, apparently did not matter to anyone who accepted Major Reno's version of the fight in the valley. If the goal of the escapade was to get "the survivors to the bluffs east of the river" the "charge" did that.

If it was to pitch into the hostiles so Custer could support Major Reno's attack by attacking behind the encampment, it did not. It did not get close to doing that. After successfully "attacking" to bluffs, and from there securing the earthen bowl the men dug by their bare fingers, tin cups and plates, dead horse carcasses, and scrub bushes, anything else that might stop a bullet or arrow. At times like those, even normally rational people become highly irrational. Yes, they even tried to hide behind bushes. Major Reno went about deploying the men he had remaining in his battalion well enough to hold out until Captain Benteen showed up nearly two hours later.

For the hostiles' part, they were not stupid. They still respected the *wasichus'* bullets. It was easier to stay out of range of the soldier's carbines and shoot at will at the scared stiff soldiers with Winchester Repeaters complements of the Indian Agency representatives. A bullet once fired does not discern who it hits, buffalo or *wasichu*.

—22—

CAPTAIN BENTEEN'S INSIGHT

To listen to or to read what Captain Benteen thought of that situation afterwards, one would think otherwise. In Lieutenant Colonel Custer's mind, command had everything to do with rank structure, and military protocol. Major Reno simply outranked Captain Benteen, and it was rank that counted in combat's chain of command.

Obviously, Captain Benteen thought differently. To his frocked mind, he knew Lieutenant Colonel Custer was out to take the glory for himself while leaving poor ol' Captain Benteen out in the cold.

To Captain Benteen, Custer did not need a reason to be accused wrongly. He had enough sins in his past that being wrong now did not matter. If the captain could make his commander, and especially this particular commander, look bad, he would.

Lieutenant Colonel Custer's troop's path from the bottom of Medicine Tail Coulee to the end of Battle Ridge is four and nearly a quarter miles further. The distance is mostly all up hill, at a very steep grade. From where Major Reno's command was then holed up on the bluffs overlooking the river and the southern end of the encampment the distance would have been about the same as the way the crow flies.

Between Major Reno's point of attack along the river and Lieutenant Colonel Custer's attempted crossing at Medicine Tail Coulee there is a gap of nearly two and a half miles. This "gap," as it is sometimes called, occurs because of the bend in the river at the point of Major Reno's attack, and the ridge line from there toward Medicine Tail Coulee.

The back side of this ridge shielded Custer's battalion as it moved north, away from where Major Reno last saw Lieutenant Colonel Custer. Along this ridge as it retreats from the river is a relatively high narrow bench shelf. It runs along the east side of the river until the coulee divides the bank, and it empties into the river below.

The bench itself could not have been easily traversed; it is narrow and heavily thicketed. It would have been almost impossible for a man on foot to move on, and would have been impossible if the man, on a horse, tried to move along its brush-covered shelf at anything other than a slow walk on the horse's part and even then it may have impassable. Facing the coulee either from the right of it, north, the terrain rises abruptly and forms a long steep climb to the ridge top perhaps a mile away. It would have been nearly impossible for a man on horseback to go up without nearly falling off the animal either over the horse's back or just to bail off because the horse faltered. This type of country runs along the east side of the river until the river bends back to the flatlands of the Little Bighorn valley, emptying in to the Powder River basin. But it is that strip of bank– almost one and a half miles long–cost Lieutenant Colonel Custer the most in terms of time and tactical covering fire support as he attacked down the coulee. With every man trying to escape the frightful scene below him, just getting out of the coulee, would have seemed no minor miracle. The hardest part unknown to those successful would be what came next, the mile long climb to the top of the ridge.

The ridge line is what Lieutenant Colonel Custer thought was shielding his movement to the north end of the encampment. Once there, he must have planned he could storm down the coulee, cross the river and smash into the back of the village, taking it by sheer 7th Cavalry horsepower.

What actually happened is he led his command into a trap as cleverly devised by the hostiles as the one sprung on Major Reno. Only the hostiles did it better in his case. The battalion Lieutenant Colonel Custer led would be surrounded on all sides for as far as the *wasichu* could see, and there was no way out.

The 7th's only chance to escape was to climb out of the coulee and try to hold out along the ridge line. Only then, if they had time to get up to the ridge before being overtaken and run down by the warriors hot on their tails could they form a skirmish line to lay down a covering fire. Some of the men might have thought that for about twenty minutes. That is all the time they had left on this earth.

Looking at what the soldier faced, perhaps, puts a different face on what those who have trouble visualizing the weightiness of the matter at hand. As far as what nearly half of the 7th Cavalry had to deal with that hot, dusty Sunday afternoon, they simply had entered into hell.

Custer's men did not have Major Reno's men with them. They did not have Captain Benteen's battalion to support them. In terms of manpower, what Lieutenant Colonel Custer faced as he attempted to cross the Little Bighorn only multiplied exponentially because of the disaster Major Reno had walked into and almost out-of-hand and had unwittingly participated in his commander's defeat.

For Major Reno, the battle lasted from around noon, when he initiated his initial attack to the arrival of General Terry and Colonel Gibbon's forces his inferno would continue for another two full days. For Custer's force the final shot was fired into the head of the last man in that battalion before 1500, 3:00 in the afternoon, at the very latest.

The survivors of Major Reno's charge and then later after Captains Benteen and McDougall's troopers arrived, though they did not know it at the time, were all trapped. The firing would be heavy and accept for the soldiers who were getting picked off or wounded with astonishing regularity no damage on the enemy had occurred.

There would be no fighting after dark. Indians did not normally fight at night. In fact, the hostiles kept near banker hours during their siege. They knew the soldiers would need water for their wounded and for the men themselves. All they would have to do is wait for them to try to get to the river so they could kill them one at a time, or however the soldiers tried to get to the river. To the hostiles, this was not very sporting or interesting, and many just got tired of it and left the matter to the younger braves to take care of these pests. It did not require the time or attention of the older men.

—23—

THE HOSTILES TAKE CONTROL

The hostiles had made no move to overrun the now fortified force after Major Reno and his men got on top of the bluff by early afternoon of the 25th, nor would they. In reality, the hostiles made no attempt at rushing the holed up men at all. They simply did not have to, where were the *wasichus* going to go? If they rushed the survivors of Major Reno's battalion, there would be a very good chance that some of the hostiles might be killed in the ensuing fight.

The hostiles may have been Stone Age men to the *wasichu*, that did not mean they were stupid. They could afford to hang back. The hostile sharpshooters could kill the careless *wasichus* that had burrowed into ground that they had dug themselves into and simply wait them out.

Their strategy was to wait the troopers out and if they would not make a break for it to the south, southeast they had little to worry about. Had the *wasichus* tried to escape using that route, the hostiles would have them out in the open and they would be easy prey. With their horses all dead and no water, they would be easy to run down and kill if that is what they wanted to do. They simply decided to play cat and mouse with those left alive and in time they would see what would happen.

Instead, they chose to shoot long range from a long a ridge that runs just north and a little east of the soldier's location. The soldiers hunkered down behind the dead horses and mules that they had killed and were using their carcasses as breastworks, waiting for an eventual attack.

On the bluffs the hostiles had a decided advantage over the fear-ravaged *wasichu*. They held the high ground and could sharp-shoot anyone who got careless inside the earthen dish. They did so with surprising efficiency. Sixty-five men would be wounded here during the entrapment, most all from what was left of Major Reno's command.

When Major Reno's force was fortified by Captain Benteen's battalion at what would seem the last moment, when everything looked to be lost by what was left of Major Reno's men, the men cheered as if the second coming of Christ had appeared to them. Major Reno's men were nearly out of ammunition, literally down to their last few rounds per man, when Captain Benteen's battalion came bursting into the perimeter of Major Reno's little earth fort from the southeast.

Where he had been, or what he had been doing since 0800 that morning did not matter now to Major Reno or his men at 1500 in the afternoon. What was important was that he was there and his three companies of soldiers were relatively fresh, they had not fired a shot all day. Nor had they been nearly frightened to death in the terrible valley fight. With Captain Benteen would be the full ration of ammunition that his troopers had carried with them.

Captain Benteen would have seemed a hero to all of them in the entrapment. There would now be plenty of ammunition for everybody at least for a while. There would even be some water that could be shared amongst the wounded men who had gone without for most of the day. Together, Major Reno and Benteen's forces would have totaled about 225 men, almost the same number as had ridden with Custer.

When Captain McDougal arrived after 1600 with the trains and ammunition packs it would seem that the problems were over. He brought with him another fresh 146 men. Now, the seven troops of cavalry had some strength, the co-joined force would swell to over 370 men. Plus, McDougall brought food and more ammunition, nearly everything they needed to hold out until Custer could get back to them, or General Terry got to the battleground except for one thing—water.

The fortress now was nearly overflowing with men and horses. On the one hand that was good, on the other it was decidedly bad. Many of the men had no place to hide from the savage heat beating down on top of them or from bullets and arrows flying into the confines of the earthen fortress. The hostiles were laying down a gulling fire and would keep it up until well after dark.

The officers and men probably never thought about it at the time, but what they had done by all locating in one place was trap themselves. What would have happened had the hostiles taken out after either General Terry or General Gibbon's commands they knew they were on their way? They could have defeated either or both of these commands the same as they just had the 7th Cavalry, had that been their thinking.

These men holed up on the bluffs would have been like rats on a sinking ship. They were anyway, the hostiles knew that. It was only a matter of time to the hostiles. The *wasichu* saw it differently.

As for the hostiles, they considered it much differently than the *wasichu* did; at least, that is what Sitting Bull said later. Sitting Bull said he wanted the *wasichus* to escape in the direction that Captain Benteen had advanced on the site. The old chief said that he would have let them leave in that direction only. The strategy was once they had gotten away they could tell the other *wasichus* what was ahead of them if they continued after the Indians in the encampment.

Whether or not the old chief was talking in his beard or not has never been satisfactorily answered. The important point was their leaving, or escaping, however one wants to describe it was a path these survivors could have used to get away; they just never did, the idea never really was considered seriously. The Indians had won the battle of their minds also; they could afford to wait on the soldiers' souls.

For the Indians' part, they could wait out the troopers and their leaders. They could continue shooting them one at a time, and not having to lose any men in the process. All the Indians had to do was stay out of range of the soldier's carbines and pluck the troopers off one at a time as they went for water or got careless and stuck their heads up to long.

Except for some sharpshooter's taking rather strenuous target practice on the morning and afternoon of the 26th along a ridge looking down into the bowl Major Reno and Benteen were stuck, the battle was over. At sunrise, on the 27th, the soldiers noticed that the last of the encampment was seen leaving the valley by the south. At nearly noon that day the remnants of the 7th Cavalry were relieved by Generals Terry and Gibbon's commands.

LAST RIDE

Those men who were relieved must have felt betrayed and abandoned as time past, as they waited for some message from Custer. As General Terry's and Gibbon's columns moved down valley a great cloud of dust followed them as they moved toward the battlefield from the north.

The first men seeing the force at first thought it was Custer's command coming back for them. Then others said, "No, it could not be them."

They would conclude it was simply another trap to get them out in the open so the hostiles could destroy them all at. They had been trapped once; they did not know Custer's command had faced the same dilemma, and rather than face that possibility happening, decided to take their chances and just sit tight.

Afterwards, it was deemed a ruse, just a mind game the Indians had won with their white enemy. The hostiles did not plan an ambush on the *wasichu* still on the bluffs because the *wasichu* had closed the escape route themselves, mentally; never attempting to get away.

On the afternoon of the 25th, Captain Benteen and his command reached Major Reno's beleaguered command sometime shortly after 1500. Captain McDougall reached the combined command just an hour later, about 1600. The last man in Lieutenant Colonel Custer's command fell sometime around 1400 maybe as late as about 1500.

Captain Weir's attempt to attack toward where he thought Custer's men were occurred about 1700. What Captain Weir saw was not the general's command, but warriors wearing dead troopers' clothing and riding their horses in celebration of the great victory. It was no ruse, but these guys, the survivors, would have believed anything.

To the Indians' way of thinking, getting all of the blue coats holed-up in one place made it all that much easier. They had them all where they could keep an eye on them. To the blue coats what happened during the next was two full days of pure unadulterated Dante's hell.

A curious aspect of the terse order is it presumes Captain Benteen and Captain McDougall had reformed as one unit, bringing that wing of the command to 321 combat-effectives. Along with Lieutenant Colonel Custer's nearly 212-man force, it would have been a combined force of about 533 soldiers and everybody associated involved in the attack on the encampment at Custer's point of attack at the river crossing.

It seems obvious the lieutenant colonel had ordered Captain Benteen to join up with Captain McDougall, and get back to where Custer was to be at the head of the Medicine Tail Coulee. That would put the reserve force close by before the general began his own attack at what he would think was the northern end of the encampment.

Though it was true McDougall's troop was attached to Captain Benteen's battalion, they were not operating in tandem together. It would not be until after 1600-hours that they would affect that link-up. It would only be then that Captain McDougall and his jackasses would finally make it into the perimeter of Major Reno and Benteen's defenses on the bluffs. The south east side, the side that stretched to the foothills of the Wolf Mountain had remained open all this day.

Of course, the *wasichu* would not have expected this and had thought it was a trap. Their thinking was that the minute they exposed their commands or open packs and trains to this open space, they would be all routed and killed out in the open. Which if they had thought about it for even a minute, they already out in the open. These men in Major Reno and Captain Benteen's commands and now even Captain McDougall had imprisoned themselves in this large earthen dish that they had carved out largely by their bare hands. They were encircled physically and mentally. They could have ridden out of the area at any time they chose, they just did not believe it, and fear would not allow them to even dare think it.

Up and until Captain Benteen and his command entered into the breastworks that Major Reno had tried to prepare with the carcasses of the animal's he had shot could have been anywhere from five to ten miles away from Captain McDougall's mules and horses and "ammo packs." McDougall did not know his location and had not sent anyone out to find him. By the time McDougall located the bluff that Major Reno's command was defending. Captain Benteen and his three troops of cavalry had been in Major Reno's support inside of the bowl for over an hour.

Author's Note: My hunch is Lieutenant Colonel Custer's force would have probably been wiped out in the village rather than where it was. In other words, it would have made not one wit of difference in the final outcome of Custer's fight that was yet to come. It would have probably been worse in terms of troops killed. Captain Benteen and his battalion would have also been wiped out to the last man. Captain Benteen would not have backed up any better than his boss did.

During the Civil War there was a term that the old timers had used when they had new boys with them going into battle. The old timers had told the young recruits that they would "see the elephant" if they lived through the next fight. The meaning of course, "seeing the elephant" was the feeling of shock and horror that they were about to experience would remind them of "seeing an elephant" for the very first time. They would never forget such an experience and if they were lucky enough to live through the grinder they were going into in the upcoming fight and they would understand. Of course many of the rookies did not live through the next fight, but the ones who did, understood from then on what the old timers meant.

Well, Captain Benteen was an old-time veteran who had not only seen the elephant, but socked the beast on his nose a time or two. There was not anything that got to this crusty, gutsy, veteran during the Civil War except the loss of his boys. He hated that for them.

Lieutenant Colonel George Armstrong Custer and his boys had taken their last ride; they just did not know it when they went down the coulee.

It seems at this exact point in the time warp some tremendous gaps in the testimony on the part of Captain Benteen, Major Reno, and the other officers with those two commanders were never fully questioned or the explanations not fully cross examined at the time of the Court of Inquiry.

As it was, Captain Benteen made it back to the point where the regiment split earlier that morning about 1400. From that point his command followed the sound of rifle fire to find Major Reno. Along much of the way he could see were they were as his path put him on higher ground than Major Reno and his men held.

His command joined Major Reno's command about one hour later. On his way into the defensive position he quickly sized up the situation and seeing that Major Reno was about at his wit's end, he quietly took charge of what was left of Major Reno's men and began deploying his own boys in defense of the saucer-like earthen dish Major Reno's boys had literally hand-dug, and were then holed-up in.

When one walks over the ground on Major Reno's Hill, one cannot help but be surprised by the size of the earthen dish, and the fact more than nearly 400 men, horses, mules, and wagons could get into such a small area.

The problem—unbeknownst to the one-time attackers and now defenders—was, of course, that the hostiles were expecting them down in the valley, had known of their advance and followed it from Fort Abraham Lincoln until that day. They did not know who came a knocking that Sunday noon, it would not have mattered. They sprang on Custer's force what he had always done to them—surprise! Custer's entire command, plus Major Reno's command, had walked into a gigantic well-planned ambush. Had the force remained together, they would have been wiped out to the last man.

That would have left Captain McDougall's troop to fend for themselves. They were still far behind the battle area waiting to be called up. Those men would have tried but they would have lasted just long enough to all get killed in about fifteen minutes.

Before attempting to enter the Medicine Tail Coulee and attacking the village, Custer had sent two messengers. First was the command's Sergeant Major William H. Sharrow; he delivered a verbal message to both McDougal and Benteen. He was dispatched with a verbal order from the commander that Benteen was to follow the sergeant major back immediately and to join up with Custer and his command. The rank of sergeant major would have attested to the earnestness of Custer's order.

This sergeant major had been the top sergeant of the 7th Cavalry for four of his eleven years of service. He was an outstanding soldier and he was totally dedicated to his boss. Without a second's thought about what

LAST RIDE

he had been ordered to do, "Find Captain Benteen and get him and his command back here as soon as he can get here," the sergeant major wheeled his tired horse around and took off in the direction of where he thought he could find the captain's battalion.

How Sergeant Major Sharrow ever found the captain without getting killed at least three or four times along the way attests to his cunning, courage and intestinal fortitude. The land between where he was and where he thought Captain Benteen was supposed to be was infested with hostile Cheyenne. He finally located the command and gave his message to Captain Benteen.

Captain Benteen asked the sergeant major to stay with his command and lead them to Custer's command. Sergeant Major Sharrow, who was no fan of Benteen's declined the offer and hurried back to join his commander. That would be the last time he would be seen alive by anyone else in the 7th Cavalry.

Almost before the sergeant major was out of sight after leaving Custer's side, the lieutenant colonel asked his brother, Captain Thomas Custer to get another courier up to the front of the column and to deliver the same message to Benteen in the event that Sergeant Major Sharrow did not get through.

Apparently, the thought occurred to the commander that the first man that had been sent, Sergeant Major Sharrow, might not find Benteen or worse be killed before he could find him to deliver the message. By the time Captain Benteen could have initiated the link-up with Captain McDougall's reinforced troop, and then set off to find Custer's battalion, literally hours would have gone by.

In fact, seven hours passed before Benteen and his battalion linked up with Major Reno at the top of the bluffs. It would be eight hours before McDougall could link up with Major Reno and Captain Benteen's position. That was as far north that they could go towards fulfilling the order of "come quick." That was four hours and four miles too late to do Custer's command any good.

—24—

CUSTER'S BATTALION GOES A-HELLIN' TOWARD DESTINY

The Medicine Tail Coulee is a long, fairly wide, sharply descending ravine. This particular day, in late June 1876, the ravine was powder-keg dry. At the mouth of the ravine it is perhaps one hundred feet from side to side at the top of the ridge where it is born.

This overgrown ravine (coulee) begins with short, steeply sloping sides that run from the top rim of the ravine down to its bottom at the river's edge. From beginning to end where it empties into the Little Bighorn River, it runs unencumbered for nearly a mile. In other times, it would put one to mind of a roller coaster run. It starts kind of slow, and then picks up speed as it nears the end. Sometimes, the sides of the coulee are just a few feet high, and at other places perhaps twenty feet in depth.

Riding down the steep recline of the coulee leading to the river below on horseback could be accomplished fairly easily. If a man on horseback took his time, and allowed his horse to lead the way this would be an easy task. The run is fairly steep at the top, though on that day, a horseman could have navigated this natural chute perfectly well even at the gallop, or perhaps, a near full run near the river's edge.

Over millennia of snowmelt and rain runoff, silt has built up in the river below forming a natural ford crossing the river at the river's edge where Medicine Tail spills into the river is at best, ankle deep. The river seems to nearly come to a stop as it plays over the slowly-rising river bottom at this point.

At its deepest point, in the middle of the natural ford, it is no more than four feet deep. The river catching the runoff from this coulee is not much in terms of rivers like the mighty Yellowstone River, or even the Powder River, into which it empties several miles to the north. Compared to these rivers, the Little Bighorn River is an orphan child.

At the top of ridge where the Medicine Tail has formed itself by cutting this natural chute, the sides of the coulee are steeply sloped. The last one or two feet along the rim of the coulee are nearly vertical. It has been eons since snowmelt and runoff chiseled out this oversized gully.

Since that day in 1876, when the 7th Cavalry blazed it for glory's sake, perhaps never again will enough snow or rain runoff fall to wash a way the memories that died in its dust and wild grasses here where the earth meets the big sky.

At several places along its run the sides try to squeeze together. The coulee bottom appears at first glance to be nearly flat and smooth; it is not. The dry buffalo grasses and prairie sage and wild flowers disguise the unevenness of its floor. The ground on the bottom of the coulee is uneven; undulating is perhaps a better word. Beneath the vegetation is sandy and loose sand mixed intermittently with loose limestone rock. Sometimes, out on the floor of the coulee, nigger head boulders and near petrified tree stumps lie hidden beneath the tall grasses and wild flowers. The vegetation in the coulee in late June on the high plains was tall, fragile, and golden dry.

It had been a dry spring, and the flora was getting a head start on curing itself out. Before the troops descended the coulee, it looked much like what a dry-lander would expect a dry creek bed, (which it really was) to look. If, in an effort to get out of this drainage in a hurry, a man on foot would have less trouble than a man and a horse trying to navigate the same up its steep and loose dry sides.

When Custer's battalion came upon the mouth of the ravine at its point of origin, it must have looked like a clear-cut road in the wilderness. To the Lieutenant Colonel this natural road to glory must have at first appeared to be heaven sent. He was sure that once on it, it would lead him to the northern end of the hostile camp.

In actuality, that was what the coulee was to the general, a highway. He was wrong of course; it was not the road to the northern end of the encampment. This natural break between the ridges would be, instead, a highway to a hell to which he and his men had never known.

From Lieutenant Colonel Custer's perspective, he was fast running out of time to support Major Reno's —with or without Captain Benteen and his men— attack nearly a mile and a half away to his south. The Lieutenant Colonel would think this natural road down to the river and across it was perfect for his purpose.

Lieutenant Colonel Custer's battalion began to move down the Medicine Tail Coulee and into glory at nearly 1245. Only thirty to forty-five minutes had passed since Major Reno began his attack on the southern end of the encampment that afternoon, Sunday, June 25, 1876, church services were about to begin.

Within minutes of moving his command about halfway down the coulee, the Lieutenant Colonel came to a small rise and for the first time saw the hostiles' encampment in its entirety for the very first time. He was shocked at what he saw for the first time! What his Crow and Ree scouts had been insisting lay in front of him was really there. Down in the valley below, going in both directions, were hundreds and hundreds of Indian lodges. This was the encampment that in the dawn's early light from the crow's nest he could not see. Only an Indian could see fifteen miles way. His scouts had said it was there. Sure enough, here it was, right in front of him! As he broke in to a clearing mid-way down the coulee, he quickly scanned the area up and down the west side of the river.

He realized, perhaps for the first time, he had miscalculated his location. The path he was on would lead him straight into the center of the largest Indian encampment North America would ever see. He made his decision instantly.

Stretching out in front of the Lieutenant Colonel were more than 2,000 teepees stretching for two miles in either direction up and down the river. He immediately ordered his troops to halt and called for Tom, his brother, to get a courier to send a message to Captain Benteen.

The first rider was the command's sergeant major, John Sharrow. He told the sergeant major to find Captain Benteen and get his command back as fast as he could.

The sergeant major moved off at the run, covering the close to eight miles, maybe even as many as ten miles, to find him on an already worn-out horse. He found the captain and relayed Custer's message. He turned and started to return to Custer's command when Captain Benteen asked the top sergeant if he shouldn't stay with his command and they could all return together.

Old timer Sergeant Major Sharrow did not think much of Captain Benteen and had gone through the command's enlisted men and told them to pick sides; as for his money, it was on "Old Curly" and they better make sure whose side they were on or they would be on his toilet paper list. Without stopping or even turning around in his saddle the old tough Sergeant Major about faced and moved away from Benteen's command and returned to his boss's side. It would be the last time these men would see their sergeant major alive.

The time it took for Sergeant Major Sharrow to search out and find the captain would have eaten up perhaps an hour may be more. However long it was, or short, for that matter, the Lieutenant Colonel grew more and more impatient. He sent a second rider with the same message. Shargeant Major Sharrow also stopped at Captian MacDougall's trains and told him to get moving toward the Medicine Tail Coulee.

Before either of the messengers can return, the Lieutenant Colonel ordered Tom for another rider to deliver the same message. As luck would have it, trooper Giovanni Martini, alias John Martin, detailed from H Troop, visa-via the volunteer from the Regimental band, and is collared by the younger Custer.

Trooper Martin was obviously the closest trooper to Tom, and the young Italian was ordered to follow him to the commander.

John Martin did not speak or understand English very well, even a little bit—neither George nor Tom seemed to remember this rather important aspect about the man—but they did know he did not speak English well. Lieutenant Colonel Custer ordered the trooper to take a verbal order to Captain Benteen.

Private Martin, Martini, had been assigned to H Troop, but that morning had volunteered to go with Custer as a messenger or extra bugler should one be needed. Lieutenant Colonel Custer's executive officer, Canadian-born W. W. Cooke, seems to be the only one that had a better idea and thought better of the idea about sending the verbal order with someone who did not speak English. Besides, written orders have more weight in a court martial if it came to that; he did not trust Captain Benteen very much.

Lieutenant Cooke obviously remembered trooper Martin did not speak English well. Cooke wrote Custer's last order out on his note pad, and gave it to Martin for Captain Benteen.

The Lieutenant Colonel told the nearly uncomprehending trooper to go find Captain Benteen and bring him back to the spot they were right then.

"Do it damn quick, man, and bring the ammunition packs when you come back!" the lieutenant colonel would say as Martini left in a cloud of dust.

For Custer's part, he could not wait; the life of Major Reno's and his own command now depended on Captain Benteen's and his battalion's support. The lieutenant colonel had two choices: He could wait for Benteen, or he could strike the encampment there and then. He was committed to do one or the other. If he waited, Major Reno's battalion would be wiped out. If he struck where he was, his chances of success were less than good.

Lieutenant Colonel Custer did what he had to do. Gathering his chosen commanders around him for a short meeting, he would have ordered a charge, telling Tom and the other captains they are not to stop until they reached and drove the horse herds away from the hostile's camp.

In support of Major Reno's column, he forms the battalion in columns of fours and attacks down the coulee. He knew his chances at saving what he could of his own five troops of cavalry hung in the balance of Captain Benteen's return with reinforcements. By now, he and the rest of the command could hear the Major Reno's rifle fire from the south, and that spurred him on, knowing those men with Major Reno would be in over their heads—if they were not already.

Lieutenant Colonel Custer must have realized he had made a tactical mistake before he had gone very far down Medicine Tail Coulee because he could see he had not reached the northern end of the hostile camp. The unfortunate point being he did not have time to find another route to the north of where he was. Where he was then, was the wrong place. On this present course, he would collide with the middle of the camp.

The note, written by Cooke, has since become famous because of its content and terseness. It is used today as an example of clarity under stress taught at West Point, as the type of field order and message officers should give during operations:

>Benteen, Come on. Big village.
>Be quick. Bring packs.
>
>W. W. Cooke
>
>P.S. Bring packs.

John Martin, among other things was a first-class trumpeter, however, when the band was ordered to stay at the Powder River Depot four days before the fight, Giovanni volunteered to be brought along as an extra bugler or courier rider for the regiment in the field if the Lieutenant Colonel would have him.

Captain Benteen was likely as not to shoot Martini out of frustration of trying to figure out what the hell he was trying to tell him.

As for the last written order Lieutenant Colonel Custer ever gave, Captain Benteen kept the order until years after the battle. Who actually had possession of the order gets muddled—like nearly everything else surrounding this battle. At first, everyone concerned with the order assumed it had been burned in a fire in Benteen's home years after the battle.

Benteen claimed that he eventually gave it to a friend in Philadelphia. In truth he probably sold it to friend, who then sold it to a New Jersey collector who later sold the famous order to another Army officer. The officer finally gave it to the West Point Academy Library, where it rests on exhibit to this day.

How long it took trooper Martin to find Captain Benteen's battalion has never been totally established. No one seems to know if he found him just down the trail five miles or ten, which is more probable. Perhaps, trooper Martin had to hunt for and follow tracks beyond Major Reno and his command. How it was that he finally did find the good captain and his men is not clearly known.

Unknown also is, did he have to fight Indians along the way? Did he have to outrun them on his horse—that would not have seemed possible—by then his horse should have been just about all used up. If he had to hide from those hostiles going to the Major Reno fight on the bluffs, he very well may not have made it. Somehow, he found the battalion, and delivered Custer's last written orders to Captain Benteen.

Finding Benteen in the first place would have been a miracle of sorts. One can only imagine what must have run through that trooper's mind at the time he was given these orders by his commanding officer. In the first place, he had probably never seen an Indian; at least, not one who was bent on killing him and lifting his hair.

The pure impossibility of even knowing which way trooper Martin began to find Captain Benteen staggers the imagination. He would not have known even where to begin to find Benteen in this country they were now in. He had never been in the foothills of the Wolf Mountains himself. On his own he would have had no idea about where Captain Benteen was sent, much less how to get to him or what would be the best way to get to him. The trail he went on to get to him must have been filled with hair-raising excitement for this green, inexperienced trooper.

At that point in time, Custer really had only one decision to make, though he had two choices within the decision. One, attack the center of the camp and hold, and in all probability be wiped out, or two, attack, but rather than stop and fight, drive on through the camp, and hit as fast as he could the hostile's horse herd out on the flats of the Valley of the Greasy Grass nearly a mile beyond the encampment.

On the move, he immediately decided. The best way to proceed was to charge straight through the middle of the camp, driving his command out onto the valley floor to drive the horse herd away from the encampment. That would have left all of the hostiles on foot. If he could accomplish hacking his way through the encampment, it would give him time to put distance between his command and the hostiles waiting for him in the encampment and his command once on the west side of the Little Bighorn River.

The hostiles who would surely attempt to dissuade him from accomplishing his new mission. At the same time, that tactic would relieve the pressure on Major Reno's command on the southern end of the encampment. It would also put Major Reno's command on the west side of the river, the same as his, or so he would think.

Perhaps, if he could make it to the hostiles horse herd and stamped it to the west, he could then come up and affect a link up with Major Reno's men. He would still have Benteen's command as a blocking force against any hostile attempt at escape to the south. By both forces being on the same side of the river and with Benteen on the east side with the river separating him from the hostiles and with General Terry and Colonel Gibbon forces coming down from the north he would have them almost totally surrounded. The step hills on the east side of the river would be nearly impossible for the women and children and old people in the large encampment to escape in that direction.

He knew that the warriors would not leave their families; they would stay and protect the people at all costs. All the 7th Cavalry would have to dig in and hold the perimeter of the encampment until their relief arrived. With Captain Benteen's battalion coming up at what he thought would be any time after his strike through the encampment, they just might get the hostiles surrounded after a fashion.

The Lieutenant Colonel could then turn his regiment on the hostiles without fear of their fleeing from his vaunted 7th Cavalry on horseback, and hold on until help arrived. No one should ever forget that Lieutenant Colonel Custer only thought of the attack. Never would he consider that he was about to be whipped and out-soldiered, or out-generaled. When the dust cleared he needed not to have fretted about the details of the future. Unbeknownst to him, the Gods of War had swung to the other side. This was now, and storm clouds were gathering and hell had a debt that its fiddler wanted paid.

Before ordering the charge, Lieutenant Colonel Custer would turn to his brother and tell him of the change in plans. They would drive through the camp and make for the horse herds out on the flats west of the village. Tom would nod his understanding and would send a trooper with the message to be passed to the other four troop commanders behind him.

Of course, we will never know what the lieutenant colonel's last thoughts were. Anything said in that regard is pure conjecture from this point on. But, having stood on the ground several times and also having walked the same ground he was then, on that day, and having studied this battle and the men who fought it for better than thirty years, I am fairly confident what his thinking must have been.

He was, by the curse of the traitorous war gods, forced into making the previous decision, he was also forced to push on and hope for the best. It was not a new position for Lieutenant Colonel George Armstrong Custer to be in. More than once he had to adjust to circumstances beyond his control in the midst of an attack. Commanders have always had to be flexible and willing to take calculated risks that other less fortunate are allowed to even think.

It is what commanders get paid to do—think on the fly and to react to the constantly changing battle picture as they progress through the battle space. That had always been the Custer way: trusting to fate, and betting on his "Custer luck" just one more time.

He leaned forward in his McClellan saddle and charged. The "Custer Luck" was like an aphrodisiac to him; it was to him, in moments like this, an opium rush to a hard-core drug user. He believed in it as much as many of the men who rode with him that day.

—25—

CUSTER'S LUCK RUNS OUT

By that time however, what was left of Major Reno's shot-to-pieces battalion had began its devil-may-care dash "charge" through the irate gatekeepers (Unkpapa-Sioux) on the south. Neither of these two battalion commanders (Custer or Major Reno) knew what had happened to the other one at that particular point in time, nor would they have ever guessed what would happen later in the span of a couple hours of that Sunday noon attack initiated by Major Reno. Major Reno would not know for sure for another two days—he could only guess—and as it turned out, Lieutenant Colonel Custer would never know.

Later when questioned by General Terry, Captains Benteen and McDougall, the other remaining troop commanders, would intimate they had no idea of the gravity either of their brother commander's desperate situations as they were unfolding. One would be lying. In the end, it would not have mattered one iota if either had. They could have done nothing about changing the outcomes, or helping either one in any way. The die had been cast, and there was going to be hell to pay no matter what any *wasichu* did, or did not do from this point on.

Captain MacDougall's order to hurry on to Lieutenant Custer's aid was countermanded by MacDougall's commanding officer, Captain Benteen. Captain Benteen ordered MacDougall and his columns fall in behind his own command and they would continue on together. Captain MacDougall complied with those orders with out incident.

That morning each company gave up additional soldiers to swell B Troop to 146 men. That made Captain McDougall's troop larger than even Major Reno's battalion including officers. Unwittingly that depleted each of the other companies going into combat that many more men short of manpower even further for the battle ahead. At the same time, ironically, though there was no way of forecasting the future, that action saved the lives of a few of the detailed men from each of the troops who were going to be otherwise wiped out with Lieutenant Colonel Custer's battalion a little later in the day.

Many of those survivors, the ones detailed from the five troops that followed him, would be promoted and become the noncommissioned officers that would help repopulate and reform the lost companies. These men would form the foundation of the new companies when they were rebuilt at Fort Abraham Lincoln after the battle. Irony would run rampant that Sunday. Several of these men, those who were detailed from their assigned troops to form the detail to support and reinforce Troop B's main support body, would be awarded the Congressional Medal of Honor for their service during the holdout and hostile siege on Major Reno Hill.

More than just a few of those survivors on Reno Hill would be alive only because their horses had failed. In each of the commands there where horses that would not make it to the battle. Some of the regiment's horses were now in terrible shape even before the regiment deployed that last time. For Custer's battalion as many as ten troopers, mostly men from C Troop, had horses play out during the sprint along the backside of the ridge with Custer before they got to the Medicine Tail Coulee. Somehow, they had made it back just in time to watch Major Reno and his stragglers be chased up the bluff. They would meet him when he got to the bluffs above the river.

These men, six to ten of them, had somehow managed not to go with

Custer in his mad dash for glory. Either their horses gave out, or they just said, "Hell no, I ain't going down that damn death trail." If these men did just not go but instead, cooled their heels and waited to see how things turned out. Perhaps, these troopers became the country's first unofficial Indian war protestors.

Which of these explanations was the most accurate has never been determined. I suspect a couple, or perhaps even more in that group, may have decided continuing on with the Lieutenant Colonel was not going to be particularly in their best interests in terms of healthy things for them to be doing on that particular Sunday afternoon. As for the men they could have been branded as cowards. That was not always the case, for when they finally did get into the Major Reno perimeter at least two of them would be awarded the Congressional Medal of Honor for their part in defense of the wounded men. At the end of the day, the one thing they knew for sure was they were alive, while some of their bunkies probably were not.

At the time Major Reno's fight in the valley commenced, Captain Benteen was some five to ten miles southwest of Major Reno's command. Captain McDougall and his reinforced B Troop, was even further away in terms of time if not distance. Lieutenant Colonel Custer's battalion could have been at least twelve or thirteen miles further away from Captain Benteen's force at that time.

Again, McDougall's supply wagons and trains would have been even further behind because of the time it would take to move the same distance because of the obstinate, ears-laid-back, wild-eyed, cantankerous mules that were hauling the ammunition packs, wagons. In addition to the "trains," his drovers had to move the spare horses up to the rest of the column when it was safe. He was at least ten miles south of Major Reno and twelve or fifteen miles, perhaps further, from Lieutenant Colonel Custer's battalion when Custer's men hit the bottom of Medicine Tail Coulee in an all-out, balls-to-the-wall attack.

For Captain McDougall, it was not so much the distance from his commander, but the time that it would take to get the mules with the packs up to the battalions that were being engaged. Captain McDougall would have had only the slightest indication of what was going on several miles to his front. The riders who went in search of Captain Benteen may have also found McDougall along the way, and generally informed him what they had told Benteen as well as what they may have known about the tactical situation as they knew it when they left Custer's side. It would have been a fluid, rapidly-changing picture to be sure.

Captain McDougall had no idea about what was transpiring just a few miles ahead of him with regards to Major Reno. He knew Benteen had been sent on a scout to the southwest of their line of march. He knew Major Reno had deployed to attack the village gate. He would have also known the Lieutenant Colonel and his command had moved off to the northeast of Major Reno. He may have even seen the command split into two different directions when Major Reno went toward the river, and Custer skirted around the ridge line to the north.

Past that, he did not know what was happening at any one place on the battlefield other than where he was. All that he knew for sure was that his pack trains containing the ammunition and other supplies would be needed—but he had one real serious problem, his mules.

In the meantime, somehow, trooper Martin-Martini, found Captain Benteen. At the gallop, he was perhaps hours away from Custer, at the trot, maybe more. Using that as a measuring stick, it would have been at least 2:30 PM before Martin reached Benteen. By then, Custer and his force are gone, blown away by the hostiles they had attempted to defeat.

Captain Benteen is clearly out of earshot of Major Reno's firefight, and will never hear the goings-on with Lieutenant Colonel Custer as his command strikes the river almost two miles further northwest than Major Reno's command. After delivering the message, Martin started to return to Custer's side. Captain Benteen stopped him, and ordered the Italian to fall in with his H Troop, and they would all go together. Of course, that is the only thing that saved Trooper Martin's life. It was not Martin-Martini's desire to stay with Benteen, he was ordered to, and not knowing what to do did as he was told. Sergeant Major would have just laughed at the captain and kept on going—sergeant majors are different cats.

As for the written order received from the commander, Captain Benteen put it in his breast pocket, "right obliqued" (about-faced, turned around) his command and moved back to the point from where he split his battalion from the regiment earlier that morning.

Here was the situation as Benteen would have known it to be: He had no idea where Major Reno was, or for that matter, where Lieutenant Colonel Custer was, and since trooper Martini could not tell him for sure because he did not speak English very well, he did the most logical thing for a commander in the field to do when faced with this situation. First, to protect his force, and second, to proceed with caution in an effort to comply with his orders. And that was what he did. No one can argue with any of that course of action.

But damn, he moved slowly. Oh God, was he slow!

To Captain Benteen's way of thinking, he was being prudent. First, he sent outriders to protect his flanks, next he sent out scouts to lead his column's point back to where they had come; then he set out trailers to cover his column's rear. To some, it may seem Captain Benteen may have dallied getting back to his original starting point.

Benteen had already marched his horses and men more than twenty-five miles that day alone. Then when Sergeant Major Sharrow found him, he about faced and marched back at least another ten or so miles, just to get back to the "trains." The facts being what they were, Captain Benteen, it could be argued, did what he should have done. He moved with caution, as quickly as he dared, based on what he knew at the time. From what Sharrow had told him, he would have expected to see a cloud of Sioux and Cheyenne, as thick as ticks on a coon dog's ear, coming over every hill he came to.

Who could argue with that? He had a perfect alibi, if he needed one, later—and he would.

Human nature, perhaps, makes us think Captain Benteen thought his commander had gotten himself into something he damn well should not have. In his stubborn mind he might have thought that, whatever the lieutenant colonel had stumbled into, he could get out of it on his own.

Captain Benteen could have let Custer stew in his own juices if it would have just been him to do the stewing. Even if he had thought that, above all else, Captain Benteen was a soldier's officer and he would not have spurned Custer's men to get even or teach his commander a lesson that he should have already known. But then again, considering the vitriol and disdain he felt for his commander, and the way he was as a man, it must have sure been tempting. You figure it out; to me it was a flip of the coin; heads, I go fast; tails, I go not so fast.

When he finally got back to the starting point of that morning, he followed the tracks the rest of the column made earlier that morning, and about five miles from there saw Major Reno on the bluffs overlooking the valley filling up with Indians. At this point, he would have been to the south-southwest and moving to the generally northerly-northeastern direction. That would have put him more or less in line with the bluff where Major Reno and the survivors of his command were heavily involved with the hostiles. Those hostiles that had finished with Custer's force by then began to close in on what was left of Major Reno's command. Benteen could see they were just barely hanging on by the barest of margins.

He moved on to where Major Reno's position was, without having to fight his way in from the south-southeast end of Major Reno's position. That portion of the battlefield appeared to be wide open. He had in the meantime dispatched riders to Captain McDougall telling him what was going on, and he should hurry as soon as he could to the point were Major Reno's command was.

—26—

THE BATTLE PLAN RUNS AMOK

After sending Major Reno's battalion into the lion's own den to kick the sleeping simba to get things going, Lieutenant Colonel Custer makes what was to become one of several miscalculations he made that day and the day before.

The result of this mistake was, of course, a real-life double nightmare for Major Reno's command unfolding before their very eyes. It would not have mattered if Major Reno struck the encampment with twice the number of men that he had and somehow sustained the attack. The outcome would have only been made worse in terms of men killed and wounded. Had Major Reno had two hundred men, the odds he faced would have been something approaching 8 to 1 rather than the 16 to 1.

On a short rise above the hills that all but hid his command, Custer watched as Major Reno moved into position to attack. As Major Reno to begin to initiate the attack, he saw Custer wave his hat over head to him just as he ordered the charge. Custer's headquarters staff gave a great hurrah, turned their horses north behind the cover of a ridge, and galloped away, still never seeing the immense size of the camp just beyond the hill to the right front of them that Major Reno had been ordered to attack. The encampment was still two and a half miles north of where the Custer's battalion was then.

As for Lieutenant Colonel Custer, as far he knew, Major Reno's attack while maybe not going to be totally successful, he figured that the affair would buy him some time. If he hurried, at the gallop, he could get to get north end of the camp and he could start his own attack.

First, he misjudged how long it would take. Custer thought he could spring a compound attack against the camp, catching them in between Major Reno's and his forces. Next he misjudged the lay of the land, and in doing so he made, perhaps, his most fatal of mistakes here. He thought he could initiate his own attack sooner than he did.

Custer would have never dreamed it would take him so long. Nearly thirty minutes would go by just to get to the end of the valley they were in. Another twenty minutes would go by, in order to get to get to the bottom of the Medicine Tail Coulee. He still would not have attacked the village. He would have to cross the river and then form his columns to hit the encampment from what he thought would be its north end. Lastly, at this juncture of the campaign, he had not considered a most important issue to a cavalryman, his horse.

These animals had been on the trail for over a month and during that time had been ridden over three hundred miles. They had been on one-third rations since leaving Fort Lincoln and in the past week had only had brackish water for drinking. During the last three days, the regiment had moved almost 100 miles, and had been on the move almost constantly day and night to just get to where they were then, at the summit of judgment day, June 25, 1876.

In other words, just getting to the soon-to-be battlefield had used up much of the horses' reserves. Now, with the battle imminent, the horses may not have enough in them to sustain their riders through the fight that was ahead. Many have argued that the horses were in good shape, having lived on a farm and ranch and having ridden stock to move cattle for a number of days on end; I doubt that. The horses were far from being prime for what lay ahead of them and their riders.

"So far, so good," the Lieutenant Colonel must have thought, he would attack them from behind, and finish them before they finished off Major Reno. He would hit them where they were not looking, he thought, from behind. Down Medicine Tail Coulee he went with a shout, "We got 'em now, boys; follow me!" The men followed with a great hurrah!

His command's horses' hooves were throwing dirt clods and raising a huge cloud of dust as they raced down the ravine. He would barely make out the sounds of gunfire coming from his left, or where Major Reno's attack was going on. He would not have known it and never would guessed those men were fighting for their very lives over the sounds of his own command's horses.

He had entered into a zone by this time that would not have allowed into his mind any alien thoughts. He was zoned in only on what he had to do. Unfortunately, he would not notice the hostiles further to his left on their way to the Major Reno fight as they went by. He would know Major Reno's command was having a whale of hard time of it. It would not be long now, and he would be in support of Major Reno and his command.

In so doing, perhaps, he would once again catch the evasive glory he so desperately craved. It was right at his fingertips, it was his for the taking, he could taste the sweetness of victory from a hard-fought victory…almost, but there was work to be done first; it would make victory all the more sweet.

It may have seemed a strange way to support your subordinate commander—moving away from the sounds of the battle just on the other side of the ridge but that was the general's plan. At the bottom of the coulee, Vic leaped into the Little Bighorn River; Lieutenant Colonel Custer could see the part of the village rising up right in front just over the bank on the far side of the river as Vic and he splashed into the river.

"Hell," he must have thought, "this village is huge; there must thousands of the red buggers here—not just hundreds."

He did not see all of them, of course; if he had, he very well may have turned and run back up Medicine Tail Coulee as fast as ol' Vic could have gotten him back up.

Some of the hostile war chiefs had considered the natural river forge would be an avenue of attack, and had gone there with men and hidden them at the river's edge in the underbrush along the slow-moving river just in case what was happening, happened. Almost grinning in mid-river, his face was set in grim determination. He felt the bottoms of his boots being splashed wet as he and the big mare waded through the deepest part of the ford. He yelled to encourage his horse, "Come on, Vic, push harder; give me all you got, a little further, and we'll be on dry ground."

By most Indian accounts, he did surprise the hostiles, but only because of the speed that his troops got to the coulee, and started down it. In the end it would not matter; they were waiting in ambush for him.

But, alas, the biggest surprise may have been what happened next. It was obvious he thought he could divert some of the pressure on Major Reno by attacking where and when he did, and he did accomplish that. He saw at once as he came down the coulee the camp spread far to the north and he was going headlong into the center of the encampment.

He would not know the die had been cast and he was about to be the next casualty. Lieutenant Colonel Custer initiating his attack when and where he did, in a roundabout way, did give Major Reno's command a little breather. In fact, it probably saved Major Reno's command from being wiped out. At least it provided enough of a respite for Major Reno to get back to the other side of the river, and then make his wild-assed retreat to the bluffs overlooking the river, and what relative safety that would afford. Little did the Lieutenant Colonel know then, or would he ever know once he started across the river the gig was up. It was a perfectly-laid trap, and he had charged cleanly into it.

About the time he would get midway across the river, the hostiles hiding in ambush opened up—on him first—for he was always out in front during an attack. With one of his British Bulldog pistol drawn and raised overhead, he led, unknowingly, his last charge. Several of the Indians in ambush would open up on him as their main target—he was like a sitting duck in one of those old-time carnival ponds.

Only one want-to-be warrior would hit his target; his name was Brave Bear, barely fifteen summers old. Brave Bear would aim straight at the lead man's chest, just as his father had advised him, for he had never aimed at or killed another human being before. Brave Bear closed his eyes (this target was so close he could hardly miss) and squeezed the trigger. The rifle's roar was so loud it hurt his ears. In that instant, the round made for killing buffalo slammed into the Lieutenant Colonel just as he started to turn around in his McClellan saddle to encourage his boys behind him. The round stuck before the young brave heard the old gun roar; rather, he felt the kick in his shoulder first. Rather than hit the lieutenant colonel dead in the heart as the young lad had planned and aimed, the round would catch the Lieutenant Colonel nearly broadside in the lower left side of his chest. At the angle of the entry wound, the lieutenant colonel sitting astride his mare would have been about three or four feet higher than the shooter.

The old Sharp's buffalo gun fired a .45-.70 caliber round. In the past, the former owner of the hand-held cannon, though now long dead and his scalp adorning someone's scalp pole, had dropped many a buffalo at far greater distances, some even upwards of over a mile away. But now, the round had traveled less than thirty yards before striking near its mark.

Sure, it was a lucky shot; not many people could hit a moving target with their eyes open, much less closed, but the results were the same as if he had been a Rebel sharpshooter with a scoped rifle at a thousand yards. The impact of the slug hit with such force it nearly catapulted the lieutenant colonel over backward off of Vic's back. The force of the round drove through both lungs and exited out the right side of his chest, then tore into and shattered his right arm.

One of the self-cocking Bulldogs the Lieutenant Colonel had carried since the Civil War whirled harmlessly high into the air and fell, disregarded, into the water beneath Vic's hooves.

It was as if a rope had been stretched in front of him, literally flipping him upside down over Vic's broad flank. The lieutenant colonel never knew what hit him. He would not feel the round that tore through him, or any pain associated with the breaking and tearing of bones and flesh. He would have been surprised at the cool stream slapping his sweat-weary face when he landed unceremoniously upside-down and headfirst into the river beneath Vic's powerful legs.

He was dead.

—27—

ALL HELL BREAKS LOOSE

At this point in the attack, a very strange thing would take place the instant after the Lieutenant Colonel was hit. The attacking force, now less than 200 men strong, would just stop. Fewer than fifty men of the force had entered or were preparing to enter the river, only a few were beside, close to him or directly behind him, when Brown Bear's shot hit him broadside.

No one, not even brother Tom, who had ridden with him since joining the cavalry in 1862 some fourteen years earlier, or even George Yates, his childhood friend who had been with him for nearly ever, had ever seen him even limp after a fight. His friends, Myles Keogh and Smith would have never expected such an astonishing thing as their boss getting hurt.

He had even managed to shoot his own horse in the head once by accident while out shooting buffalo (obviously not the one he was riding that day or Dandy, his favorite; he had several). He narrowly escaped injury from that event, and later, narrowly escaped adorning some teepee with his scalp when a war party happened by about a mile from where the mishap occurred. Waiting with bated breath, the lieutenant colonel sat by his dead horse until a patrol picked him up.

During the Civil War he had many horses shot out from under him during battle. Some say as many as seventeen horses where killed beneath him, three on one day, but he had never been shot off of his horse.

He'd had only one minor injury in all that time; a piece of shrapnel had cut into his right thigh during a charge early in the Civil War. Ever to use his time wisely, the then Captain Custer finagled a thirty-day convalescent leave back home to marry the love of his life, Elizabeth "Libby" Bacon, and to go on a short honeymoon, before resuming his "war." Past that and the time a bull buffalo tried to gore him while he was riding it down to kill, he was injury-free.

But that was then, and at that moment, while attacking the village, he was hit and was face-down—not a good sign. The sight simply shocked everyone in his command to a sudden stop. The impact of the slug was as if he had been slapped by a giant fly swatter from his horse's back. His brother was the first to react to the general's demise. They were nearly right beside each other at the time. Tom characteristically was always beside the general.

In a flash, Tom was off his own horse and pumping his legs as fast as they would carry him through the nearly waist-deep water to get back to his brother, who was now floating lifelessly face-down in the river. By the time Tom got to his brother, other men had ridden ahead of the two men down in the water to protect the rescue of the commander. The telltale sign of the seriousness of the wounds were evident in the red-colored water churning around the injured man's lifeless body.

Swinging the man face-up, Tom stared into the general's face, looking for signs of life. "Autie, Autie," he would scream at the blank and glazed-over eyes. No sound would leave the Lieutenant Colonel's lips. He was fully unconscious or dead—Tom could not tell which; if not dead, life fading quickly from his body, bright red blood was bubbling out of his two chest wounds onto Tom's chest and arms as he held his brother.

With tears filling his eyes, Tom had seen enough wounds in his time to know that his brother had "bought the farm." Tom, seeing the blood flowing from the wounds and the lifeless expression on his brother's white face, was instantly brought back to reality with sounds of gunfire becoming more and more intense to his front. He grabbed the reins of Vic and, with a Herculean effort, Tom just barely got his brother's body flung over Vic's broad back. He would not leave his brother to be butchered by these fiends who were now jumping into the river to fight the men protecting him and the commander. He led the horse to the east side of the river while other men protected the two officers with their own horses and bodies.

The firing from the far side of the river grew in intensity; those hostiles already in the river began shooting point blank into the soldiers in the river and on the other bank. The hostiles' fire was being answered with volley shots from the front columns of troops. Not many shots could be fired in the configuration that the battalion was then in. It was not enough to slow the red men down and they were gaining the advantage of the lack of converging fire that the front fours could manage.

How could so much go so wrong so fast in such a short time? Less than ten minutes have pasted since the Lieutenant Colonel entered the river? Now, the entire column was stuck where it now was. The men in the rear companies did not know what had happened or why the advance all of sudden went dead. They could hear the sounds of the carbines and Winchesters being fired. All they knew for sure was that something had gone wrong and the column was like the ribs of an accordion on the inward push, they were collapsing on top of those men in front of them. If that was not enough, some of the soldiers could see the hostiles moving in on their left flanks. These were the hostiles who had crossed the natural forge on moments before in an attempt to beat Major Reno's men to the top of the bluff. When they heard and then saw that Custer's men were coming down the coulee behind them, the warriors reversed their course and attacked them from the side.

Poor Lieutenant Sturgis' horse started to spook when the firing broke out along the river. At the morning meeting of the officers he had been detached from M Troop and ordered to act as Captain Custer's second in command C Troop. The poor horse and rider were a perfect match for one another. Neither the beast, nor the man, were used to the gunfire or the screams and sounds of battle. The Lieutenant's horse bolted, taking the young shave-tail officer into the bowels of hell—thankfully, death came quickly for the young man.

Young Jack had barely been a month out of the Academy. His father was the actual commander of the 7th Cavalry and would blame Custer for his son's death. For his part in the matter, Lieutenant Colonel Custer was way past the point of caring at this instant in history. The body of young Jack was never recovered—it did not any longer exist, except in pieces.

As the intensity of what was occurring in the river reached almost a riotous scene, another horse bolted toward the Indians, taking that rider to his instant death among the attacking angels of death.

Tom, leading the way back to the east side of the river, was trying to direct his C Troop's covering fire for those men still in the river. Captain Smith and his F Troop had witnessed the river action before ever getting into the river, and had already directed his troop to unhorse and provide a covering fire for the now-fleeing men.

Troops E and F tried fighting a delaying action while the other three troops started back up the coulee only to be stopped by the red mass coming up from behind them. The men in those two troops were the ones who would pay first. Nearly twenty-five percent of both troops would be killed within fifty to seventy-five yards of the river's edge. There, the bodies, or what was left of them, (after the women and elderly had had their way with them) would be scattered from the river to nearly 200 yards back up the coulee, and the sharply-rising slope leading to what is today called Battle Ridge.

It would be as close as Custer's command would get to the encampment for the rest of the day. During the madness going on around them, the soldiers in the lead troops tried to reorganize themselves and form a protective firewall. Those men still horse-backed had the toughest time; three or four regrettably green-broke horses bolted and ran into the village, their riders of course to suffer a similar fate as Sturgis. All of these men were killed instantly and mutilated when they were yanked from their saddles. These men would never be identified after the battle—they no longer resembled men but instead were just pieces and parts of what were once the bodies of men. Several of Tom's Troop C men would be killed in their valiant try to keep the hostiles at bay as their troop commander got his brother back to the east side of the river.

The two troops of cavalry, E and F, tried to hold back the red waves of humanity that can only be likened to a tsunami literally smashing over those closest to the river. The skirmish line attempt was useless. Just seventy-seven men stood against this first onslaught of 1,200 warriors. Each and every one of them bent on destroying every *wasichu* they could get their hands on. Killing the *wasichu* would not have been enough. These men were going to be brutalized when they got their hands on them.

The encampment was emptying out like a beehive of swarming killer bees after the proverbial honey bear. These red men came literally boiling across the river to overwhelm the soldiers on east bank of the Little Bighorn River. Only a few of this first wave of warriors were on their war ponies. Nearly all at this point had not even had time to put their war paint on, adorn their horses, or grease and braid their hair. Many had not had time to dress appropriately as a warrior should when he goes to war. Some merely stripped naked, picked up their weapons, and took off for the sound of the gunfire. They would be joined by hundreds of other warriors, all headed in the same direction with only one thought on their minds: Kill the *wasichu* who had dared attack their village.

The attackers-now-turned-skirmishers braced for the first wave as best as their sergeants had taught them. Those soldiers brave enough, or too shocked to move as they watched the spectacle unfolding before their very eyes died quickly. There was nothing brave about the way they died. They were literally torn from limb to limb, dead or alive.

Those men further back from the river and up the side of the slopping hill who could run, did. They mounted their broken-down horses and tried to get on up the steep slope. These men going up that hill with a tired horse were not going to outrun a warrior on foot. What they would accomplish, though, was to add a few minutes to their lives. Some of the men's horses broke loose from the holders, leaving the troopers on foot—these men too died quickly, either by the Indians arrows or club, or by their own pistols aimed at their temples or hearts.

It would not matter which, dead was dead.

Man after man, line after line of troopers would try to form—only to be trampled beneath the feet and unshod hooves of the Indians' war ponies or overtaken and killed. No skirmish line could be established for more than a single un-aimed volley by the frightened troopers.

As the troop commanders withdrew from both the river and over the north side of Medicine Tail Coulee would order a squadron sergeant to deploy a short skirmish line. Time after time, as each line would try to set up, they would be quickly flanked, attacked from the rear, or simply overwhelmed and smashed by the onslaught at their front. Soon these men realized that no matter what direction they tried to set up, to stop and face the enemy and fire a volley into the flood coming at them was near instant death.

The Indians were playing a game with the soldiers; it was as old as man himself—cat and mouse. You stop, you die; you run, you live a little while longer, maybe. Nearly half of the troops in E and F fell at the hands of their enemy playing this deadly game. Surprisingly, the hostiles reported that many of these *wasichu* fell by their own hand, or at the hand of a bunkie.

—28—

KEOGH TAKES OVER

Captain Keogh's "Wild Eye" troop was stationed directly behind Smith's F troop when all hell broke out at the head of the column. Quickly scanning the terrain and his troop's rear, the Irish-born mercenary sized up the situation immediately. He could see other warriors coming in through the trees and attacking on the column's left flank. What would have surprised him most was that so many were now not only forming on their exposed left flank but the column's rear was starting to take fire.

It was obvious that things up in front of the column were not going well. But, he and his men had not even fired a shot yet and a couple of the boys had been shot out of their saddles just sitting where they were in column. From where he was he could see what was going on. Those men still in the river were the only ones keeping the commander and young Tom alive for the next few minutes. The time those poor brave souls stole from the Indians by staying put and fighting as best as they could, would be all the time the rest of the men would ever get in that lifetime.

These men, perhaps only four or five now, would be named as missing in the next roster call. Their bodies were never seen again.

In a blink of an eye it seemed, the hostile force was now growing exponentially by the second on all sides of the command except one—the north. Hundreds of the red demons were now in the river, and hundreds more were somehow coming down behind the troops still in the Medicine Tail Coulee. Keogh realized that if the command was to survive, it would have to make a break; they would have to get out of the coulee and make a run up the steep sides of the ridge, running to the northeast of Medicine

LAST RIDE

Tail Coulee.

It was a hard way to go, but it appeared to him it was the only way out of this death trap that they were now in. The terrain was very steep, and while the footing for the horses was solid enough, the horses were beginning to play out. They had put in a day of marching already and it was just now not even 1:30 in the afternoon.

As for the men with Custer, they would never know those hostiles coming down the coulee behind them were the same ones who had been fighting—or were on their way to fight Major Reno's men in the valley nearly at the same time. These warriors flooding down the coulee now and up the river on the east side of the river had heard the firing, and had gone to the sound of the gunfire, compounding the force the soldiers had to face.

It would not have mattered how they got there—there was no need for answers now, only debts to be paid. The pony soldiers were going to pay off their debts today, in full.

At the river's natural ford, the hostiles seemed to almost be fighting themselves to get into action. The few soldiers still alive on the banks of the river were still trying shield the command as they withdrew from the ford. Their pistols long since empty, these desperate men may have taken to clubbing at the hostiles with their carbines, trying to keep them at bay. The matter was settled quickly as each soldier was either shot at point-blank range or became a living pin cushion for the hostiles' arrows that would be let loose on them.

Those men still trying to stay in their McClellen saddles were repaid by being pulled from their horses and hacked to death, turning the gentle Little Bighorn River into a river running red with the blood of the dead soldiers.

During the past twenty minutes of the fight, surprisingly, only one or two warriors were killed here while literally hundreds of shots had been fired by the *wasichu* during that time.

Those soldiers who were lucky enough to withdraw to the far shore ran headlong into the hostiles coming down the coulee behind the now-doomed command. Many of these men where filled with arrows, or clubbed to death, or just outright shot and scalped before they could get turned around to answer the hostiles' fire and wrath. These men would be in near panic as they made their way out of the coulee and then up the side of the steep ridge in front of the Little Bighorn River in order to put distance between them and the enemy behind them.

Those left on the near side of the river to cover the withdrawal were doomed—it would not matter; when the hostiles got to them in the next few moments their pain and fear would ironically end. The stark terror each man would feel in the mere seconds he had left in this world would make the moments seem like cruel, horrifying hours.

Without a moment's hesitation, Captain Keogh automatically assumed command. He was not the next ranking officer in the battalion, but he took charge after Lieutenant Colonel Custer went down. For Keogh's part, though his Indian-fighting experience was sorrowfully limited—he would not need more; more battle experience with the Indians would not matter now. What mattered now was that someone kept their wits about them and got as many men as possible back far enough away from the enemy to form some kind of defense to take advantage of the trained firepower they still had left.

Captain Myles Keogh had been a warrior's warrior nearly his whole life. War was war, and fightin' was fightin', even a hardheaded, tough-talking Irishman knew that. Keogh was as tough as they came, and he was just mean enough to try and do just that, if put in the position to do. Picking up the mantle of command was not something alien to the man. He had been in more battles than anyone else left in the command, and he was good at giving orders.

The problem was he was fresh out of choices. His ever-shrinking force could not escape from the overpowering force that was now closing in on three sides of him and the men. The last side the north side of the coulee was quickly filling with hostiles. He and the troopers would have to make a break now and try to get to the top of the ridge or die where they were.

There was no front, the hostiles were rolling up his flanks and killing his rear-echelon skirmishers before he could get any kind of sustained line of fire established. No sooner would he get a line of skirmishers assembled, than the Indians were killing them; or, the poor bastards (the troops) were killing themselves. The only way out was to run out on to the sloping ridge and then back along to the ridge top to the northeast. Hopefully from there they could get north to the end of the ridge where they might affect an escape with what few men he could get out of the entrapment.

For the next forty-five minutes, the time it took to get out of that damnable coulee and up the side of that miserable slope, Captain Keogh would direct the withdrawal. He would be cut off from Captains Smith and Yates who were still struggling with the hostiles coming out of the camp. He would deploy each of the troops he had left just long enough for the others to get a few yards farther before having to reform the rear guard. It did not take long to see that this tactic was not going to work if he was going to save the as many as he could. There were just too many warriors in amongst his companies to get cleanly away and the hostiles were starting to catch up with the front of his retreating men.

It would not be long, and he would be out of maneuvers and tricks and lastly, troops. Captain Keogh had been a brevet general cavalry officer during the Civil War for a reason—he, like his now-dead boss, had no fear in his heart. When pushed hard, whoever did the pushing had better be ready for trouble—for Keogh would strike like a two-headed rattlesnake at the closest target. Today, however, even though he had that same fighting spirit and grit that builds in a fighting man's chest in a fight he was beaten before he ever got started, he was smart enough to see that.

—29—

CAPTAINS SMITH AND YATES PULL OUT

Captains Smith and Yates, commanders of E and F Troops had been directly behind Tom Custer's C Troop when it hit the river. They had seen their commander go down and Tom Custer jump into the river and retrieve the body. Almost mesmerized they watched the younger brother flop his brother into the Vic's saddle and casually lead the horse to the other side away from the hostiles.

Captain Yates grasped the situation immediately and ordered his troop to deploy across the bench leading down to the river and to provide covering fire for Tom and his command. Captain Smith being a part of Yate's light battalion followed suite. These commanders had pulled out of the coulee and deployed as covering fire for C Troop as it made its way back up the coulee and out onto the sloping terrain just north of the coulee.

No one had to tell them what to do next, these men were old hands at laying down a covering fire. They ordered their sergeants to do what they wanted done. They understood if they stayed a second longer than was necessary that they could loose not only their commands but that the rest of the retreating companies would be totally exposed from the rear. How much time they could spend keeping the hostiles back or at least slowed down until the battalion could get up to the ridge top was down to mere minutes. Twenty-five percent of the men in each of these troops would be killed within five minutes of trying to form a skirmish line.

Captain Yates and the lieutenant colonel had always been close friends. Seeing his life-long friend fall must have shattered the man. Men of war get used to seeing men get killed; normally it just comes with the job—seeing other men die. After a while a man may start to believe it will always be someone else who will be killed. Men get used to, even callused to death and can almost act as if it did not happen if they see enough of it. As for Yates and Custer they had fought the Civil War side-by-side for four long years. They had ridden thousands of miles across the plains and chased hundreds of Indians in the years since. All that while through all those fights and hard times they had been constant companions and the closest of friends. Even their wives were like sisters.

A couple years before, the two had even taken out life insurance policies, together with all of Custer's inner circle, as a lark. The men saying then those insurance policies were a pure waste of money, the women thinking perhaps, something else. Keogh, always one to out do everyone else took out a $10,000 policy on his life (double that of anyone else) and named the beneficiary as himself. That of course would not work and his brother who was still in Ireland would get the policy paid in full.

Like Yates, Smith's troops while mostly foreign-born, they were the pride of the regiment. Custer ever one to build espirit de corps among the 7th Cavalry had ordered that all troops would as near as possible ride color matched horses. Smith's Troop was given the grays. They were the most distinguishable of the all. Gray was not a common color for a horse then or now. As such they were supposedly the best troop in the 7th. At a distance the horses looked almost white, easily the most distinguishable in battle. It was a way to instill pride into the untested regiment. Smith's troopers were known as the "Gray Horse Troop," Troop E, McDougall's old troop. It had changed only recently when Lieutenant McDougall had been promoted to captain was transferred to command B Troop.

All of the soldiers' mounts were nearly exhausted, and had not wanted to leave smell of fresh water. It had been three days since the horses had been watered with anything better than the brackish water they found in the Wolf Mountains.

—30—

BREAKING OUT OF DEATH'S GRIP

The moment would pass as C Troop withdrew from the river's edge, followed by Keogh's "Wild Eye," and the general's own brother-in-law, Lieutenant "Jimmy" Calhoun's L Troop would bring up the rear. Outside of Tom, his brother, and George Yates, "Jimmy" the Custer's closest friend. Lieutenant Calhoun had married Margaret, the colonel's little sister only three years before.

Lieutenant Calhoun was blond and six feet tall, quiet, and reserved. He owed his commission, and command of a troop to the lieutenant colonel, his brother-in-law. He had been a non-commissioned officer during the Civil War. He said once if the time ever came when the Lieutenant Colonel needed him, he would not be found wanting for a better man. His time was coming, soon. Whatever their relationship with the commander was, it did not matter. All of their fates were sealed.

Within minutes, the hostiles were hacking and butchering the men closest to them as they attacked the fleeing *wasichu* who by this time were staggering up the hill leading away from the river. Here and there the pony soldiers stood their ground, barely getting off a few partially-aimed shots. They died where they stood, some before they could even get off a second shot from their single-shot carbines. It was only minutes before the officers tried again to distance themselves from the demons charging headlong into the now-rattled men and frightened horses.

After only a few minutes, both Yates and Smith ordered the troopers to disengage and get what was left of the troops back in the saddle. Those who could get to their mounts did. Those who could not either killed themselves where they stood, or let the Indians save them the effort. Little more than half the men survived from both troops—they would not last another hour.

The troopers with Smith and Yates tore up the side of what would become known as Battle Ridge, trying angle off to their right to cut off the distance Keogh's Wild Eye, Tom Custer's C Troop, and Calhoun's L Troops were going along the west side of the ridge line. Try as they could, they could not close the distance put between them while they covered the retreat.

Riding to the north, about 300 to 400 yards from the river now, they were angling toward the line of retreating soldiers maybe a quarter mile further away. They had gained a little distance between themselves and the hostiles. Now the problems were that those hostiles who had been on their way to Major Reno and his battalion were running their troopers down.

The Indians were somehow getting between them and the rest of the command. Captains Smith and Yates continued up the slope they had to cut further to their left, drawing them toward the river in order to avoid running into the hostiles that had wedged themselves between them and the troops of L, C, and I. The hostiles had cut them out of the herd as neat as a cowboy cuts a critter from the herd for branding. The closer they swerved toward the river the more hostile fire they encountered from warriors pouring from the river and up to where the troops now were. They had to turn away from that course that they were then on and try to go straight toward the rest of the command. That meant that both horse and man would be worn out as the grade in this area of the battle space was particularly steep.

Try as they might, the men could not outrun the enemy. Now the hostiles were literally riding among them, kicking soldiers off their mounts here and there for the warriors on foot to deal with. The further they went, the more hopeless it seemed to become. The only way to escape what was behind the troops now was to continue to flank the slope as soon as they could and make a break away from the hillside covered with thousand of hostiles to the north east. Just as Yates and Smith's troopers started to come around the northern base of the hill that at its top would become the site of what is now called Custer's Last Stand Hill, they would see what Captain Keogh and Captain Custer were yet to see.

Unsuspecting and totally shocked, what was left of Smith's and Yates men saw them first—nearly 2,000 more Indians waiting to attack. The Ogalalas' war chief, Crazy Horse, had gathered his braves at the northern end of their encampment and had moved a mile or so down the western side of the Little Big Horn River before crossing at another natural ford. Then he worked back up the hills on the east side of the river to the point that Captains Yates and Smith were then trying to withdraw to. By the time the pony soldiers got there, Crazy Horse and his warriors were there to greet them.

Captain Yates took his command of two companies on a diagonal path up the side of the hill that would become known as Battle Ridge. Because of the path that they were on was easier once they reached a small saddle between the Battle Ridge and the next run of hills to the north of Battle Ridge. When Captain Yates and 1st Lieutenant Smith got to the saddle, they saw the Crazy Horse's warriors waiting *en mass* for them and the others not yet to the northern edge of the ridge. What the two officers saw stopped dead in their tracks as it did the few men that were with them.

They all knew what was in store next. The end was near and that they had come to the end of any hope of escaping to the north. Almost as if not accepting what they saw, or perhaps, not ready to quit, some of the men headed up the side of the hill just below Battle Ridge–this little teat like knoll would become known as Custer's Hill.

This was not the time to waste thinking about being dead or alive. The two troop commanders just had time to do something that might get them, and their men out of this situation. They could see though going farther was useless. The further they cut to the northwest of the ridge the more Indians they faced, and the more that were coming up the hill trying to cut off all avenues of escape by continually striking their flanks and getting closer and closer to the soldiers.

Captain Yates would halt his F Troop, and somehow manage to form a skirmish line in a small saddle running northeast to southwest nearly 400 yards from the top of the Custer Hill. Smith's men fell in with those of Yates' troops and formed up with them to try and establish a skirmish line facing the hostiles who were only two hundred yards away and as luck would have it and as the hostile war chief had planned it, just out of range of the cavalryman's carbine.

Only a few men, perhaps as few as six or seven went running up the side of the hill that would become their final resting ground.

The Indians sat just out of range of the carbines, waiting. Those with the Winchester repeater rifles could pick the soldiers off one at a time with impunity. The soldier's carbines were no match to the range and fire power of the Winchester. At the same time the warriors started closing in, using the gullies and ravines to shield their movements from the soldiers. By laying on their backs or sides the hostiles could shoot arrows into the huddling mass without fear of getting shot by some lucky *wasichu*.

What was left of Yates Troop had become isolated from those survivors with Captain Smith. These men would make a dash to a deep ravine just to the south of their current position. Once there, perhaps they could hold out a little longer or even escape unnoticed by the warriors.

—31—

THE DEEP RAVINE IS A DEATH TRAP

It was a bad idea, once in the ravine it became evident that they were indeed trapped like fish in a barrel. No sooner had the few men from Yates and Smith's troops clamored into the ravine than the warriors, who had been working their way up from the river below to the ridge top unseen, attacked these unsuspecting soles. Things did not get better at that point for those men now trapped in the deep ravine; they truly had nowhere to run. Once the soldiers still alive realized that the ravine was full of warriors a few had tried to climb up the steep sides of the ravine only to be shot in the back by the warriors in the ravine with them or being drug out of the ravine by the warriors waiting for them at the top. These men wasted what life they had left fighting or simply trying to surrender to the hostiles.

Back up the ridge, somehow Captains Smith and Yates had managed to bring what was left of their commands up to tie in with Keogh and TW Custer's men.

L Troop was totally gone, all had been killed. Remnants of TW Custer's C Troop and Keogh's Wild Eye and the few men that Yates and Smith had drug up the hill was all that was left. Those still alive could see what lay ahead of them if they continued any further than where they were. A few minutes before Smith and Yates got to the top of the hill Lieutenant Calhoun's troop had been literally swamped out in the middle of the prairie as it deployed along the ridge. They also witnessed that rather than fight to the end, the men that were left, perhaps as many as a dozen, maybe a few more, simply turned their weapons on themselves, or, were standing in groups and shooting each other before the Indians could get to them. So befuddled and astonished were the hostiles that they just stopped and watched Calhoun's soldiers' final act of desperation. Though the largest of any of the troops in regiment, it was also packed full of men who had very little service time and were largely green to the ways of the West.

The Indians as a people did not even have a word in their vocabulary for such things as an individual among their people taking his or her own life. But to see mass suicides as they occurred amongst these *wasichu* simply stopped them in their tracks. These men would hardly be worth scalping to the warriors on that portion of the battlefield. Those who came later to this place would not know what the warriors had witnessed and they would take care of scalping these spiritless *wasichu*.

What Keogh and TW Custer may have thought as they raced along the ridge top of Battle Ridge was that maybe they could escape out into the northern end of the plains ahead that they could get the command or what was left of the command out of harms way. From where they were at that time it would not appear to be any Indians at the end of the ridge. It was a chinch that they could not go back toward where they had come, especially after they had just watched Lieutenant Calhoun's men fall. The only avenue left was that at the end of the ridge. Perhaps, when they got there, they could strike to the northeast and get away with what was by now a pitiful few men.

—32—

THERE IS NO ESCAPE

The two captains, Custer and Keogh, might have just started to relax if Captains Smith and Yates had not reached the northern face of battle ridge before they did, and saw what was waiting for them on the next hill and what would be their front when they got there —1,500 more Indians. The problem they would encounter in the next few minutes would surprise them.

The end of the ridge became to what was left of the battalion, the unit's guidon. They raced toward it and immortality. Being the lead troop, TW Custer's C Troop saw first what was ahead, and veered still further to the left to avoid running straight into the hundreds more hostiles waiting for them on the next ridge. There seemed to be more in front of them than had been behind. Everywhere Captain Custer would have looked, the Indians were coming straight toward them, as if this small gaggle of survivors were magnets.

The only way out appeared to be at the end of the ridge they were on. With the fall of Lieutenant Calhoun's L Troop, the back door was swung wide open and the flood of hostile humanity was nearly amongst them. There was nothing to stop the hostiles coming in behind the survivors now huddled together on the lip of Battle Ridge and sloping down Custer Hill northwest face. Some of the men would do as Calhoun's troopers had done. Most would try to fight, but the numbers were too great against them. These men, their guns were empty or the breeches were frozen shut from fouled ammunition, they had given so much of themselves to just get to where they were that some were totally physically exhausted nearly unable to move. Many of those, if not all would have some earlier wound that would be leaking life juices from their bodies as stared down at what lay before them. The gods of war would not take pity on them, for there is no such thing as mercy to the gods of war.

The men in the Keogh's Wild Eye's would go next. Keogh and his boys withered under a hail of arrows. Those left wounded by that ploy would become targets for the younger braves. The blowout on the back side of the ridge in only invited the hostiles to pile in on top of these men and finish them off, many being killed in hand-to-hand combat.

Captain Keogh and his men had a time of it at the end. After all but one or two of his men had fallen, the tough little Irishman stood daring the hostiles to get close to him, his pistol empty, his left knee shattered by a bullet, he stood swinging a carbine he held on to by the barrel, at whoever got too close. That little game ended badly for Keogh, and a hostile shot him in the chest with one of his own men's carbine rifle from across the blowout.

Long after the fight, the Indians would tell of the best fighter in that last group of men, they would identify Captain Keogh by fighting spirit only, his name was unknown.

The Wild I Troop was gone, not one man was left standing. Only the wounded or unconscious men who could not move or fight any longer were left. The warriors set about taking care of that situation. No *wasichu* would leave that field of battle except as ghosts moving on wind into the spirit world.

Now, only the few survivors on Custer Hill, remnants of E, C, F—and somehow, the four civilians were still alive. Both of the Custer's little brother, Boston; their nephew, little Autie Reed; the newspaper man, Mr. Kellogg; and the half-breed scout, Mitch Bouyer had somehow managed to stay away from bullets or arrows. At the end they were with the command that day kneeling or squatting to avoid being too big a target. One by one they would go down dead; or lay wounded waiting for the end to come.

Only a few of the men with Yates and Smith would reach the summit of Battle Ridge, perhaps as many as or six or seven men out of the two troops. All that was left now were the survivors of E, and F, a few of TW

Custer's C men, and maybe less than one or two of the Wild I Troop.

These men were all that was left to try to fend off the thousands of red men. As for the officers still standing, Yates, Smith, and TW Custer were all that were left out of the sixteen who had only an hour or so before been alive and well. Tom Custer managed to unhorse his brother and lay him close by, standing in front of him, protecting him from God only knows what.

The rest of the men took up positions as close as they could around their fallen leader. They would not cost much these who remained; they had only minutes left before they fell beneath the hooves, lances, arrows, axes, tomahawks, and bullets of the victors.

They would end their day trying to form a skirmish line, and would be killed in place as they prepared to meet the enemy to their front, which by now a front did not exist. There were literally thousands, not hundreds of Indians around these last fifty-four soldiers.

The end would come fast. The Indians had taken to staying just out of range of the carbines, and sneaking up on the soldier's blind sides and shooting arrows into the frightened men. One by one the soldiers went down. Occasionally, an Indian would dash into the mash of survivors to count coup on one or more of the live soldiers, and then dash away while the stunned men only watched as the warrior ran back to his friends. The stunned soldiers did not fire at the fleeing warriors, instead just stared blindly at the enemy's back time and time again as they made their mindless dashes with impunity.

It was back to cat and mouse for the Indians. It was a great day to be a Sioux or Cheyenne warrior, poking fun at these frightened *wasichu*. To an Indian, it was a sign of mighty power. Counting coup on a live enemy was even more prestigious than killing an enemy to the hostiles. Killing could come later-displaying their courage was more important. Most of the wounded men lay quietly, a few of the dying graveled on their own. The final rush was mostly hand-to-hand with those that resisted, and then it was over, almost before it started.

Captains Yates, Smith and TW Custer fell protecting the leader's body. Before going down, though wounded, TW reached down, cocking the general's second British Parrot Bulldog as he did. Gently, he placed it to the general's temple, and pulled the trigger. It was the last sound Tom ever heard.

In the final rush that occurred just then, one of the hostiles crushed the back of Tom's head in with a stone headed war club mallet just as he pulled the trigger. Tom's body fell over the top of the brother.

Captain Yates was next, and he too died trying to fend off the last rush a carbine, swinging it madly over his head before a Cheyenne lance caught him full in the chest. He too fell at the feet of his life long friend, friends to the end.

"Fresh" Smith was clubbed with the butt end of one of his own men's carbine, knocking him out, but not killing him. When the fighting was all but finished, and the Indians were going about the wounded, finishing them off, Captain Smith would regain consciousness suddenly. He would sit up, aim his pistol at no one in particular, and attempted to shoot his pistol; it was empty. Apparently, still badly dazed by the blow to the head, he just sat on the ground, staring off into the distance, not realizing he was not shooting anyone. A warrior closest to him yanked the weapon from his hand and shot him between the eyes at point-blank range—blowing the back of his head off with a nearby carbine that was loaded.

For Lieutenant Colonel Custer, it wouldn't matter—he was dead, and had been for almost an hour; he would have never regained consciousness from the wound he received. To his brother, Tom, and the others making their way along the ridge line, it would not have mattered a great deal. They were alive, and they might still have a chance to save what was left of the command if they could have made it to the end of the ridge they were on and strike north and east away from the ridge line.

—33—

THE MISSING MEN

Two of the sixteen officers killed that day (out of thirty-one in the field) could not be positively identified: Second Lieutenants James "Jack" Sturgis and Henry Moore Harrington. Only part of Sturgis' blood-soaked shirt was found in the village after the battle by some of General Terry's men. His name was hand-stenciled into the collar of the bloody, tattered shirt.

For poor Lieutenant Harrington, not even that was found. He may have been one of the very few who almost got away. No trace of his body was ever found by the burying parties or by the surviving members of the 7th Cavalry who formed the burial details. Later, even in some cases years later, when skeletal remains were located, Harrington's remains were never identified. Since then, more remains were found and buried in the national cemetery on the battlefield, but none were ever identified as Lieutenant Harrington. His body just disappeared.

Even as late as 1951, remains were found; none were thought to have been Lieutenant Harrington. The Indians said no *wasichu* left that field alive, and from that day to this there seems to be a solid truth to their statement. One warrior, who had lost a son earlier in the battle who had gone to fight against Major Reno's men, had captured a soldier who was with Custer's command. The warrior killed the man and then, while the fighting was going around him, butchered the man like one would butcher a buffalo or steer, leaving the pile of butchered meat in one heap and bones and entrails in another heap on the side of the hill. That could have been Lieutenant Harrington. One thing is certain: The man was there, and he died there; he did not get away. He just was not in a form recognizable to his friends and bunkmates.

—34—

RETRIBUTION

Long before Lieutenant Colonel Custer rode down into the valley of the Greasy Grass from the Wolf Mountains he was an honest to goodness real-life hero. His star may have fallen on hard times during his years out on the plains, and it may have gotten tarnished a little bit towards the end of his life, but nonetheless he was a bona fide hero. After his last fight, he would become the guideon for western settlement and the stuff legends are made of.

From that time on he would become a tool used to spin the yarn of American lore and hero worship. Many an Indian who had nothing whatsoever to do with the battle died for no other reason than retribution for some red brethren killing someone named Custer, or Son of the Morning Star, or Old Iron Ass.

This country was young, largely unsettled, and had lost its focus on settling the rest of the lands to the west. It was just coming out of an economic depression. The country needed to expand, or it would collapse in on itself. Gold had been found in the Black Hills, first by greedy gold miners and prospectors, and then by Custer's expedition into that beautiful, untamed country in 1874—both technically illegal. But then, who honored treaties? Not the U.S. government. The Fort Laramie Treaty signed six years earlier in 1868 forbid white men into the Black Hills. Did the government try to stop the Black Hills gold rush? No. They sent Lieutenant Colonel Custer's 7th Cavalry to push the Indians out of their sacred grounds.

Lieutenant Colonel Custer and the 7th Cavalry had been instrumental in protecting the opening of the Black Hills for the prospectors. The prospectors were so grateful they even named a settlement after this one-time heroic general—Custer, South Dakota, in 1874. Nebraska named a county after the man, as did Oklahoma and Colorado.

As for a national focus, the Civil War had badly abused nearly all the peoples of this land except the American Indian. What America needed right then was someone who could spur their imaginations, someone who could become their hero. They did not need to ask Lieutenant Colonel Custer twice; he was the man for that job, dead or alive.

There is just something about his name that permeates the spirit of us Americans, then, and even now. Eastern folks back then loved reading the things he wrote, and the things written about him. He, in his own mind, as well as the most of the white folks back in the East, was one of the heroes the people needed. For glory's sake, while alive, he scrambled at the chance.

But alas, it was more than just glory that drove this heroic, brave, and cavalier soldier. He loved the opportunity to command, and he lusted for combat. In addition to those two things, he had been badly treated by his former commander, who had somehow managed to become the president of the United States. Important people were beginning to have second thoughts about this once-famous Civil War commander, and now-famous Indian fighter.

His star had been tarnished, perhaps rightly so. He was an odd fit as a soldier; he disliked immensely taking orders from officers he did not respect or who tried to rein him in. He would have been even an odder fit had he tried to live his life as a civilian.

As for his latest falling out with his commander in chief, he had to try to still the troubled waters between the two of them. Lieutenant Colonel Custer had to clear himself of the debacle in Washington. His thinking, perhaps, was one more good fight with the Indians, and everybody would forget the mess he had created at his own hand. Maybe, just maybe, he could leave the Army and with Libby in tow could settle maybe in New York City, a city they both loved and that had loved them back. Who knew, maybe politics was where his next war would be fought and then if his timing was right, maybe he could run for the presidency of the

United States of America. Perhaps he even thought he could do a better job than his boss was doing at the present time.

Later, after the 7th Cavalry's fiasco in Montana, his government and his superiors would use his fall to finally push for the white settlement of the Indian's unseeded lands. A little tragedy like the "Massacre of Custer, and the whole 7TH Cavalry" would help the populace push harder on in the settlement of the frontier. Be he alive, or be he dead, Lieutenant Colonel Custer was the man.

Libby Bacon Custer gave the country the sacrificial lamb, her husband, a real-life war hero. Lieutenant Colonel Custer, with receding hairline, light-blue eyes that burned with an uncommon flare, a bushy mustachio that covered thinly-lined lips, thinning reddish-blonde hair, gave, as his part for his country, his life. He became a legend, bigger than the life he had lived—a life we white folks wanted to be romantic enough to believe in then, and even now, after all this time.

Is it any wonder the truth got muddled up in the falsehoods and half-truths of that day? Those fables and falsehoods, bald-faced lies, and half-truths have perpetuated and churned around until this very day. The truth of what happened that day is still partly hidden in the dark shadows of the American frontier's history.

For the Army's part, it has had the self-serving history of shifting responsibility to those who were not able to defend or protect themselves. It was always best if the scapegoat died before standing to face his accusers, or to tell his side of the story, to protect those who really messed up. Again, Lieutenant Colonel Custer, then dead, was the man the Army used to cover up its shortcomings. Major Reno would become the Army's live scapegoat for the Indians' annihilation of Custer's five companies; he would be the less able to defend himself. That statement will surprise some of the less initiated.

Many superior officers, not on the battlefield at the time, thought Major Reno should have come to the aid of the general. Perhaps he should have, and if he had been able to at the time, he would have, and so would have Captain Benteen.

Custer's wife also thought Major Reno had failed her husband, his commander, in George's hour of need. There was evidence that indicated that he indeed should have attempted to come to Custer's aid, but given the truth to the matter that has been written in earlier chapters, that evidence is mostly hearsay and not based on the circumstances that Major Reno faced at any time during his part in the battle. Short of publicly accusing the major, Libby set out to destroy the man.

As has been pointed out, Major Reno and his command were not able to come to anyone's aid. Before Captain Benteen arrived, they could barely protect the wounded troopers and themselves at the time. Major Reno's command had taken nearly eighty percent casualties in the first two hours of the fight and had shot all of their horses and were using them as barricades. What in the world good would a handful of worn-out troopers on foot, having to run four miles, do to help Custer in the situation he was in? Even if they had known where he was or what his situation was, they would have been in potentially the same position the moment the hostiles turned their attention on them.

Except for one brief blink of an eye, and two minor details, Major Reno might have had a moment to go to the aid of his commander. That assumes of course, he knew for sure where his commander was—and had a way to get to him. The bald-faced truth was, he did not know where his commander was; and, even if he did, he did not have a way to get to him.

Even if he had known where he was, it would have been too little, and too late. Lieutenant Colonel Custer's fight was over before Captain Benteen had rescued Major Reno. Major Reno's battalion was down to less than twenty able-bodied men. Major Reno had nearly sixty men missing—thirty-seven killed along with twenty-two missing that he did not know if they were alive or dead along with about fifty who were wounded. What would he do with his wounded? Who would stay with them while he and his band of marry men went out looking for his boss? All Major Reno knew for sure was that when they left the valley after they had retreated, he had more wounded than unwounded and he presumed the others were dead.

At the moment in question he could not have known the only reason he and what was left of his command was alive was because Lieutenant Colonel Custer had attacked in support of Major Reno's attack in the valley…down Medicine Tail Coulee. He did not know Medicine Tail

Coulee from Niagara Falls. He had never seen it had never heard of it before and damn sure would not have known that is where his boss had decided to attack in support of his attack.

At the very moment Major Reno reached the bluffs, Lieutenant Colonel would have been facing his own command's summary defeat at the river's edge more than two miles away. As it turned out, it was that attack by Custer's battalion which took most of the pressure away from Major Reno's beleaguered front. The lieutenant colonel's attack though no real surprise to the Indians, did divert many of the Indians from attacking Major Reno's depleted command in force, and would delay them from finishing off the rest of them.

Within a half-hour of Lieutenant Colonel Custer's attempted river crossing at Medicine Tail Coulee, Major Reno would have had mere minutes only to come to his commander's assistance. By the time he could have gotten even a mile, the commander would have been dead, and his command would be strung out nearly four and a half miles away—what was left of it was running for its life. In the end, it would not have mattered; Custer's force was gone, cut down like grass on the Montana prairie hay field.

SAVING CUSTER

Major Reno and Benteen assumed, correctly, that Custer's command was somewhere north of them. They also guessed it was Custer's force on the edge of Battle Ridge, but they did not know for sure. What would it have mattered? They could not have helped, no matter where he was; they could not get to him—they had shot their horses.

If you have never done it, sometime, try looking at something under glaring summer sun four or five miles away. Do it on a bright, very hot day, while trying to imagine a dust storm between you and the object you are trying to see. Try to imagine someone painted in awful colors, half-naked, and screaming at the top of his lungs, with hate in his eyes for only you—what is it you see? What do you see for sure? What do you hear? What these men heard, and what they saw, and had seen would have been more than enough to keep them where they were.

It could have very well been General Terry's command showing up a day earlier than he was supposed to, just like Custer had. It could be Custer's force making for an escape to the north. What Major Reno's command knew for sure was there were 4,000-4,500 very determined and extremely angry cold-blooded killers between where they were and where, maybe, Lieutenant Colonel Custer and his men were thought to be. Getting to him would be akin to crossing the Atlantic in a paper raft during a hurricane.

To try to get where Custer's men were would have been suicide. Though they could count the number of hostiles that had been killed by their own weapons on one man's hand, they were very low on ammunition. Now that is amazing, it is hard to imagine the survivors were almost out of ammunition for no more damage than they had inflected on the enemy. They were literally down to a few rounds for each man. They had only killed eight hostiles in the valley fight against Major Reno, afterward not one hostile was found wounded or dead near Major Reno's hand-scooped fortress. Until Captain Benteen got to Major Reno's position, Major Reno didn't have enough able-bodied men to do anything tactically, and by that time only an hour, maybe an hour and a half later, Major Reno and his men where done in.

At this point in time if what was left of Major Reno's command had attempted to go to some undefined location to support his commander they would have been wiped out to the last man. Major Reno had failed to complete his mission. His going anywhere, or his doing anything other than what he was doing at the time, would have only compounded an already impossible situation. His lack of command experience in a combat environment from the very beginning was only the tip of the iceberg if we were innumerate his short comings at this point.

The fact is, he had no idea what to do next other than to keep his head down and hope and pray that he did not get stuck with an arrow and killed. As for his men, they were left to their own devices; luckily these survivors' officers and noncommissioned officers were on the ball enough to keep the better part of his men still alive until Captain Benteen and his battalion got into the perimeter they were squirreled into.

Major Reno did not know anything about where his commander was. In his mind his boss could be anywhere. He would not have known that nearly four and a half miles away what was left of Lieutenant Colonel Custer's command was at that very moment being offered up as living sacrifices to an angry god of war. He could not have seen clearly anything that was going on at the end of what would become known as Battle Ridge. It had been a cloudless, hot, clear day. On the northern prairies, distance and clarity sometimes get distorted and mirages can rise up out of nowhere from the terra firma on days like this one. The heat radiating from the ground would make things appear that are really not there at all. To Major Reno's overly stressed mind things he thought were real could have only been figments of his imagination.

By the time Major Reno and Captain Benteen had barricaded themselves into their little earthen dish, those who were unlucky enough to be with what was left of Lieutenant Colonel Custer's command would be looking into the bright and shinny faces of Crazy Horse and perhaps another 1,500 Ogalalas warriors. If what was about to happen to these men had not already happened, Major Reno and Captain Benteen would have been no more the wiser

It would have been over before Benteen rescued Major Reno; they just did not know it. All that was left for the Indians to do was to count coup, take scalps and other unmentionable souvenirs, and to celebrate. The Indians had their ways to get even with enemies, alive or dead. They made sure the enemies did not bother them again in this life, or the one after.

Captain Weir's D Troop tried a fool hearty attempt to find Lieutenant Colonel Custer, after Captain Benteen joined Major Reno around 1500. The attempt was short-lived and very nearly disastrous, had it not been for Captain Benteen's charge with his battalion on foot into the assaulting Indians, Captain Weir's attempt to break out and go to his commander's aid would have ended the same way as it did for Lieutenant Colonel Custer's did.

That was the last attempt that could be made, far too late to have helped at all. Captain Weir's heart was in the right place, but the end had already been decided for Lieutenant Colonel Custer's command hours before. At the end, Captain Weir would owe his life to a man who hated Captain Weir's hero. The smart answer was to stay put, and protect what was left of Major Reno's exhausted, but now, reinforced command.

Captain Benteen's command was spent also, even though they had not fired a round in anger or self-protection until they came into the breastworks of Major Reno's command. That day alone, they had spent the last twelve hours in the saddle in the past two days, and nearly thirty-eight of the forty-eight hours before that.

Major Reno, even with Benteen and McDougall's troops, the rest of the 7th Cavalry could not have overcome the four miles between the commands. Had they tried they would have risked the obliteration of what was left of the 7th Cavalry Regiment. Common sense clearly shows that though Major Reno could be suspect of marking time rather than advancing to the commander's position, he could not be accused of cowardice or dereliction of duty like Libby accused him and Captain Benteen.

There is no evidence pointing to Captain Benteen being less than willing to risk his own neck, or his force, for that matter, to do his duty. Many things can be said about Captain Benteen's dislike and open defiance of Lieutenant Colonel Custer at most every turn. But no one can deny the man had the courage of a rabid mongoose fighting a pit full of cobras. Benteen was a fighter; he was worse when he had his blood up. Then, the man became a rabid, raging, slobbering, dirt-pawing, head-tossing maniac.

Along the bluffs and later, leading his three troops of cavalry on foot into the Indians massing round the Weir's D troop to save them will attest to that. What Weir had taken upon himself to do, and what Captain Benteen and his men did to save them from that valiant but stupid act, attests to Benteen's clear-headedness and ability to alter events by sheer human will and intestinal fortitude.

He could hate with the same intensity, and he hated Custer with a magenta-purple passion. This grandfatherly-looking man, with what appears to be a kindly face with soft friendly eyes, had the heart of a serial killer with ice water running through his veins. At the same time, Captain Benteen would not lose control of himself or of a situation when under extreme pressure as he was under that day on the Little Bighorn River. He, like the commander he hated, was fearless and a warrior who would rival anyone on that field that day.

Men begged, and later swore under oath to the captain's refusal to take cover for his own safety during the Court of Inquiry. They said it was almost as if he defied the enemy to shoot him. He stayed up on his feet, moving among his soldiers, giving them encouragement and steadying those who were near the breaking point with the words of a man talking to his sons, as if this was an everyday occurrence and that they could do whatever they had to.

Captain Benteen took command from Major Reno in order to secure the area around Major Reno's hill. Major Reno was more than ready to relinquish control to Benteen. Remember this was the first time meeting hostile Indians who very much wanted to kill him. Several of the officers —Godfrey, Hare, Varnum, and Edgerly—would later testify at the court of inquiry in 1879, he was real nervous and if not cowardly, then timorous the whole time. Both Varnum and Hare were there at the valley fight, and then up on the hill with him, and said the same thing about Major Reno. Benteen, in private would say as much, but in public was less critical of him, saying that when he reached the major and his command on the bluff, the major was indeed nervous and excited, but that once he calmed down he was fine, "though by no means heroic." The major had been overcome by the fighting, and had or very nearly had lost control of his all faculties.

Of the charges brought against Captain Benteen, in his unflappable way, he denied he did anything against orders. And in the end, who could argue with that? He did only what he was ordered to do, scout the watersheds five to ten miles to the south of where the regiment split.

Captain Benteen said he had no idea what his commander's battle plans were (that seems to be a misstatement of the whole truth and nothing but the truth) but almost acceptable in light of what transpired once on the hill with Major Reno, and what the men who served with him told the same court of inquiry. It was he who kept most of the rest of the command alive for the remainder of the battle. He stated to the court of inquiry he had no idea that both of the other wing commanders would be so totally overwhelmed.

That was the truth. How would he have known differently? What Captain Benteen might have thought, and what he knew for a fact are different things.

When Major Reno was overwhelmed, and even later Custer also, could not that have been predicted by anyone on that battlefield wearing a blue uniform at that time. He himself had not seen the encampment until after the Indians had left the valley, so he had no reason to believe any differently than Lieutenant Colonel Custer did when the Lieutenant Colonel ordered him to scout the areas south from where they had stopped at 0800 before the battle. While he thought it a dumb order, who was he to argue with the commander on the substance of it?

Had he been able to "come quickly, and to bring up the ammunition packs"—as the last written orders from Custer ordered him to do, his, and probably Major Reno and Captain McDougall's commands would have fallen. Captain Benteen would have been wrong no matter what he did, or did not do. Damn it! And that is the truth.

—35—

SOMEBODY'S TO BLAME

There is no one to blame except George Armstrong Custer for what happened that day. In this case, Major Reno's and Captain Benteen's accusers would have had to be there in that situation, as it was unfolding before them to understand the dilemma facing both officers. It was much easier to sit in an office smoking big, fat cigars, and second-guessing the commanders in the field who, when decisions had to be made under tremendous stress of the moment, made them, and did the best they could.

As for Major Reno, a hundred and twenty-five years or so ago, they did not know what it was that made men crack under pressure. They would not even consider there was such thing as a man simply "losing it," and not being able to protect himself—much less lead a command. The Army had a name for it all right, but it was the wrong name. They called it cowardice; today we call it combat operational stress syndrome. It could, and did strike men then, just as it does today. The impact of combat stress of that day is very apparent today, even if it was not considered then or accepted.

Combat Operational Stress can turn brave men into mindless jellyfish, unfit for useful duty. Far less than well-trained and battle-hardened men could become a suicidal mob. Major Reno and Captain Benteen were working under the protection of their own lucky star. They would be very lucky that most of their seven troops survived the rest of the day on the 25th, much less the day of the 26[th,] and the morning of the 27[th,] before relief would finally arrive the afternoon of the 27th. It was nothing short of a modern-day miracle for those who survived.

Two things worked in Major Reno and Captain Benteen's favor: one, as unbelievable as it sounds, the hostiles got tired of fighting and killing on the 25th. On the 26th, the Indians toyed with the remaining force—where were these white men going to go? The hostiles had them in a hole—all they had to do was wait, and get them one by one when they tried to make a break, or went to get water. The Indians could have taken them whenever they wanted, if they were willing to pay the price in Indian blood. And two, in the afternoon of the 27th, General Terry and Lieutenant Colonel Gibbon's commands came into the valley and the Indians knew that long before the *wasichu* did and broke camp and headed south away from potential danger. Sitting Bull was in the hope that what the commands found on the hillsides beside the Little Sheep River would deter the *wasichu* coming down the valley, scaring them bad enough to leave his land.

It was as simple as that.

If there is a silver lining in the way Custer's fight panned out it is that when Custer attacked when he did, it saved Major Reno and his men.

His command would have been wiped out completely within the hour by the hostiles who were on their way to him, some 1,000 to 1,200 of them, from up the Medicine Tail Coulee and across the ridges toward where he was them. In addition to the 1,200 or so who had attacked his command at the edge of the encampment. These new warriors would have been in position to flank him, had they not stopped, and gone to the sound of Lieutenant Colonel Custer's gunfire that he had initiated.

When the hostiles heard the gunfire from the river, they turned around and came down behind Lieutenant Colonel Custer's men as they attacked down the Medicine Tail Coulee.

This movement completely blocked any chance of retreat from the way Lieutenant Colonel Custer's battalion had attacked, back up Medicine Tail Coulee. This action on the part of the hostiles forced all of the troops to move off to the north across and up a very steep hill to get to the ridge line perhaps one-half to a mile away from the river. As for Major Reno's command, those still able to fire a weapon were placed on line being just able to hold off the frontal attacks, and when time permitted to attempt to dig breastworks with whatever they could get their hands on; tin cups, plates, and their fingers. Here they would stay, barely hanging on by their fingertips.

By the time it was over three days later, both Captain Benteen and Major Reno would encounter another eleven men killed, and a total of sixty-eight would be wounded. All totaled for the strike in the valley and the fight on the hill, there were forty-eight men killed and sixty-eight more wounded; of those men wounded, five would die of their wounds on the way back to Fort Lincoln.

From the surviving two commands, including B Troop, 433 men would ride into battle, 318 would ride out under their own power, and two were unaccounted for.

The one question that begs to be asked here is: "How many of those men left for dead in the valley were really dead?" Or were they just "left for dead" when Major Reno made his frantic retreat —he called it a "charge"—to the bluffs overlooking the river for safety? Does it matter? What would you call it?

It is known for sure at least two of Major Reno's men could not stop their stampeding horses during the initial charge, and flew headlong into the midst of the attacking Indians. Their life expectancy was less than two seconds amongst those folks. That question will go unanswered except for the Indian's accounts of the valley fight. A goodly number of the men left were killed by the Indians going about the bodies of the fallen, counting coup, killing, and scalp the slain.

—36—

AFTER-EFFECTS

There are a few things that could have altered the debacle on the Little Bighorn that might have been averted had a lesser man commanded the 7th that day. What would have happened if Custer had not pushed his way into the history book is hard to say. It could have gone worse for the Army than the loss of five companies of cavalry. They could have lost a lot more.

It has been conjectured it could have gone the other way with the Army winning the fight. The Army might have won that fight if Custer hadn't gone after them when he did. The odds are had General Terry's force reached the valley first, the same thing that had happened to Custer would have happened to General Terry and Gibbon's commands. The only thing that would have change is that part of this command was on foot and would have probably completely helpless in short order.

General Crook had already tested the Northern Cheyenne of Lame White Man and Crazy Horse's Ogalala Lakota and was found wanting. Crook wouldn't have tried a second time; he had learned his lesson about fighting the best light cavalry in the world. He was still licking his mental wounds from the first battle on the Rosebud a week before.

Had Gibbon's force run into the encampment, his command very well could have been wiped out to the last man. They were a much smaller force, and except for two troops of cavalry, were totally on foot. They were infantry.

There would be clashes in the next few years with the Indians to be sure, and there would be scores of settlers killed, and Indians killed by the hundred. But for all tense and purposes, the Indian Wars really ended

LAST RIDE

June 25-27, 1876, in the Valley of the Greasy Grass, thanks in a large part to Lieutenant Colonel George Armstrong Custer, and five troops U.S. Army's 7th Cavalry.

If Lieutenant Colonel Custer had it do over, I'd bet he would have done it differently, don't you? Funny thing about fighting wars, and men dying, they don't get do it over until they get it right. They do it once, and if they are lucky, they walk away with a few scratches, lumps and limps they will learn to cope with for the rest of their lives.

If they are not lucky, and they can find the pieces of what once was left of these men, they bury them, and put a stone over their head, telling folks who they might have been, and others will talk about gallantry and bravery displayed on the fields of fire.

And you know what? If you could ask all the men who died in all the wars, if they would want to be called dead heroes or be alive to be old men, what do you think they would choose? What would you choose? The problem here, of course, is soldiers don't get the choice. They just do what they are ordered, and hope things turn out okay.

Custer's command did not fall because he disobeyed his orders. It has been argued and debated he had; but in the final analysis, when one reads those orders and understands the circumstances surrounding General Terry and his field commanders, and then applies that knowledge to those orders, he simply did not disobey his orders. Too many have tried to deface Custer wrongly by playing that card—that dog won't hunt.

There is the argument Custer failed because he divided his force that fateful morning, and he lacked the manpower to stop a superior force on the side of Custer Hill. That idea does not work either. How did the survivors—there were only fifty-four or fifty-six left out of the command by then— get to the end of Battle Ridge? Those who were left ran for their lives and died because there was nowhere else to run. The Indians had them right where they wanted them, tethered at the end of a very short leash.

It is true he split his force—actually he did not just divide his force into two parts. Circumstances at the time demanded he quarter it—sending one battalion (of 175 men) with Benteen; one battalion (112 men) with Major Reno, a third wing with the wagon trains and pack animals (146 men) with Captain McDougall, and finally taking with him the remainder of the force, five troops totaling 213 men, with him. In his command, he divided it, putting Captain Yates in command of a small battalion and he in command of the other three troops.

The lack of manpower at the time he deployed was not an issue he would even consider until it was too late. His military and scouting intelligence he trusted was almost non-existent at the time he divided his command. He was still trying to find the hostiles. In a sense, up until he ordered Major Reno's attack of the southern end of the camp he did not know, or even consider, the Indians would be massed in the kind of strength he encountered. Some say there were between 1,000 to 1,500 lodges, plus several hundred single warrior huts when they were told to expect no more than 300 to 400 lodges all together.

Though Custer's force was a lot light of having anywhere near enough men and firepower at the end of Battle Ridge—eighty percent of his own force had fallen by then—if he could have had his combined force, and fought from that standpoint the same thing would have probably happened. He was simply out-manned, from start to finish.

But, instead of 272 graves across the battlefield, there could have been just as easily 334 more. Terry wanted Custer to take four companies of 2nd Cavalry with the 7th when it left Fort Abraham Lincoln, Custer rejected the idea—he wanted only the 7th with him. In the end what was left of his command would be out-manned at the end at least 60 to 1, and with those two troops he would have still been out-manned and outgunned 25 to 1. The difference it would have made would have been like spitting in the ocean to raise the water volume.

Custer did the only thing he, as a military man, could do under the circumstances he encountered when his scouts found the hostiles—he initiated his attack and he attacked—leaving history to sort out the rights and wrongs of it.

Unfortunately, we humans who write our own history seldom get things right the first time. There were just too many men who would hide behind this tragedy, and blame everything on a dead man. Someone once said, "Nothing noble comes from tarnishing a hero," and I have to agree.

Custer failure was not for the fact that Major Reno and Captain

Benteen hated their commander or because their commander did not like them —they loathed him—and would not come to his aid, especially Captain Benteen, if his hair had been on fire under normal circumstances. The fact that Captain Benteen dallied back for literally hours when the issue was still up in the air is beside the point of the argument. Had his entire force gone up to Custer's aid, they could not have gotten there from where they were when he started his attack, had they been able to they would have fallen right along side of Custer and his boys. His battalion saved Major Reno's battalion, and thus kept the 7th from being totally wiped out.

Captain Benteen was not a coward; he was a realist who hated Custer. The hostiles could have just as easily gone through Major Reno and Benteen's command on the hill as they had ridden over the top of what was left of Custer's force had they have wanted, and he knew it. If what was left of Major Reno's battalion and his command could have come to his aid; there was a very small window of opportunity to do so—he knew that too. Had they, they too would have met his very same end.

At the same time, their commands were spent from having faced exactly what Custer's men were facing that moment on Battle Ridge. The entire force was at that moment as useless as teats on a boar hog to Custer and his boys.

They were dangerously close to being totally overwhelmed themselves by very angry and very hostile Unkpapa and Minniconjoux, and Black Foot Lakota Indians. They could have been on the other side of the moon for all the help they could have been to Custer's command that afternoon. What is more, they were only lucky what happened to Custer—though they didn't know it then—didn't happen to them later in the afternoon, or in the early evening of the 25th after the Indians had taken Custer out. They were doubly lucky for sure on the next day, the 26th when the Indians started massing to the front of Major Reno-Benteen-McDougall's troops at sunup and started getting serious about it nearly three hours later. Finally, apparently out of boredom, and the fact they had gotten word Terry's command was on its way into the Greasy Grass, the Indians broke up and went their own ways.

Some have argued his horses were worn out, and totally at the end, used up. Captain Benteen had said the same thing about his command's horses. Major Reno's were either totally used up, or serving the purpose of barricades to keep the Indians at bay. Horse carcasses do not stop bullets. As for Custer's horses, they were in as bad a shape as everybody else's were—they had been on the move since early morning, and had not rested or watered or eaten for two days. What is more, they had been ridden hard for more than a month and more the 700 miles to get to the battlefield.

It was not for the fact he had ordered his one platoon of Gatling guns to be shipped off to parts unknown. The gating guns were heavy, hard to manage, often mechanically unreliable, and purely defensive weapons, not offensive weapons in that day. One could not charge with gating guns on horseback, for example. The battle they were going to be engaged in was going to be at best a running gun fight from the backs of worn-out cavalry horses going full-tilt—hardly the place for Gatling guns.

As it turned out, they never got into a defensive posture where they could have used the guns effectively. They were in a running gunfight for sure, but it was more like a wild-assed dash to the rear to save their lives retreat, rather than a gut curdling, clod-flying cavalry charge.

That being said however, the taking of the Gatling guns could have avoided Custer's defeat. But, only because they would have made it impossible for him to get to the battlefield until after the time General Terry and Colonel Gibbons would have gotten there. Gatling guns did not travel well, and the time it would have taken Lieutenant Colonel Custer's men to get the Little Bighorn would have been measured a day or two longer rather than a day shorter.

What would he have found had he gotten there two days later would have been the same General Terry found when he got there, only it would have been him and Colonel Gibbon laying naked and dead in the valley of the Greasy Grass rather than them finding him naked and dead on the side of a hill.

It was not because he refused General Terry's offer of four more troops of 2nd Cavalry Gibbon's offered (120 men), or the two companies of infantry (135 men) of Terry's to go with him. More is not always better. In this case, the same argument could be made about saving the command as the one used for the Gatling guns. It would have slowed him down, and made it impossible for him to get there ahead of the other generals.

Based on the intelligence he was given before moving out, the regiment he had all the men he would need. His thinking, of course was he would meet up with an equal number of the hostiles, and his 7th Cavalry, even though they numbered almost half of the authorized strength, he could have beaten 800 Indians with 637 men that moved with him.

In his mind—and who could have argued with him based upon the information that they had at that time—this action was totally a cavalry mission. He needed to move, and move quickly, when he found them. He would fight them with men who he had commanded.

Infantry, foot soldiers, (the Indians called them walk-a-lots) do not move quickly, or at least, not as quickly as horse cavalry. They would have been too slow to keep up with his line of march once he got on the Indians' trail. He had to move or miss the chance of hitting the enemy fast before they split up, and scattered to the directions of the wind. That, and that alone, was his motivation for moving in the manner he did, for dividing his force the way he did, for deploying them as he did, and even taking one troop of greenhorn untested cavalry troop with him (L Troop), so the others would not have to be hampered with them.

Following are the written orders he deployed with the night of the 22nd when he met with General Terry that one last time on the river steamer Far West. He had not been ordered otherwise.

"Strike them if you find them, drive them back to the agencies and reservations, or kill them."

Custer followed his orders the best he could. His commander knew he would, or die trying, and that honestly bothered General Terry a great deal.

The following reproduction is a copy of the orders Brigadier general Alfred E. Terry had delivered to Lieutenant Colonel Custer on the morning of June 22, 1876. Since the disastrous defeat of George Custer at the Little Bighorn, this set of orders has been at the center of an ongoing debate as to whether or not Lieutenant Colonel Custer disobeyed Terry's orders.

In a not-so-confidential letter to Generals Sherman and Sheridan after the battle, General Terry inferred Lieutenant Colonel Custer had indeed disobeyed his orders. From my point of view, the argument he disobeyed his orders is purely ridiculous. General Terry was covering his hind parts with that statement. General Terry specifically authorized Lieutenant Colonel Custer to use his own judgment at every turn that the Lieutenant Colonel made. One may question Lieutenant Colonel Custer's judgment; but not his authority to judge, or his obedience or disobedience in following his orders.

GENERAL ALFRED E. TERRY'S OFFICIAL WRITTEN ORDERS

Headquarters of the Department of Dakota
(In the Field) Camp at Mouth of Rosebud River,
Montana Territory

June 22nd, 1876

Lieutenant-Colonel Custer, 7th Cavalry Colonel

The Brigadier General Commanding directs that, as soon as your regiment can be made ready for the march, you will proceed up the Rosebud in pursuit of the Indians whose trail was discovered by Major Reno a few days since. It is impossible to give you any definite instructions in regard to this movement, and were it not impossible to do so the Department Commander places too much confidence in your zeal, energy, and ability to wish to impose upon you precise orders which might hamper your action when nearly in contact with the enemy. He will, however, indicate to you his own views of what your action should be and he-desires that you should conform to them unless you shall see sufficient reason for departing from them.

He thinks that you should proceed up the Rosebud until you ascertain definitely the direction in which the trail above spoken of leads. Should it be found (as it appears almost certain that it will be found) to turn towards the Little Bighorn, he thinks that you should still proceed southward, perhaps as far as the headwaters of the Tongue and then turn toward the Little Horn, feeling constantly, however, to your left, so as to preclude the escape of the Indians passing around your left flank.

The column of Colonel Gibbon is now in motion for the mouth of the Bighorn. As soon as it reaches that point will cross the Yellowstone and move up at least as far as the forks of the Big and Little Horns. Of course, its future movements must be controlled by circumstances as they arise, but it is hoped that the Indians, if upon the Little Horn may be so nearly enclosed by the two columns that their escape will be impossible. The Department Commander desires that on your way up the Rosebud you should thoroughly examine the upper part of Tullock's Creek, and that you should endeavor to send a scout through to Colonel Gibbon's command.

The supply-steamer will be pushed up the Bighorn far as the forks of the river is found to be navigable for that distance, and the Department Commander, who will accompany the column of Colonel Gibbon, desires you to report to him there not later than the expiration of the time for which your troops are rationed, unless in the mean time you receive further orders.

Very respectfully,
Your obedient servant,
E. W. Smith, Captain
18th Infantry A. A. J. G.

These orders were written within hours of Lieutenant Colonel Custer's departure on his last campaign. The previous evening there had been a meeting of General Alfred Terry, General John Gibbon, Major James Brisbin, and Lieutenant Colonel Custer on the steamboat *Far West*. The proposed purpose of the meeting was to develop a plan of attack against hostile Sioux known to be in the Rosebud-Little Bighorn Region. The above text is reproduced from page 462 of the Annual Report of the Secretary of War for 1876, which is House Executive Document for the second session of the Forty-fourth Congress (Serial volume 1742). From these hand-written orders above it is clear General Terry had given Lieutenant Colonel George A. Custer complete authority to act in his own best judgment. These orders say nothing about waiting for either of the other units in the field, or to join up with either before engaging the enemy.

General Terry, who is rather a disappointment after reflection on him and the type of job he did during the campaign, tried to infer it was Lieutenant Colonel Custer and Lieutenant Colonel Custer alone who caused his and his command's defeat. In the end, it was. But not in the way the story is often told. Everything from hearsay, to fiction, and everywhere in between, is what gets told.

But for General Terry to infer Lieutenant Colonel Custer disobeyed orders lowers my estimation of this already questionable officer, who up to this time and then forever afterward was a picture of truth and honor, it is too bad he was just slow, disorganized, and unpopular as a commander.

After all, it was General Terry who literally begged Sheridan, and the President of the United States, U.S. Grant, to allow Lieutenant Colonel Custer back to his command of the Montana wing of the operation. The reason being of course is that General Terry had even less experience with Indians than did Major Reno, which was absolutely none. It seems everyone wanted to distance themselves from Lieutenant Colonel Custer after his defeat, General Terry included.

That shouldn't surprise anyone. Most folks don't want to be to close to the fire—lest they get burned; or, in this case blamed for failure. Had General Terry's orders specifically stated Lieutenant Colonel Custer was to wait, the Lieutenant Colonel would have waited. He would have hated it and may have even cussed a bit, but, he was a soldier, and he would have waited. Soldiers do what they are told to do, even if they don't like it.

Well, maybe that needs to be qualified a little bit; Custer would have waited. Benteen and Major Reno were not on the same plain as Lieutenant Colonel Custer, nor was General Terry for that matter or Colonel Gibbons. Generals Sherman and Sheridan —and even President U.S. Grant were, and they would stand up for Lieutenant Colonel Custer, when others would not, though at different times they too would indict him publicly when it suited their political purposes.

—37—

CULPABILITY

The reasons Lieutenant Colonel Custer failed that afternoon were fairly straightforward and simple:

• First and foremost, he lacked communications with his battlefield commanders during the deployment of their troops and during their engagements with the Indians once the battle began. He ultimately had no communication with the other forces in the area.

Normally, in times like that, you just did the best you could; communication was only possible by courier, smoke signals, and mirrors. Usually, if a courier from another command could not get through, and if he did not get one out, the commander could not communicate and he was cut off from the rest of the outside world.

• Second, and this was as serious as the first reason, he lacked reliable, current intelligence on his enemy. Custer and his superior officers had totally underestimated the strength of the Indians in the field against them. It is a wonder that any of the troops survived that summer after the fights on the Rosebud and Little Big Horn Rivers. For Lieutenant Colonel Custer's part, he had been given poor (inaccurate) intelligence by his commanding officer (General Terry) concerning the number of warriors his regiment would be facing when and if he found them.

That latest intelligence had been completed by Major Reno's scouting expedition over a month old and before Custer had left Fort Abraham

Lincoln. This intelligence did not give how many of the enemy to expect. Major Reno's scout of the region never saw an Indian only the tracks of those on their way to the Rosebud and Little Bighorn valleys. Since Major Reno had no Indian fighting experience and he had no desire to get any, he never got close enough to them to actually see them.

No one in either General Terry's or Gibbon's commands had found anything that would change the estimated number of enemy warriors that they would face. As late as 22 June 1876, only three days before the fight on the Little Bighorn when the three commanders had met that last time, Terry had not changed the estimate, nor had there been any updating of that intelligence. There had been no word from General Crook's command that had been moving from the south out of Fort Laramie. They, the three northern plains commanders, did not know where Crook and his command really was.

Custer was told to stay in touch by his commander and had even been given a couple, three couriers for that purpose. While he had located the tracks of a large party moving through the region on the 24th, he had not located the party itself. He would not have known if this was the party that Major Reno had located on his scout the month before or if this was an entirely new contingent moving on to a general location.

History does not record what it was that Lieutenant Colonel Custer thought when he discovered the tracks on the afternoon of the 24th. He never sent the couriers to General Terry, apparently, because he had not seen the encampment himself. Up to that point in time, none of the men in his command had, either—no *wasichu* had. Custer had no fear of man or beast and it was difficult for him to understand why other men did frighten easily. In this instance, tracks of an enemy did not scare him or make him want to send couriers to tell somebody about tracks. He would wait until he had something to substantiate his findings to report. Since he personally did not really have a first hand knowledge of the Indian's presence and in what numbers, he really did not have anything to report.

Conversely, Major Reno had not seen the enemy a month earlier but had seen the tracks of somebody moving into the Rosebud basin. That had been enough for him to return to Fort Lincoln. Major Reno did not have to see the enemy to know that danger was lurking near by.

That said, by itself, it was a main difference between Custer and Major Reno. Custer knew no fear. He was not afraid of shadows or tracks and backed down from no one. Major Reno, of course, was and always did.

However, from the actions of some of his officers and men in the command and from those of his Indian scouts and guides, we can surmise what the effects were and history does record the outcome.

On the Powder River General Terry had given Custer his last written orders. They do not or did the record of the conference the night before shed any light as to how many he should expect to find if he did catch up with the Indians.

It was suggested at the time that the estimate of 800 possible hostile warriors might be somewhere higher than 1,000 to maybe even as high as 1,200. But there was no hard evidence it would be more than that number. From that time on until Custer's regiment attacked the encampment the 7th Cavalry was out of contact with the other forces that were close at hand. Although Generals Crook and Terry were no more than 40 miles apart; they may have well as been on different planets.

Unknown to Custer was the fact that Crook had learned the hard way just a week before, the 17th of June, on the Rosebud River just how hard it was to go against the Lakota and Cheyenne. General Cook's force thought that their disastrous brush had come at the hands of Two Moon's Cheyenne warriors. They were wrong, of course: Though there were Cheyenne there, the assault on them was led by the war leader of the Ogalala Teton Lakota, Crazy Horse. Crook and his men would not know the difference, but what would they know? All Indians looked alike to them.

When it came time, it was as if the 7th Cavalry had fallen into a time warp. Had Custer known the size of the camp in terms of warriors (thousands rather than hundreds) and that "Red Beard" (General Crook) had been defeated by a 1,500-warrior-strong force only a week before, he would not have deployed on the encampment on the 25th—he was bullheaded maybe, but stupid, never.

There still would have been a battle for sure, perhaps on the 28th or shortly thereafter when the three Army columns may have very well linked up and perhaps have Crook's command as a reserve if it had still been in the area. The Indians would have been allowed to move south perhaps. The fight would have probably occurred in the same location (the Rosebud) as General Crook had fought this savage juggernaut only a week prior to the 25th.

The U.S. Army was in the field for one reason, to punish the all Indians not still on the reservations. Make no mistake about that. That was their mission: push and punish the Indians back to the reservations and to keep them out of the Paha Sapa or Black Hills. That was what the U.S. Army was out to accomplish.

• Third, neither Custer, nor any of the other battlefield commanders leading their under-manned and under-armed armies against the Indians up and until that time respected the fighting capabilities of the hostiles.

• Fourth, tactically, the *wasichu* were out-generaled. The battle would have been better staged had the other commanders been rejoined with Custer. He could be counted on to do as he was ordered to do. He would carry his orders to the limit. And yet, for all that happened that Sunday afternoon in late June, Custer's battle plan was a good one.

Given the facts that he was working with, as discussed throughout these many chapters, the plan almost worked. Had he known what the real situation was to his front, he would have waited. Against his carnal nature, most assuredly, but his military sense would have him wait until the commands could reunite and they could attack it in force. His answer was to attack always. It would have agitated him to tears possibly, but he would have waited.

In the end, it was his obligation as a commander to have known. He was not a stupid man. He went with what he knew and trusted fate for everything else. On this test day, his answers were proven to be wrong. Hindsight is always twenty-twenty; had Lieutenant Colonel Custer waited for the other generals to join up with him, the losses on the U.S. Army's side when the fight did come would have possibly been higher, but distributed across three commands, not just his soon-to-be-undeservedly-famous 7th Cavalry. The defeat of the Northern Plains hostiles may have been assured then and there, rather than a year or two later.

    Who is to say? There could have been a tremendous defeat for the U.S. Army and there might have been indeed an Indian Nation in the heart of the United States. Imagine that! What Generals Crook and Terry, Colonel Gibbons, and Lieutenant Colonel Custer would have brought to that fight would have been nearly 3,300 fighting men. Moving in tandem against the hostiles the Army may have destroyed Crazy Horse and Two Moons in one fell swoop.

    The U.S. Army may have won a battle that pitted Terry's and Gibbon's, Cook's and Custer's commands fighting together instead of piece meal like the Army had a habit of fighting the Indians. The Army's commanders just did not get it. The sheer size of the forces garnered together would have made a difference. What Generals Gibbon and Crook and Terry would have brought to the fight were three thousand more men. One would think more than enough for a fair fight. Perhaps, it would have been enough.

—38—

HUNKA HEY!
"IT IS A GOOD DAY TO DIE"

It is often written in many of the writings about the battle that the soldiers gave a good accounting of themselves during the battle. Presumably, that means that the soldiers killed as many or even scads more of the warriors than the hostiles killed of Custer's men—that simply was not so. From the start at the south end of the village where Major Reno led his battalion into the bowels of hell to the finish on Battle Ridge, the Indians had the soldiers by the short hairs.

Four Lakotas played a significant part in the defeat of Custer and the 7th Cavalry. They were Sitting Bull, Gall, Crazy Horse, and Rain-in-the-Face. Though Sitting Bull was never in the battle, he was the Medicine Man who predicted that the Indian people would win a major battle against the *wasichu*. Crazy Horse, Gall, and Rain were war leaders of the Lakota and ferocious fighters both against Major Reno and Custer. Crazy Horse never allowed pictures to be taken of him as he was afraid the picture would lock up his spirit. There is no picture that can be authenticated as one of this truly amazing man.

If ever a surprise attack (it was not one, not even close) turned into a desperate fight for the attackers' very lives, this was it. It was payback time! The Indians kept up overwhelming force, in terms of firepower and manpower from the outset long before the term or even the concept became popular. They fired first and never stopped shooting or attacking until the last soldier fell at the end of Battle Ridge. The soldiers for their part never stopped retreating long enough to mount any kind of resistance.

In Major Reno's official report he stated as much saying, "I only counted 18 dead Indians." I truly doubt that he even counted that many, or half that many. Not because I am saying that he was lying, but how could he have told them apart from his own scouts and the Sioux and Cheyenne in the physical condition in which any of them left on the field after the battle would have just looked like a dead Indian, much the same as white dead men looking like white dead men. There would have been no uniforms to distinguish the live "good Indians" from the dead "bad Indians" is the point. The Indians left on the field after the battle would have been his own. The attackers did not leave any.

That fact cannot be written enough times, or, said with enough emphasis to empress the reader of this history concerning the Battle of the Little Bighorn. There was not an instance during the battle that Indians were ever threatened or were out manned or out gunned. The Indians won because once engaged in battle, they never allowed the soldiers to regroup long enough to mount any kind of defensive perimeter or skirmish line. Not only when Major Reno attacked, but also, when Custer attempted to cross the Little Bighorn River at Medicine Tail Coulee's natural ford.

Had Major Reno attempted to make a stand on the edge western side of the Little Bighorn River where he was driven to ground, he too would have met the same fate as his commander and his men would during the next couple of hours. It was only because of Custer's attack that caused the Indians to be distracted long enough so that what was left of Major Reno's men could make a desperate retreat. Major Reno had nerve enough to call it a "charge" in his after action report. It was far from that—it was a mad-assed, wild-eyed, screaming, every man for himself, un-glorious, gut wrenching retreat.

Major Reno would never guess why the Indians let him go and would never admit it long afterwards. His own report says as much when he said that apparently the lieutenant colonel was supporting me from the north rather than from behind my attack.

His retreat (charge) was so wild in fact that over thirty wounded men would be left to the mercy of the Indians. Along with that number another 19 were left because they did not have horses. The men, alone to fend for themselves would make it back to Major Reno Hill later that night. It was a day that no mercy would be given to the *wasichus* left out in the open or unprotected. The Indians notion of mercy was a bullet in the brain or an arrow in the heart and an enemy's hair in his hand.

KILLED IN THE VALLEY FIGHT AGAINST MAJOR RENO & HIS MEN

LAKOTA

UNKPAPAS	SANS ARCS	OGALALA	TWO KETTLE
1. Swift Bear	1. Two Bears	1. White Eagle	1. Chased-by-Owls
2. White Buffalo	2. Standing Elk		
3. Long Road	3. Long Robe		
4. Hawk Man			

SHAHIYELA OHMESEHESO (Northern Cheyenne)

Whirlwind

KILLED FIGHTING CUSTER'S BATTALION

LAKOTA

UNKPAPAS	SANS ARC	OGALALA	MINNECONJOUX
1. Rectum (Guts)	1. Long Dog	1. Many Lice	1. High Horse
2. Red Face	2. Elk Bear	2. Bad-Light-Hair	2. Long Elk
3. Cloud Man	3. Young Skunk		
4. Black White Man			

SHAHIYELA OHMESEHESO (Northern Cheyenne)

1. Left Hand
2. Black Cloud
3. Swift Cloud
4. Noisy Walking
5. Hump Nose
6. Lame White Man
7. Owns-Red-Horse
8. Flying By
9. Bearded Man (Mustache)
10. Limber Bones
11. Black Bear

A total of thirty-two Indians were killed in action during that bloody Sunday afternoon! As far as is known, the above is the complete list of Indians killed in action against the soldiers at the Little Sheep River fight. No number of wounded has ever been established, even to this day, nor is there an official number for wounded hostiles who died after the encampment left the valley.

An interesting side bar here: Only thirty-two Indians were killed. If the idea is to lose less than the enemy, it was a pitiful few if you are a *wasichu* trying to call a catastrophe a draw. In comparison to the 272 or so of the cavalry, scouts, and civilians who were lost during the battle—it almost does not sound like a fair fight. It was not. The hostiles clobbered them. It was not until long after the battle was over that the Indians knew whom they had killed. When asked by the *wasichu*, most of the Indians just said nothing. What difference did it make? Dead is dead, and that was the way the Indians wanted it that day.

Only a few, even 30 or 40 years later, would ever say who of the warriors might have killed Custer himself. That presumes of course that he died on Battle Ridge. The Indians knew better; he died at the natural ford at Medicine Tail Coulee on the Little Sheep River, one of the first to fall. It was his men who took him to the top of the hill with them as they ran from the river.

The following are names of Lakota who have been mentioned or actually took credit for killing "The Famous 'Injin' Fighter":

Red Horse
Little Knife
Brown Back
Walks under the Ground
Fast Eagle
White Bull
Brave Bear
Wooden Leg

Some of the Indians said Walks under the Ground was seen riding Custer's mare, "Vic," after the fight. How they would know "Vic" was Custer's horse is a mystery, since only very few "knew" him when they would have seen him alive, much less dead.)

White Bull, the father of my dad's carpenter, was convinced to the day he died that he put the final coup de grass on the *wasichu* soldier chief, a bullet in the brain, though at the time, he did not know who he was. In fact, White Bull thought that it was another soldier who was chief because of the medallion he had around his neck. It was a Saint Christopher medal worn by Captain Myles Keogh. The "medallion" he was wearing was strong medicine and Indians did not go against a man's strong medicine, dead or alive, if they knew of it before hand. The tough-talking Captain Keogh very well may have been the last living white man on the ridge when he finally met his end. Only a few other men where not mutilated—Indians respected fearless fighters; they would have seen a few that day.

The Indians thought that a young brave by the name of Brave Bear shot Custer as he came across the river. At least, he is given credit for the act. Indians are generally very picky about who gets what coup when they count things up. It is pretty important that they get things right. White Bull had never personally met Custer so he wouldn't have known him on the battlefield that day; he did not know Keogh either. At the end, the hostiles were shooting the pistols of the *wasichus* into the brains of the slain, making sure they were all dead. That is probably the reason that the men on Major Reno Hill thought that the fighting on Battle Ridge went on as late as it did (around 5:00 or 5:30). I am convinced that the Indians were just celebrating their victory at that time. They had lots of ammunition.

Wooden Leg, a Shahiyela warrior, the most notable, backs this up saying that it was not until weeks later that they (the Indians) knew who it was that they had defeated that day on the Little Bighorn.

—39—

TAPS
7th CAVALRY REGIMENT
OFFICERS AND ENLISTED
KILLED IN ACTION

The following pages list a compilation for each element of the 7th Cavalry that fell during the battle at the Battle of the Little Big Horn. Usually, casualty lists are just names of individuals who were killed during an engagement and units they were attached to, and if lucky, the cause of death.

As time goes on, we tend to forget what happened and are only reminded by marble or granite stones that may have the names of the fallen etched into the stone marker. As we gaze at the names we barely read the names of the men who are written on the list that sometimes get enshrined in stone. In time, the names become just words. They have no form and we do not even associate the name with someone who was once a viable, living, breathing, smiling face, who was once someone's son, or husband, or brother. If you knew the man, it hurts too much; if you did not, they are bad memories of another time—when we once considered the eternal questions, "Why was it them and not us?" Later, these names just become words on a piece of rock.

This list that follows is an attempt to give the names of the fallen some form, some shadow of depth, that perhaps, the reader can identify as belonging to a man who died in a cause of this country's development.

HEADQUARTERS COMPANY

Military Personnel

1. General George A. Custer. Commander.
2. 1st Lieutenant William Winner Cooke. Regimental Adjutant (Canadian-born, acclaimed the best horseman, best shot, and fastest runner in the regiment) well over six feet tall, he was a close member of the Custer family. When killed he was 36 years of age, 6' 2" tall, brown eyes, brown hair, and a native Canadian.
3. George E. Lord, Assistant Surgeon. A civilian contract doctor paid $100.00 per month. He died with Custer's battalion. Was to be commissioned a 1st Lieutenant on 26 June 1876; he was killed on the 25th and his body not recovered.
4. Corporal John J. Callahan, killed while with Doctor Lord acting as the doctor's steward. He was 23 years of age, 5' 7" tall; gray eyes; dark hair; 3 years 9 months of service. His home record was Massachusetts.
5. Sergeant Major William H. Sharrow. He was 32 years of age, 5' 8" tall, blue eyes, brown hair, 11-years service. He was born in England.
6. Chief Trumpeter Henry Voss. His body was found near the river; he would have been perhaps one of the first troopers to fall after Lieutenant Colonel Custer, commanders kept their buglers closer by. His approximate age was 34-35; he was 5' 9" tall, blue eyes, light hair, 16years service, Germany.
7. Trumpeter Henry C. Dose, detailed from Troop G to ride with Custer's battalion that day as a messenger and second bugler, killed near the Medicine Tail Coulee. He was 27 years of age, 5' 6" tall; gray eyes, brown hair; 5.5 years service: born in Germany.
8. Sergeant Robert M. Hughes; Assigned to Headquarters Company from K Troop. Of the three Hughes on that field that day, two were killed in action, one wounded, none of these men by the same sir-name were related; this one carried Lieutenant Colonel Custer's battle flag. He was 36 years of age, 5' 9" tall; blue eyes; brown hair; 8years service, born in Ireland.

CIVILIANS

9. Boston Custer. Brother of George and Thomas Custer. Contractor-guide, $100.00 per month, he was 26-28 years of age, born in Michigan.
10. Henry Armstrong "Autie" Reed. He was the nephew of George A. Custer. His job on the campaign was officially a civilian drover for the quartermaster corps assigned to the trains he was 18 years of age. He was born in Michigan.
11. Mark Kellogg. He was a newspaper reporter for the Bismarck, Dakota Territory, Tribune, and the New York Herald. Generals Sheridan and Terry had told Lieutenant Colonel Custer that they did not want a reporter to accompany the expedition. Just before leaving Fort Abraham, Custer relented the man's begging to be taken and allowed him to go. He was 43 years of age, 5' 7" tall, brown eyes, brown hair. He was a widower who left two children, both girls.
12. Mitch Bouyer. He served as a civilian-Lead Scout for battalion. His salary was $150.00 per month. He was 39 years of age when he was killed. His mother was full blooded Santee Sioux, father French Canadian.

BATTLEFIELD CASUALTY FIGURES
FOR THE HEADQUARTERS
AND HEADQUARTERS COMPANY

Officers KIA	2
NCO KIA	3
Enlisted KIA	2
Civilians KIA	2
Scouts & Guides KIA	2
Contract Surgeon	1
Headquarters Co KIA	12
Assigned to the Regimental Rolls	27
Present for duty on 25 June 1876	9
Detailed to HQ Company 25 June 1876	3

COMPANY C OFFICERS

1. Captain Thomas Ward Custer, Commanding Troop C. He served as his brother's Aide de Camp on the last day. He was 31years of age, had light brown hair; gray eyes; was 5' 10" tall. Native state was Michigan. He left his family a life insurance policy from New York Life $5,000.
2. 2nd Lieutenant Henry Moore Harrington. His body was never recovered It is thought that during the initial charge down the Medicine Tail Coulee that his horse bolted from the excitement the charge and the firing going on around that forward group. The horse bolted and ran into the village. He was 27 years of age and was on his third campaign since joining the regiment. He had 4years active service, was married with two children-a boy and a girl; a native of New York. His wife received a pension of $15.00 per month and $30.00 per month for the children.

NON-COMMISSIONED OFFICERS

1. 1st Sergeant Edwin Bobo. He was 31 years of age at the time his death; was 5' 6" tall; had hazel eyes and brown hair; he had 9years service was married and had two children; native Ohio.
2. Sergeant Jeremiah Finley. At the time of his death he 35 years of age; was 5' 7" tall; grey eyes; brown hair; had served for 15years He was married with three children. In civilian life he had been a tailor and made Lieutenant Colonel Custer's buckskin jacket for the campaign. He was from Ireland.
3. Sergeant George August Finckle. Like most NCO's; he was older than the average trooper; at the time of his death he was 32years of age; tall for a cavalryman; 6' 1" tall; had gray eyes and dark hair. Though older he had only 4 years service in the United States. He was a native Germany where he had served as a captain in German army.
4. Corporal Henry E. French. He was 26 years of age; was 5' 6" tall; had brown hair and hazel eyes with 4years service. He was born and raised in New Hampshire.

5. Corporal John Foley. He was 25 years of age; was 5' 9" tall with blue eyes and prematurely graying hair with 3 years service. His body was located near the ford at the end Medicine Tail Coulee. From its location he would have been one of the first to fall from Custer's battalion. He was from the state of Maine.

6. Corporal Daniel Ryan. One of three Ryan's in the regiment though none were related. At the time of his death he was 25 years of age; he was 5' 7" tall; he had enlisted from the state New York.

ENLISTED TROOPERS; COMPANY C

7. Trumpeter Thomas J. Bucknell. 27 years of age; 5' 8" tall; gray eyes; light hair; 6 years service; Ohio.

8. Trumpeter William Kramer. 27 years of age; 5' 6" tall; gray eyes; brown hair; 8 months service; Pennsylvanian.

9. Saddler; George Howell. 30 years of age; 5' 6" tall; gray eyes; dark hair; 3.5 years service; prior to coming into the service he had been a harness maker; hailed from New York City; New York.

10. Blacksmith; John King. 27 years of age; 5' 5" tall; gray eyes; brown hair; 9 months service; born in Switzerland.

11. Private Fred E. Allan. 28 years of age; 5' 8" tall; brown eyes; black hair; 2.5 years service; native of England)

12. Private John Brightfield. 23 years of age; 5' 9" tall; brown eyes; brown hair; 6 months service; Indiana.)

13. Private Christopher Criddle. 25 years of age; 5' 8" tall; gray eyes; brown hair; 9 months service; Virginia.

14. Private George Eiseman. 22 years of age; 5' 5" tall; blue eyes; dark hair; 4.5 years service; Pennsylvania.

15. Private Gustave Engle. 27 years of age; 5' 8" tall; brown eyes; brown hair; 9 months service second tour when killed; native of Germany.

16. Private James Farrand. 37 years of age; 5' 8" tall; dark eyes; black hair; 5 years service; originally from Illinois.

17. Private Patrick Griffin. 28 years of age; 5' 9" tall; dark eyes; dark hair; 3.5 years service; from Ireland.

18. Private James Hathersall. 27 years of age; 5' 6" tall; blue eyes light hair; 5.5 years service; England.
19. Private John Lewis. 30 years of age; 5' 8" tall; gray eyes brown hair. 9 years service; Pennsylvania.
20. Private Frederick Meier. 32 years of age; 5' 6" tall; hazel eyes; brown hair; 6 months service; Germany.
21. Private August Meyer. 24years of age; 5' 6" tall; blue eyes; brown hair; 8 months service; Germany.
22. Private Edgar Phillips. 23 years of age; 5' 6" tall; brown eyes; brown hair. 9 months service; Massachusetts.
23. Private John Rauter. 30 years of age; 5' 9" tall; blue eyes; dark hair; 2.5 years service; Switzerland.
24. Private Edward Rix. 26 years of age; 5' 6" tall; gray eyes; brown hair; 2.5 years service; Massachusetts.
25. Private James H. Russell. 24 years of age; 5' 5" tall; gray eyes; brown hair; 2.8 years service; Indiana.
26. Private Ludwick St. John. 28 years of age; 5' 9" tall; gray eyes; brown hair;15 years service (that is not a misprint—the boy; I mean; the man; joined the service at age of 13 years old) in the 9th Missouri Cavalry during the Civil War. Missouri.
27. Private Samuel S. Shade. 29 years of age; 5' 9" tall; blue eyes; brown hair; 9 months service; Pennsylvania.
28. Private Jeremiah Shea. 22 years of age; 5' 6" tall; gray eyes; brown hair; 9 months service; England.
29. Private Nathan Short. 22 years of age; 5' 7" tall; gray eyes; brown hair; 9 months service; Pennsylvania. His body was found several miles from the battle field over on Rosebud Creek about three or four weeks after the fight. He was one who almost got away.
30. Private Alpheus Stuart. 34 years of age; 5' 0" tall; gray eyes; dark hair; 6 years service; New York.
31. Private Ygnatz Stungewitz. 29 years of age; 5' 8" tall; blue eyes; light hair; 2.7 years service; Russia.
32. Private John Thadus. 22 years of age; 5' 7" tall; black eyes; dark hair; 10 months service; North Carolina.
33. Private Garrett Van Allen his given name is Van Allan; his mother had

a tombstone cut for him with the name Niver; her remarried name. 30 years of age; 5' 7" tall; brown hair; blue eyes. 2 years 3mos service; New Jersey.

34. Private Oscar L. Warner. 36 years of age. 5' 6" tall; hazel eyes, brown hair;12 years service; Indiana.

35. Private Willis B. Wright. 22 years of age. 5' 7" tall; blue eyes; brown hair; 8 months service; Iowa.

36. Private Henry Wyman. 36 years of age. 5' 6" tall; brown eyes; dark hair; 3 years service with cavalry; served first with Navy; dates unknown. Massachusetts.

BATTLEFIELD CASUALTY FIGURES FOR TROOP C

Officers KIA	2
Non-commissioned officers KIA	6
Enlisted KIA	29
Wounded in Action (detailed to pack trains)	4
Died of Wounds	1*
Missing but presumed dead	1

(*Listed as MIA on some roles, trooper Nathan Short, see number 29 above, the soldier's body was found and identified later.)

TOTAL KIA: 39

* Died of wounds; Private James C. Bennett (5 July 1876) Assigned To Company on the morning May 17, 1876; 66 Present for Duty to the Company on the morning, June 25, 1876; 43

COMPANY E OFFICERS

1. 1st Lieutenant Algernon Emory (Fresh) Smith, Commanding
2. 2nd Lieutenant James Garland Sturgis. Body never recovered. 22years age, 5' 9" tall, brown eyes, dark hair, 2-mo. active service, home record; New Mexico.

NON-COMMISSIONED OFFICERS

1. 1st Sergeant Frederick Hohmeyer. Nude when found, recognized only by his name on his sock; 32years age; 5' 7" tall; gray eyes; light hair; 6 years service; Germany.
2. Sergeant John S. Ogden. 31 years of age; 5' 8" tall; gray eyes; light hair; 4 years service; Massachusetts.
3. Sergeant William B. James. 27years of age; 5' 9" tall; hazel eyes; light hair; 4 years service; Wales.
4. Corporal Thomas P. Eagan. Enlisted as Thomas Hagan. 28 years age; 5' 5" tall; gray eyes; sandy hair; 2.5 years service; Ireland.
5. Corporal Henry S. Mason. 29 years age; 5' 11" tall; gray eyes; sandy hair; 6 years service; Indiana.
6. Corporal George C. Brown. 25 years age; 5' 5" tall; brown eyes; brown hair; 4 years service; Maryland.
7. Corporal Albert H. Meyer. 24 years age; 5' 8" tall; blue eyes; light hair; 2.5 years service; Germany.
8. Trumpeter Thomas F. McElroy. 31 years age; 5' 5" tall; blue eyes; dark hair. He had served during Civil War; was wounded and then reentered the service in 1870; 6years service. Native land; Ireland.
9. Trumpeter George A. Moonie. 21 years. age; 5' 6" tall; hazel eyes; dark hair; 1-yr. service; Massachusetts.
10. Private William H. Baker. 27 years age; 5' 9" tall; blue eyes; brown hair. 6 years service; married; one child; Illinois.
11. Private Robert Barth. 25 years age; 5' 10" tall; gray eyes; brown hair; 3 years service; Germany.

12. Private Owen Boyle. 33 years age; 5' 6" tall; gray eyes; dark hair; 14 years service; Ireland.
13. Private James Brogan. 27 years age; 5' 8" tall; hazel eyes; brown hair; 6years service; Pennsylvania.
14. Private Edward Conner. 30 years age; 5' 5" tall; hazel eyes; brown hair; 9 years service; Ireland.
15. Private John Darris. 30 years age; 5' 6" tall; blue eyes; brown hair; 15 years service; New York.
16. Private William Davis. 25 years age; 5' 6" tall; gray eyes; brown hair; 1.5 years service; Illinois.
17. Private Richard Farrell. 24 years age; 5' 9" tall; gray eyes; brown hair; 7 months. service; Ireland.
18. Private John S. S. Forbes. Assumed name; John S. Hiley. He was 27years age; 6' 0" tall; hazel eyes; brown hair; 4 years service. Was born in either England or Scotland.
19. Private John Heim. 24 years age; 5' 1" short; brown eyes; light hair; 6 months. service; from Missouri.
20. Private John Henderson. 27 years age; 5' 8" tall; gray eyes; light hair; 3 months. service; from Ireland.
21. Private Sykes Henderson. 27 years age; 5' 8" tall; brown eyes; brown hair; 6 years service; Pennsylvania.
22. Private William Huber. 23years age; 5' 7" tall; gray eyes; light hair; 1.5 years service; Germany.
23. Private Andrew Knecht. 23 years age; 5' 6" tall; hazel eyes; brown hair; 2.5 years service; Ohio.
24. Private Patrick O'Connor. 24 years age; 5' 5" tall; blue eyes; light hair; 2.5 years service; Ireland.
25. Private William H. Rees. 32 years age; 6' 1" tall; gray eyes; sandy hair; 4.5 years service; Pennsylvania.
26. Private Edward Rood. 28 years age. 5' 7" tall; hazel eyes; black hair; 2.5 years service; New York.
27. Private Henry Schele. 33 years age; 5' 6" tall; blue eyes; sandy hair; 9 years service; Germany.
28. Private William Smallwood. 24years age; 5' 8" tall; brown eyes; brown hair; 1.5 years service; Indiana.

29. Private Albert A. Smith. One of the three Smiths in Troop C. All totaled, there were 10 men claiming their last name was Smith in the 7th Cavalry on the day the battle. At the end of the day there were only half that many left alive. Private A. A. was 38 years age; 5' 6" tall; gray eyes; brown hair; 8.5 years service; supposedly a native New York; enlistment papers list that city as his home of record and is where he enlisted.

30. Private James Smith; (1). Age unconfirmed; enlisted in 1861 on re-enlistment documents in 1874 his listed age was 22 years age. If the later is accurate; he would have been 11 years old on first enlistment; will go with the listed age in '74 (22). 24 years age; 5' 6" tall; hazel eyes; brown hair; 2-14 years service; from Ireland. His real name was never known—What was an Irishman doing with an English handle; if not trying to hide who he really was? We shall never know; his secret died with him.

31. Private James Smith; (2). 29 years age; 5' 4" tall; hazel eyes; black hair; 1.5 years service; Massachusetts.

32. Private Benjamin F. Stafford. 29 years age; 5' 5" tall; brown eyes; black hair; 2-6 years service; Massachusetts.

33. Private Alexander Stella. 23 years age; 5' 6" tall; brown eyes; black hair; 1.5 years service; formally from the nation of Greece.

34. Private William A. Torrey. 26 years of age; 5' 4" tall; gray eyes; light hair; 1 month service; Massachusetts.

35. Private Cornelius Van Sant. 26 years of age; 5' 7" tall; blue eyes; brown hair; 4 years service; Ohio.

36. Private George P. Walker. 24 years of age; 5' 6" tall; gray eyes; brown hair; 1.5 years service; Rhode Island.

BATTLEFIELD CASUALTY FIGURES FOR E TROOP

Officers KIA:	2 (One body never recovered)
Non-Commissioned officers KIA:	7
Enlisted KIA:	29
Missing, but presumed dead:	0
Total KIA:	38

LAST RIDE

Assigned to Company on the morning, June 25, 1876: 61
Present for Duty to the Company on the morning, June 25, 1876: 38

COMPANY F OFFICERS

1. Captain George W. Yates. Commanding.
2. 2nd Lieutenant William Van Wyck Reily. Second-in-command; 22 years of age, appointed to the Naval Academy at the age 16 in 1870; forced to resign because he was deficient in math and science two years later. Re-joined the Army in October 1875, and transferred to the 7th Cavalry in January 1876, 1.5 years service, Washington, D. C.)

NON-COMMISSIONED OFFICERS

1. 1st Sergeant Michael Kenney. At the time his death he was 26 years age, 5' 7" tall, gray eyes, brown hair, he was at the end his second enlistment 5.5 years in the service. He was from Ireland.
2. Sergeant Frederick Nursey. He joined the cavalry at 23 years age; he was 5' 5" tall, had blue eyes and light hair. He had 5 years service at the time of his death. He was from England.
3. Sergeant John Vickory. Used the listed alias after he had deserted during the Civil War from an artillery unit, he re-enlisted under the name John Vickory and re-entered the war, this time with 2nd Massachusetts Cavalry, later enlisted with the 7th Cavalry under the same name. Real name was John H. Groesbeck. At the time his death he was 29 years age, was 5' 10" tall, he had blue eyes and brown hair. Young, when he first joined at 15 years age. He had 14 years in the Service. Originally from Canada.
4. Sergeant John K. Wilkinson. He was 28 years age when he fell with Custer's command. He was 5' 8" tall, had gray eyes, brown hair. His real name was John R. not John K. as listed on the Battle Monument. He was

married; his widow received $8.00 per month until she remarried two years later. He had 4.5 years in Service, Originally from New York.

5. Corporal Charles Coleman. 25 years age, 5' 5" tall, blue eyes, dark hair, 2.5years in service, Indiana.

6. Corporal William Teeman. His name was listed as William Teeman on the monument, it was an alias. His real name was William A. Adams. Adams was the one he used to get into the Artillery eight years before; he deserted and then joined the cavalry using the name Teeman. At the time his death he was 30 years age, he was 5' 9" tall, and had gray eyes and brown hair. All totaled he had 8-years in the service. He was born in Denmark.

7. Corporal John Briody. He was 28 years age; was 5' 5" tall; had brown eyes and dark hair, 3.5 years in service; born in New York.

ENLISTED TROOPERS F TROOP

8. Trumpeter Thomas N. Way. 29 years age; 5' 7" tall; hazel eyes; dark hair; 4 years service; Pennsylvania.

9. Farrier Benjamin Brandon. His real name was Robert Nelson; he had deserted (twice) and used the alias now listed on the battle monument. One the oldest enlisted men in the regiment. At the time his death he was 45 years age; 5' 6" tall; had hazel eyes and black hair. His total service time was 6 years counting time in 17th Infantry. Originally from Kentucky.

10. Blacksmith James R. Manning. 33 years of age; 5' 8" tall; hazel eyes; dark hair; 3 years service; Georgia.

11. Private Thomas Atcheson. 38 years of age; 5' 5" tall; hazel eyes; dark hair; 10 years service; Ireland.

12. Private William Brady. 28 years of age; 5' 6" tall; blue eyes; brown hair; 9 months. in service; Pennsylvania.

13. Private Benjamin F. Brown. 27 years of age; 5' 9" tall; hazel eyes; light hair; 4 years in service; Kentucky.

14. Private William Brown. That was an alias; his real name was never known. He was 33 years of age; he was 5' 5" tall; with blue eyes and brown hair; 9 years in service. Born Germany.

15. Private Patrick Bruce. 32 years of age; 5' 5" tall; blue eyes; brown hair; 9 years in service; Ireland.
16. Private Lucien Burnham. 25 years of age; 5'8" tall; gray eyes; red hair; 3.5 years in service; New York.
17. Private James Carney. 33 years of age; 5' 4" tall; gray eyes; black hair; 3.5 years in service; England.
18. Private Armantheus D. Cather. 26 years of age; 5' 8" tall; gray eyes; brown hair; 3.5 years in service; Pennsylvania.
19. Private Anton Dohman. 26 years of age; 5' 2" tall; gray eyes, brown hair; 5 years service; Germany.
20. Private Timothy Donnelly. 22 years of age; 5' 6" tall; blue eyes, dark hair; 9 months. service; England.
21. Private John Gardner. Listed as William Gardner on battle monument. He had served as a lieutenant during Civil War in an artillery unit. He was 31 years of age; 5' 7" tall; had blue eyes and light hair. All totaled he had 14 years in service. He was Canadian, perhaps; though he was born in Germany.
22. Private George W. Hammon. 24 years of age; 5' 8" tall; blue eyes, brow hair; 2.5 years service; Ohio.
23. Private John P. Kelly. 28 years of age; 5' 6" tall; hazel eyes, brown hair; 9 years service, Ireland.
24. Private Gustave Klein. He had used at least two other alias names, the one he died with is as listed on the Battle Monument. He was 29 years of age and stood 5' 7" tall; he had blue eyes and light hair. He had been in the military in the United States for 10 years. As his name indicates he was born in Germany.
25. Private Herman Knauth. 38 years of age; 5' 8" tall; blue eyes, brown hair; 4.5years service; Prussia.
26. Private William H. Lerock. 26 years of age; 5' 5" tall; hazel eyes, dark hair;11 months. service; New York.
27. Private Werner L. Liemann. The name that is listed on the Battle Monument was Liemann. He had used at least three alias names besides the one listed there. He was 26 years age at the time of his death. He was 5' 5" tall with blue eyes and brown hair. He had been in the cavalry 4 years His enlistment paper said he was born in Germany.

28. Private William A. Lossee. 26 years of age; 5' 5" tall; gray eyes, light hair; 9 months. service; New York.
29. Private Christian Madsen. His name is different on the battle monument, listed there as Christian Madson, and elsewhere, as Christian Madsen. Could have been just a mistake by the engraver. He was 28 years of age, 5' 11" tall with blue eyes and light colored hair (blonde), 3.5 years service. Born in Denmark.
30. Private Francis E. Milton. Entered the service as a 13-year-old. At the time his death he was 23 years of age. He was 5' 7" tall; had blue eyes, light hair. He had 10 years service to his credit at the time of his death. Born in Michigan.
31. Private Joseph Monroe. 25 years of age; 5' 6" tall; brown eyes, black hair; 10 months. service; born in France.
32. Private Sebastian Omling. 38 years of age; 5' 5" tall; hazel eyes, light hair; 5 years service; born in Bavaria.
33. Private Patrick Rudden. 23 years of age; 5' 6" tall; blue eyes, brown hair; 10 months service; New Jersey.
34. Private Richard D. Saunders. 5' 9" tall; blue eyes, brown hair; 10 months service. Born in Canada.
35. Private Francis W. Sicfous. 24 years of age, 5' 5" tall, gray eyes, light hair, 9 months in service; Pennsylvania.
36. Private George A. Warren. 35 years of age; 5' 10" tall; hazel eyes, brown hair; 10 months. service; Indiana.

BATTLEFIELD CASUALTY FIGURES FOR TROOP F

Officers KIA: 2
Non-commissioned officers KIA: 7
Enlisted KIA: 29
Missing but presumed dead: 0
Total KIA: 38
Assigned to the Company on the morning of May 17, 1876: 68
Present for Duty to the Company on the morning of June 25, 1876: 38

COMPANY I OFFICERS

1. Captain Myles Walter Keogh. Commanding.
2. 1st Lieutenant James E. Porter. West Point graduate, 1869; assigned 7th Cavalry 1869. He was survived by wife and two small sons.

NON-COMMISSIONED OFFICERS

1. 1st Sergeant, Frank E. Varden. An alias; also known as Frank E. Noyes. He was 31 years of age; 5' 10" tall; blue eyes, brown hair; 10 years service; hailed from Maine.
2. Sergeant, James Bustard. 30 years of age; 5' 6" tall; hazel eyes, light hair; 6 years service; Ireland.
3. Corporal, John Wild. 27 years of age; 5'10" tall; hazel eyes, brown hair; 3 years service; New York.
4. Corporal, George C. Morris. 25 years of age; 5' 6" tall; brown eyes, brown hair; 8 months service, Massachusetts.
5. Corporal, Samuel F. Staples. 27 years of age; 5' 6" tall; brown eyes, dark hair; 3.5 years service; Massachusetts.

ENLISTED TROOPERS, I TROOP

6. Trumpeter, John McGucker. 40 years of age; 5' 5" tall, hazel eyes, black hair; 10 years service, New York.
7. Trumpeter, John W. Patton. 24 years of age; 5' 3" tall; brown eyes, brown hair; 3.5 years service, Pennsylvania.
8. Saddler Henry A. Bailey. 24 years of age; 5' 7" tall; gray eyes, brown hair; 3.5 years service; Rhode Island.
9. Private John D. Barry. 26 years of age; 5' 7" tall; gray eyes, dark hair; 8 months. service; Ireland.
10. Private Joseph F. Broadhurst. 25 years of age; 5' 5" tall; brown eyes, dark hair; 2.5 years service, Pennsylvania.

11. Private Thomas Conners. 30 years of age; 5' 7" tall; blue eyes, dark hair; 5.5 years service, New York.
12. Private Thomas P. Downing. Miss-represented his age at time enlistment, said he was 21, he was only 17. At the time of his death he was 20 years age; he was 5' 8" tall; he had blue eyes, sandy hair. He had 3years service. Born in Ireland.
13. Private Edward Driscoll. 26 years of age; 5' 6" tall; hazel eyes, light hair; 3 years service, Ireland.
14. Private David C. Gillette. 24 years of age; 5' 5" tall; blue eyes, light hair; 2.5 years service, New York.
15. Private George H. Gross. 31 years of age; 5' 6" tall; blue eyes, light hair; 4 years service, Germany.
16. Private Adam Hetesimer. 29 years of age; 5' 7" tall; blue eyes, black hair; 8 months service; Ohio.
17. Private Edward P. Holcomb. 31 years of age; 5' 6" tall; black eyes, black hair; 3.5 years service; Connecticut.
18. Private Marion E. Horn. 22 years of age; 5' 6" tall; hazel eyes, brown hair; 3 years service; Indiana.
19. Private Patrick Kelly. As listed on the Battle Monument; again could have been a chisel mistake; his real name was Edward H. Kelly. He was 35 years of age; stood 5' 5" tall, had gray eyes and brown hair. He had 10 years service at the time of his death. Born in Ireland.
20. Private Henry Lehmann. 37 years of age, 5' 4" tall, brown eyes, dark hair, 3.5 years in service, Germany.
21. Private Edward W. Lloyd. 24 years of age, 5' 6" tall, gray eyes, brown hair, 3.5 years service, England.
22. Private Archibald McIlhargey. His real name was McEllargey. Never determined why he used the alias. He was married and had two children. His wife received a pension $10.00 per month until she remarried. She received $2.00 per month for one the children. He was 31 years of age when he was killed. He was 5' 5" tall; brown eyes and dark hair; 3.5 years service. Born in Ireland.
23. Private John Mitchell. He was married and had two children. When he was killed he was 34 years of age. He was 5' 6" tall; had blue eyes and brown hair. He had been in the service 10 years when he was killed. He

was in Major Reno's command but had carried the second message from Major Reno to Custer's column and stayed with him. Born in Ireland.
24. Private Jacob Noshang. 24 years of age, 5' 5" tall, hazel eyes, brown hair; 3.5 years in service, Ohio.
25. Private John O'Bryan. 25 years of age, 5' 6" tall; blue eyes, brown hair; 3 years in service; Pennsylvania.
26. Private John Parker. 27 years of age; 5' 7" tall, with gray eyes and light hair; 3 years in service; England.
27. Private Felix James Pitter. 26 years of age; 5' 6" tall; hazel eyes, brown hair; 2.5 years in service, England.
28. Private George Post. 28 years of age; 5' 7" tall; blue eyes, light hair; 10 years service; Michigan.
29. Private James Quinn. 26 years of age; 5' 6" tall; blue eyes, red hair; 4 years service; New York.
30. Private William Reed. 33 years of age; 5' 10" tall; gray eyes, light hair; 9 years service; Maryland.
31. Private John W. Rossbury. 27 years of age, 5' 6" tall, hazel eyes, dark hair, 4 years service; New York.
32. Private Darwin L. Symms. 24 years of age; 5' 9" tall; blue eyes, brown hair; 9 months service; Canada.
33. Private James E. Troy. 27 years of age; 5' 5" tall; gray eyes, brown hair; 5 years service; Massachusetts.
34. Private Charles Van Bramer. 26 years of age; 5' 9" tall; gray eyes, dark hair; 4 years service; New Hampshire.
35. Private William B. Whaley. 27 years of age; 5' 6" tall; brown eyes, dark hair; 2.5 years of service; Kentucky.

BATTLE STATISTICS FOR I TROOP

Officers KIA	2
Total KIA	37
Non-commissioned officers KIA	5
Assigned to Company on 17 May 1876	65
Enlisted KIA	30

Present for duty on 25 June 1876   37
Missing but presumed dead   0

COMPANY L OFFICERS

1. 1st Lieutenant James Calhoun. Commanding.
2. 1st Lieutenant James E. Porter. Second-in-command. Appointed to the 7th Cavalry in 1869; He had two small sons, one just four months old when he was killed. That son died before his first birthday and his second son in a mining accident in 1903. His wife received a pension of $17.00 to 30.00 until her death in 1915.
3. 2nd Lieutenant John Jordan Crittenden. Appointed as a fill-in for Lieutenant Edwin Eckerson who was in the process of joining the regiment from his old station in the southwest where he was fighting Apaches. Eckerson was an interesting man. Lieutenant Crittenden came to the 7th Cavalry from the infantry and had lost an eye during a hunting accident. He was 22 years old at the time of his death. He had been in the cavalry less than two months at the time of his death. His father a Lieutenant Colonel wanted his son's body buried with the men he commanded. New York.

NON-COMMISSIONED OFFICERS

1. 1st Sergeant James Butler. His remains were first located and identified near the Medicine Tail Coulee by Lieutenant Godfrey, Commander of K Troop. He was surrounded by many spent shell casings which indicates that he had kept the enemy away from him for a time. Oddly, he was buried in an unmarked grave. In 1905, his remains were identified and they were interred in the Custer Battlefield National Cemetery, he was married. His wife received a $12.00 pension (later $18.00) until her death in 1914. He was 34 years of age; 5'5" tall; gray eyes, black hair; 6 years service; New York.
2. Sergeant William Cashan. 31 years of age; 5' 9" tall; blue eyes, brown

LAST RIDE

hair; 9 years service; Ireland.
3. Sergeant Amos B. Warren. 27 years of age; 5' 10" tall; hazel eyes, brown hair; 3 years service, New York.
4. Corporal William H. Harrison. 31 years of age; 5' 7" tall; hazel eyes, dark hair; 7 months. service; Massachusetts.
5. Corporal John Seiler. 26 years of age; 5' 8" tall; gray eyes, light hair; 4 years service; Bavaria.
6. Corporal William H. Gilbert. 25 years of age; 5' 7" tall; blue eyes, brown hair; 2.5 years service; France.

ENLISTED MEN, L TROOP

7. Trumpeter Frederick Walsh. 25 years of age; 5' 7" tall; hazel eyes, brown hair; 3 years service.
8. Blacksmith Charles Siemon. 33 years of age; 5' 7" tall; gray eyes, brown hair; 9 years service; Denmark.
9. Saddler Charles Perkins. 28 years of age; 5' 10" tall; black eyes, dark hair; 8 months service, Maine.
10. Private George E. Adams. 30 years of age; 5' 8" tall; blue eyes, light hair; 7 years service; Pennsylvania.
11. Private William Andrews. 33 years of age; 5' 6" tall; blue eyes, brown hair; 9 years service, Prussia.
12. Private Anthony Assadaly. 34 years of age; 5' 3" tall; blue eyes, dark hair; 11 years service; Prussia.
13. Private Elmer Babcock. 20 years of age, 5' 6" tall; brown eyes, brown hair; 9 months service; New York.
14. Private Ami Cheever. He had used two aliases: Chreer (Register Enlistments during his enlistment and as Hester elsewhere; 27 years of age; 5' 11" tall; gray eyes; brown hair; 4 years service, Pennsylvania.
15. Private William B. Crisfield. He had two aliases; Cristfield and Christfield; 41 years of age; 5' 7" tall; gray eyes, black hair; 18 years service; England.
16. Private John L. Crowley. Was enlisted under the name of John Duggan (name on Battle Monument); 27 years of age; 5' 9" tall; gray eyes,

dark hair; enlisted in the Navy in 1873, how he got to the cavalry is not known; 1 year service; Massachusetts.

17. Private William Dye. 26 years of age; 5' 9" tall; brown eyes, black hair; 9 months. service; Ohio.

18. Private James J. Galvan, had two aliases; J. J. Galvin and Calran; 28 years of age; 5' 6" tall; gray eyes, dark hair; 8 months service; England.

19. Private Charles Graham. 41 years of age; 5' 6" tall; blue eyes, brown hair; 10 years service; Ireland.

20. Private Henry Hamilton. 33 years of age; 5' 6" tall; blue eyes, brown hair; 8 years service; Ohio.

21. Private Weston Harrington. 21 years of age; 5' 8" tall; brown eyes, brown hair; 3.5 years service; Ohio.

22. Private Louis Hauggi. 25 years of age; 5' 9" tall; brown eyes, light hair; 2.5 years service; Germany.

23. Private Francis T. Hughes. 22 years of age; 5' 7" tall; blue eyes, brown hair; 1 year service, Kansas.

24. Private Thomas G. Kavanagh. He had been a sergeant but busted into the ranks for being AWOL; 32 years of age, 5' 11" tall; blue eyes, brown hair; 8 years service; Ireland.

25. Private Louis Lobering. 41 years of age; 5' 6" tall; blue eyes, brown hair; 16 years service; Germany.

26. Private Charles McCarthy. 31 years of age, 5' 7" tall; blue eyes, brown hair; 8 years service, Pennsylvania.

27. Private Peter McGue. 27 years of age; 5' 4" tall; brown eyes, brown hair; 1 year cavalry service and 4-yrs before the infantry and the artillery; New York.

28. Private Bartholomew Mahoney. One of three brothers to fight in the battle; he was the only one of the three to be killed; 30 years of age; 5' 10" tall; hazel eyes, dark hair; 3.5 years service; Ireland.

29. Private Thomas E. Maxwell. 25 years of age, 5' 5" tall; Blue eyes, brown hair, 3.5 years service; Pennsylvania.

30. Private John Miller. One of four men with the last name Miller (none related) assigned to 7th Cavalry; only two of the four took part in battle; 26 years of age; 5' 8" tall; hazel eyes, brown hair; 6 years service; Pennsylvania.

31. Private David J. O'Connell. 32 years of age, 5' 7" tall; dark eyes, brown hair; 2 years service; Ireland.
32. Private Oscar F. Pardee. His enlisted name was John Burke, that was the inscribed on the Battle Monument, his real name was Pardee; 24 years of age; 5' 8" tall; brown eyes, brown hair; 3 years 6 months service; New York.
33. Private Christian Reibold. Aliases; Reinbold and Riebold; 26 years of age, 5' 6" tall; gray eyes, light hair; all together about 2 years service. He had a habit of deserting; New York.
34. Private Henry Roberts. 26 years of age; 5' 9" tall; blue eyes, light hair; 3.5 years service; England.
35. Private Walter B. Rogers. 29 years of age; 5' 8" tall; brown eyes; dark hair, 3 years service; Pennsylvania.
36. Private Charles Schmidt. 26 years of age; 5' 8" tall; brown eyes, brown hair; 3.5 years service; Germany.
37. Private Charles Scott. 25 years of age; 5' 9" tall; blue eyes, brown hair; 2.5 years service; Scotland.
38. Private Bent Siemonson. 26 years of age; 5' 5" tall; blue eyes, light hair; 4.5 years service; Wisconsin.
39. Private Andrew Snow. 23 years of age; 5' 5" tall; hazel eyes; black hair; 9 months service; Canada.
40. Private Byron Tarbox. 24 years of age; 5' 6" tall; gray eyes; brown hair; 9 months service; Maine.
41. Private Edmond D. Tessier. 29 years of age; 5' 7" tall; hazel eyes; dark hair; 10 years service; Canada.
42. Private Thomas S. Tweed. 22 years of age; 5' 5" tall; gray eyes; brown hair; 9 months service; New York.
43. Private Johann Michael Vetter. 23 years of age; 5' 9" tall; blue eyes; light hair; 8 months service; Germany.

BATTLE STATISTICS FOR L TROOP

Officers KIA 3
Non-commissioned officers KIA 6
Enlisted KIA 37
Missing but presumed dead 0
Total KIA 46
Assigned to L Troop on the morning 25 June 1876 69
Present for duty on the morning 25 June 1876 46

CUSTER'S BATTALION BATTLE STATISTICS

Officers KIA 11
Non-commissioned officers KIA 27
Enlisted KIA 129
Civilians Killed 2
Guides and Scouts Killed 5
Total MIA (Officers only) 2
Total MIA (enlisted only) Unknown
Total KIA, Lieutenant Colonel Custer's Battalion 176

THE FOLLOWING TROOPERS WERE KILLED IN ACTION UNDER THE COMMAND MAJOR MARCUS RENO

COMPANY A CIVILIANS AND SCOUTS

1. Frank C. Mann. Civilian, Chief Packer, killed, on the hill top fight with Major Reno's men. Age unknown, Maine.
2. Charley Reynolds. Civilian-Chief Scout, $100.00 per month. A close personal friend of both Mrs. and Lieutenant Colonel Custer's, acclaimed

LAST RIDE

as the best scout on the plains and the second best shot in the Regiment next to Winner Cooke, detailed to ride with Major Reno that morning and was killed trying to re-cross the river. He and Isaiah Dorman were killed within 30 feet of one another. 34 years of age, 5'8" tall, brown hair, blue eyes.
3. Isaiah Dorman. Civilian-interpreter, grew up with the Indians that were being attacked, his body was badly slashed and shot with many arrows, scalped of facial hair.
4. Bloody Knife. Mixed-blood Indian, his father Unkpapa Sioux, his mother Ree. (39-years of age, he was born in Dakota Territories. Shot in the head and killed in the timber near Major Reno before Major Reno re-crossed the river, was thought to be Lieutenant Colonel Custer's favorite scout.
5. Bob-Tailed Bull. Was a full-blooded Ree Indian. First leader of the Ree scouts. 35years of age. Cut of before reaching the timber by Sioux, killed in valley fight near the timber.
6. Little Brave. Listed also as Little Solider. Arikara Indian scout. Killed in valley, stories vary as to where. Rode with Major Reno that day.

OFFICERS

7. 2nd Lieutenant Benjamin Hubert Hodgson. 32 years of age; joined the 7th Cavalry 1870; on extended duty from then until May 1876; he was killed during Major Reno's retreat from river. His horse had run-off on him and he grabbed a stirrup one the troopers making his get-away, drug across the river and then shot as he tried to escape on foot.
8. James M. DeWolf. Acting Assistant Surgeon; 33 years of age; he had enlisted at age 17 in 1861, discharged for disability in 1862 for gunshot wound. Resigned his one-third pension in and enlisted in1864, discharged 1868, enlisted same day, Idaho Territory as James DeWall, discharged in 1871, and enlisted same day as James De Wolf, transferred to Harvard School of Medicine, graduated from the school of medicine in June 1875, and took the Army's medical examination for assistant surgeon, failed. He was killed by gunshot wound through the abdomen and wounded six times in the head and face. He was 5' 8" tall, gray eyes, light hair; Pennsylvania.

NON-COMMISSIONED OFFICERS

None

TROOPERS

9. Corporal James Dalious. 25 years of age, 5' 10" tall; brown eyes, dark hair; 3.5 years service, Pennsylvania.
10. Private John E. Armstrong. Killed in valley during initial assault on village, his headless body was found in the valley, his head near the southern end of the village. 40 years of age, 5' 8" tall; blue eyes; brown hair; 11 years service, Pennsylvania.
11. Private James Drinan. 23 years of age, 5' 7" tall; gray eyes, brown hair; 1-5 years service, Ireland.
12. Private James McDonald. 22 years of age; 5' 6" tall; gray eyes, brown hair; 9 months service, Massachusetts.
13. Private William Moodie. Also known as Moody and Moony; 35 years of age, 5' 8" tall; gray eyes; brown hair; 1.5 years of service, Scotland.
14. Private Richard Rollins. 27 years of age; 5' 11" tall; blue eyes, brown hair; 3 years 9 months service; Kentucky.
15. Private John Sullivan. 25 years of age; 5' 6" tall; gray eyes, brown hair; 1.5 years service, Ireland.
16. Private Thomas P. Sweetser. His body was never recovered, at least not enough of it to recognize. He went by two other names, Switzer and T. F. Sweetser. 26 years of age; 5' 8" tall; blue eyes; brown hair; 7 months of service, Massachusetts.

BATTLE STATISTICS FOR TROOP A

Total enlisted KIA   8
Total officers KIA   1
Scouts and Guides   6

Contract Surgeon   1
Total KIA   16
Assigned to Troop on morning of 17 May 1876 58
Present for duty on the morning 25 June 1876 Un-known

COMPANY G OFFICERS

1. 1st Lieutenant Donald McIntosh, Commanding; 38-yrs of age. Born in Canada, mother was full-blooded Indian; served during the Civil War, appointed to 7th Cavalry in 1867. By nearly all accounts he was popular with his brother officers and troops, though he had a stick burning between him and Col Samuel Sturgis the 7th Cavalry commander. He was killed during the break-out from the valley fight with Major Reno's men.

NON-COMMISSIONED OFFICERS

1. Sergeant Edward Botzer. 31 years of age, 5' 6" tall; blue eyes; brown hair; 10 years service, Germany.
2. Sergeant Martin Considine. 29 years of age, 5' 7" tall; blue eyes; brown hair; 1.5 years service, Ireland.)
3. Corporal James Martin. 31 years of age, 5' 5" tall; gray eyes; brown hair; 3.5 years service, Ireland.
4. Corporal Otto Hagemann. 27 years of age, 5' 9" tall; brown eyes; brown hair; 3 years 9 months. service, Germany.

ENLISTED TROOPERS, A TROOP

5. Farrier Benjamin J. Wells. His body was found in the water close to where Lieutenant McIntosh was found (on the east bank of the river, one of the few not found by the Indians, he was fully clothed. Killed when his

horse bolted during the initial attack; (33 years of age; 5' 6" tall; blue eyes, fair hair; 11 years service; Illinois.
6. Saddler Crawford Selby. 31 years of age, 5' 5" tall; gray eyes, brown hair; 1 year service; Ohio.
7. Private John J. McGinniss. 26 years of age, 5' 7" tall; gray eyes, sandy hair; 1 year service; Massachusetts.
8. Private Andrew J. Moore. 26 years of age, 5' 8" tall; blue eyes, dark hair; 4.5 years service; New Jersey.
9. Private John Rapp. He is listed elsewhere as Ropp or Papp; 28 years of age; 5' 10" tall; blue eyes, dark hair; 2 years 9 months. service, Germany.
10. Private Benjamin F. Rogers. 29 years of age; 5' 10" tall; blue eyes, brown hair; 4.5 years service; Kentucky.
11. Private Henry Seafferman. 37 years of age; 5' 7" tall; hazel eyes, brown hair; 4 years service; Germany.
12. Private Edward Stanley. 26 years of age; 5' 9" tall; blue eyes, brown hair; 8 months service; Massachusetts.

BATTLE STATISTICS FOR G TROOP

Total enlisted KIA   12
Total Officers KIA   1
Total KIA   13
Assigned to G Troop on the morning of 17 May 1876: 73
Present for duty on the morning of 25 June 1876: 47

COMPANY M OFFICERS

None

NON-COMMISSIONED OFFICERS

1. Sergeant Miles F. O'Hara. Killed in the skirmish line when Troop M deployed in the valley fight with Major Reno's battalion; 25 years of age; 5' 8" tall; gray eyes, light hair; 3-5 years service; Ohio.)
2. Corporal Henry M. Cody. This name was an alias, real name was Henry M. Scollin; body was worked over pretty well by the squaws after he was killed; 25 years of age; 5' 7" tall; blue eyes, brown hair; 2.5 years of service; New Hampshire.)
3. Corporal Frederick Stressinger. Name on Battle Monument is Streing; that is wrong it should be Stressinger. 24 years of age; 5'5" tall; gray eyes, light hair; 3 years 9 months. of service; Indiana.

ENLISTED TROOPERS, M TROOP

1. Private Henry Gordon. 25 years of age; 5' 6" tall; brown eyes, brown hair; 3.5 years service, England.
2. Private Jacob Gebhart. He is listed as James J. Tanner on Battle Monument; wounded severely scaling the bluffs out of the valley, died on the 26th; 27 years of age; 5' 8" tall; brown eyes, black hair; 9 months of service; Pennsylvania.
3. Private Henry Klotzbucher. He was wounded during the retreat from the river, helped to a dense patch of undergrowth by a couple of troopers from his troop and given a canteen water; his wound in the stomach looked fatal to them and they had to leave him, telling him they would come back, they did, he had died in the mean time; the hostiles had not found him and had not mutilated his body; 28 years of age; 5' 6" tall; brown eyes; brown hair; 2 years 9 months service; Germany.
4. Private George Lorentz. He was killed in the attempted escape from the valley, a trooper who witnessed his death said that Private Lorentz was shot in the back of the neck and the bullet came out his mouth. 25 years of age; 5' 7" tall; gray eyes, brown hair; 3 years service, Germany.
5. Private William D. Meyer. One of four Meyers to die that day during the

battle, none related. Bullet entered his right eye. Body not mutilated; 26 years of age; 5' 9" tall; blue eyes, light hair; 3.5 years service; Pennsylvania.
6. Private George E. Smith. One of ten men named Smith on the battlefield that day; five of whom where killed and two wounded. This one's horse stampeded into the direction of the hostiles camp, his body was never recovered; 26 years of age; 5' 6" tall; gray eyes, brown hair; 9 months service; Maine.
7. Private David Summers. Killed during the retreat from the valley; 28 years of age, 5' 8" tall; blue eyes; sandy hair; 3 months service, Missouri.
8. Private Henry James Turley. His horse broke and stampeded during the rush to escape the valley into the Indians, when found after the battle, a hunting knife had been driven fully into his right eye, other than that, he was not mutilated; 25 years of age, 5' 4" tall; brown eyes, black hair; 3.5 years service; New York.
9. Private Henry C. Voight. He was shot in the head during the stand-off on the cliffs overlooking the valley; he and trooper Gebhart (Tanner) (see # 5 above) were buried in the same grave. 21years of age, 5' 5" tall; blue eyes, brown hair; 2.5 years service; Germany.

BATTLE STATISTICS FOR M TROOP

Officers KIA	0
Non-commissioned officers KIA	3
Enlisted KIA	7
Enlisted Missing	2 presumed killed
Total KIA	12

Assigned to M Troop on the morning of 17 May 1876: 66
Present for duty on the morning of 25 June 1876: 55

LAST RIDE

THE FOLLOWING CASUALTIES
ARE ACCOUNTED FOR AS KILLED IN ACTION
UNDER THE COMMAND CAPTAIN FRED BENTEEN

COMPANY D OFFICERS

None

NON-COMMISSIONED OFFICERS

None

TROOPERS

1. Farrier Vincent Charley. 28 years of age; 5' 10" tall; hazel eyes. red hair; 5 years service, Switzerland.
2. Private Patrick M. Golden. Several stories surround this man's death, the most notable one is that he was wounded four times before being shot in the head and killed as he was standing and firing near his rifle pit firing at whatever seemed to be hostile. He was buried in his rifle pit; 27 years of age; 5' 9" tall; blue eyes; brown hair; 4.5 years service, Ireland.
3. Private Edward Housen. Private Housen's last name was an alias. His real name was Dellienhousen, he had deserted a few years before and re-enlisted as just Housen; apparently he went also by the Hansen for he (this same man) also went by that name; 28 years of age; no description of physical characteristics are shown. He was in and out of trouble the entire time in the service; at time of his death he was making up time lost by desertion. He had been in and out of the Army since 1867; Pennsylvania.

BATTLE STATISTICS FOR D TROOP

Enlisted KIA 3
Officers KIA 0
Assigned to Troop on the morning of 17 May 1876   67
Present for duty on the morning of 25 June 1876   49

OFFICERS

None

NON-COMMISSIONED OFFICERS

None

TROOPERS

1. Private Juilien D. Jones. He was killed during the defense of Major Reno Hill perimeter; shot dead center in the heart by and Indian nearly a thousand yards away—lucky shot; killed him just the same; 27 years of age; 5' 6" tall; gray eyes, dark hair; 6.5 years of service; Massachusetts.
2. Private Thomas E. Meador. 25 years of age; 5' 5" tall; brown eyes, brown hair; 4.5 years service; Virginia.)

BATTLE STATISTICS FOR H TROOP

Total number of enlisted men killed   2
No Officers killed; no wounded
Total KIA   2

TROOP K OFFICERS

None

NON-COMMISSIONED OFFICERS

1. 1st Sergeant Dewitt Winney. 31 years of age, 5' 4" tall; gray eyes, brown hair; 4 years service; New York.

ENLISTED TROOPERS

2. Trumpeter Julius Helmer. 25 years of age; 5' 9" tall; gray eyes, brown hair; 10 years service, Germany.
3. Private Elihu F. Clear. He was killed trying to scale bluffs onto Major Reno Hill; 33 years of age, 5' 6" tall; blue eyes, brown hair; 10 years service; Indiana.

BATTLE STATISTICS FOR K TROOP

Non-commissioned officers KIA   1
Total number of enlisted men killed   2
No officers killed; no wounded.
Total KIA   3
Assigned to K Troop on the morning of 17 May 1876   73
Present for duty on the morning of 25 June 1876   44

COMPANY B OFFICERS

None

NON-COMMISSIONED OFFICERS

None

ENLISTED TROOPERS

1. Private Richard Dorn. His body was not discovered for fifty years, an arrow head was still embedded in his spine when found; listed as missing (un-recovered), presumed dead; 23 years of age, 5' 9" tall; gray eyes, brown hair; 4.5 years service, Michigan.
2. Private George B. Mask. 27 years of age; 5' 4" tall; gray eyes, brown hair; 3.5years service; Pennsylvania.
3. Private Herod T. Liddiard. He was assigned to E Troop but assigned that day to Troop B and pack train escort; he was killed on hill top during the siege. 25 years of age; 5' 5" tall; blue eyes, light hair; 3.5 years service; England.

BATTLE STATISTICS FOR B TROOP

No officers were killed wounded, or missing
No non-commissioned officers were killed, wounded, or missing
Total Enlisted KIA   3
Total Enlisted KIA Benteen's Battalion   9

Note: There were 68 men listed as wounded, all assigned to Major Reno and Captain Benteen's commands that resulted from the attacks on the breastworks on Major Reno Hill. Nine would die of their wounds on the way back to Fort Abraham Lincoln or shortly afterwards.

TOTAL BATTLEFIELD STATISTICS FROM THE FOUR U.S. CAVALRY ELEMENTS THAT WERE IN CONTACT WITH THE HOSTILES AT THE LITTLE BIGHORN RIVER BATTLE

Officers KIA	13
Non-commissioned officers KIA	35
Enlisted KIA	197
Civilians Killed	6
Guides and Scouts Killed	5
Total MIA (officers only)*	4
Total MIA (enlisted only)	Unknown
Total Died as results of wounds	9
Total WIA but surviving	57
Total KIA, 7th Cavalry	266

OFFICERS NOT ACCOUNTED FOR, BUT PRESUMED KILLED

1. 2nd Lieutenant Harrington
2. 2nd Lieutenant Sturgis
3. 1st Lieutenant T. L Porter
4. Contract Surgeon Dr. Lord

ENLISTED WHO DIED OF WOUNDS SUSTAINED DURING BATTLE BUT DIED EN ROUTE TO FORT ABRAHAM LINCOLN OR WHILE IN HOSPITAL AT THE POST

1. M Troop. Private Frank Braun. He was wounded but would die of those wounds October 4, 1876. 28 years of age; 5' 6" tall; hazel eyes, fair hair; 8 months service; Switzerland.
2. A Troop. Private George H. King. There were two Kings killed during

the fight that day, this one was wounded but died of his wounds on the steamer, Far West, July 2, 1876. 28 years of age; 5' 10" tall; hazel eyes, brown hair, 6 years service, Pennsylvania.

3. C Troop. Private James C. Bennett. Assigned to pack train detail that day, gun shot to spine and paralyzed below the point of injury; died July 5, 1876 on the steamer, Far West. He is not listed on Battle Monument. 28 years of age, 5' 6" tall, gray eyes, dark hair; 6 years service; Ohio.

4. H Troop. Private William George. Fatally shot through the left side, severely painful, during the defense of Major Reno Hill, lived for 9 days before succumbing to wounds. 26 years of age; 5' 9" tall; blue eyes, sandy hair; in and out of service several times, served late in Civil War; later with two other regiments before the 7th Cavalry last enlistment in May 1875. All totaled he had about 6 years service time from 1864 through 1876; Kentucky.

5. H Troop. Corporal George Lell. Was wounded fatally during the defense Major Reno Hill during the 25th, died on the 26th; 29 years of age, 5' 9" tall; blue eyes, dark hair; 2 years 9 months service; Ohio.

6. I Troop. Private David Cooney. Shot through the right hip during hilltop fight, he had been assigned to pack train escort earlier in the day. Died of wound July 20, 1876 at Fort Abraham Lincoln. 28 years of age; 5' 5"tall; gray eyes, dark hair; 3.5 years service, Ireland.

—40—

THE CONGRESSIONAL MEDAL OF HONOR (AWARDED TO SOLDIERS AFTER THE BATTLE OF THE LITTLE BIGHORN)

The Congressional Medal of Honor was originated in July 1862. Up and until then the U.S. military had only one medal awarded for bravery and valor, the Purple Heart, and it was awarded only to enlisted men.

General Washington, during the Revolutionary War designed the award and presented it to three soldiers who displayed valor during the war. That award fell into disuse for more than eighty years and a new award was issued during the early years of the Civil War to award soldiers for valor in action against an enemy force. The Congressional Medal of Honor became the highest award the United States Congress can award for services above and beyond the call of duty for the U.S. fighting man.

Initially, it was awarded to only enlisted men; officers were not awarded the "Medal." In fact, officers were not awarded any medals for fear that they would let the "winning" of awards cloud their otherwise good judgment when under the stress of combat. That policy changed by 1877, and officers could be awarded the Congressional Medal of Honor. It was the only medal available until the start of the First World War.

Since its origination in 1862, 3,429 service members have been awarded the nation's highest military award. During that one battle, twenty-eight of those medals were awarded for actions on the hills overlooking a little stream in southeastern Montana. As a passing note of interest, Captain Thomas Ward Custer, commander of Troop C, 7TH Cavalry, is one of only nineteen men to have been awarded the Congressional Medal of Honor twice. Both awards granted for actions during the Civil War (the first in 1862, the second in the spring of 1865).

Nearly two years would pass before someone got around to looking into the actions of the several of the individual men who survived the Battle of the Little Bighorn. As a result of the investigation of the after action reports twenty-eight men were awarded the Congressional Medal of Honor for their actions during the stand on Major Reno Hill. Those men awarded the medal were obviously the survivors of the Major Reno's fight in valley and then Major Reno's and Benteen's defense of the remnants of the command on top of the bluffs overlooking the river. For their part they were dug in holding off the off the Lakota. As for the Lakota and Shahiyela warriors who had boxed the remaining *wasichu* in, it was a game of cat and mouse that they were playing with the soldiers. They knew that sooner or later they would need water for themselves and for the wounded.

It was a deadly serious game and the Indians stayed just out of range of the soldier's carbines and took shots of opportunity at the soldiers inside their barricades with their longer ranged repeaters. They would wait until the men behind the breastworks tried to sneak down the bluff to get water from the river and then try to pick them off one or two at a time. They had shot at and wounded several playing that game without them being hurt in return. To the Indians it was fun and also practical— they had them right where they could keep an eye out for those attempting to get to the river and would send an arrow or a bullet at those brave or desperate enough to try for the river.

For the soldiers' part, they were just trying to hang on until relief arrived, either in the form of Lieutenant Colonel Custer or General Terry. Up to that point in time, none of the survivors, officers included, knew where either of those commands was. They were just hoping that one of them would get to them before the hostiles killed those that were alive.

The soldiers for as much as they did not like the "ol' man" they respected him. As strange as it is to say it, it was true. They hated him and loved him at the same time.

During that time, when what remained of Major Reno's battalion (Troops A, G, and M) were literally pinned into the ground, many men were wounded and the entire command and stuck out in the middle of the prairie in the boiling sun for two days they needed water.

To remedy this serious problem for the command, someone would have to chance going to the river through the hostiles and bringing water back up the hill. Those men who either went on their own or volunteered carried the precious fluid in whatever they could carry it back in (cooking pots and anything else).

It was a highly risky proposition and nearly impossible task; a few would not make it. But if the command were to survive, water would have to be secured. This problem was compounded by Captain Benteen's command being held "captive" and with Major Reno's shot up crowd. The two commands were pinned to the ground they were on, that was all they would have until the Indians would come back in force to finish them off, or so they thought.

The Indians tell the story a little differently. At the end of first the day the Indians had formed a virtual wall around the men of Major Reno and Captain Benteen on three sides, the north, the west, and the south. They left the east side open so the soldiers had they wanted to could have escaped in that direction but that direction only.

Of course, the soldiers did not know that. Just because they could not see any hostiles in that direction and they had not been attacked from that direction—it did not mean, in the *wasichus* mind at least, that they were not there.

The Indians that holding the *wasichu* in check were there, but on the other three sides. The east side was clear; it was the way out of the trap and freedom. They did not have to; to the Indians, it was enough the remnants inside of Major Reno's goofy barricade of dead horses thought they could be attacked at any moment aside from just a few guards left to watch the place and the rest went to the party and to celebrate the victory over the pony soldiers.

Out of pure dumb luck, or twisted fate, this combined force was surrounded and kept holed up until the Indians withdrew from the valley during the afternoon and evening of the 26th and the morning of the 27th by a hand full of warriors until the other members of the tribes had left the Valley of the Greasy Grass safely.

During those nearly two and a half, days the men in the battalions thought that they were surrounded. Of those men cornered behind their defenseless positions, many of the men volunteered go back to the river to get water for the command. That meant of course fighting through the Indians if necessary to get to the river, load up with what ever they had brought to fetch the water in and to bring it back to those in the barricades. To say it was very dangerous work is to give new definition to understatement. Carefully and with look-outs guarding their paths the individual soldiers would sneak down to the river, fill whatever containers they had to be filled. Then carefully they would carry their precious cargo back up the steep sides of the bluff to the injured and others inside their defensive lines. These men, time and time again, exposed themselves to death to save the command. Sometimes they made it and sometimes they did not. They would get stuck with an arrow in the back or a bullet for their trouble.

Earlier, but after Benteen's battalion reached the position he found Major Reno's survivors (fewer than twenty uninjured men) were bravely holding off hundreds of warriors that had started to gather along a long and higher ridge line that ran parallel to the area that Major Reno had gathered his shot up force. The ridge would be later called Sharpshooters Ridge in memory of the hostiles that kept the soldiers hunkered down behind decaying and stinking carcasses.

There were several of the men who had deployed with Custer's battalion whose horses had played out as they were on their way to Medicine Tail Coulee. These men were left a foot to fend for themselves and were lucky to still be alive when Major Reno and what was left of his command scaled the bluffs to their present position.

They had hidden from the hostiles and when Major Reno and his men reached the top of the bluff they had hurried in to their fortress with them. A number of these men who had been left behind displayed outstanding courage and valor once deployed into the defensive lines with Major

Reno's men.

From Major Reno's battalion (Troops A, G, and M) eighteen men were awarded the Congressional Medal of Honor. From Benteen's battalion (Troops B, D, H, and K) another nine were awarded. Of the eight men who were left behind five would be awarded Medals of Honor awarded. They had been men assigned to Captain Tom Custer's troop.

No medals were awarded posthumously; no one on Battle Ridge was awarded the medal–there were no witnesses and no survivors.

7TH CALVARY TROOPERS AWARDED THE CONGRESSIONAL MEDAL OF HONOR FOR VALOR

Troop A—
Captain Myles Moylan

1. Bancoft, Neil, Private
2. Harris, David W. Private
3. Rogan, Patrick, Sergeant
4. Roy, Stanislaus, Sergeant

Troop H—
Major F. Benteen

1. Geiger, George H., Sargent
2. Michlin, Henry, Private
3. Voit, Otto, Private
4. Windolph, Charles, Private

Troop B—
Captain Thomas McDougall

1. Callan, Thomas J., Private
2. Criswell, Benjamin, Sgt
3. Cunningham, Charles, Crpl
4. Hutchinson, Rufus J., Sgt.
5. Murray, Thomas, Sergeant
6. Pym, James, Private
7. Stivers, Thomas W. Private
8. Tolan, Frank, Private
9. Welch, Charles H., Sergeant

Troop D—
Captain Thomas Weir

1. Brant, Abram, Private
2. Deetline, Frederick, Private *
3. Harris, David, Private
4. Holden, Henry, Private
5. Scott, George B., Private

* Blacksmith

Troop C—
Detailed from T. Custer

Troop E—
Detailed from Capt. Fresh Smith

1. Hanley, Richard P. Private
2. Thompson, Peter, Private

1. Evans, William, Private
2. Bell, James, Private

Troop G—
Commanded by Lt. D. McIntosh**

1. Golden, Theodore, Private
2. Stewart, Benjamin, Private

**Killed in the valley fight, Lieutenant Wallace commanded the troop on Major Reno Hill.

Within a year, three officers who were also commanders of companies in either Major Reno's or Benteen battalion's during the battle of the Little Bighorn were awarded the "Medal" in actions against the Nez Perce in western Montana, or against these same Sioux with the reformed 7TH. These officers were:

1. Captain Miles Moylan, Troop E
2. Lieutenant Edward Godfrey, Troop K
3. First Lieutenant Charles Varnum, Chief of Scouts.

If the Battle of the Little Bighorn was a clear defeat for the U.S. Army, it was a disastrous one for the 7th Cavalry Regiment. Of the 597 enlisted men and thirty-one officers in the regiment 263 were killed. Fifty-nine, were wounded and thirty-one were missing. Of those reported as missing, twenty-five turned out to be the Indian scouts that Custer released just prior to going into battle. Later, as many as nine other men would succumb to their wounds sustained in the fight on Major Reno Hill, but they were not part of the initial KIA list for the battle. The final number

LAST RIDE

of 7th Cavalry for the battle is plus or minus one or two of 272. Fifty wounded, and four or five missing but presumed dead:

1. 2ND Lt. Sturgis, Troop E
2. 1st Lt. James Porter, Troop I
3. 2ND LT Henry M. Harrington, Troop C
4. Dr. Lord

Two sets of remains were found many years later, and not positively identified. These remains would be buried in the National Cemetery at the Little Bighorn National Monument.

—41—

LIEUTENANT BRADLEY'S GRUESOME FIND

Author's Note: I did not place the following material in the main body of this book for a couple reasons. One, it is a little gruesome and I did not want this material to detract from the main theme of the telling of Custer and the 7th Cavalry's last ride. You may have thought it strange that the book skipped this part while you were reading. Please, forgive me; I have taken a little bit of author's license here, because the facts do not make much sense when standing alone. The conversations between Bradley and Nowlan are from my own thoughts as to what they must have said to one another as they surveyed the battlefield on horseback that first time.

Second, I had second thoughts about it in terms of what this chapter would add to the body of the story I was trying to tell. While what you will read here is true and can be verified from a number of sources, it would only serve to distort, somewhat, what we already know—all of the men who rode with Custer perished. While it is important to know the reasons why an American Civil War and frontier icon and his men died, it is infinitely more important to also know that their deaths were not the only ones to be mourned. In the harshest of realities, Lieutenant Colonel Custer and his battalion only signaled the beginning of the end and slow death by strangulation of a whole race of people, the American Indian. The white man had been doing it for years, ever since the first white settler stepped foot on American soil; while Custer did not start it, his ghost would have been able to see the end of their rights as a free people from Custer Hill on the Little Big Horn ridge that looked down on the Valley

LAST RIDE

of the Greasy Grass.

The battle of the Little Big Horn was a savage, horrifyingly brutal, and murderous affair. Ask any veteran of any war if that is not true still today...unfortunately, all battles are. This one was no different. The sight of men bent on killing one another is a horrific thing. In Custer's case, had the shoe been on the other foot and he would have won and in the aftermath their would have been 267 dead warriors laying on the side of those hills it would have been no less so.

I personally doubt though there would be a national monument to mark the occasion. It was only this past year (2002-2003) that the American Lakota and Shahiyela were even allowed to place a monument of their own on the top of Battle Ridge. The National Monument placed by the National Parks Service has been there nearly a hundred years. On it there is not one word about the American Indians killed that day, or why the battle was fought.

Now I ask you, "What is wrong with that picture?" We have monuments all over the South and in a few places in the north where monuments commemorate hundreds of battles dating back to the American Revolution and before even. The famous battles of Yorktown, Lexington, Concord, and only a few years later at Gettysburg, Vicksburg, Antietam, the list is nearly endless. North and South alike, British and Colonialists, French, Spaniards and Mexicans, even Canadians—hell, we fought them all and put monuments up wherever we had a fight. Sometimes, we even let the former enemies put them up next to ours.

Why would it take a hundred and twenty-five years before the white man would let the American Indian have one of their own on that ground?

As for the *wasichu* killed that day, and in no way to justify their deaths as anything other than honorable, let me say that the white men on that field that day were mostly hard, hard men. They had seen hard times in their lives. Many had fought wars in Europe prior to coming to this country. Some of those had been veteran Civil War soldiers and were now on the American frontier fighting Indians. That was all they knew—war and fighting. They had been through it before. In terms of death, they had seen far worse happen in number for battles fought during that time before this day. The other men had tested the frontier and up and until that day, somehow, had managed to live through everything that life had passed their way.

What I am saying is this, these men, all of them, except for maybe a couple civilians and a newspaper man knew the score and they acted accordingly. They could be as mean as a sow bear with a sore ass when she feels threatened. When a situation arose that depended on them to be mean, they damn sure could rise to the occasion and be as mean as anything you ever saw.

If they had not responded in such a way they might not see the next sunup. Even it they did, there was no guarantee that they would live to see even the next sunset. For many of these men, their time had run out. Past that, it doesn't matter much what happened and where, or how.

The reader, ought to know it was no picnic or Sunday afternoon social that they were attending and at the end they just ended up dead....

First Lieutenant James Bradley and Lieutenant Henry Nowlan, 2nd U.S. Cavalry, were Colonel Gibbon's lead scouts and the first soldiers to locate the battlefield on the 27th of June 1876. They were sickened by the appalling scene that they and their Crow and Ree scouts encountered on the slopes of what has become known as Battle Ridge and Custer Hill. Somehow, the nearly overwhelming stench of the dead soldiers and horses covering the hillside went almost without comment. It was the way in which the men were butchered, obviously after they were killed. That can be understood. It would have been the last thing that they would have expected to see, the 7th Cavalry butchered on the ground lying where they were last left by their conquering foe. These sloping hills that led away from the east side of the Little Bighorn River were covered with death.

After the scouts realized what it was that they had been looking at from the other side of the river, those in this party were in shock. Lieutenant Bradley's first view of the horrific scene was with the aid of his field glasses from the valley floor nearly a mile away from the west edge of the river. At first, he did not know what he was looking at. He paused before passing the glasses to his second in command. "Take a look up that hill and tell me what you see."

He passed his looking glasses to Nowlan. Lieutenant Nowlan looked at where Lieutenant Bradley had been pointing. He adjusted the center gear on the glasses and stared through them for a long time, scouring the distant hillside. As he brought the glasses down he looked at Lieutenant Bradley with a confused look on his face.

"Hell's fire, Lieutenant; if I didn't know better I'd say it looks like bodies of dead men. But, how can that be?"

"The only ones around here are the 7th Cavalry and they are supposed to be here today. That looks like men lying out there on the hill side. Looking back up the slope with his naked eye, he took off his straw hat and shaded his eyes from the sun with the wide brim. "It is too far away to be sure, sir. But God in heaven, it looks like bodies to me. Damn...a lot of them."

Lieutenant Bradley nodded, "At first, I thought it was buffalo entrails, or perhaps, hides that the Indians might have just left after a hunt."

"But the longer I look, the more I think the same thing you just said, it looks like bloated white-skinned bodies." Shaking his head, Lieutenant Bradley passed the glasses around to the other scouts. His men were confused as he was at what they saw through the lieutenant's glasses.

He could not make it out clearly for sure, nor could have even considered that it could be the bodies of butchered soldiers that speckled the hillside. If the Indian scouts who were with him could make out what he was seeing, they just would not say. One would suspect that more likely than not, the Ree scouts did know what those shapes were.

They were afraid of being right...better to be positive than to be right, or wrong. The Indians did not want to send the wrong message or make the soldiers think that they had known all along what they would find.

The distance from where both of the soldiers were then; on the west side of the river to on up the hillside, was still too far away to be sure just what it was that they had seen. It tweaked their curiosity and they decided to investigate farther. Lieutenant Bradley ordered his men to be ready for a surprise attack that could come from any direction. He unsnapped his holster and checked his carbine to ensure it was ready for action should the need arise and he had to shoot first.

They crossed over the river and started up the steep hillside on the east side. As they crossed, the river the party drew closer together. The entire party was on full alert. Their carbines were locked, cocked, and loaded. Their pistols were checked and their holsters unbuckled in case they had to react quickly. If what they had seen were indeed bodies of dead white men, they did not want to join them because they had not been ready for an attack. They had been told to expect hostile action and to avoid it at all costs by General Terry. He did not have to tell them twice. They may not have the luxury of the choice.

They were expecting hostiles to charge straight at them from any direction at any moment. The hillside was curious; they could smell death hanging in the air as it does. A large swarm of carrion birds was gliding on invisible thermals overhead. Cautiously, the scouting party moved up the banks of the river and onto the bench leading away from the river. The threat of ambush never materialized, nor did the spookiness of the area desert them.

The patrol's horses were starting to act up, shying at the waves of grass as it rolled across the hillside in front of them. By the time 1st Lt. Bradley and his scouting party crossed the river and began to ascend the nearest hillside, they could smell the mixture of odors that death brought as it hung over the hot ground ahead of them.

Perhaps no further than a quarter of a mile after crossing the stream, they saw the first slain man's remains lying in the blood-soaked tall grass. It was the body of a lone naked white man. His body was pocked with arrows. His head, though severed from the main torso, was upside-down lying close by.

The grisly detached mass had been scalped. The man's thighs were slashed from hip to nearly the kneecap. The man's private area had been violated; his penis had been severed, his private area had been pocked

LAST RIDE

with arrows.

The right had and forearm had been tomahawked off up to the elbow. There was no means available for possible identification of the poor fellow lying in front of them in the hot sun for nearly three days. The corpse's skin had turned a blackish, almost freakish color. The open wounds on the body had become home to thousands of little black flies that were feasting on his flesh and dried blood.

Not far away lay another corpse. It too had been mutilated beyond any hope of identification. A little ahead of it, another man's body was lying face-down. Each man was as grotesquely flayed-out as the first.

A little ways farther up the hill, more remains could be seen. To the patrol, it did not look like there had been any attempt to fight a coordinated battle. It seemed to these men that the dead men had been just run down and killed where they now lay.

All along the hillside, more and more bodies began to appear as the scouting party ascended the hills. Here and there dead horses and every now and then a saddle or cavalry horse blanket with the markings of the 7th Cavalry could be identified. Sometimes, the remains of these bodies lay alone and sometimes in heaps of three to six dead men lay willy-nilly close together. Sometimes, they could not guess what part of a leg or an arm belonged to which man. If the bodies were headless, who would know or how could they guess which one went to which body.

First Lieutenant Bradley's men were living their worst nightmare. Reality struck the two scouting party lieutenants over, and over again. The bodies were the bodies of men from the 7th Cavalry. The markings on the disused equipment, the canteens, horse bridles and saddles even, a few horse blankets that lay strewn across the area had the marking of the 7th Cavalry on them.

As they closed in on the bodies of the ones closest to the river and then on up the hillside to the upper edge of what would become known as Custer Hill; it looked as if the whole 7th Cavalry could have been whipped out to a last man. The mere idea of it saddened and sickened the men. How did this happen?

Of course, they had no answers. Tears freely ran down the officer's faces. Here and there they thought that they had known a man whose body was lying naked in the dried grass, but they could not be sure.

The lieutenants were overcome as much by the sight of all these dead men and horses as they were demoralized by the reality of what had occurred. As they scanned the hillside, all they could see was dead soldiers.

Lieutenant Nolan asked Lieutenant Bradley, "Sir, do you think this carnage can continue on over to the hills beyond the ground were we are now standing?"

Lieutenant Bradley just shook his head in disbelief. "God in heaven," Bradley mumbled. "What if they killed everybody in the 7th?" The thought of idea jarred both men back into reality.

"We better get back to the colonel and tell him what has happened up here."

Lieutenant Bradley though as shocked as Lieutenant Nolan was, simply shook his head and closed his eyes trying to clear his mind. "God-almighty," he thought to himself, "what in the hell did we stumble into here?"

Sweat was beading up and rolling off his forehead. He reached up and removed his hat, wiping the sweat away with the sleeve of his shirt. Squinting up at the before-noon sun, he dabbed the top of his almost-bald head with his forearm. Shading his eyes with his campaign straw hat he scanned the hillside again. Looking across the hillside, shaking his head in dismay he looked down at his hands on the short pommel of his saddle. Sweat dripped of his nose on to his weathered hands. Blinking, he patted his mare's neck before looking back at Lieutenant Nolan.

It was a long time before he could find his voice enough to even begin to talk.

It was nearly too much to even contemplate. The 7th Gone! "How in the hell could this have happened?" he muttered as if he was asking a rhetorical question and really did not expect an answer.

"Where the hell is Custer, Major Reno, and Benteen? Are they dead too?" Bradley had no answers.

Lieutenant Bradley kept those thoughts to himself. From what little he had seen thus far; and they had not even started, it looked like the 7th had been gunned down before they had a chance to turn and fight.

By the looks of things, it looked like there were hundreds of dead scattered from hell to breakfast along this hillside. The only things alive were a few of the horses that had not been killed at the top of the hill.

Lieutenant Nowlan started riding along a line that led to the far end of the ridge nearly a mile in the distance. From where they were then, it looked like some sort of a fight had taken place there. A lone war lance stood at the end of the ridge. A feather at the top of the lance waved quietly in the mid-morning breeze. Maybe from that point, Nowlan could see what had happened. How many more men he would find between where he was then and by the time he got to the lance, he did not know. Lieutenant Nowlan had the first four men in their party with him and had ridden maybe a hundred yards when he halted the patrol and ordered the men to dismount and go it on foot. The dead men and horses were spooking their own animals. It would be best to walk than to risk the horses stepping on the remains of a dead man.

Spreading out and going up the steep grade toward the hill where the lone lance served as guideon, the scouting party began its grisly count. It was there at the top of the long ridge that they encountered the men who had made their last stands.

Just below the ridge, maybe 400 yards distance, they counted the remains of a number of solders who had fallen in what seemed to them as a skirmish line. These men were found space out across the swell between Battle Ridge and another ridge line running perpendicular to the main ridge.

Bradley and Nowlan pondered the area between the two ridge lines. It appeared that the men were spread so thin that there was no way that these few men found here could have countered the massive attack that was initiated against them at this point. With nowhere to run, they would have fallen almost without a fight after just one volley from their single shot carbines.

It appeared that the men had tried to hold their ground and were killed where they stood. These men where part of Captain Yates and Smith's Troops. Less than a dozen men to counter a space of two hundred yards and perhaps as many as 2,000 mounted hostile cavalry. Incredible odds! It was obvious though that these men tried to hold the line and had not tried to evade what was asked of them. Their intentions mattered not.

Continuing up the slope from this point the officers' encountered three civilians who would be later identified as Boston Custer and Autie Reed, close by was the newspaperman Mr. Kellogg and the regimental surgeon Doctor Lord. Though the young men were naked and had been scalped and defaced; enough of them remained that made them recognizable. Their bodies had been ravaged. Each boy's body had paid a price in death. There were multiple arrows shot into each, the nearly two- foot-long slashes ran down each of their thighs. The now-characteristic amputations of their male gender parts and other cuttings that were evident on nearly all of the bodies that they had seen to this point did not set them apart from what Bradley and Nowlan's scouts had seen on the bodies of the soldiers. It was sad nonetheless; these lads were just boys, really—one just eighteen, the other not much older. But their lives had been sheltered ones and they had not seen the harsh realities of life on the prairies until they were part of its toughest lesson.

Mr. Kellogg had not escaped anything not visited upon all of the others. He too had lost most of his clothing, his hair and male parts as well, the same for Doctor Lord.

A few yards back up the hill from them, between the remains of three other men, were the remains of Mitch Bouyer. He was recognized only by his well-known leather vest. Though now covered in blood, the vest was still in place. Unfortunately, he was known by the Lakota and Shahiyela as a traitor to his people. He had lived with them and they had treated him as one of their own for years. The red brothers did not take kindly to traitors. His body, when found, would have only been recognizable by some article of clothing. There was not much else that would have allowed him to be identified any other way.

Slowly, the party came up the hill to what is generally called Last Stand Hill and Battle Ridge, counting as they came. Once on top, they spread across and back down the slope and started toward the southern end of the ridge until they crossed over Medicine Tail Coulee and continued on until they saw no more remains to be counted. Rejoining at the top of the coulee the officers carefully added together their totals. When they had completed this circuit, the patrol had counted 175 men and six or eight officers dead.

They had also counted about eighty head of horses that were also dead. Several more of the horses were injured. Some lay in agony. Others were just too worn-out, not only by their injuries but from the ordeal that they had just gone through. Out of kindness to the horses, they were shot in the head rather than left to die. Totaled, this horse count came out to 97 head that were dead or had been destroyed by the patrol themselves. The scouts would not know, but the Indians had chased the horses down the slopes leading to the river during the battle. The horses would be easy to catch once they got to fresh water. The Indians could always use extra horses, especially big strong cavalry horses.

Only one horse, this one with four arrows and three gun shot holes in him, was left standing near the summit of the last knob at the north end of the ridge. The horse was smallish by cavalry standards and did not seem to be bothered by the fact that a couple of his wounds were freely bleeding.

Either during the fight or afterwards, the saddle had become loose and had slipped underneath the horse's mid-section. It was still there when the scouting party got to the horse. There was what appeared to be a serious bullet wound just behind the horse's right shoulder. The animal's blood was still fresh, draining down his side and onto the ground where he stood. Smeared blood had dried around the wound and was evidenced on the saddle right stirrup leather straps that attached to the body of the saddle and the covered stirrup.

One of the soldiers with Lieutenant Nowlan recognized the little chestnut and knew his owner. "That's Captain Keogh's horse, sir: that horse there is Comanche," the soldier said.

Upon reaching the animal, they saw that the name on the saddle identified its owner. It was indeed Captain Myles Keogh's little gelding. His master was lying nearby; his right knee had been shattered by the round that caused the wound in the horse, answering the question as to what had caused all the additional blood that had dried on Comanche's side. A killing wound to Keogh's chest had dropped the man for the last time.

His body was not defiled past the shattered knee wound and the point-blank round into his heart. Around his neck was a Catholic medal and in his pocket was the Medallion of St George given to him by the Pope. The Indians left those artifacts with the dead captain, touching nothing on his body. Not only was Keogh a man of powerful medicine—his medallion in his pocket and the Saint Christopher medal around his neck—he was a tough man and he died like his men, to his last breath. Later, the Indians would comment on the man with the big medicine who was so courageous at the end of the fight.

Nearby Captain Keogh lay the remains of First Sergeant Frank Noyes (alias, Varden), a Civil War veteran and a man who had served for fifteen years; Sergeant James Burtard (alias Bustard) and little 25-year-old John Patton (alias Patten) who stood only five-feet-three-inches tall were lying next to the captain and his horse. They had fought to the end as had all the men in this sector of the battle.

At the end, it may well have been hand-to-hand as the men would have expended their twenty-four rounds of ammunition for their carbines and were down to using their single action pistols. The troop's horses would have either been released by the holders to put more guns on the line or perhaps they would have chased away by the rising tide of warriors coming up on all sides of Keogh and the Wild Eye's line.

The warriors who fought against this part of the line said of the Keogh's Troop, "The men here did not quit, did not beg for mercy; they did not run." Instead they said that they begrudgingly moved back up the slope to the top of the ridge and stood their ground when they had run out of bullets to fire. Many of the Indians said, "These soldiers along this line died fighting with their bare hands. They had big medicine from their leader."

The lone horse standing on the ridge top had somehow not bled to death and was standing nearby his master, Captain Myles Keogh. The horse was not the only horse left standing when the patrol got to him. As many as eighty head had to be put down by the men here because of their injuries. That many more cavalry mounts had been killed during the fight. What was left of Custer's mounts had run down the slope towards the river. A few of the mounts were grazing perhaps a quarter mile away from the last stand area and though most were injured they were still too frightened to let any man get very close to them.

LAST RIDE

Note: Comanche was spared. He would become the symbol of the 7th Cavalry and nursed back to health by the regimental veterinary doctors. He would be curried and brushed daily, given a healthy portion of oats and fresh hay every day; his leathers would be polished and his brass would sparkle as he led the 7th Cavalry Regiment in all of its parades. He lived to be about 37 years old and from the 25th June 1876 to the day he died he would never be ridden again. To this day he stands in a glass-encased glass cube in the rotunda of the University of Kansas. So, in effect, it is true: Comanche was the only horse to survive the battle.

Near the top of the big hill, perhaps as many as seventy men, probably even a few more, had been pushed up the hill to this point, hemmed in on all sides, and ultimately slaughtered.

These men could see the end was coming and a few of them saw also what appeared to be a way out the trap. As many as twenty men would make a break toward an area a little north and just west of where they were on the ridge top of the ridge. Since that time, where these men tried to escape has become known as the deep ravine. It is hypothesized that about that many men ran into the ravine thinking that they would make their escape by running down it, even it led back toward the encampment and all of those angry hostiles.

It was wrong headed of course; the hostiles had been using the ravine and ones like it in the area to get to the top of the slope that the soldiers had just left. In the ravines the hostiles could shoot arrows into the soldiers trapped ahead of them without exposing themselves.

Once in the ravine, these soldiers were now in a real pickle. The hostiles were in there with them and as the men tried to turn and run back the way they had come they were met by hostiles coming down behind them. Several of the men would try to crawl up the sides of the ravine but the sides were to steep and they kept falling back into the hostiles waiting for them in the bottom of the ravine.

Afterwards, when their bodies were found, the burial parties had said that they could see the marking of men's claw marks on the sides of the walls where they had tried to crawl out of the ravine. Those who fell there could have been the remnants of E Troop, the Gray Horse Troop, with a few others who had risked a chance of getting away.

The rest of the battalion were now in a terrible position, they had nowhere to run, they were out of ammunition, what happened next would be as if the hostiles were going to slaughter a herd of buffalo or the *wasichu* a herd of Indian ponies. These last men were like tethered goats on short ropes at the end of their lives. With nowhere to go, they had run out of places to run.

Most would have been without ammunition and sensing the end was near perhaps. The hostiles still ever cautious because there was no sense getting killed needlessly either used their more modern rifles with much greater range than the carbine possessed or continued to rain arrows down upon the survivors until all firing stopped on top the ridges. Those men not dead would have been too injured to offer any resistance to the warriors as they broke down on the final group of men. Those not dead would soon be.

It would be nearly three days before the remains of the men who lay across this battle area knoll were found. What was found were the exposed, bloated, and disfigured bodies of dead and butchered white men of C Troop and parts of E and F Troop.

When Lieutenant Nowlan assessed the area, he quickly assumed that these bodies belonged to Lieutenant Colonel Custer's 7th Cavalry because of the markings on the saddle blankets and other equipment still lying littering the battlefield.

After confirming this find, Lieutenant Bradley immediately sent two of his Indian guides back with a message to his commander that it appeared that the whole command had been wiped out. Within two hours, both Colonel Gibbon and General Terry forces arrived on the battlefield and came up to the findings of Lieutenant Bradley and his second in command 2nd Lieutenant Nowlan.

This day, the 27th of June 1876, like the day three days before, was hot and dry. It was mid-morning. By the time the Terry and Gibbon had arrived on the battlefield, Lieutenant Bradley had completed his initial survey of the area and had personally counted 197 dead on his final count (he could not be sure of the number as some of the bodies were in parts or pieces.

As gruesome as it was, the heads of four men had been located in what would have been the encampment that the hostiles had just left. The faces on the gory masses could not be identified, nor were the bodies of the four ever found in total. He reported that he had located the body of Lieutenant Colonel Custer at the end of what is now known as Custer Hill, at the northwestern end of Battle Ridge.

Most of the remains of the men of Custer's command were located the afternoon of the 27th between Medicine Tail Coulee and the end of the Battle Ridge. A few of the slain men were found up towards the top of the coulee and a few more found in the opposite direction, heading toward Major Reno's hill. Apparently, these men had attempted to get back to the rest of the command and had fallen short of that goal.

Of the casualties found that day, only a very small handful of the nearly 200 bodies (they had not located all of them) that had been located at that point had not been mutilated. That is not to say that these few men's remains were in pristine condition. Quite the contrary, what it means is that, at least of few of the corpses were almost recognizable by men who had known them when they were alive. The slain soldiers' bodies had been through a battle and dead bodies do not last long in the heat under the best conditions. Now, badly abused by combat and all that had been done to them afterwards, and then lying out in the sun, they really had not done well.

The significance of what the white men considered as abuse was not really anything of the sort to the avenging hostiles, at least, not totally. Much of what was done to these bodies only exhibited the extreme and complete disdain and utter contempt the hostiles held for the *wasichu* who had attacked them this one last time.

Mostly, the mutilation was the handy work of the women who did what the whites considered barbaric: the smashing of heads with stone mallets (unless the man was killed by such a weapon during the fight), the amputations of fingers and penises, ears, noses, jaws, arms and hands, lower legs, and such.

After the fight, in some instances, the Indians would run across a *wasichu* who was not dead. Of course, they were perfectly capable of taking care of the situation themselves and at least in the case of Major Reno's translator Dorhman, were quite efficient. One simple slice with a trader's knife put an end to the matter.

The throat-slitting (the Sioux were known by their Indian enemies, the Crow, as the "Throat Cutters" for good reason; they nearly always cut the throats of all they killed) was like leaving their calling card, so others would know who had done the deed. The other mutilations—deep gashes across the right arm (Cheyenne—"the Cut Arms" as they were known—also on occasion took the whole right arm up to the elbow); slitting a nostril (the "smeller tribe"—Arapahos), gashing down the thighs, or across a body's caves or down a victims thighs, merely identified "others" who had counted coup of the dearly departed.

Two full days of lying in the hot sun does amazing and horrifying things to human remains, combat or no combat. Decomposition starts within only a few hours, for starters. The situation gets worse from there on, until the remains return to from whence they came (...ashes to ashes...dust to dust...) or parts are devoured by birds of prey, coyotes, or wolves.

Within hours after being exposed to the hot sun, a dead body can start to swell from the gases percolating within the body's cavities, the skin begins to change colors—ranging from stark ghostly white if the wounds that caused the death are allowed to drain enough blood, to an ashen gray and later, to almost black, to, in the later stages of decomposition, almost translucent.

At that stage of decomposition, the skin and other tissues covering the stomach cavity starts to expand from the gases expanding in the stomach and intestines. Shortly thereafter, the tissue starts popping wide open, spilling out the foulest odors one can imagine.

Mass migrations of tiny little black flies seemingly just pop up out of the ground, or from the wounds of the corpses in numbers that defy counting, to surround anything dead. These little insect vultures gorge themselves on blood and soft tissues (eyes and mouth areas, ears, nose, and deep into the wounds of the fallen). Not long after that, fly eggs are hatched and thousands and thousands of maggots also fight for food in these areas. Everyone on that field would be literally covered with thousands and thousands of these little critters.

Add to that, the injuries sustained in combat of the fallen, everything from gun shot wounds and puncture wounds from arrows and spears, smashed-in heads and butchering; scalping and body mutilations, the sight of the dead on this battlefield would resemble something worse than Dante's Inferno come true.

To go along with these human dead would have been nearly one hundred dead horses soaking up the same boiling sun during those same two or three days the slain soldiers had. Their bodies were going through the same decaying processes as their former owners.

The vast majority of soldiers, including officers, had been, for the most part, mutilated almost beyond recognition. At the end of the fight the injured men that were among those still alive were in no condition to defend themselves. These were put out their misery by the hostiles with the aid of government-issued axes (issued from the reservations that the hostiles had just left) that was used to chop across the eyes or forehead or, a stone mallet whap in the face or on the back of the head. The young boys in the village used some of the soldiers' bodies for target practice for arrows.

When these dead were identified, many of them looked like their bodies had been used as pincushions for all the arrows in them. Some were positioned on their knees and elbows after being stripped naked and their buttocks were exposed and their backsides used for target practice, leaving the man's backside bristling with arrows.

Most, if not all of the men had their private male part removed and that pelvic area shot full of arrows. Some men were nearly butchered, with legs, arms, and heads taken off, leaving only a torso for identification. A few of the dead had been indeed butchered and the remains just left in a pile for the carrion birds and wolves to take meals from.

Thomas Custer's body was an example of the brutality that was visited upon the men who fell that afternoon. Naked when found, only a few feet from the pile of bodies that contained his brother, the younger Custer was laying naked, face-down. According to Cheyenne folklore, they considered it bad luck to leave an enemy face-up. His back was bristling with arrows; the back of his head, though obviously scalped (only a few hairs on the nape of his neck remained) had been smashed nearly flat with a stone mallet. In that condition, he was of course unrecognizable from behind. No one could identify the corpse.

When the body was turned over to see if identification was possible, it was found that he had been slit from stem to stern and horizontally across the midsection so that his entrails rolled out of the stomach cavity when he was rolled over. His throat had been slashed (a Lakota trademark) so severely that his head nearly came off. He had been scalped and then shot in the top of his head with an arrow that literally could not be removed.

About Arrowheads: Arrowheads are identified by the type and size of point used. The arrowheads differed depending on the target, for shooting game, small stone (flint) arrowheads were usually shorter than an inch to an inch and a half long. These shorter arrowheads with narrow ears (from side-to-side) were used, making it easier to remove the point so it could be used again).

For hunting larger game, buffalo, for example, or shooting humans, the Indians used longer steel-headed points that were twice as wide at the base of the arrowhead (the ears) than the shorter flint game point and longer from tip to notch. They could get these arrowheads from the reservation store keeps for trading their furs and such. One of the advantages the Indians liked in the steel points was that the steel pointed ears on the steel arrow point had a tendency to bend when pulled back through muscle and bone, locking the head of the arrow neatly in place rather coming right back out through the same hole it had made. If it was pulled out of the same hole it had made upon entering the tissue, serious injury could be sustained. The removal of the steel arrowhead by pulling it back out of the wound hole was made impossible because of the bending of these ears; they mechanically locked the point of the arrowhead into the victim, be he man or beast.

The alternative was then to drive the arrowhead still attached to the shaft all the way through the wounded victim. That caused great pain to the victim and sometimes death because by doing so, vital organs and other soft tissues could be destroyed.

Someone in the burial party had tried to remove the one in Tom's head by pulling it out. He could not, so the man broke off the shaft as close to the skull as possible, and buried him that way in the same hole next to his brother.

Only Captain Thomas Ward Custer's tattooed initials "TWC" on his right forearm identified his corpse. He had other tattoos; the wound caused by the non-surgical but nonetheless successful removal of his heart obliterated the tattoo of double eagles on his chest. In addition to his chest being ripped open, his penis had been hacked off. That was not uncommon. The native plains victor nearly always whacked off a man's manhood. The male organ held some sort of mystic power to the Indians. If they removed an enemy's penis, he would not be able to procreate in the next life and the Indian would not have to fight him or his offspring again.

The heart was taken out sometimes and eaten so that the warrior who killed him could take on the fighting spirit of the victim.

Normally, that job was left to the Indian women, but in this case probably not. What they did with such trophies, one can only guess. If Mr. Rain-in-the-Face removed the heart, he could have done it for two reasons: one out of disgust and disdain for an enemy, and also, out of respect for a warrior. Tom would not have saved the last bullet for himself. As for Rain-in-the-Face, he was pestered relentlessly on that issue. To his credit, he would never say to a white man if he had kept his promise to the younger Custer. Many suspect that he did.

Does it matter?

Back before the 7th had left on their last march, Tom Custer had been stationed at Fort Robinson, Nebraska, where he first ran into Rain and finally at Fort Abraham Lincoln in North Dakota. He had tricked Rain-In-The-Face (just "Rain" for short) into going into a sutler's store and had captured him and slapped leg and wrist irons on him and put him in jail for being a renegade. Rain told him that the next time they met he would cut his heart out and spit it into his face.

What few whites realized at the time was that Rain was a man of his word. At the Little Bighorn, these two men met again apparently, for the last time at the end of Battle Ridge. For years afterward, Mr. Rain never discussed the matter for as long as he lived, nor did any of the other hostiles on the battlefield that day. The fact that Captain Thomas Custer's body had sustained many terrible wounds, one can only assume that Mr. Rain got his two cents worth in during their last meeting.

As for the older Custer, it must have been something else that kept Lieutenant Colonel Custer's body in mostly one bloated, decaying corpse that day. George Armstrong Custer was acclaimed to be a very successful "Injin fighter." He had been fighting Indians for nearly eight years and had lived to tell about it. That was notable enough. In those days, there were not many that could make that boast.

But Custer was not a famous Indian-fighter to the Indians. Those who knew him or of him did not respect him as a mighty warrior. Killing one's wife and children and burning their homes and destroying their food supply, fibbing to them, was not a good way to build a credible reputation. Killing all of a people's horses in the dead of winter, as he had ordered on the Washita, did not make one a particularly famous individual among the Indians camped there on the Little Bighorn River that Sunday afternoon. There would have been a few who had been in that Southern Cheyenne winter camp those long-gone years a go. Maybe none of them would have known it was Morning Star who had attacked them again until after the fight; some, not until weeks later.

The general consensus is that Lieutenant Colonel Custer's body was one of the few bodies whose was not mutilated beyond recognition. For years, even up to today, the story that one usually hears is that it was a strange occurrence that only he was not mutilated. "It must have been because of the great respect the Indians held for this famous "Injin fighter."

LAST RIDE

The truth is about the only fight that Custer clearly won while on the plains was down on the Washita River in the Oklahoma territory all those years before. You will remember that then, he had claimed to defeat and kill 102 Tse-tsehese-staeste, Shahiyela, in the process. He and his men had in fact killed 102 Shahiyela. The dead were women and children and old men, mostly. He had also killed nearly 900 horses, destroyed tons of dried buffalo meat; burnt all of the tents and buffalo robes that the people of poor old Black Kettle, Chief of this Tyospay branch of the Southern Shahiyela in the dead of winter, 1868.

The story, when told the *wasichu* way, left out those parts. The parts not talked about made little boys want to grow up to be just like Lieutenant Colonel Custer, the hero. When told the way it really was, it put a different slant on the episode and was not discussed in front of children and women folk. What was done to the soldiers at the Little Big Horn River just normally is not discussed. Most times, it serves as no purpose either way. The thing it taught the *wasichu* was that it was hard to "outdo" an Indian in what they could do to the remains of a human being.

Somehow, wives feel better if they know that their husbands had "just died" while fighting the Indians, as if it was a natural thing to do. It sat better with the women if you did not go into the details, even if they asked to know. They did not like to hear that her man had been killed and hacked to bits and pieces in the process.

The truth of the matter was, of course, something quite a bit different. It was all in the perception that we *wasichu* have of men fighting to the death on a battlefield on the frontier. If they were killed, they just died; the details about the death need not be gotten into in mixed company.

As for Lieutenant Colonel Custer's remains, the truth was something different than we have been lead to believe. George Custer, like everyone else, had been stripped naked and was lying stark naked out in the hot sun for nearly three days with only one sock partially on. Indians never wore socks so they did not have any use for them, and when they were taking a *wasichu's*, if the sock came off with the boot, that was one thing; if it stayed on the foot when they took off the boot, they threw it away.

Second, he had several wounds. The man's body had multiple holes in it from that shot hitting him were it did in the lower left side of his chest.

The round was no small matter, traveling through his lungs and heart and out the right upper side of his torso, entering his right arm near the arm pit, shattering the upper end of the humerus, and finally exiting the right upper arm. The four wounds caused by that one round would have mangled him pretty good.

He had also been shot in the left temple, which probably meant that there was also an exit wound that would have removed part of his skull on the right side. It is said by some that he did not have powder burns on his face. That is hard to believe; his skin on the side of his face would have been singed, as would his hair and possibly his eye brows. If the round would have taken off part of his head at least one of his ear openings (exterior acoustic meatus) and probably both (if he still had both) had been reamed out with an antler awl. One of his fingers had been cut off, probably for his wedding ring. His male organ was also missing. In addition to those "secondary wounds," his private area had been used for target practice and had numerous arrows penetrating his lower pelvic area.

He was found in a face-up semi-supine position. That was a bad sign—face-up means to those initiated in Indian sign that the body was held in disdain, at least by the Lakota. Could it have been because someone, or perhaps a few of the folks cleaning up after the warriors had done their work, recognized the "famous Injin Fighter"? Or was he in that position possibly because he had a bullet hole in his left temple? Indians did not respect folks who looked as though they had killed themselves rather than fight. Since Custer had died earlier at the river, whoever put the round in his head after he was dead probably did his remains a favor of sorts. The Indians did not do to him what they did to his brother Tom, for example. The Indians did not want to face Tom again in this life or the next. George Custer was not scalped, again probably because his hair was short and he had started to prematurely go bald. Indians did not usually take scraggly, stubby-haired scalps; they could not use them for anything and they looked funny once off the head.

So, why has the legend about the general's body not being mutilated persisted?

You have to know that the survivors on that battlefield that day and for the rest of their lives would never totally divulge the condition of the commander's physical condition, mostly out of respect for Libby Custer, and in telling her that he was dead, trying to make it sound as if he had just gone to sleep, thinking happy thoughts.

Nearly all of the initial injuries were life-ending, save for the missing trigger finger that Kate Big Head, a Lakota woman, or one of the other squaws had hacked off. The antler awl jammed into his ear canals would not have killed him. It would have hurt like hell, had he been alive, but it would not have killed him. The obvious conclusion from the rest of his wounds was that he would have bled out; that would have been messy. In reality, his wounded body would have just blended with all of the other carnage and desecrations heaped on those found around the lieutenant colonel's body.

The men who saw the condition of his body would never for the rest of their lives tell the truth of his physical condition for fear of upsetting his lady, Libby. Had she ever found out, it would have driven her insane. Privately, among themselves, they would write of it back and forth to one another but would never speak of it publicly.

Not talking about the condition of Custer's body was, perhaps, a chivalrous thing to do. It was simply an effort to spare his lady any more pain for the loss of her husband. Men lived by a different code in those days. Even for women today this would be too much, and it certainly would have been in those days. In a very real way, it probably robbed history of the facts surrounding his death. It is enough probably to know that he was found with his men.

Lieutenant Bradley also located Benteen and Major Reno's commands on what is now known as Major Reno's Hill later that morning just over four miles south and west of Custer Hill. Both General Terry and Gibbon saw these two officers and got their side of the action, as they purported it to be. Both men were visibly shaken at the news that Custer's command had been completely destroyed. It would not be until the next day, the 28th, that the two commanders got over to where their commander's body was found.

When Captain Moylan, B Troop commander, viewed the battlefield on the 28th, he identified the remains of Lt. James Calhoun (L Troop

Commander and brother-in-law of the two Custer brothers) before burial. Captain Moylan and Lt Calhoun, the Custer's brother-in-laws, had also been close friends. Moylan was married to Calhoun's sister.

As a new member of the former "Custer Inner Circle," Moylan had of course become friends with Calhoun's wife, Custer's sister, Maggie. Writing her afterwards, Captain Moylan told her that her husband had not been mutilated. That was not the whole truth anymore than what Libby had been told about her husband's body. It was his attempt to soften the blow for a friend's wife.

For Custer's part, he was a big boy; he knew what the deal was. Within a few months of the battle, in the final act of this story, Major Reno would request and be granted a Court of Inquiry. The Court would not convene until 1879, nearly three years after the battle. There were no pending charges against the man until then concerning his part in the battle.

He had requested the Court of Inquiry in an effort to clear his name in any wrong doing at the battle site. At the conclusion of the proceedings, he and Captain Benteen were found innocent of all charges brought against then. For the most part, the damage had been done to Major Reno's career and his honor. Both men had soiled reputations to live down. Captain Benteen would overcome the difficulty of the talk about his part in the battle and would live any wrong doing down and go on to be promoted to brigadier general when he retired.

Captain Benteen's military bearing, his ability to act on his feet when threatened by an enemy and his sheer tenacity of spirit left him unscathed. His Army record reflected no black-mark for his part in the fight. He was sited for bravery and when it was all over, who could have argued with him except those men that knew the difference.

Captain Benteen when facing the charges of acting to slow or not following his orders from his commander could with a straight face say, "I did follow my orders of my immediate commander, Major Reno. Major Reno ordered me to stay with him and to help protect the command."

Major Reno would not be so lucky; his undoing was his own fouled character traits as a man and a commander. Concerning the battle, part of the fuss could have been because Custer's wife who by her own hand had nearly single-handedly created a folk-legend that has lasted until this day.

LAST RIDE

Libby lived another 57 years after her general's death and wrote several books about his exploits on the Western frontier. She always pushed for her husband to be a hero and legend that they both thought he was in real-life. Libby, his loving and doting wife, was largely responsible for the Court of Inquiry of Major Reno and Captain Benteen concerning their failure to support Lieutenant Colonel Custer.

The Army needed a scapegoat to cast the dubious eye away from how it was handling things in the war with the Indians. In Libby's mind, not only had Major Reno and Benteen tried to cover up their own presumed failings in her husband's death, several other notable officers had the same opinion on the matter.

Several other "friends" of the dead lieutenant colonel tried to cast eyes away from their part in the matter: President Grant, for one, openly said the day he heard the news that Custer's defeat, "as a sacrifice of troops brought on by Custer himself; that was wholly unnecessary—wholly unnecessary." Later he would change his tune, but for the time being he blamed Custer—he was still mad at him for what he said about his brother to the Congressmen.

Generals Terry, Sherman, Sheridan, and Crook (Red Beard), as well as other officers: Lieutenants De Rudio, Godfrey (later a general officer), and Luther Hare and Wallace all had their shots at the late Lieutenant Colonel Custer. However, this author has not made a final conclusion regarding General Terry. The man seemed to talk out of both sides of his mouth at the same time. If he seemed confused it was because he was.

Lieutenant Varnum would rise up on the side of the 7th Cavalry's commander, as would Captains McDougall, Weir, and Moylan. Much later, even Lt. Godfrey would come over to their side, though it was much later, after most of the dust had settled. It was the politically correct thing to do. There could be little lost of a man's career for setting the record straight once and for all after it was all over.

George Armstrong Custer was, before his death, a heroic figure in real life. He was even more qualified as a battlefield commander leading and deploying troops into combat. He had spent his entire adult life doing that one thing, and he was very good at what he did. On his worst day before this day, he could not have so badly calculated his battle plan that he would lose his whole command.

There was more to it than he ridding blindly down Medicine Tail Coulee in some wild-eyed gut -wrenching charge, seeking glory, and taking with him 212 men to their deaths.

For Libby's part, she would have never understood the full impact of her husband's commitment to this country, or to the Army he served, or even the glory he craved. She would have never understood what happens when men are bent on killing one another during the heat of battle. She only knew that her beloved "Autie" was dead and it had to be someone else's fault. To her, someone would have to pay—as if that paying would make everything else seem right.

No matter what she might have thought, or tried to do, it would never bring back her "Autie." For all the wrong reasons, Libby was right even though she was wrong, there was more to it all than she would ever know or understand.

General Sheridan went along with that thesis and as a result subtly, under the table like, blamed Major Reno for Custer's defeat and death. He was charged for not acting prudently on the information he had to save Custer. As we have seen, neither Major Reno, nor Captain Benteen knew or claimed not to know where Custer was. That is only partially the truth.

Both men knew where he was. Each had communicated with him, or he with them. Messages had been passed, either through written message or verbal dispatch telling each of these officers what their commander expected of them.

Who is to say what would have happened had these two men done what their commander had wanted them to do?

Could they have put the hostiles on the defense rather than the offense? Or, would both Major Reno and Benteen's commands been annihilated along with their commander's? Finally, had they done what he ordered them to do, would his five troops have been so easily defeated?

There are real answers to those questions, not only guesses and what ifs. The reason is as obvious to most military men as it is not to civilians. The 7th Cavalry was on the verge of being routed and destroyed totally had either of the surviving commander did anything other than exactly what they did; orders or not. Did they disobey their orders?

Yes—by Captain Benteen not getting back on Custer's trail as the general intended him to. By doing so, did they save their commands? Yes. Is that how it should be done? No!

That tactic of moving slowly was by Benteen's design, his silent protest. As it turned out, he was too far away to come to the aid and support of Custer's battalion. His being late is what saved Major Reno's shot-up battalion. At the same time it doomed Custer's battalion as he attacked down the coulee.

By Major Reno not attacking hard enough against the back of the encampment, the major enabled the hostiles to withdraw their forces from Major Reno's front. That limited attack allowed the hostiles to slip down behind Custer's command closing off all avenues of retreat up Medicine Tail Coulee. That forced the Custer battalion to retreat up the sides of the steep hills leading away from the river.

After Custer committed to attack down the coulee without Benteen's support, which he was expecting at any minute, the die had been cast. Nothing anyone did was going to save Lieutenant Colonel Custer and his five troops. To send troops to find him would have been dereliction of duty by both Major Reno and Benteen to both of their individual commands.

Lieutenant Colonel Custer's orders would have been impossible to carry out once both officers failed to meet their commander's orders when he ordered them to do so. For that part they were right. The rest of their claims are purely fiction and poppycock that the powers to be accepted in order to cover up the Army's complicity in failing the 7th.

Later, when Captain Benteen viewed Custer's body, he is reported to have said something to the effect, "There that son-of-bitch is...well, at least he won't fight again." He hated Custer, his being dead was not enough for Captain Benteen's hate to be abated.

Major Reno was just glad to be alive. I am satisfied that they could not have helped him once the window of the attack closed. It would not have been high on either man's list of things to do that Sunday afternoon. One, because unfortunately for him, Major Reno turned out to be a coward, and the other, Captain Benteen, let his personal feelings stand in the way of doing his duty.

For Major Reno part he was the odd man out. Kind of a weird duck in his own right, he was easy to blame, he was a drunk. At the end of his career, four years later, Major Reno was drummed out of the service in 1880. It was not until 1967, long after his death, that his record was corrected and he was given an honorable discharge.

Go figure; the man is found guilty on five counts of conduct unbecoming an officer: drunk and disorderly; window-peeking on the post commander's daughter, and trying to take undue advantage of a brother officer's wife while the other officer was detailed to other duties during a Court Martial in 1881. For those offenses just cited, he was dismissed from the Army.

Oddly enough, Major Marcus Albert Major Reno is one of only three officers buried with the men of 7th Cavalry Regiment who died on Custer's Hill (Second Lieutenant John Jordan Crittendon is another—his father, an infantry colonel, wanted his son buried where he fell; and young Second Lieutenant John Sturgis). All other identifiable officers were buried in either Arlington National Cemetery; or, in their home states, or other national cemeteries. There was a forth officer, whose remains were never identified or recovered, those of 2nd Lieutenant Harrington perhaps he was buried in someone else's grave or along with several others.

As for Custer and his brother Tom (who had been twice awarded this country's highest military award, the Congressional Medal of Honor, for valor in face of the enemy during the Civil War) they faced the enemy 'til the end, each in their own way: both fighting as they always had, and always together.

Today, standing along the battle ridge, standing there quietly with your eyes closed, if you listen carefully you can still hear the ode to the 7th Cavalry, their jaunty "Gary Owen."

I know...I have heard it sounding on the winds that blow along the ridge top. Standing there looking down along the ridge, you can almost catch a glimmer as each Troop of the 7th riding along under their own Stars and Stripes Troop swallow-tailed guideon flowing on the wind as they push on toward their last ride.

For the Indians' part, all that they knew was that the pony soldiers were attacking the villages, and that they must be stopped and killed. To that end, the Indians in that encampment were totally dedicated.

Plus, on the other side of the coin, all of Custer's officers were dressed very similarly to him. In the heat of battle, it would have been difficult to pick one officer out from all of the others; they were all dressed and looked alike (to the other races, white people look alike also). Most of the officers were wearing deerskin shirts that day, even Benteen and Major Reno. Custer, of course, was wearing both the pants and the jacket. His brother officers stuck to their government-issue riding britches and wore the deer hide shirt to look uniform to the general.

Think about that for a moment. There were 31 officers in the 7th Cavalry Regiment that day, 13 of those officers are with Custer's battalion; for the most part of the 4,000-4,500 to even as many as 5,000 on the field that day maybe only a hundred of the Indian warriors that had heard of the "Long Hair" Custer. Of that number, maybe fewer than a dozen of them would have ever seen him in person and fewer still would have ever been close enough to talk to him in order to be able to identify him at any distance at all, to notice his physical appearance or even his mannerisms.

Put him in with 212 others, all dressed basically the same, save for the buckskin jacket and britches that he wore (the other officers wore just buckskin jackets); they would have never known he was there, nor would they have cared; if they had known. They would have no way had knowing that it was he attacking them right at that moment that he did.

To those Indians at the southern end of the village, they may have thought it to be "Red Beard" (General Crook) attacking them again. The Indians knew him and they had attacked him a week earlier and had scared him badly. He may have been coming back for "seconds" for all the Indians would have known if it was. Maybe he was a sore loser, and wanted to get even with them. They did not know who was knocking on their back door, it did not matter—they were going to deal with them.

It would not be until long after the battle and the tribes had split and moved on far away that they would know they had beaten Custer and the vaunted 7th Cavalry. When the general was un-horsed at the ford at the river most of them would not have known him then from O'Leary's cow.

The Indians would not have guessed that one of their own had done what countless numbers of Confederate soldiers had tried to do and failed to do each time.

Had they have known, they would have thrown a party right then. The point is, they did not know and there was work to be done.

Had they known who it was that they had killed; it would not have mattered to them one way or the other. The Indians did not think that way; the *wasichus* were attacking their homes and family members just like they always did; and for that, they would pay handsomely for doing it.

The Indians who were there on the day of the battle told other whites what had happened. It was not the kind of story that white folks would want to hear about their hero, then or even now.

In the end, it should be said that Lieutenant Colonel Custer did what he had to do, and in so doing, it got him killed (maybe, inwardly; just maybe, he knew it would). He had no choice but to do what he did. Few soldiers have ever gone through situations like the one he faced that day and lived to tell about it.

—42—

OFFICIAL REPORTS OF THE BATTLE
(Published Records of the Surviving Commanders)

After the battle, there were many reports and news stories written in which the 7th Cavalry had gotten its nose bloodied. In addition to those, many officers directly attached to, or in one way or another, in command of a unit, wrote official reports concerning the battle and their knowledge of the matter. There were also many officers, and even a few soldiers, who wrote what they either witnessed, or thought about the battle, and the scene found two days after the battle on Battle Ridge. Most of these were, of course, unofficial writings; some were never meant to be published as factual reports. Some were even just thoughts or explanations to questions by the writer. In some instances the writer was not even at the battlefield and wrote only what he surmised had happened after hearing the story second- or third-hand.

Add to all of those types of notes and writings, and there were many such reports; the morass of "eyewitness" accounts, the conjecture of other military experts of the day, (who had no first hand knowledge, just opinions) and the yellow-penned journalists out to sell papers, and you have room for miss-truths and outright lies being told at every corner. Stupidity and cover-ups were running almost neck-to-neck throughout the Army. No one wanted to get splattered when the "bull let go," and good men's hearts turned stone cold on the issue of Custer's defeat, to defend or deflect possible incriminations aimed at themselves. It was every man—officers for the most part— for himself.

The following reports are in and of themselves interesting because if studied, you can see that even those men directly involved in the battle were somewhat confused about the whole thing, or were trying to dodge the shadow of blame that might be cast on them at some later time.

The Commander of the Expedition, General Alfred Terry, had even written a letter to Sheridan in which he suggests Lieutenant Colonel Custer openly disobeyed his orders. Colonel John Gibbon indicated in his letters and writing concerning the event intimates or hints as much. However, there were one or two general officers who were old Indian fighters, who had years of experience in fighting the Indians who said the tactics Lieutenant Colonel Custer tried to implement at the Little Bighorn, illustrated the genius the man had for tactically initiating an attack. He was just overwhelmed by superior numbers, outgunned, and his men out fought.

Those generals, Oliver Otis (O.O.) Howard and Nelson Miles saw the event differently. Historians can say what they will about these two generals, but they were generals of reputation for tactics and battlefield strategy not only during the Civil War, but also in fighting the Sioux, Cheyenne across the northern plains, the Nez Perce in the northwest, and the Apache in the southwest. I believe I will trust their judgments on this matter of tactics rather than General Terry, who had never been on an Indian campaign until he by choice chose to stay with Gibbon rather than go with Custer. He knew Custer would find and would fight the Indians and he did not want to be there when he did. He did not think he could keep up with Custer's movements after the 17th of June physically, and did not want to slow him down. So, he chose to ride the river boat *Far West* for a few more days, meet up with Colonel Gibbon and march with him to the proposed battlefield—that is what he did, folks. He knew Custer would find the Indians, and he had never fought against the Indians himself—and out of a natural instinct of self-preservation that is what he did.

As for Colonel Gibbon, John Gibbon was a fighter, he would go a round with you much as Custer would, but he was more laid back and more apt to pick his fights than to fight where the enemy wanted to fight.

To Custer, it did not matter where he fought, he would come at the enemy wherever he was. It did not matter; if he found them, he wanted to reach out and touch them.

Unfortunately, what we find within the officer corps remaining in the 7th Cavalry was that many of the surviving officers of the 7th Cavalry after the battle were trying to dodge blame any way they could. There were exceptions to be sure. Lieutenants Weir, D Troop, and J. J. Crittenden were two, Captain McDougall, B Troop another who had tried to come to the aid of their commander. However, even those officers who claimed to be close to their commander at some time or another sold him out either to make a profit, or to protect their own careers.

Lieutenant E.S. Godfrey, commander of K Troop, was one such man. He was young at the time and was perhaps cast under Custer's spell when he was early in his career—but he did cast dispersions upon the facts, when he did not need to and caused needless confusion on the matter. He would later become the General of the Army and later still the noted "expert" on the battle at the Little Bighorn. For the most part, I think Lt. Godfrey was trying to do the right thing all the time, I believe he got confused toward the end of his life and said some things he did not mean.

The official commander of the 7th Cavalry, Colonel Sturgis, had an ax to grind in the aftermath of the battle since his only son was killed and his body never recovered at the battle. He can be somewhat excused for his reaction to the news of the battle. He died not knowing what had happened to his son, and had more reason than most to be a little antagonized by the entire affair. He never forgave the Lieutenant Colonel in his son's death. And until his dying day, the commander blamed Custer's tactics and manhood for it.

Not that it would have mattered to Custer, if he had known, and obviously not after the battle, he was dead. But even if he had been successful and Colonel Sturgis' son had still been killed. Custer's reply would have been, "Sir, men die in battle, and as sorry as I am for the loss of your son, sir, I lost a lot of good men besides your son."

Soldiers get paid for fighting and winning its nation's wars; sometimes they get killed in the process. It is part of the business of putting on the uniform of your country. While it is infinitely better to have someone else die for his country or beliefs than it is for yours; if you are a soldier, you know the risks and accept them. They go with the job.

The decision to attack the Indians was Lieutenant Colonel Custer's alone. Given his orders, and based on the face-to-face council of General Terry in front of Gibbon and the other officers present Colonel Custer knew what he was supposed to do under the circumstances as they (the officers present on the *Far West* thought them to be). He did what he had always done, he gathered his command, formed them up, and then went hell bent for leather until he found, and attacked the enemy. One would expect nothing less from him, not his immediate superior, General Alfred Terry, not Colonel John Gibbon, not his subordinate commanders, Major Reno or Captain Benteen or the 700 plus soldiers he led. That was the reason why he was commanding that day. In true Custer form he did his best. He devised a plan for battle, and to the best of his ability tried to implement that battle plan—it was his decision alone, and he must be responsible for the outcome.

Had he survived the battle himself and still losing it, he would have — and you would not have had to go looking for him— stepped up and taken the responsibility for its failure. He would have faced his accusers, and not been found guilty of dereliction of duty. Custer did not hide from responsibility for his actions, blame others when things went wrong, or shed fame when it came his way. In the end it came down to one thing— honor, and if nothing else Lieutenant Colonel (brevetted, Major General) Custer died with his honor and dedication to duty in tact.

So blame him for a lot of things, blame him for being a pompous ass, call him names if you must, debate his tactics, but do not ever question his honor or fidelity to his country.

LAST RIDE

BENTEEN'S OFFICIAL REPORT

As published in the *Annual Report of the Secretary of War*, 1876, Forty-Fourth Congress, first session house executive document no. I serial volume 1742 (Pages 479 – 480) 3 Bb—report of Captain F. W. Benteen, Camp Seventh Cavalry, July 4, 1876:

Sir:

In obedience to verbal instructions received from you, I have the honor to report the operations of my battalion, consisting of Companies D, H, and K, on the 25th ultimo. The directions I received from Lieutenant-Colonel Custer were, to move with my command to the left, to send well-mounted officers with about six men who should ride rapidly to a line of bluffs about five miles to our left and front, with instructions to report at once to me if anything of Indians could be seen from that point. I was to follow the movement of this detachment as rapidly as possible. Lieutenant Gibson was the officer selected, and I followed closely with the battalion at times getting in advance of the detachment. The bluffs designated were gained, but nothing seen but other bluffs quite as large and precipitous as were before me. I kept on to those and the country was the same, there being no valley of any kind that I could see on any side, I had then gone about fully ten miles; the ground was terribly hard on horses, so I determined to carry out the other instructions, which were, that if in my judgment there was nothing to be seen of Indians, valleys, &c., in the direction I was going, to return with the battalion to the trail the command was following. I accordingly did so, reaching the trail just in advance of the pack train. I pushed rapidly on, soon getting out of sight of the advance of the train, until reaching a morass; I halted to water the animals, who had been with4ut water since about 8 p.m. of the day before. This watering did not occasion the loss of fifteen minutes, and when I was moving out the advance of the train commenced watering from that morass. I went at a slow trot until I came to a burning lodge with the dead body of an Indian in it on a scaffold. We did not halt. About a mile farther on I met a sergeant of the regiment with orders from Lieutenant Colonel Custer to the officer in charge of the rear-guard and train to bring it to the front with as great rapidity as was possible. Another mile on I met Trumpeter Morton, of my own company, with a written order from First Lieut. W. W. Cook to me, which read:

"Benteen, come on,
Big village. Be quick. Bring pacs.
W. W. Cook
P.S. Bring pacs."

I could then see no movement of any kind in any direction; a horse on the hill, riderless, being the only living thing I could see in my front. I inquired of the trumpeter what had been done, and he informed [me] that the Indians had "skeedaddled," abandoning the village. Another mile and a half brought me in sight of the stream and plain in which were some of our dismounted men fighting, and Indians charging and recharging them in great numbers. The plain seemed to be alive with them. I then noticed our men in large numbers running for the bluffs on right bank of stream. I concluded at once that those had been repulsed, and was of the opinion that if I crossed the ford with my battalion, that I should have had it treated in like manner; for from long experience with cavalry, I judge there were 900 veteran Indians right there at that time, against which the large element of recruits in my battalion would stand no earthly chance as mounted men. I then moved up to the bluffs and reported my command to Maj. M. A. Major Reno. I did not return for the pack-train because I deemed it perfectly safe where it was, and we could defend it, had it been threatened, from our position on the bluff, and another thing, it savored too much of coffee-cooling to return when I was since a fight was progressing in the front, and deeming the train as safe without me.

Very respectively,

F.W. Benteen, Captain Seventh Cavalry
Lieut. Geo. D. Wallace, Adjutant Seventh Cavalry

MAJOR RENO'S OFFICIAL REPORT

As published in the Annual Report of the Secretary of War, 1876 Forty-fourth Congress, First Session House Executive Document No. I Serial Volume 1742 (Pages 476 – 480) Headquarters Seventh United States Cavalry, Camp on Yellowstone River, July 5, 1876:

E. W. Smith, A. D. C. and A. A. A. Gen.:

The command of the regiment having developed upon me as the senior surviving officer from the battle of the 25th and 26th of June, between the Seventh Cavalry and Sitting Bull's band of hostile Sioux, on the Little Bighorn River, I have the honor to submit the following report of its operations from the time of leaving the main column until the command was united in the vicinity of the Indian village:

The regiment left the camp at the mouth of the Rosebud River, after passing in review before the department commander, under command of Bvt. Maj. Gen. G. A. Custer, lieutenant-colonel, on the afternoon of the 22nd day of June, and marched up the Rosebud 12 miles and encamped; 23rd, marched up the Rosebud, passing many old Indian camps, and following a very large pole-trail, but not fresh, making 33 miles; 24th, the march was continued up the Rosebud, the trail and signs freshening with every mile, until we had made 28 miles, and we then encamped and waited for information from the scouts. At 9:25 PM, Custer called the officers together and informed us that beyond a doubt the village was in the valley of the Little Bighorn and in order to reach it, it was necessary to cross the divide between the Rosebud and the Little Bighorn, and it would be impossible to do so in the day-time without discovering our march to the Indians; that we would prepare to march at 11 PM. This was done, the line of march turning from the Rosebud to the right up one of its branches which headed near the summit of the divide. About 2 AM on the 25th the scouts told him that he could not cross the divide before daylight. We then made coffee and rested for three hours, at the expiration of which time the march was resumed, the divide crossed and about 8:00 AM the command was in the valley of one of the branches of the Little Bighorn. By this time Indians had been seen and it was certain that we could not surprise them, and it was determined to move at once to the attack. Previous to this, no division of the regiment had been made since the order had been issued on the Yellowstone annulling wing and battalion organizations, but Custer informed me that he would assign commands on the march. I was ordered by Lieut. W. W. Cooke, adjutant, to assume command of

Companies M, A, and G; Captain Benteen of Companies H, D, and K. Custer retained C, E, F, 1, and L under his immediate command, and Company B, Captain McDougall, in rear of the pack- train.

I assumed command of the companies assigned to me, and, without any definite orders, moved forward with the rest of the column, and well to its left. I saw Benteen moving farther to the left, and, as they passed, he told me he had orders to move well to the left, and sweep everything before him. I did not see him again until about 2.30 PM. The command moved down to the creek toward the Little Bighorn Valley, Custer with five companies on the right bank, myself and three companies on the left bank, and Benteen farther to the left, and out of sight.

As we approached a deserted village, and in which was standing one teepee, about 11:00 AM, Custer motioned me to cross to him, which I did, and moved nearer to his column until about 12.30 AM [PM?] when Lieutenant Cook, adjutant, came to me and said the village was only two miles above, and running away; to move forward at as rapid a gait as prudent, and to charge afterward, and that the whole outfit would support me. I think those were his exact words. I at once took a fast trot, and moved down about two miles, when I came to a ford of the river. I crossed immediately, and halted about ten minutes or less to gather the battalion, sending word to Custer that I had everything in front of me, and that they were strong. I deployed, and, with the Ree scouts on my left, charged down the valley, driving the Indians with great ease for about two and a half miles. 1, however, soon saw that I was being drawn into some trap, as they would certainly fight harder, and especially as we were nearing their village, which was still standing; besides, I could not see Custer or any other support, and at the same time the very earth seemed to grow Indians, and they were running toward me in swarms, and from all directions. I saw I must defend myself and give up the attack mounted. This I did. Taking possession of a front of woods, and which furnished, near its edge, a shelter for the horses, dismounted and fought them on foot, making headway through the woods. I soon found myself in the near vicinity of the village, saw that I was fighting odds of at least five to one, and that my only hope was to get out of the woods, where I would soon have been surrounded, and gain some high ground. I accomplished this by mounting and charging the Indians between me and the bluffs on the opposite side of the river. In this charge, First Lieut. Donald McIntosh, Second Lieut. Benjamin H. Hodgson, Seventh Cavalry, and Acting Assistant Surgeon J. M. De Wolf, were killed.

I succeeded in reaching the top of the bluff, with a loss of three officers and twenty-nine enlisted men killed and seven wounded. Almost at the same time I reached the top, mounted men were seen to be coming toward us, and it proved to be Colonel Benteen's battalion, Companies H, D, and K. We joined forces, and in a short time the pack-train came up. As senior, my command was then A, B, D, G, H, K, and M, about three hundred and eighty men, and the following officers: Captains Benteen, Weir, French and McDougall, First Lieutenants Godfrey, Mathey, and Gibson, and Second Lieutenants Edgerly, Wallace, Varnum, and Hare, and Acting Assistant Surgeon Porter.

First Lieutenant De Rudio was in the dismounted fight in the woods, but, having some trouble with his horse, did not join the command in the charge out, and hiding himself in the woods, joined the command after night-fall on the 26th.

Still hearing nothing of Custer, and, with this re-enforcement, I moved down the river in the direction of the village, keeping on the bluffs.

We had heard firing in that direction and knew it could only be Custer. I moved to the summit of the highest bluff, but seeing and hearing nothing sent Captain Weir with his company to open communication with him. He soon sent word by Lieutenant Hare that he could go no farther, and that the Indians were getting around him. At this time he was keeping up a heavy fire from his skirmish line. I at once turned everything back to the first position I had taken on the bluffs, and which seemed to me the best. I dismounted the men and had the horses and mules of the pack-train driven together in a depression, put the men on the crests of the bluffs, and which seemed to me the best. I dismounted the men and had the horses and mules of the pack- train driven together in a depression, put the men on the crests of the hills making the depression, and had hardly done so when I was furiously attacked. This was about 6:00 PM. We held our ground, with a loss of eighteen enlisted men killed and forty-six wounded, until the attack ceased, about 9:00 PM. As I knew by this their overwhelming numbers, and had given up any support from that portion of the regiment with Custer, I had the men dig rifle pits, barricade with dead horses and mules, and boxes of hard bread, the opening of the depression toward the Indians in which the animals were herded, and made every exertion to be ready for what I saw would be a terrific assault the next day. All this might night the men were busy, and the Indians holding a scalp- dance underneath us in the bottom and in our hearing. On the morning of the 26th I felt confident that I could hold my own, and was ready, as far as I could be, when at daylight, about 2.30 AM, I heard the crack of two rifles. This was the signal for the beginning of a fire that I have never equated. Every rifle was handled by an expert and skilled marksman, and with a range that exceeded our carbines, and it was simply impossible to show any part of the body before it was struck. We could see, as the day brightened, countless hordes of them pouring up the valley from the village and scampering over the high points toward the places designated for them by their chiefs, and which entirely surrounded our position. They had sufficient numbers to completely encircle us, and men were struck from opposite sides of the lines from where the shots were fired. I think we were fighting all the Sioux Nation, and also all the desperadoes, renegades, half-breeds, and squaw-men between the Missouri and the Arkansas and east of the Rocky Mountains, and they must have numbered at least twenty-five hundred warriors.

The fire did not slacken until about 9:30 AM, and then we found they were making a last desperate effort and which was directed against the lines held by Companies H and M. In this charge they came close enough to use their bows and arrows, and one man lying dead within our lines was touched with the coup-stick of one of the foremost Indians. When I say the stick was only ten or twelve feet long, some idea of the desperate and reckless fighting of these people may be understood.

This charge of theirs was gallantly repulsed by the men on that line, lead by Colonel Benteen. They also came close enough to send their arrows into the line held by Companies D and K, but were driven away by a like charge of the line, which I accompanied. We now had many wounded, and the question of water was vital, as from 6:00 PM. the previous evening until now, 10:00 AM, about sixteen hours, we had been without.

A skirmish line was formed under Colonel Benteen to protect the descent of volunteers down the hill in front of his position to reach the water. We succeeded in getting some canteens, although many of the men were hit in doing so. The fury of the attack was now over, and to our astonishment the Indians were seen going in parties toward the village. But two solutions occurred to us for this movement; that they were going for something to eat, more ammunition, (as they had been throwing arrows,) or that Custer was coming. We took advantage of this lull to fill all vessels with water, and soon had it by camp- kettles full. But they continued to withdraw, and all firing ceased save occasional shots from sharp-shooters sent to annoy us about the water. About 2:00 PM. the grass in the bottom was set on fire and followed up by Indians who encouraged its burning, and it was evident to me it was done for a purpose, and which purpose I discovered later on to be the creation of a dense cloud of smoke behind which they were packing and preparing to move their village. It was between 6:00 and 7:00 PM that the village came out from behind the dense clouds of smoke and dust. We had a close and good view of them as they filed away in the direction of the Bighorn Mountains, moving in almost perfect military order. The length of the column was full equal to that of a large division of the cavalry corps of the Army of the Potomac as I have seen it in its march.

We now thought of Custer, of whom nothing had been seen and nothing heard since the firing in his direction about 6:00 PM on the eve of the 25th, and we concluded that the Indians had gotten between him and us and driven him toward the boat at the mouth of the Little Bighorn River. The awful fate that did befall him never occurred to any of us as within the limits of possibility.

During the night I changed my position in order to secure an unlimited supply of water, and was prepared for their return, feeling sure they would do so, as they were in such numbers; but early in the morning of the 27th, and while we were on the qui vire for Indians, I saw with my glass a dust some distance down the valley. There was no certainty for some time what they were, but finally I satisfied myself they were cavalry, and, if so, could only be Custer, as it was ahead of the time that I understood that General Terry could be expected. Before this time, however, I had written a communication to General Terry, and three volunteers were to try and reach him. (I had no confidence in the Indians with me, and could not get them to do anything.) If this dust were Indians it was possible they would not expect any one to leave. The men started, and were told to go as near as it was safe to determine whether the approaching column was white men, and to return at once in case they found it so, but if they were Indians to push on to General Terry. In a short time, we saw them returning a note from Terry to Custer saying Crow scouts had come to camp saying he had been whipped, but that it was not believed. I think it was about 10:30 AM when General Terry rode into my lines, and the fate of Custer and his brave men was soon determined by Captain Benteen proceeding to the battle-ground, and where was recognized the following officers, who were surrounded by the dead bodies of many of their men; Gen G. A. Custer, Col. W. W. Cook, adjutant; Capts. M. W. Keogh, G. W. Yates, and T. W. Custer; First Lieuts. A. E. Smith, James Calhoun; Second Lieuts. W. V. Reily, of the Seventh Cavalry and J. J. Crittenden, of the Twelfth Infantry, temporarily attached to this regiment. The bodies of Lieut. J. E. Porter and Second Lieuts. H. M. Harrington and J. G. Sturgis, Seventh Cavalry, and Asst. Surg. G. W. Lord, U. S. A., were not recognized; but there is every reasonable probability they were killed. It was more certain that the column of five companies with Custer had been killed.

 The wounded in my lines were, during the afternoon

and evening of the 27th, moved to the camp of General Terry, and at 5:00 AM of the 28th I proceeded with the regiment to the battle-ground of Custer, and buried 204 bodies, including the following-named citizens: Mr. Boston Custer, Mr. Reed (a young nephew of Lieutenant Colonel Custer,) and Mr. Kellogg, (a correspondent for the New York Herald.) The following-named citizens and Indians who were with my command were also killed: Charles Reynolds, guide and hunter; Isaiah Dorman, (colored,) interpreter; Bloody Knife, who fell from immediately by my side; Bobtail Bull, and Stab, of the Indian scouts.

After traveling over his trail, it was evident to me that Custer intended to support me by moving farther down the stream and attacking the village in flank; that he found the distance greater to ford than he anticipated; that he did charge, but his march had taken so long, although his trail shows that he had moved rapidly, that they were ready for him; that Companies C and L, and perhaps part of E, crossed to the village or attempted it; at the charge were met by a staggering fire, and that they fell back to find a position from which to defend themselves, but they were followed too closely by the Indians to permit time to form any kind of a line.

I think had the regiment gone in as a body, and from the woods from which I fought advanced upon the village, its destruction was certain. But he was fully confident they were running away, or he would not have turned from me. I think (after the great number of Indians that were in the village,) that the following reasons obtain for the misfortune; His rapid marching for two days and one night before the fight; attacking in the day-time at 12 in., and when they were on the qui vire, instead of early morning; and lastly, his unfortunate division of the regiment into three commands.

During my fight with Indians, I had the heartiest

support from officers and men, but the conspicuous services of Bvt. Col. F. W. Benteen I desire to call attention to especially, for if ever a soldier deserved recognition by his Government for distinguished services he certainly does. I enclose herewith his report of the operations of his battalion from the time of leaving the regiment until we joined commands on the hill. I also enclose an accurate list of casualties, as far as it can be made at the present time, separating them into two lists: A, those killed in Lieutenant Colonel Custer's command; B, those killed and wounded in the command I had.

The number of Indians killed can only be approximated until we hear through the agencies. I saw the bodies of eighteen, and Captain Ball, Second Cavalry, who made a scout of thirteen miles over their trail, says that their graves were many along their line of march. It is simply impossible that numbers of them should not be hit in the several charges they made so close to my lines. They made their approaches through the deep gulches that led from the hill-top to the river, and, when the jealous care with which the Indian guards the bodies of killed and wounded is considered, it is not astonishing that their bodies were not found. It is probable that the stores left by them and destroyed the next two days was to make room for many of these on their *travois*. The harrowing sight of the dead bodies crowning the height on which Custer fell, and which will remain vividly in my memory until death, is too recent for me not to ask the good people of this country whether a policy that sets opposing parties in the field, armed, clothed, and equipped by one and the same Government should not be abolished.

All of which is respectfully submitted.

M. A. Major Reno, Major
Seventh Cavalry,
Commanding Regiment.

GENERAL TERRY'S OFFICIAL REPORT ON THE CUSTER DISASTER

As Published in the Senate Executive Document No. 81 Serial Volume 166 [Telegram] Philadelphia, July 8, 1876:

General William T. Sherman, Washington, D.C.

The following just received from Drum, and forwarded for your information, Chicago, Ill., July 7, 1876 —1:10 AM:

General P. H. Sheridan, U.S.A., Continental Hotel
The following is General Terry's report, received late at night, dated June 27:
"It is my painful duty to report that day before yesterday, the 25th instant, a great disaster overtook Lieutenant Colonel Custer and the troops under his command. At 12 o'clock of the 22nd instant he started with his whole regiment and a strong detachment of scouts and guides from the mouth of the Rosebud; proceeding up that river about twenty miles he struck a very heavy Indian trail, which had previously been discovered, and pursuing it, found that it led, as it was supposed that it would lead, to the Little Bighorn River. Here he found a village of almost unlimited extent, and at once attacked it with that portion of his command, which was immediately at hand. Major Reno, with three companies, A, G, and M, of the regiment, was sent into the valley of the stream at the point where the trail struck it. Lieutenant Colonel Custer, with five companies, C, E, F, 1, and L, attempted to enter about three miles lower down. Major Reno, forded the river, charged down its left

bank, and fought on foot until finally completely overwhelmed by numbers he was compelled to mount and re-cross the river and seek a refuge on the high bluffs which overlook its right bank. Just as he re-crossed, Captain Benteen, who, with three companies, D, H, and K, was some two (2) miles to the left of Major Reno when the action commenced, but who had been ordered by Lieutenant Colonel Custer to return, came to the river, and rightly concluding that it was useless for his force to attempt to renew the fight in the valley, he joined Major Reno on the bluffs. Captain McDougall' with his company (B) was at first some distance in the rear with a train of pack mules. He also came up to Major Reno. Soon this united force was nearly surrounded by Indians, many of whom armed with rifles, occupied positions, which commanded the ground held by the cavalry, ground from which there was no escape. Rifle-pits were dug, and the fight was maintained, though with heavy loss, from about half past 2 o'clock of the 25th till 6 o'clock of the 26th, when the Indians withdrew from the valley, taking with them their village. Of the movements of Lieutenant Colonel Custer and the five companies under his immediate command, scarcely anything is known from those who witnessed them; for no officer or soldier who accompanied him has yet been found alive. His trail from the point where Major Reno crossed the stream, passes along and in the rear of the crest of the bluffs on the right bank for nearly or quite three miles; then it comes down to the bank of the river, but at once diverges from it, as if he had unsuccessfully attempted to cross; then turns upon itself, almost completing a circle, and closes. It is marked by the remains of his officers and men and the bodies of his horses, some of them strewn along the path, others heaped where halts appeared to have been made. There is abundant evidence that a gallant resistance was offered by the troops, but they were beset on all sides by overpowering numbers. The officers known to be killed are Lieutenant Colonel Custer; Captains Keogh, Yates, and Custer, and Lieutenants Cooke, Smith, McIntosh, Calhoun, Porter, Hodgson, Sturgis, and Reilly, of the cavalry. Lieutenant Crittenden, of the Twelfth Infantry, along with Acting Assistant Surgeon D. E. Wolf, Lieutenant Harrington of the Cavalry, and Assistant Surgeon Lord are missing. Captain Benteen and Lieutenant Varnum, of the cavalry are slightly wounded. Mr. B. Custer, a brother, and Mr. Reed, a nephew, of Lieutenant Colonel Custer, were with him and were killed. No other officers than those whom I have named are among the killed, wounded, and missing.

It is impossible yet to obtain a reliable list of the enlisted men killed and wounded, but the number of killed, including officers, must reach two hundred and fifty. The number of wounded is fifty-one. The balance of report will be forwarded immediately."

R. C. DRUM,
Assistant Adjutant-General
P. H. Sheridan,
Lieutenant General

—43—

NEW YORK TIMES NEWSPAPER STORY

Right from the start, the news of Custer's demise was surreal and overstated. The facts of the battle were never completely told at that time and even up to this day we still haven't gotten an unblemished report that makes total sense. Least-wise, not one that accurately told all the facts that were known. Little tide-bits would be added or deleted from time-to-time to meet the satisfaction of the writer or historian.

The truth of the matter is that not all the facts were known at the time. Some of the facts that were known were covered up to protect the guilty or to protect those still living. What statements of facts that were reported could have been facts or figments of someone's imagination—as was usually the case.

To illustrate this, the following article appeared in the *New York Times Newspaper*, published two weeks after the fiasco in the southern corner of the Montana Territory. The lateness of the report could be blamed on the fact that news traveled slowly in those days. What the article points out though, is a perfect example of misstated truths and half-truths.

In the first sentence it says that "Major General..." Well, he was not then Major General George Armstrong Custer. He was Lieutenant Colonel George Armstrong Custer the day he died. In the same sentence, it says that his whole command was killed. We know that is not the truth of the matter either. Next, it goes on to say, in this same sentence, that the Indians were under the command of Sitting Bull. The point of the matter is that Sitting Bull never got out of his tent that day when the battle was going on.

That phrase alone "…under the command of Sitting Bull" was another example of not understanding the way things worked with the Indians. First of all, Indians didn't command anybody, the Indians followed whom they wanted, when they wanted to, and then did what they wanted to do after they got there.

Another big mistruth was that it was Sioux fault for Custer getting killed that day. As if to say that the Lakota were the only ones to strike. That is a little mistake, understandable perhaps, considering it was written by Easterner *wasichus*. No Easterner would have known or ever heard of the Gross Ventres, Blackfeet, or Ohmeseheso, or even Shahiyela, Arapaho, or any other lesser tribes that were camped beside the Little Sheep River that Sunday morning. It was easier to just lump them all together and call them "Sioux" rather than what they were known out on the plains by their many enemies–Cut Throats, or by the different tribes that represented the Teton Lakota Nation: Ogalala, Brule, Minneconjoux, Hunkpapas, Sansarcs, and Santees.

About the truest sentence in the beginning of the article is, "that Custer was a soldier in the truest sense of the word." He was. No one should ever question that. He was not a great general, but he was a fighter, and he deserved better than he got then and now. If he was anything, he was a soldier, and a good one.

The article only mentions the fact, in sort of a, "Oh, by the way," manner that, "George Armstrong Custer was killed." It did not say where he was killed, or how, just that he and "his whole command" were. Then, the article spends a great deal of space talking about the exploits of the fallen soldier during the War Between the States eleven years earlier. That is sad. There was so much that should have been said about him and the plight of the Indians in their quest for some sort of official recognition by the United States government.

Something should have been said about the broken treaties between them and the white man, about the starvation of the Indians brought on by their being forced off their ancestral lands and their being forced to live like paupers, about the plundering of the buffalo herds by the white man. These great herds by the way had managed to feed these same Indians for thousands of years without ever making them go hungry. The white man managed to kill nearly all of them in about four years.

NEW YORK TIMES NEWS

July 7, 1876

Major Gen. George A. Custer, who was killed with his whole Command while attacking an encampment of Sioux Indians under command of Sitting Bull, was one of the bravest and most widely known officers in the United States Army. He has for the past fifteen years been know to the country and to his comrades as a man who feared no danger, as a soldier in the truest sense of the word. He was daring to a fault, generous beyond most men. His memory will long be kept green in the many hearts. Born in New-Rumley, Harrison County, Ohio, on the 5th of December 1839, he obtained a good common education, and after graduating engaged for a time teaching school. In June, 1857, through the influence of Hon. John A. Bingham, then member of Congress from Ohio, he obtained an appointment to the United States Military Academy at West Point, and entered that institution on the 1st of July of the year named. He graduated No. 34 in one of the brightest classes that ever left the academy. Immediately upon leaving West Point he was appointed Second Lieutenant in Company G of the Second United States Cavalry, a regiment which had formerly been commanded by Robert E. Lee.

He reported to Lieut. Gen. Scott on the 20th July, the day preceding the Battle of Bull Run, and the Commander in Chief gave him the choice of accepting a position on his staff or of joining his regiment, then under the command of Gen. McDowell in the field. Longing for an opportunity to see active service, and determined to win distinction Lieut. Custer chose the latter course, and after riding all night through a country filled with people who were, to say the least, not friendly, he reached McDowell's headquarters at daybreak on the morning of the 21$^{st.}$ Preparations for battle had already begun, and after delivering his dispatches from Gen. Scott and hastily partaking of a mouthful of coffee and a piece of hard brad he joined his company. It is not necessary now to recount the disasters of the fight that followed. Suffice it to say that Lieut. Custer's company was among the last to leave the field. It did so in good order, bringing off Gen. Heintzelman, who had been wounded in the engagement. The young officer continued to serve with his company, and was engaged in the drilling of volunteer recruits in and about the defenses of Washington, when upon the appointment of Phil Kearny to the position of Brigadier General, that lamented officer game him a position on his staff. Custer continued in this position until an order was issued from the War Department prohibiting Generals of Volunteers from appointing officers of the regular Army to staff duty. Then he returned to his company, not, however, until he had been warmly complimented by Gen. Kearny upon the prompt and efficient manner in which he had performed the duties assigned to him. At the same time the General predicted that Custer would be one of the most successful officers in the Army. Nor were these predictions without a speedy realization. With his company Lieut. Custer marched forward with that part of the Army of the Potomac which moved upon Manassas after its evacuation by the rebels. Our cavalry was in advance, under Gen.Stoneman and encountered the rebel horsemen for the first time near Catlett's Station. The commanding officer made a call for volunteers to charge the enemy's advance post. Lieut. Custer was among the first to step to the front, and in command of his company he shortly afterward made his first charge. He drove the rebels across Muddy Creek, wounded a number of them, and had one of his own men injured. This was the first blood drawn in the campaign under McClellan.

After this Custer went with the Army of the Potomac to the Peninsula and remained with his company until the Army settled down before Yorktown when he was detailed as an Assistant Engineer of the left wing, under Sumner. Acting in this capacity he planned and erected the earthworks nearest the enemy's lines. He also accompanied the advance under Gen. Hancock in pursuit of the enemy from Yorktown. Shortly afterward, he captured the first battle-flag ever secured by the Army of the Potomac. From this time on he was nearly always the first in every work of daring. When the Army reached the Chickahominy he was the first man to cross the river; he did so in the face of the fire of the enemy's pickets, and at times was obliged to wade up to his armpits. For this brave act Gen. McClellan promoted him to a Captaincy and made him one of his personal aids. In this capacity he served during most of the Peninsula campaign, and participated in all its battles, including the bloody seven days fight. He performed the duty of marking out the position which was occupied by the Union Army at the battle of Gaines' Mills. He also participated in the campaign which ended in the battles of South Mountain and Antietam.

Upon the retirement of Gen. McClellan from the command of the Army of the Potomac, Custer accompanied him, and for a time was out of active service. He was next engaged in the battle of Chancellorsville, and immediately after that fight he was made a personal aid by Gen.'. Pleasonton, who was then commanding a division of cavalry. Serving in this capacity he took an active part in a number of hotly-contested engagements and marked himself as one of the most dashing, some said the most reckless, officers in the service.

When Pleasonton was made a Major General his first pleasure was to remember the valuable services of his Aid de Camp. He requested the appointment of four Brigadiers to command under him, and upon his recommendation, indorsed by Gens. Meade and Hooker, young Custer was made a Brigadier General and assigned to the command of the First, Fifth, Sixth, and Seventh Michigan Cavalry. He did noble service at the battle of Gettysburg. He held the right of line, and was obliged to face Hampton's division of cavalry, and after a hotly-contested fight, utterly routed the rebels and prevented them from reaching the trains of the Union Army, which they hoped to capture. Custer had two horses shot under him in this fight. Hardly had the battle concluded when he was sent to attack the enemy's train, which was trying to force its way to the Potomac. He destroyed more than four hundred wagons. At Hagerstown, Md., during a severe engagement, he again had his horse shot under him. At Failing Waters, shortly after, he attacked with his small brigade the entire rebel rear guard. The Confederate commander Gen. Pettigrew was killed and his command routed, with a loss of 1,300 prisoners, two pieces of cannon, and four battle flags. For some time after this fight he was constantly engaged in skirmishing with the enemy, and during the Winter which followed in picketing the Rapidan between the two armies. He participated in the battle of the Wilderness in 1864, and on the 9th of May of the same year, under General Sheridan, he set out on the raid toward Richmond. His brigade led the column, captured Beaver Dam, burned the station and a train of cars loaded with supplies, and released 400 Union prisoners. Rejoining Grant's Army on the Pamunkey, he took an active part in several engagements. After the battle of Fisher's Hill, in which he did most important service, he was placed in command of a division, and remained in that position until after Lee's surrender. At the ever-memorable battle of Cedar Creek his division was on the right, and not engaged in the rout of the morning, so that when Sheridan arrived on the field, after the twenty-mile ride, he found at least one command ready for service. His immediate order was "Go in, Custer!" The brave young General only waited for the word, he went in and never came out until the enemy was driven several miles beyond the battlefield. Nearly one thousand prisoners were captured, among them a Major General. Forty-five pieces of artillery were also taken. For this service Custer was made a Brevet Major General of Volunteers. Sheridan, as a further mark of approbation, detailed him to carry the news of the victory and the captured battle flag to Washington. From this time on his fortune was made, and he continued steadily to advance in the esteem of his superiors and of the American people. When the rebels fell-back to Appomattox, Custer had the advance of Sheridan's command, and his share in the action is well described in the entertaining volume entitled; With Sheridan in His Last Campaign. The book in question says: "When the sun was an hour high in the west, energetic Custer in advance spied the depot and four heavy trains of freight cars; he quickly ordered his leading regiments to circle out to the left through the woods, and as they gained the railroad beyond the station he led the rest of his division pell-mell down the road and enveloped the rain as quick as winking. Custer might not well conduct a siege of regular approaches; but for a sudden dash, Custer against the world."

After many another dash of the same kind as that described, Custer was mustered out of the volunteer service on the 1st of February, 1866, and on July 28 of the same year he was appointed General of the Seventh United Sates Cavalry, and since that time has been almost constantly engaged in duty upon the frontier.

Recently he has contributed several interesting articles to the magazines. Of his personal appearance, I Newhall, in With Sheridan in His Last Campaign, speaks as follows: "At the head of the horsemen rode Custer of the golden locks, his broad sombrero turned up from his hard, bronzed face, the ends of his crimson cravat floating over his shoulder, gold galore, spangling his jacket sleeves, a pistol in his boots, jangling spurs on his heels, and a ponderous claymore swinging at his side. A wild, daredevil of a General and a prince of advance guards." This description will be recognized by those who knew Gen. Custer as exceedingly true to nature. He was not a great General. He was a great fighter. His place in the Army will not easily be filled.

—44—

THE COURT MARTIAL OF MAJOR MARCUS A. MAJOR RENO

Major Marcus A. Major Reno was tried and convicted by Court Martial board of his peers twice, once, about ten months after the battle of the Little Bighorn. Often the story is told that he stood a court martial for his service during the battle, or for his lack thereof.

That is false. He stood before a court martial for what he didn't do during the battle—follow orders. It didn't seem to matter that the man failed to follow orders and by doing so, sealed the fate of five companies of U.S. Cavalry. Most historians report that it was for his actions during the battle that he stood before a court martial board (apparently they didn't have time to check the record for themselves). As surprising as it seems it wasn't because of his battlefield actions, though perhaps they should have been, but alas the Army works in mysterious ways sometimes.

He was tried for, "Conduct unbecoming an officer and a gentleman," of all things, probably justifiably so.

The situation unfolds this way—Shortly after the battle, Major Reno had been made commander of the 7th Cavalry at Fort Abercrombie, Dakota Territory. Near Christmas time, on or about December 18th, 1876, Major Reno apparently made a romantic pass at Mrs. James M. Bell, the wife of one of Major Reno's Troop captains who was detailed elsewhere, leaving Mrs. Bell alone on post. From what is written about this woman in this situation, she had been alone a long time and apparently was not opposed to "visitors" or at least up and until Major

LAST RIDE

Reno presented himself in probably a drunken stupor on the evening in question. The problem seemed to be that Major Marcus Reno seemed to think that she and he could spend the Christmas Holidays together.

This woman shunned Major Reno then and then again a few days later when she did not invite him to a party that she was giving later in the month (New Years Eve). The good Mrs. Bell could have been a bit of "a rounder," history does not say for sure, one way or the other. Lest we assume too much by reading between the lines of what little is written about this woman, I dare not say too much.

However, knowing human nature and also knowing that most men like women in more than conversational venues, and usually women like men in other ways also, and being that Major Reno was by all known sources a male, we can assume that the good major having been a bachelor for some three or four years by that time (his own wife had died in 1872) it would not have been surprising today for anyone to make a little suggestive, however, inappropriate, talk to Mrs. Bell. Especially, if one thought that she was of rather loose character and bawdy reputation, which she apparently was. And if, as is suggested, Mrs. Bell, may have been a little loose by those then rather prudish standards. He may very well have tried to seduce the lady in question, however probably not in public, as she charged. Especially, if he, Major Reno, being a drunk by nature, was drunk at the time. Apparently, that was the case also. We all seem to be a little bit less than what we ought to be when we partake in the devil's brew.

It could have happened and it probably did. Mrs. Bell, did not like his particular unwanted advances (while apparently she didn't mind those advances by other officers) and reported the officer and charged him with " conduct unbecoming." while her good captain was off post doing army business.

The charges were ultimately dropped, but it took nearly a hundred years, long after his death. The good record of Major Marcus A. Major Reno was expunged of the charges and his records cleared of the said charges.

In passing, Major Reno is the only surviving 7th Cavalry officer who fought in the battle to be buried with those officers (only three) and enlisted men who fell at the Little Bighorn. That softens the usually harsh negative line I usually hold on this man—somewhat, though not entirely. It was his final wish. He could have been buried most anywhere, even Arlington National Cemetery, but he chose a lonely little cemetery in nowhere Montana to spend his eternity. I am not sure what that says about this man.

I wonder why he would want to be buried there. He never said why in his last days. The following are the court martial proceedings captured from the records of the 47th Congress, Second Session, and Senate Report Number 926, In the Senate of the United States, January 16, 1883. Nowhere do the charges go anywhere near the Little Bighorn Battlefield and his part in that battle. One can only guess what the good major had in his mind when he made that request.

47th CONGRESS, SECOND SESSION
SENATE REPORT No. 926
IN THE SENATE OF THE UNITED STATES

January 16, 1883. —Ordered to be printed. MR. HARRISON, from the Committee on Military Affairs, submitted the following report (to accompany bill S.2190):

> The Committee on Military Affairs, to who was referred the bill (S2190) for the relief of Marcus A. Major Reno, respectfully report:
>
> An inquiry addressed to the Secretary of War asking for the military record of Major Reno, and for any other facts in the possession of the department appearing upon the subject of the relief asked for by him, was answered on the 9th instant by transmitting the military record of Major Reno and also certain proceedings before courts-martial which were convened: The first, March 8, 1877, at Saint Paul, Minn.; the second November 28, 1879, at Fort

Meade, Dakota. The committee does not deem it necessary to state at length the military history of this officer. He was graduated at the United States Military Academy July 1, 1857, and his record shows that he performed valuable and even distinguished services in the war of the rebellion, and also in Indian wars since. The proceedings had by the two courts martial before which he was tried, as has been mentioned above were as follows:

Headquarters of the Army, Adjutant-General's Office Washington, May 8,1877.
Before a general court-martial which convened at Saint Paul, Minn., March 8,1877, pursuant to Special Orders No. 22, Headquarters Department of Dakota, Saint Paul, Minn., February 20,1877, and of which Col. WILLIAM B. HAZEN, Sixth Infantry, is president, was arraigned and tried—Major MARCUS A. MAJOR RENO, Seventh Cavalry.

CHARGE. — Conduct unbecoming an officer and a gentleman."

Specification 1st.—"In this: that he, Maj. Marcus A. Major Reno, Seventh Regiment of Cavalry, being in command of the military post of Fort Abercrombie, Dakota, garrisoned in part by Company F, Seventh Regiment of Cavalry, under command of Capt. James M. Bell, did, during the temporary absence from the post of the said Captain Bell, in disregard of his honor and duty as commanding officer, visit the quarters of the said Bell, and then and there, take improper and insulting liberties with the wife of the said Captain Bell, by taking both her hands in his own, and attempting to draw her person close up to his own. This to the scandal and disgrace of the military service, at Fort Abercrombie, Dakota, on or about the 18th day of December,1876."

Specification 2d. — "In this: that he, Maj. Marcus A. Major Reno, Seventh Regiment of Cavalry, being in command of the military post of Fort Abercrombie, Dakota, garrisoned in part by Company F, Seventh Regiment of Cavalry, under command of Capt. James M. Bell, did, during the temporary absence from the post of the said Captain Bell, in disregard of his honor and duty as commanding officer, visit the quarters of the said Bell, and while the wife of said bell was passing through the storm screen connecting the said quarters with the adjoining set of quarters, take improper and insulting liberties with her, by placing his arm around her waist. This to the scandal and disgrace of the military service, at Fort Abercrombie, Dakota, on or about the 21st day of December 1876.

Specification 3d.—"In this: that he, Maj. Marcus A. Major Reno, Seventh Regiment of Cavalry, being in command of the military post of Fort Abercrombie, Dakota having along of all the officers of the garrison, failed to receive an invitation to a social gathering held by invitation of the wife of Capt. James M. Bell, Seven Regiment of Cavalry, during the absence from the garrison of the said Bell, did say to Mr. John Haselburst, post trader at Fort Abercrombie Dakota: 'This means war! Mrs. Bell has thrown down the gauntlet, and I will take it up. Perhaps these people do not know the power of a commanding officer,' referring thereby, and intending to be understood to refer, to Mrs. Bell's purposely excluding him from the list of her invitations, and did further say: 'I will make it hot for her (meaning Mrs. Bell), I will drive her out of the regiment," or words to that effect, thereby dishonorably and maliciously threatening to use his power as commanding officer of that post to revenge himself upon the said Mrs. Bell for her failure to invite him to the social gathering as aforesaid. This to the scandal and disgrace of the military service, at Fort Abercrombie, Dakota on or about the 25th day of December, 1876.

Specification 4th. –In this: that he, Major Marcus A. Major Reno, Seventh Regiment of Cavalry, being in command of the military post of Fort Abercrombie, Dakota, did write, or did cause to be written, and did sign and send to the Rev. R. Wainwright, who was at Fort Abercrombie for the purpose of holding Divine service, and a guest in the quarters of James M. Bell, Seventh Regiment of Cavalry, a communication in words and figures, as follows:

Dr. Wainwright:
Sir:

My attention having been again called to the subject of your holding service, I am convinced it is in the interest of peace and harmony that you should not do so. I need scarcely assure you of the deep regret with which I made you acquainted with this decision.

Very Respectfully, M.A. Major Reno
Major, Seventh Cavalry,
Commanding

Paraphrasing to save the reader the agony of reading further—Then there is a part in which Major Reno and Dr. Wainwright had a discussion concerning the matter and Major Reno charged that, "Mrs. Bell was like a spoiled egg...you cannot hurt it. She is notorious in the regiment as a loose character; and did further say that Captain Benteen and Lieutenant Wallace, all of the Seventy Regiment of Cavalry had had occasion to witness it or be a part of it." For which brought:

Specification 5th.—"In this: that he Maj. Marcus A. Major Reno, Seventh Regiment of Cavalry, being in command of the military post of Fort Abercrombie, Dakota, did, in and interview with the Rev. R. Wainwright, urge him to leave the quarters of Captain Bell when he was a guest, and did say those things mentioned above. Causing of course, "the injuring of the good name and repute of the said Mrs. Bell, and in fulfillment of the threats made by the said Major Reno, as set forth in the foregoing third specification." And again, bringing scandal and disgrace of the military service."

This also brought forth—

Specification 6th.—Paraphrasing again for the same reason as 5th Specification above-
"...thereby to express an intention to assail the reputation of the wife of Capt. James M. Bell and to assert that her reputation was bad and of course to the disgrace of the military service."

And lastly, finally, almost the last...

Specification 7th—Paraphrasing again..." Major Marcus A. Major Reno willfully, and maliciously attempted to and did endeavor to annoy and humiliate the wife of a brother officer in his absence and to stop the religious service should Mrs. Bell be allowed to play the organ during the service." This to the scandal and disgrace of the military service, at Fort Abercrombie, Dakota.

With all of this disgracing going on, one wonders how anything else of importance got done.

All of which Major Marcus A. Major Reno Commander 7th Cavalry pleaded, "Not Guilty."
The findings were that he was indeed found guilty of all seven charges by a board of his peers.

SENTENCE

The court does, therefore sentence him, Major Marcus A. Major Reno, Seventh Cavalry, "To be dismissed [from] the service."

PART II. The following are the orders of the Secretary of War (concerning this matter):

WAR DEPARTMENT, May 8, 1877.

The proceeding in this case having been forwarded, under the 106th Article of War, to the Secretary of War, have been most carefully considered and have been submitted to the President who approves the proceeding, findings, and sentence, but is pleased to mitigate the latter, "to suspension from rank and pay for two years from the 1st of May 1877."

Major Reno's conduct toward the wife of an absent officer, and in using the whole force of his power as commanding officer of the post to gratify his resentment against her, cannot be too strongly condemned; but after long deliberation upon all the circumstances of the case, as shown in the record of the trial, it is thought that his offenses, grave as they are, do not warrant the sentence of dismissal, and all its consequences, upon on who had for twenty years borne the reputation of a brave and honorable officer, and has maintained that reputation upon the battle-fields of the rebellion and in combat with Indians. The President has therefore modified the sentence, and it is hoped that Major Reno will appreciate the clemency thus shown him as well as the very reprehensible character of the acts of which he is found guilty.

GEO. W. McCRARY
Secretary of War.

By command of General Sherman:
E.D. TOWNSEND
Adjutant-General

That Court Martial, in and of itself, was the full extent of the conduct of Major Reno's conduct close to the time he was on the battlefield of the Little Bighorn with Custer. As you can see, it had nothing to do with the battle, but with a tussle he had with one of his officer's wife. He was put out of the Army for two years from May 1, 1877 until May 1, 1879. He was back on duty, this time at Fort Meade, Dakota on May 1, 1879.

By then, though, Major Reno was a full-blown drunk and the end was in sight for barely six months from that date, he would be run up on charges for, "Conduct unbecoming an officer and gentleman." This time it was for drunk and disorderly conduct and fighting with a brother officer (junior grade to himself). Just a few months prior to that he had been caught window peeking at his commander's family late at night, for which charges were also brought against him.

Again, the good major pleaded, "Not Guilty."

Again, he was found guilty of all charges, by a board of his peers; three specifications this time, instead of the seven the first time. But, alas, the good Major had run out of favors, and he was once and for all put out of the service by order this time by the President Rutherford B. Hays on April 1, 1880. Things moved slowly back then, didn't they? But that is not the end of the story of Major Reno. In 1956, long after his death, Congress in its infinite wisdom, reversed the order of the court martial and cleared his record for all time—they dropped all charges as though the incidents in which he was indebted of, ten in all, never happened—maybe they never did. Congress, after all said they never did. So, who knows?

What we don't know is, "What happened to the infamous Mrs. Bell after all of this happened?" Before the 7th left for their date on the Little Bighorn, Captain Bell was on detached service back east, lucky for him he missed out on the battle in which he would have probably been killed. What bothers me is that he was still on detached service back east at the time this event happened between her and Major Reno. That was two years after the fact and Mrs. Bell was still out west without her husband.

What I wonder is how did she manage that; and why did the Army allow her to live in government quarters all that time? That was not the first time Mrs. Bell had been tied to such an event with an officer, doubtfully it was the last. Perhaps, I will look into that matter at another time.

—45—
THE CUSTER LEGACY

LAST RIDE

LIEUTENANT COLONEL (BREVET MAJOR GENERAL) GEORGE ARMSTRONG CUSTER

From the farmlands of the rich Ohio valley,
To the land of the Wolverine you grew solid and true.
On the Hudson at West Point you yearned to go.
A horse soldier's life you chose as your own.

From Maryland's quiet countryside,
Throughout the South you fought the Rebel band.
From the Bull Run to Appomattox Court you flew.
At Gettysburg, Antietam, Winchester, Cold Harbor too.

On fiery, ragging stallions you led for Ol' Glory's sake.
No quit, nor fear, nor doubt as you drove your enemy.
With a vanquished enemy's cutlass in the one hand
Custom-made British Bulldog Parrots for the other.

You led your pony soldiers in blue through the fiery haze.
You slew those who tried to break this country's back.
More than five score charges made amidst the fog of war.
Leading men as they should be led, the only way you knew.

Battle after battle, year after year, 'til it was o'er.
You stayed the course, were loyal, valiant, and true.
With brother Tom at your side, and Libby always near by.
The history you and your boys made you never knew.

Year after year, bones grown weary of the fight.
How many fiery mounts you lost, you never knew.
How many men died, you never stopped to count.
And always your voice was for war.

Then, one day, it was o'er ,
There was no more war.
What's a nation to do,
With a man who only knew war?
To Texas and southern plains you lead the 7th Cavalry.
To fight, Apache, Comanche, Kiowa, upon desert plains.
Along snowy banks of the Washita in Oklahoma,
You killed Black Kettle's Cheyenne one wintry morn.

Not much glory in the trail you left that day.
Your voice was for war, you made it plane for all to see.
The light cast by Son of Morning Star dimmed ever more.
Leaving Major Elliott's men to stand and die alone.

You lost something that day when you left those men.
Your honor at stake, never fear, your country cried 'more'.
Free us from the red man, so we can take his Mother Earth.
We have crops and kids to raise we said, and gold to dig.
In Kansas you punished Arapaho, Pawnee and Cheyenne.
You left them breathless; your voice was for war.
Across Kansas, Colorado, 'Braska flats, into Lakota land.
Son of Morning Star's pony soldiers came to destroy.

Into lands of the Teton, Wind River, and Devil's Tower.
On to the Yellowstone, the Wolf Mountain divide.
You drove the mighty Lakota–Minneconjoux, Sans Arc, Ogalala
Across the lands of the Big Sky, the Powder and Tongue.

Into the sacred lands of the Lakotas.
Along the banks and streams of their Black Hills.
In the dark red soil and along sacred streams,
You found wasichus' lust for golden dust.

From the Cut Throat Sioux
The Wasichu stole their scared Hills.

LAST RIDE

Though not alone, the "Long Hair" would be remembered
The "Long Hair," he stole what man can never own.

On that last ride along the Little Sheep they struck.
For the pain the wasichu caused for many moons,
Bore by a people who wanted to just to be free.
Was that too much to ask, just to be free?

From Fort Abraham Lincoln your blue legions came,
Now though only a shadow of glory past.
With you in the lead as their fearless leader,
How could the mighty 7th fail?

Across the baron plains you came,
Pushing man and beast harder and faster still.
Down the Wolf Mountain divide you pushed your men
Into the valley of the Greasy Grass you flew.

With your battle flags waving in the wind,
The swallow-tailed guideon too.
"Attack, Benteen and Major Reno from the south."
"McDougall stay with the trains."

"Bro Tom, C Troop, form on me,
Yate's F and Smith E and Keogh's Wild I too,
Oh Jimmy, "Jimmy Boy," bring on L,
Our scouts and Indian guides and little Autie and Boston.

Down into the Medicine Tail Coulee you charged,
Leading men the way leaders do.
At the front of the charge, not behind,
That was never the Custer Way.

On the broad strong back of mighty Vic,
You gave a mighty last hurrah.

JAMES CLINTON HUNGERFORD

Into the Little Sheep River you went
Leading your men as you always did.

The river was too wide dear General,
The other side you never reached.
Swiped off Vic's back with one near canon shot.
You never saw it coming, nor heard the final roar.

Laid low by young Brave Bear boy, nowhere yet a man.
Oh, the stories they would tell would make you roar.
You became a near saint, still to this day!
Your name itched on white marbled stone.

To all who should read that cold old stone,
Here on this day, June 25, 1876, the 7th fell.
You and your gallant 7th took its last ride,
Your loves of this world are no more.

For in the death of a soldier
Lies but a lonely lost memory.
A hope no more,
For those who knew.

For those who believed
That no matter what
Custer would find a way.
To win, his voice was for war.

For you General your end was kind—final.
You left behind only a wife, who loves you still.
Perhaps too, left an unclaimed red son, you never knew.
Who could have known, who could have guessed?

The cloud of battle long since cleared.
On the edge of Battle Ridge a nude General lay dead,

LAST RIDE

His blue eyes searching a bluer yet sky.
For some unknown answer, unimportant now.

The peaceful Little Sheep River untouched,
By terror men felt keeping him company lay nearby,
Ran red as it gently slides by the lonely hill where you fell.
Its secrets ever safe, never to be told. Oh! If only it could talk.

Wasichus lay in heaps, one by one, and some two by two.
They gave up their ghost at the red man's hand.
Perished as they sped on foot, with fear in their hearts,
On warn-out steeds all the same at battle's end.

Close by brother Thomas,
Perhaps the bravest, truest friend.
Captains Yates, Smith, and Keogh stood tall
Defending you, you never knew, to their last.

Not far away,
Little brother Boston and Autie Reed lay.
Their young lives now but sorrowful memory.
Troopers died—one by one, some together, all—alone.

Not one *wasichu* escaped,
The god of battle had his fill.
Respected no *wasichu*, nor bred, nor deed,
Displayed impartiality in the offering, taking all.

Death on the battlefield
Indeed, an individual, lonely end.
At peace now, these sleeping men lie.
True brothers now, both white and red.

The senseless fight now o'er.
Their bodies destined now to turn to dust,

Their spirits beyond the stars.
Friendlier now, as time passes them by.

What were their names, tell me, what where their names?
Remember their names, see their faces, hear them laugh.
We fight not to forget there are no winners' this day.
Just tears of lovers who have dried and gone their own way.

So too, little children's broken hearts.
What of the moms and dads,
Their dreams for you
Now like the wind.

Do you here the bugle sound
And the red man's willow flute?
So many years have past,
No memory of a soldier or brave remain.

Now, gone forever
Beneath the bluest Western sky.
A cold white piece of stone marks the place
To tell one and all that a U.S. 7th Cavalryman fell near by.

High above
The Red men's names
As if on eagle wings gliding high.
They came to fight and die.

Protecting their homes and loves.
Resting places still unknown,
Beneath the same endless blue sky,
The winds of summer blow across Battle Ridge.

Hear the drum roll and hollow bone flute,
A lost lover's sorrowful moan.

Sleep deeply dear warrior
Brave and true.

Listen! Don't you hear? Look! Don't you see?
The pipes, they're a blowin' "Gary Owen."
There go the boys in blue, on white billowin' clouds,
A chasin' Ol' Fanny…"Old Iron Ass" hisself, on that last ride.

General George Armstrong Custer, "Fanny" to his friends and his battalion of the 7th Cavalry took that last ride, together, that fateful Sunday afternoon in late June of 1876. Custer was a man of incredible valor and nearly unbelievable eye-popping bravery, honor be-damned.

Honor does not win fights or wars. Custer understood that as few in his time did. Honor gets good men killed during battle. To put a point on it, there is damn little honor in killing your fellow man, be he red or white. War is nasty work, not many are cut out for it—Custer understood that, and he was cut from its broad harsh cloth. That is the long and the short of it. Men like Custer win battles and are the ones that project military might on their country's enemies. In the end, it protects our way of life, sometimes, more often than not, at the forfeit of their own life.

An experienced solider once put it this way, "Hit the other fellow as quick as you can, where it hurts the most, and where it will do the most good…when he ain't lookin'." That is what Lieutenant Colonel Custer attempted to do, he knew about war and how to defeat the enemy. His plan failed and he died trying to implement it.

Generating and projecting your force is the first goal among equals. If you are not equal, it should be done as rapidly and effectively as you can; you might still win. If you are not equal, (Custer's force was not anywhere near equal to the force he had to fight) the consequences that he faced ranged from a simple strategic embarrassment to a gigantic military disaster.

Unwittingly, Lieutenant Colonel Custer achieved both. His regiment's defeat was obviously not what he had planned. His defeat was brought on by the uncontrollable circumstances that he faced, probably knowing full well it would lead to his regiment's defeat and even his own possible death.

In the truest Custer form, he did what he always had done in that situation, he charged. Throwing caution to the wind, he led his band of brothers the only way he knew—at the front into the hottest point of the attack. He was the point of the lance in this last fight just as he had been in every fight since Manassas so many years before. What you always got from George Armstrong Custer, as a friend, or mortal enemy, was his best, always his best. And that, my friends, was pretty damn good. Who has the right to ask for more?

—46—

EPILOGUE

My fascination for Custer really started for me as a young boy growing up on our farm in the panhandle of northwest Nebraska. During the summer of 1952, my dad was building a house on the little place where we lived on the outside of Alliance, Nebraska.

He had gotten to the fine wood finishing part, and had decided that kind of work was a little too precise for him. Dad was like a bull in a china cabinet when it came to woodwork or near anything that required he be precise. Dad was not a precise kind of man. His way of handling that situation was to "let it ride" until my mother got after him, and told him to hire someone to do the finish work. Dad finally decided Mom was right, and that he had to have some help in building the Knotty Pine bookcases, and big bay window with a built-in storage bench in the living room if he was going to get along with the woman.

Shortly afterward, Dad in his imperturbable way brought home an honest to goodness, real live, full-blooded American Minniconjoux Sioux Indian. Of course, I did not know that was what Mr. Levi was until the next day, when he proudly began listing his pedigree. From there he started telling me stories about his ancestors as if to prove his point.

About all I could brag to him about me was I was my dad's kid, and my dad had said we Hungerford's came from a long line of Englishmen. Somewhere, back 700 or 800 years before, there was a guy named Sir Thomas from Hungers Ford on the Frome River, in Somerset County, England. The man had somehow managed to become a knight and the very first Speaker of the House of Commons, the year of 1200 and something. Since the early 1600s we Hungerford's had helped settle this country, and had, somehow picked up a strain of Irish bull-headedness.

My uncle, who was always telling stories about our family tree, had said somewhere back in time, after we got to America, and the birth of his great, three times removed, grandmother, we had also picked up some strain of "Injin" blood in us too. I did not understand any of that then, and besides I was as gullible as Thanksgiving turkey, I always believed my uncle. I never quite understood any of that, of course, being a little kid then. I was not real sure just what that implied at the time, but nonetheless, it seemed to impress this American Minniconjoux Sioux Indian working on my dad's bookcases.

Mr. Levi White Bull, finish carpenter, "par excellence" was a true craftsman. He was hired to do the work Dad knew he could not.

It was a big deal to me because he was the first Indian I had ever really known. I had seen them as we drove by them, and Dad had told me about who these people were living on the outskirts of our little sleepy town. As for Mr. Levi, he was —aside from being a terrific wood worker—a great storyteller, which was much more important to me.

When I knew Mr. Levi, as I called him, he was already in his early to middle seventies. I couldn't tell for sure, and it would not have made any difference to me anyway. He just looked real old, but then, everybody looks old to a little kid. Even now, when I am all grown up, it is still kind of hard to guess an Indian's age because they seem to age differently than white folks.

Mr. Levi's skin color reminded me of wet iron clay straight out of the Paha Sapa (the Black Hills of South Dakota). He had a very dark reddish-brown complexion, had big, droopy, sad-looking, dark-brown eyes. His great big dark red proboscis (as I remember that nose) covered a goodly portion of the center of his face. When a big toothy smile appeared beneath that tremendous nose, and when he laughed out loud, the act itself would divulge that Mr. Levi had several missing teeth and a few heavily yellow-stained ones.

He carried deep pock marks on his dark brownish-red round old wrinkled face. His long, black hair had streaks of gray running through it, which he pulled back "Injin style" he laughingly would say, as he tied it in the back of his head. On top of all of that hair he would plop an old sweat-stained Montana Sheriff's cowboy hat. The hatband was an Indian-worked leather strap. He was a big man, nearly as tall as my dad, who was more than six feet tall. He seemed taller somehow. It must have been his worn-out old cowboy boots, along with his rotund belly that seemed whiskey-barrel hard.

He always showed up at the farm, early enough for breakfast before setting off to craft his trade. Dad and he would sit after breakfast for a few minutes, and talk about what God only knows and then he would work all day.

Mr. Levi never used a power tool—he did not have any. Skillful hands made all of his cuts and miters on those bookcases and on the picture window bench. Every day he would arrive, carrying his bag of tools and at dusk, after Dad paid him for his labor for the day, he would leave the same way he showed up, walking down the dusty old dirt road back toward town.

I was a little boy of six or seven, with willing ears, an inquisitive mind and an imagination that was on the warpath. Mr. Levi fueled it all. To this day, I still remember ol' Mr. Levi working for several days on those bookcases and the bay window bench and my setting beside him the entire time listening to him telling stories about his life.

Among the many stories he told me which I never forgot was about a great battle the Indians won against a great pony soldier named Custer. In between him hand-rollin' his own cigarettes (a lot of folks did that in those days) and me running errands for him, he told me Indian stories.

The errands I ran for him ranged from fetching him a drink of water every now and then to looking for left-handed hammers or wood stretchers. He may have sent me on them because little kids ask a lot of dumb questions or if I interrupted him to much. The real reason he had me running all over the place was probably because he was having fun watching "a little squirt run hither and yon" to help an ol' "Injin" with his work. He would always ask me if I wanted to first; of course, and I always did.

I would not have known then even what ol' Mr. Levi was telling me, and would not have had anyway to check out his story, even if I would have had the inclination to check him out. I know he told me a lot of things about the Indians ways, things about their old ways of doing this and that, about catching' fish with his bare hands, or how to make arrow heads out of flint, and the way "Injins" think about things being so different from the way *wasichu* see the same things.

The one thing that has stuck in, even now—after nearly fifty years—is the Custer and the 7th Cavalry story up on the "Greasy Grass" as he called it, in Montana. He told me his father had been in that famous battle, and it was his father who passed the story on to Levi when he was a little boy about my age. It would be several years later before I could confirm his story.

Mr. Levi's old daddy, "White Bull" —Indians did not have first names in the "olden days"— was on that battlefield the day when Custer struck their camp. Daddy White Bull was a nephew of Buffalo Bull Who Sits (Sitting Bull), the famous Medicine Man of the Lakota, and not the war chief nearly everyone says he was.

Levi's father was an important man as Minniconjoux Lakota war chief. He is sometimes credited with the killing of George Armstrong Custer, but, he did not, I found out later—see Chapter 17. As I remember it, hours passed for him to tell me the story of how the "Injins" rubbed out many blue coats, finally killing them all on the hilltop overlooking the valley of the Greasy Grass, above the Little Sheep River.

I remember sleeping closer to my English shepherd dog "Shep" that night. Mr. Levi really told a good scary story. The whole time he never stopped his work to talk, so he kept me on my toes moving along with him as he worked. I would find out later it was very unusual for an Indian to even tell of the fight on the Little Bighorn with a *wasichu*—they just did not do it. Many of my Indian friends later in my life would never even say anything about it when I asked them. Why Mr. Levi did, I never would find out.

As for whatever happened to my old "Injin" friend, well, unfortunately, things don't always work the way we would like or that they should. Life, I have found, is not particularly fair about that sort of thing. Before Mr. Levi left our farm he had handcrafted two beautiful bookcases my stepmother uses to this day, nearly fifty years later.

Shortly after leaving the farm, poor ol' Mr. Levi was murdered by an inebriated Native American over a cheap bottle of wine in an alley out behind a run-down bar in that little town where I had grown up in.

Sadly, that was an unfortunate ending for Mr. Levi White Bull, the son of a famous American "Minniconjoux" Lakota war chief. (Later, I would learn that there were two "White Bulls," on that battlefield that day: one a Lakota (Sioux), Minniconjoux, the other a medicine man a Tse-Tsehese-Staeste Cheyenne, those who are hearted alike).

I still remember going out to our barn after I overheard dad telling my mother ol' Mr. Levi was dead, and then preceded to tell her how he had been in knife fight out in back of the Last Frontier Bar. A fitting end to the old man's life, I suppose in looking back at it now. Then, I remember going out to the barn and getting into the farthest corner stall, slumping down on the freshly laid straw with ol' Shep and crying. I do not think my dad ever knew about that; or how important ol' Mr. Levi was to me then, or ever. He was my first; lifelong friend I remember and his stories have stayed with me since then.

Years later, in college, having nearly forgotten all about Mr. Levi by then, I studied history, and found that I was particularly drawn to Western Frontier History. Thinking back on it now, it might have been the spirit of ol' Mr. Levi White Bull who drove me to the plains of Americana. A few years later I walked over that battlefield upon the Greasy Grass as a young man. I remember talking to the spirit of Mr. Levi that first time. It was almost like going to church. Years after that, I had walked those same grounds again—but by then, I had read and studied maybe a hundred different accounts of that fateful day George Custer's 7th Cavalry charged into the history books.

I have sat on the Battle Ridge on more than a few occasions chewing the sweetness out of a stunted stem of wild oats, or maybe a blade of buffalo grass, wondering, while looking off in the distance at the setting sun. I have sat there among the ghosts of the battle past, hoping that if I stayed long enough the answer might come to me on the breath of the wind.

What I came up with is this: It is not so much it happened then, and the battle is only a distant memory now. Most of us white folks want to believe it was something it was not. It was not a glorious fight to the end. Once, real live men, both red and white, died in a true tragedy in the saga of settling the West. That event is now, unfortunately, only a footnote in the American story.

What is important now; is why it happened, and what happened as a result of that happening. Perhaps, the next time we get into that situation we will have come far enough down the evolutionary trail to find a different means of handling similar situations.

But, do not count on it.

I remember one night sitting on a blanket of buffalo grass, listening to the prairie winds washing up the sides of those hills like slow-rolling surf on a sandy wind blown shore at night. Everything was peaceful and quiet, the earth covered with a beautiful blanket of stars.

I was hoping then, the breeze flowing over the crest of the hill where most of Captain Miles Keogh's boys, the Wild Eye (Troop I) fell would reveal the secrets of Custer's Last Stand. Mariah, the wind god, remained silent that night. The "Everywhere Spirit" just was not talking.

As I looked down into the quiet of the valley of the Greasy Grass, I thought of how many things can change without really changing. The valley was the same as I had always remembered it. The grasses were the same as they had been for a million years. Yet the place had changed. Paved roads, the tombstones along Battle Ridge more faded, walkways, parking lots, and people wandering at all times of day and night around have changed a boyhood's vision.

Growing up and living where we did as a child—on the Great Plains—was a perfect place to study our frontier past. After settling my own family close to an old frontier fort, Fort Robinson, just west of Crawford, Nebraska, I began to start tracing the last ride of Custer and the 7th. During those years, I learned and heard more of those days on the northern plains and about the life and times of the American frontiersmen, and his struggle against nature, including the American Plains Indian. And...

I wonder, have we as a nation of people of all colors and creeds—Americans—in short, taken a lesson from this storied event and applied it to today's life? Or, do we really care anymore, if we ever did in the first place? Will, what we can learn from our past, make us better for what that past teaches? Unfortunately, I am not romantic or fool hardy enough to believe we learn much from our past mistakes.

People die in wars, most unjustly—all, too young. I have seen in this life on other fields of battle the senseless death of men. It is not unusual; it is accepted and expected that men—rather, young men and boys—die in wars.

In the final analysis it is no less tragic than it was on the hillsides of a place called the Little Bighorn, then or now. On the balance scales of life before or since then, the number of deaths on that day was not a big deal. The ve-ho-e (another name for white people), as our Indian enemies knew us to be, were the losers on that field of battle. To the Red Americans, on the heels of victory that day came crushing defeat, poverty, the loss of ancestral lands and the disappearance of a whole way of life within mere months of Custer and the 7th's defeat.

The ve-ho-e recovered quickly and struck harder still at what we, as a nation, have never understood. The Indians in our path crumpled like dry grass beneath our soldiers' boots and their horse's hooves—like the buffalo, they have nearly perished.

We, the *wasichus*, fought for and won—or did we? Do not get the idea that I am a dove. I am not. I am, and have been described as, an owl in hawk feathers by an Indian friend of mine. I have been on one to many battlefields to feel anything but pure shock at what man can do to his fellow man.

I had the advantage and distinct privilege, though I did not know it at the time, of growing up with several Indian boys and young men. I learned more about them and their ways during those early years of my life. Their friendships and their names have been a blessing to me and have stayed with me all these years. Life has separated me from those boyhood friends I used to pass my youth with.

There were several: Johnny Cedar Face, Percy Brown Otter, Timothy Good Shot, Lester Weasel Bear, Russell Thigh, Ivan Chase In Winter, Lester Dreaming Bear, Booger Horse; and his son, Bobby Whirl Wind Horse (who by the way was Ogallala Sioux. He named his first son, Cray "Z" Horse), Moses Charging Thunder, Ike Black Elk, Joe American

Horse, Paul Little Hill, Wendell Bird Head, Frankie Pushtonequa, Arthur Half Hide and Willie Garnier. It is my hope that the spirit of Levi White Bull and my boyish remembrance of long ago friends has guided my fingers over the keys of my computer of these past few pages.

SELECTED REFERENCES

The following is a list of works used in part in developing a basis of understanding of the events that occurred during George Armstrong Custer's life leading up to the last battle that he was a part of. Further this list includes works of author's who wrote about his life and times and those who were his family and associates. It is by no means exhaustive. Many prominent secondary works were helpful to the understanding of the man and the times in which he lived.

BOOKS

Ambrose, Stephen A.; Crazy Horse and Custer First Anchor Books Edition, 1996.
Bachrach, Deborah, Custer's Last Stand: Opposing Viewpoints (Great Mysteries), 1990.
Custer, Elizabeth; Tenting on the Plains, University of Oklahoma Press, 1994.
Custer, G. A.; My Life on the Plains, Bison Books, University of Nebraska Press, 1966.
Daily, Edward L.; From Custer to MacArthur, Turner Publications, Paducah, KY, 1995.
Frost, Lawrence A.; The Custer Album, Superior Publishing Co. Seattle, WA. 1984.
Godfrey, E. S., Custer's Last Battle, Outbooks, 1976.
Graham, W. A., The Story of the Little Big Horn, Stackpole Books, Military Publishing Company, 1994.
Gray, John S., Centennial Campaign: The Sioux War of 1876, University

of Oklahoma Press, 1988.
Greene, Jerome A., Battles and Skirmishes of the Great Sioux War, 1876-1877, University of Oklahoma Press: Norman, 1993.
Geene, Jerome A., Nez Perce Summer 1877, Montana Historical Society Press, 2000.
Hook, Jason, To Live and Die in the West, Osprey Publishing, 1999.
Johnston, Terry C., Sioux Dawn, St. Martin Press, 1990.
Johnston, Terry C., Trumpet on the Land, Bantam Books, 1995.
Lecki, Shirley A., Elizabeth Bacon Custer and the Making of a Myth, Shirley A. Leckie, 1993.
Marquis, Thomas B., Wooden Leg, Bison Books, University of Nebraska Press, 1931.
Merington, Marguerite, The Custer Story: The Life and Intimate Letters of General George A. Custer and His wife Elizabeth, 1987.
Michino, Gregory, The Mystery of E Troop, Mountain Press Publishing Company, 1994.
Military History, Congressional Medal of Honor Society, 2000.
Miller, David Humphreys, Custer's Fall, Meridian Book, 1992.
Monaghan, Jay, Custer, Bison Books, University of Nebraska Press, 1971.
National Archives, The Register of Enlistments, USA, Record Group 94.
Nichols, Ronald, Men With Custer, CBH&MA, 2000.
Sandoz, Mari, Battle of the Little Big Horn, University of Nebraska Press.
Sandoz, Marie, The Long Flight (Cheyenne Autumn), University of Nebraska Press.
Seventh Calvary Association, Fort Sill Oklahoma.
Sklenar, Larry, To Hell with Honor, University of Oklahoma Press: Norman, 2000.
Urwin, Gregory J. W., Custer Victorious, Blue and Grey Press, 1955.
Van de Water, Glory Hunter, Bison Book, University of Nebraska Press, 1988.

NEWSPAPERS AND JOURNALS AND WEBSITES

Little Big Horn Associates Newsletter
New York Times; July 07 1876-Microfilm Archives-New York, NY
Research Review: The Journal of the Little Big Horn Associates
The Battle of the Little Big Horn, 1876, Web site: http://www.ibiscom.com/custer/htm.
Web site: GeneralCuster.net
http://www. thehistorynet.com/images/1997/03973_11.htm
American History, Digital Item Display, Website:
http://lcweb2.locgov/gov/cgi-bin/query/I?presp:149:./temp
Annual Report of the Secretary of War 1876, pages 476-480,
    Web site: http://www. ibha.org/Major Renorep.htp
Colorado Historical Society, 'library@chs.state.co.us'
Denver Public Library, 'http://gowest.coalliance.org'
Colorado Historical Society, Stephen H. Hart Library, www.coloradohistory.org
History of the 7th Cavalry Regiment, 2001. Web Site: http://www.metronet.com
Major Marcus A. Major Reno, http://majorMajor Reno.com/Major Reno.html.

Printed in the United States
67131LVS00005B/98